MOBILE

⚜

Produced in cooperation with
Mobile Area Chamber of Commerce
451 Government Street
Post Office Box 2187
Mobile, Alabama 36652
(205) 431-6951

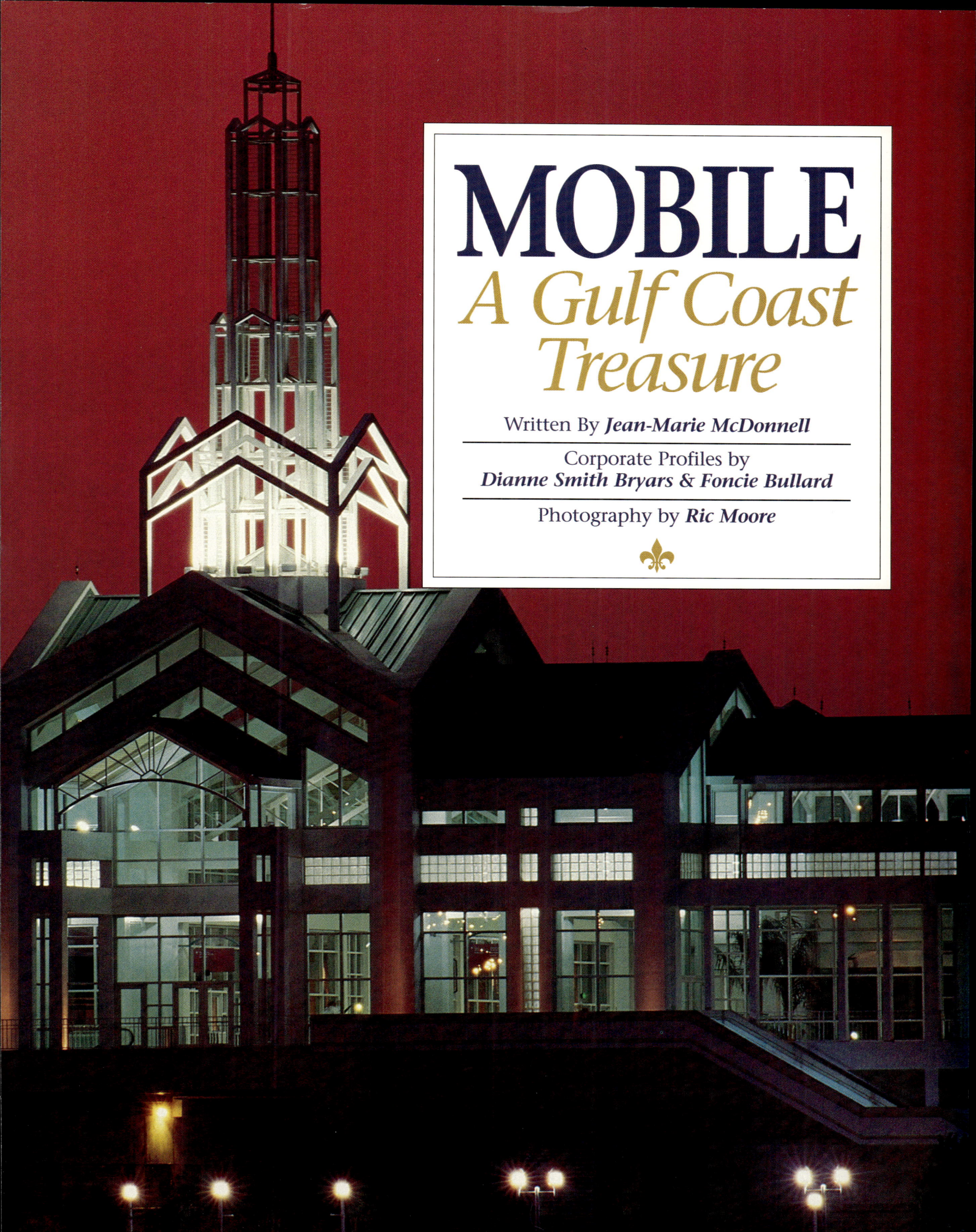

MOBILE
A Gulf Coast Treasure

Written By *Jean-Marie McDonnell*

Corporate Profiles by
Dianne Smith Bryars & Foncie Bullard

Photography by *Ric Moore*

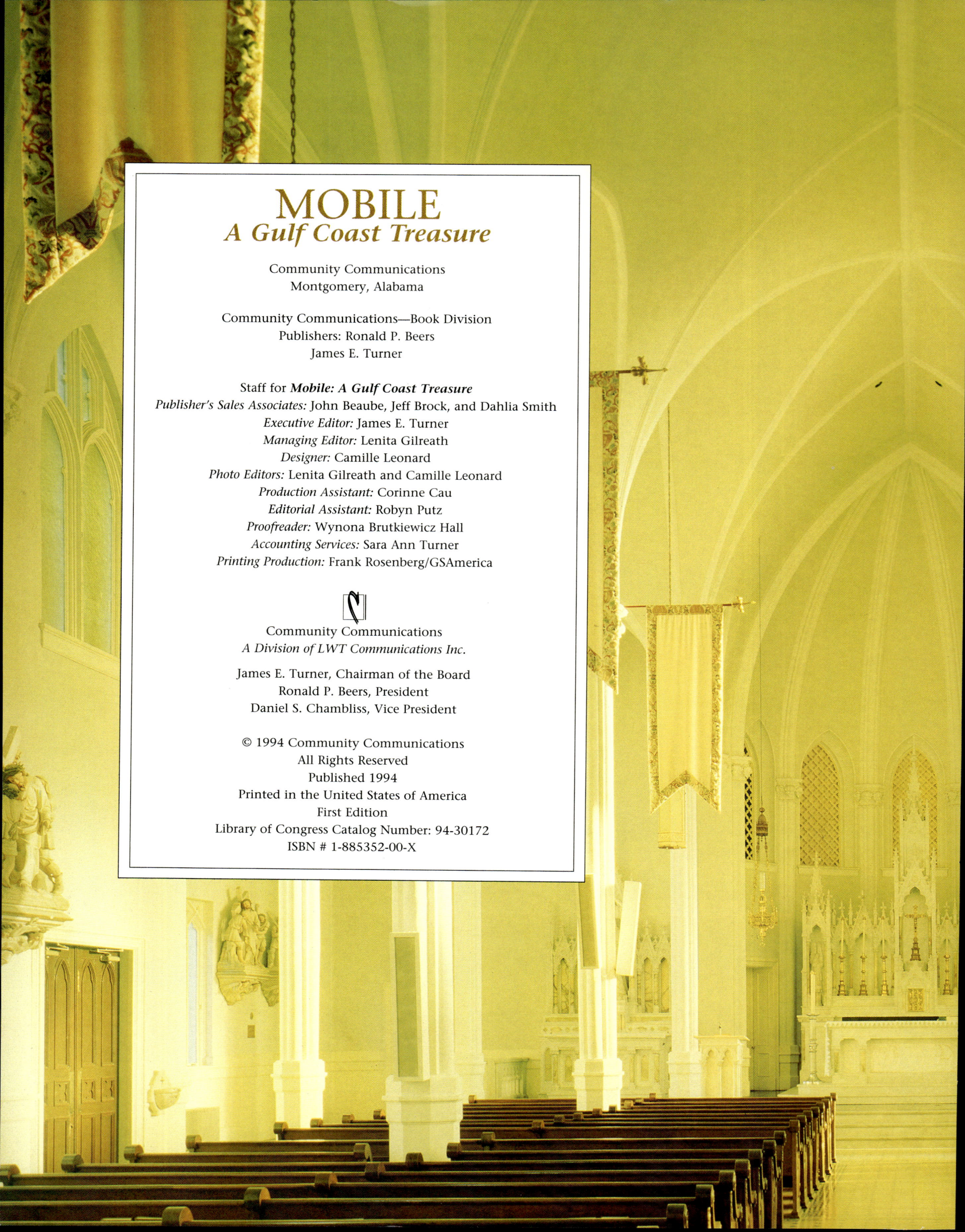

MOBILE
A Gulf Coast Treasure

Community Communications
Montgomery, Alabama

Community Communications—Book Division
Publishers: Ronald P. Beers
James E. Turner

Staff for **Mobile: *A Gulf Coast Treasure***
Publisher's Sales Associates: John Beaube, Jeff Brock, and Dahlia Smith
Executive Editor: James E. Turner
Managing Editor: Lenita Gilreath
Designer: Camille Leonard
Photo Editors: Lenita Gilreath and Camille Leonard
Production Assistant: Corinne Cau
Editorial Assistant: Robyn Putz
Proofreader: Wynona Brutkiewicz Hall
Accounting Services: Sara Ann Turner
Printing Production: Frank Rosenberg/GSAmerica

Community Communications
A Division of LWT Communications Inc.

James E. Turner, Chairman of the Board
Ronald P. Beers, President
Daniel S. Chambliss, Vice President

© 1994 Community Communications
All Rights Reserved
Published 1994
Printed in the United States of America
First Edition
Library of Congress Catalog Number: 94-30172
ISBN # 1-885352-00-X

Contents

A GULF COAST TREASURE

Part I

Foreword
Page 10

Preface
Page 12

Acknowledgments
Page 13

**Cover photo by Ric Moore.
Cover inset by Dave Hamby.**

Chapter 1
A BACKWARD GLANCE
"Damn the torpedoes! Full speed ahead!"
Those may be the most famous words with which Mobile is associated, but Admiral David Farragut's assault represents only one of many times that Mobile's rich assets have made it a coveted prize. In all, six flags have flown over the city.
Page 16

Chapter 2
DOWNTOWN
A second Golden Age.
Not since antebellum times when cotton was king have spirits been so high or things looked so good.
Page 28

Chapter 3
PEOPLE
Men and women who have made their mark.
Hank Aaron hit his first ball here. Jimmy Buffett was raised here too. Fewer may recall that an international chess champion and Thomas Edison's right-hand man were both educated here; or that the nation's first black T.V. camerawoman was a Mobile native.
Page 40

A Gulf Coast Treasure

Chapter 4
ATTRACTIONS
Hospitality Southern-style.
Wrap-around porches with creaky swings. Stoops. Park benches. A shady canopy of oaks to stroll under. They all seem to invite people to stay awhile. Tourists and newcomers tout the city's friendliness as an intangible benefit, but one of its strongest commodities. And there is lots to see and do here.
Page 52

Chapter 5
MARDI GRAS
You can bet your Moon Pie the first parades were staged here.
For 10 days before Lent the city sheds its dignity as thousands of Mobilians join in the revelry. Balls, receptions, and other functions begin in November and last through April.
Page 68

Chapter 6
THE DELTA
A natural gem.
The Mobile-Tensaw Delta, a vast wilderness of seemingly endless water trails, lying within minutes of downtown Mobile, was a treasure prized by early American Indians and today is prized by sportsmen, lumbermen, scientists, and all those who value nature and its vast array of surprises.
Page 80

Chapter 7
THE PORT & WATERWAYS
A maritime heritage and an international outlook.
Shipping interests connect this city to seaports throughout the world, giving it a global view, while thousands of miles of inland waterways keep it in touch with the pulse of the nation.
Page 90

Chapter 8
MOBILE ON THE MOVE
Industrial muscle. High-tech capabilities.
Plentiful raw materials such as natural gas, water, and timber, plus ease of transportation and a friendly business climate, make Mobile a choice location for many kinds of businesses and commerce.
Page 100

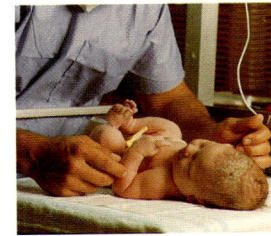

Chapter 9
HEALTH & EDUCATION
Mobile's two biggest employers help keep mind and body in shape.
Mobile County has the state's first public school system. Its medical society is more than 150 years old. Such milestones point to Mobile's commitment to health and education.
Page 108

Contents
MOBILE'S ENTERPRISES
Part II
❧

Patrons
Page 234

Bibliography
Page 235

Index
Page 236

Chapter 10
NETWORKS
The area's transportation, communications, and energy firms keep people, information, and power circulating inside and outside the area.

Mobile Gas, 122-123; The Mobile Airport Authority, 124-125; South Central Bell, 126-127; WKRG-TV, 128-129; Contel Cellular, 130; WBLX AM and FM Radio Stations, 131; ST&T, Inc., 132; Alabama Power Company, 133

Page 120

Chapter 11
MANUFACTURING, DISTRIBUTION, & TECHNOLOGY
Producing and shipping goods for individuals and industry, manufacturing and distribution firms provide employment for many Mobile area residents, while the technical firms contribute to the high-tech community.

Inchcape Shipping Services, 136-137; Jeffreys Steel Company, 138-139; QMS, 140-141; Courtaulds Fibers, 142; Cooper/T. Smith Corporation, 143; Hoechst Celanese, 144; Mobile Paperboard/Recycled Fibers of Alabama, 145; Warrior & Gulf Navigation Company, 146; Degussa Corporation, 147; Equity Technologies Corporation, 148; QF, Inc., 149; Mobile Aerospace Engineering, Inc., 150

Page 134

Chapter 12
BUSINESS & FINANCE
Mobile's business, insurance, and financial community offers a strong base for the area's growing economy.

Mobile Area Chamber of Commerce, 154-155; First Alabama Bank, 156; Hiller Investments Incorporated, 157; AmSouth Bank, 158; Warranty Corporation, 159; SouthTrust Bank, 160; Pete Peters and Associates, 161; Colonial Bank, 162

Page 152

Chapter 13
PROFESSIONS

From law to architecture, advertising to consulting, Mobile's professional firms are recognized as leaders in their fields.

Adams and Reese, 166-167; Miller, Hamilton, Snider & Odom, L.L.C., 168-169; Johnstone, Adams, Bailey, Gordon and Harris, 170-171; Lewis Communications, Inc., 172; Lyons, Pipes & Cook, P.C., 173; Gottlieb, Barnett, & Bridges Engineering Consultants, 174; Sirote & Permutt, P.C., 175; Richardson, Daniell, Spear & Upton, P.C., 176

Page 164

Chapter 14
BUILDING GREATER MOBILE

From concept to completion, the Mobile area's building and real estate industry shapes tomorrow's skyline and neighborhoods.

Cummings and White-Spunner, Inc., 180; White-Spunner Construction, Inc., 181; Lane, Lyons, Burton & Bullock, Inc. Real Estate, 182; Thompson Engineering, 183; J. S. Walton & Co., Inc., 184; Hosea O. Weaver & Sons, Inc., 185; McAleer-Rogers-Willard, Inc., 186; David Volkert & Associates, Inc., 187; Vance McCown Construction Company, Inc., 188; Brett Real Estate, 189; Southern Earth Sciences, Inc., 190; The Buyer's Agent, 191; Roberts Brothers, Inc., 192

Page 178

Chapter 15
EDUCATION & QUALITY OF LIFE

Educational and religious industries, recreation, and leisure-oriented companies all contribute to the high quality of life in the Mobile area.

University of South Alabama, 196-199; Coastal Land Trust, Inc., 200; St. Paul's Episcopal School, 201; Spring Hill College, 202; UMS-Wright Preparatory School, 203

Page 194

Chapter 16
HEALTH CARE

The Mobile area's progressive medical community is shaped by compassionate, caring, keen minds and modern facilities.

University of South Alabama Hospitals, 206-209; Bay Area Plastic Surgery, 210-211; Saad Enterprises, 212-213; Providence Hospital, 214; Cardio-Thoracic and Vascular Surgical Associates, 215; PrimeHealth, 216; Mobile Infirmary Medical Center, 217; Blue Cross and Blue Shield of Alabama, 218; Springhill Memorial Hospital, 219; Mobile Bay OB-GYN Associates, 220; Partial Hospital Institute of America, Inc., 221; Cardiology Associates of Mobile, P.C., 222; Pulmonary Associates of Mobile, P.A., 223; Cogburn Health Center, Inc., 224; The Mobile Heart Center, 225; Anesthesia Services, P.C., 226; Mobile Orthopedic Center, 227

Page 204

Chapter 17
THE MARKET PLACE

The area's grocers and their suppliers, as well as the hospitality industry, vitalize the economic life of the Mobile community.

Barber Dairies, 230; Holiday Inn Downtown, 231; Delchamps, 232

Page 228

FOREWORD

Anyone who has ever visited Mobile or lived here understands what we mean when we refer to it as a "treasure" on the Gulf of Mexico. Mobile is historic, romantic, and beautiful, yet it has become very much a New South city, one that has successfully entered the arena of global competition and one whose future prospects have already been labeled very good by those who professionally make such predictions.

In fact, this book was undertaken because it marks a very important period in Mobile's history. It is a celebration of nearly a decade of steady, upward economic growth. It is a sneak preview of downtown and waterfront development programs that rival those of the most progressive cities in the nation. And it's an opportunity for us to showcase some of the successful ventures that were cultivated and launched in the late 1980s which have now come to fruition. Some of those ventures are in the form of new or expanded businesses that you'll read about in the business profile section.

The words and pictures in this book invite you to use your imagination to sample our fresh seafood, take a leisurely boat ride through our magnificent delta area, catch a Moon Pie at one of our festive Mardi Gras parades, or visit one of our history-laden antebellum homes. It's a story about one of the oldest and finest cities in the South.

So read on, and you'll soon discover why Mobile is considered a Gulf Coast treasure.

Winthrop M. Hallett III
President
Mobile Area Chamber of Commerce

PREFACE

I think of all the things I love about this area and wonder how I ever managed to leave it for more than a decade to see the rest of the world and to find my way in life.

I love the long avenues of majestic live oaks; the peanut man with his wares; the Government Street cannon; the gargoyles in the form of eagles atop the *Mobile Press Register* building; the camellias with names like Dr. Tinsley and Professor Sargent; the late fall, which brings black-eyed Susans, red basil, and gray-blue tufts of ageratum growing wild along the roadsides; hot sand under foot; backyards from Citronelle to Bayou La Batre with amber-green scuppernongs hanging thick on the vine and with figs whose brown skins encase ruby-red centers and crunchy seeds.

And I love the storytelling tradition. Hearing my father tell over and over again how his mother, maid, and five of his brothers were strung out like the tail of a kite as they struggled against the wind to reach a cottage behind the Grand Hotel during the 1916 Hurricane. And how the family jewels were lost. And how they were unburied after nine days of prayer.

This book owes a lot to the memory of my father, who was a reporter for the *Mobile Press Register* for more than 27 years. Most people remember him by his maritime column and his trademark beret. It also owes a lot to my mother, who has a keen appreciation for good writing. It especially owes to those who reviewed the manuscript and, drawing on their fields of special expertise, offered their comments. ⚜

Jean-Marie McDonnell

ACKNOWLEDGMENTS

One of the most rewarding things about doing a book on Mobile is having the opportunity to work with the people who live here. People helped in so many ways. I was impressed not only with their kindness, but also with how many bright minds we have here. While I could not write this book without the help of many people, they bear no responsibility for any error in the text.

Special thanks go to George H. Schroeter and his staff at the Local History and Genealogy Division, Mobile Public Library, where I spent many months doing the research for this book. Thanks also go to Annette Huddle, reference services manager, Mobile Public Library, and her staff.

Tom Ellis, Peggy Jeffrey, Mary Morgan Toulmin, and my mother, Ruth McDonnell, kindly proofed the manuscript before it went to my editor at Community Communications. Their knowledge of the area and appreciation of the English language were of immeasurable help. My editor Lenita Gilreath's good sense of humor and constant encouragement helped make the lonely life of a free-lance writer more bearable.

Many thanks also go to each of the following for reviewing the manuscript in their areas of expertise: Sue Alexander, internal communications coordinator, and Sarah Teague, public affairs manager of the Alabama State Docks; Dr. Ian W. Brown, University of Alabama professor and curator of Gulf Coast archaeology for the Alabama Museum of Natural History; Roger Clay, Alabama Game and Fish Division nongame wildlife biologist; Dr. George Crozier, Marine Environmental Sciences Consortium, Dauphin Island Sea Lab; Myrna Bayne, Elaine D. Klotz, and Vangalia Kordomenos with the Mobile County Public School System; Wayne Dean, Mardi Gras historian who reigns as the fourth Chief Slacabamorinico; Monde Murphy Donaldson, alumni and parent relations director, Spring Hill College; Dr. Samuel Eichold, Eichold-Heustis Medical Museum of the South founder; J. Renee Eley, Office of Special Events, City of Mobile director, and her staff; Jack Friend, historian; Eva Golson, City of Mobile Department of Tourism, and her staff; Jay Higginbotham, City of Mobile municipal archivist; John Hall, assistant director of the Alabama Museum of Natural History; Mark C. McDonald, Mobile Historic Development Commission director; John C.H. Miller Jr., Mobile Downtown Redevelopment Commission chairman; Paul Moser and William Everett Smith, Geological Survey of Alabama; Amy Oliver, development director, and Pat Ryan, senior horticulturist, Bellingrath Gardens; Randy Roach with the U.S. Fish and Wildlife Service; Elizabeth Sanders, director, Main Street Mobile; Dr. Michael Thomason, University of South Alabama professor and head of the USA Photography Archives; Walter Tatum, chief marine biologist with the Marine Resources Division of the Alabama Department of Conservation and Natural Resources; Richard K. Wallace, Alabama Cooperative Extension Service, Sea Grant Extension, Mobile; and Wilbert J. Wetzel, Office of Community Services manager.

Others who helped include Jean Galloway, Mobile Arts Council director; Vic Knight, Senior Bowl public relations director; Tom Mason, of Tom Mason Communications; Len Motykiewicz, director of racing, Mobile Greyhound Park; Sage Lyons, Coastal Land Trust; and Lee Schissler, president and CEO, Mobile Convention & Visitors Corp.; and Jean Yuille, retired school teacher.

The following people opened their archives to me or provided me with materials that were not otherwise readily available: Don Brady, South Alabama Regional Planning Commission executive director; Dr. Semoon Chang, Center for Business and Economic Research director; Hillary H. Jeffcoat, district chief United States Department of the Interior, Geological Survey, Water Resources Division; Jim Martin, vice chairman, Mobile Black Chamber of Commerce; Chichi Terney, the papers of Mobile historian John Glennon; the staff of the Mobile Historic Preservation Society; and the staff of the Mobile Area Chamber of Commerce.

This book would not have been possible without the support of the Mobile Area Chamber of Commerce, Winthrop M. Hallett III, president. I particularly appreciate the encouragement I received from him and from Jodi Zielinski Swiderek, vice president communications/community development.

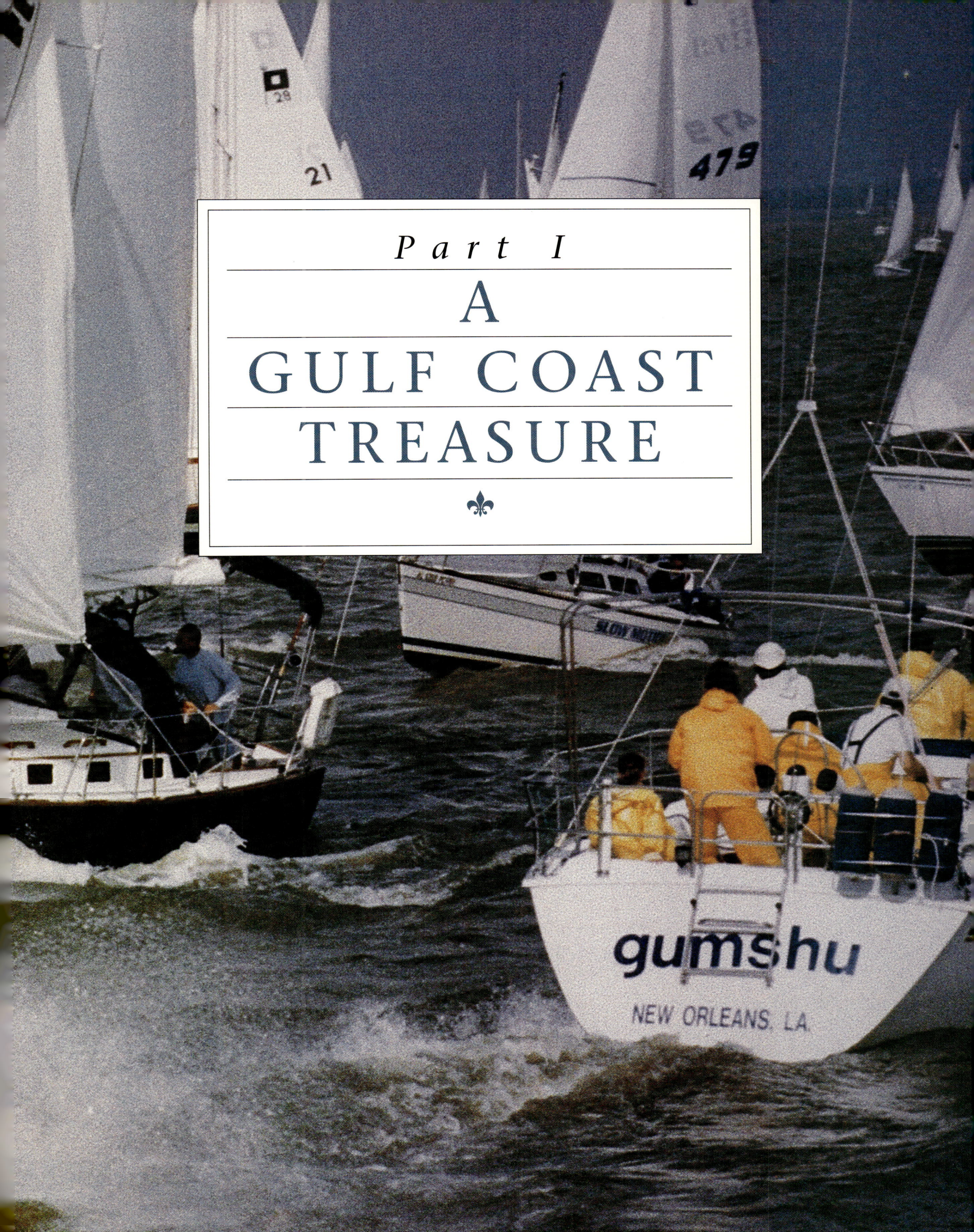

Chapter 1
A BACKWARD GLANCE

"Damn the torpedoes! Full speed ahead!"

A Gulf Coast Treasure

The inscription "He who founds a city builds himself a lifelong monument" on a Bienville Square marker honors Jean Baptiste le Moyne d'Bienville, a Frenchman who established Mobile at its present site in 1711. Now as in the past, the park offers a shady retreat for its visitors. Photo courtesy of the University of South Alabama Archives.

On the previous page
An angel in Magnolia Cemetery stands sentry over the graves of the many people who helped shape Mobile's dramatic history. Photo by Dave Hamby.

On the previous page, inset
The French, the British, the Americans, the Spanish, and the Confederates each claimed Mobile. A sixth flag (not shown) belonging to the Republic of Alabama flew over the city for a few weeks in 1861 before the state aligned with the Confederacy. The flag, which bears a woman holding a flag, is rarely flown. Photo by Ric Moore.

Early explorers of the Mobile Bay area found neither gold nor silver nor fountains of youth. They, and others like them in the centuries that followed, however, found an even greater treasure along the sunbaked Gulf Coast.

Mobile (pronounced *moh BEEL*) lies in that area of the country between east Georgia and the Mississippi River, which was the cradle of the earliest Spanish exploration and the first permanent French colonization. The bay's exploration in 1519 was concurrent with Hernando Cortés's triumph over the Aztec kingdom in Mexico and predated the Pilgrims' landing on Plymouth Rock by a hundred years.

The bay's easily defended harbor, linked to an extensive, navigable river system, led to an interior with natural riches—an abundance of crystal-clear springs, large stands of timber, a wealth of game and fur-bearing creatures, relatively fertile soil, and a temperate climate. The area's lack of gold cooled the interest of early explorers. But the area's many assets made it a prize coveted by later explorers seeking to expand the empires of their mother countries.

Thus it is that Mobile's history unfolds like a drama. It is a city of which historian Peter Joseph Hamilton (1859-1927) once wrote, "born in romance, cradled in chivalry, baptized in fire, educated in commerce, it is made for greatness."

Mobile's precarious position on man-made boundaries between nations and its bountiful resources drew the area into controversy as one country and then another claimed it for its own. The Spanish, the French, the British, the Americans, and, for four years, the Confederates, have all claimed Mobile. The Spanish and American flags each flew over her for two periods, and, if the American claim under the Louisiana Purchase is correct, it belonged to France twice. A sixth flag belonging to the Republic of Alabama flew over Mobile from January 11, 1861, to February 4, 1861, after the state left the Union, but before it joined the Confederacy.

Mobile's position between Pensacola and New Orleans ensured the city would be spiced with an international flavor to retain a unique taste. Hamilton noted, "Modern Louisiana was never under the English flag, and Florida was not under the French, except in part as the temporary fruit of war, while the Mobile country saw and honored all five standards."

Spain's Admiral Alonso Álvarez de Pineda visited in 1519. Pineda's fleet of four ships remained in Mobile Bay for more than a month while repairs were made. During that time Pineda mapped the area and kept a written account. He also traded with the Indians on the shore of Mobile Bay. On a 15-mile trip up the Mobile River, he counted more than 40 Indian villages.

In 1540 Hernando de Soto's expedition visited Mauvila, an Indian city in the Mobile-Tensaw Delta that was later to give Mobile its name, but whose location remains enshrouded in mystery. A battle ensued, leaving thousands of Indians dead. Though only a handful of de Soto's men died, the psychological and logistical effect was devastating. De Soto abandoned plans to rendezvous with a supply ship in Mobile Bay for fear of mutiny.

Tristan de Luna's brief attempt to settle the area between 1559 and 1561 was the most ambitious colonization effort in the New World to that date. He had sailed from Veracruz, Mexico, with 13 ships, 500 soldiers, 1,000 colonists, and 240 horses. Before he could unload, a hurricane struck and most of his supplies were lost. Had he succeeded, the colony would have been the oldest in the United States, predating Saint Augustine by four years.

In 1699 European ships again sailed into Mobile Bay, but this time the sailors were French, not Spanish. Pierre Le Moyne d'Iberville led the expedition and was accompanied by his brother Bienville, who was destined to succeed d'Iberville as governor of the French capital.

Iberville's charge, like that of so many other adventurers, was to find the mouth of the fabled Mississippi and to build a fort so that other nations would be barred from access to the extensive waterway and its tributaries.

In his February 3 journal entry, Iberville wrote of his exploration of the bay. He named the island guarding the bay's mouth "Massacre Island" because he found the remains of 60 bodies there. He later renamed the island "Dauphine." It is now known as Dauphin Island.

When Iberville landed on the mainland, he saw buds swelling on the trees as the first hints of spring touched Mobile County: "I found all kinds of trees, oak, elm, ash, pines, and other trees I do not know, many creepers, sweet-smelling violets, and other yellow flowers, horse-beans . . . hickories of a very thin bark, birch (the high ground not being subject to flooding), traces of Indians and some huts, from which they had moved no more than six days before."

He and his men continued west to set up Fort Maurepas on Biloxi Bay at what is now Ocean Springs, Mississippi. His visit to Mobile Bay must have left a lingering impression, for he returned to the area when the fort failed.

The new settlement, built in 1702 on Twenty-Seven Mile Bluff, a location 26 miles north of the present city, was named Fort Louis de la Louisiane and called "La Mobile."

This was a glorious point in Mobile's history. The tiny fort reigned as the capital of French Louisiana with a domain stretching from Canada to the Gulf of Mexico and from the Appalachians westward to the Rockies. Toward the end of its second decade, the French capital was moved to Biloxi and then in 1722 to New Orleans.

Throughout Mobile's early history, the colonists feted the Indians and showered them with presents at an annual gathering. As many as 2,000 Indians would descend upon the city during these "congresses" to trade furs and negotiate prices for the upcoming year.

The French strived to ensure the permanence of the new colony by bringing in women. A shipload of 23 potential brides arrived aboard the *Pélican* in 1704. The new arrivals detested, among other things, corn, a staple in the New World diet. The fracas they caused has been recorded in history as the Petticoat Rebellion.

The Mobile River flooded in 1710, swamping the settlement, so the French capital of Louisiana was moved the following year to the site where the city of Mobile now stands. The French constructed a wooden fort there in 1711. An impressive brick fortress was constructed between 1724 and 1735. Fort Condé was rebuilt

Horse-drawn carriages at Fort Condé treat guests to a ride from an era gone by. Photo by Ric Moore.

in honor of the bicentennial and lies in downtown Mobile close to the waterfront.

French ships carrying slaves from Africa arrived in Mobile aboard the *Africaine* in 1721, marking the first large introduction of African slavery to the Louisiana colony. Though the United States outlawed the importation of slaves in 1808, a shipload arrived aboard the *Clotilde* in 1859 as a wager to see whether they could be smuggled in.

The repercussions of the French and Indian War against the British and the close of the Seven Years' War in Europe were not felt here until the warring powers signed the Treaty of Paris in 1763.

Through the treaty, England acquired all of France's holdings east of the Mississippi River except New Orleans. Thus Mobile changed hands, and the new owners renamed the fort "Fort Charlotte" in honor of England's queen. Spain was given New Orleans and the land west of the Mississippi.

During the American Revolution, fighting in Alabama was limited to the Mobile Bay area. The Spaniards sided with the Americans against the British, so Bernardo de Gálvez, Spanish governor of Louisiana, set out to capture Mobile. He bombarded Fort Condé, and the British surrendered March 14, 1780.

Gálvez's overall plan, according to local historian David E. Denny Jr., was to seize British-held Pensacola. To anchor his plans, Gálvez garrisoned a fort across from Mobile on the east side of Mobile Bay atop a high bluff. The area is still known as Spanish Fort.

British General John Campbell ordered four attacks on the outpost in late 1780 and early 1781, all of which were repulsed. With Mobile and that point west to the Mississippi secured, General George Washington's troops could continue to travel through the Mississippi and Ohio rivers. Pensacola surrendered to Gálvez May 9, 1781.

Though the United States claimed Mobile Bay as a part of Louisiana purchased from the French in 1803, the Spanish continued to occupy the city. The Spanish forces were finally ousted April 14, 1813, when President James Madison sent 600 soldiers to reclaim the city. Not a shot was fired.

Throughout the colonial period and into the early 1800s, Indian raids and settler reprisals were common. One of the most brutal conflicts occurred August 30, 1813, when the Creeks stormed Fort Mims in northern Baldwin County across the bay from Mobile. In response, General Andrew Jackson crushed the Creek nation at the Battle of Horseshoe Bend on March 27, 1814. After the battle, Jackson pushed toward Mobile and made his headquarters at the site where the Battle House now stands. The Indians lost half of Alabama in postwar treaties. After the War of 1812, settlers flooded into the state looking for land to grow cotton.

High times and hard times characterized Mobile as it matured from a rough frontier town into a city of culture and charm. During the nineteenth century, yellow fever cut into the city's population, while fires cut great swaths through the city and demolished hundreds of buildings at a time. Mobile lost a tenth of its 2,700 residents within two months to illness, prompting the city to purchase the Church Street Graveyard in 1820. The Fire of 1919, in which more than 200 houses were lost, was the city's last major blaze.

As early as 1826, Mobilians recognized a need for public education and created a school commission board. Ten years later Barton Academy, a splendid Greek Revival structure on Government Street, was constructed, but because of inadequate funding, it was rented to private concerns that charged tuition. Numerous tuition-free parochial schools filled the gap.

Reconstruction brought educational opportunities for blacks. Blue College, operated by the American Missionary Society, opened its doors in 1865. It was renamed the Emerson Institute. Mobile County Training School, founded in 1880, also provided an education for black students.

Beginning in the 1820s, the fur trade gave way to the cotton trade, and Mobile prospered. During the decade the city's population quadrupled to 12,672 residents, and cotton exports increased from 103,065 bales to 440,102 bales.

An ebullient sense of optimism and hedonistic sense of prosperity marked the time. The city took pride in a thriving intelligentsia whose focal point was the home of Octavia Le Vert, a woman whose charisma defies explanation. Nationally and internationally known actors, poets, musicians, writers, artists, and politicians met in her parlor to exchange ideas. One of her most faithful correspondents, judging by the thick stack of letters preserved by the Historic Mobile Preservation Society, was U.S. statesman and orator Henry Clay. The queen of Mobile society's popularity waned after the Civil War because she entertained Union soldiers.

An interest in theater caught on during the 1800s and flourished. The earliest record of theater documented in Mobile dates to 1808 when a traveling company from Charleston played. The first theater built in the city with the first regular company opened December 24, 1824, under the direction of Noah Ludlow. The Mobile Theatre was built on part of the site of Fort Condé at the northwest corner of Royal and Theatre Streets, the latter taking its name after the erection of the theater. Sections were also provided for blacks and for quadroons. Theater reached its height in Mobile during the 1840s and 1850s when the city rivaled Charleston, Saint Louis, and New Orleans as the theatrical center of the South.

As its American Revolution bicentennial gift to the nation, the City of Mobile partially reconstructed Fort Condé as it stood under French dominance. Today costumed guides offer the official city welcome to thousands of tourists each year. Photo by Ric Moore.

The Tennessee *fought the entire Union fleet for more than two hours before surrendering. Farragut may have won the Battle of Mobile Bay, but the city remained a Confederate stronghold until the spring of 1865. Photo courtesy of the University of South Alabama Archives.*

Cotton merchants James, John, and Samuel Battle, established in 1852 what was perhaps the most opulent hotel in the Southeast. The Battle House on Royal and Saint Francis Streets was fitted with modern conveniences—the 240 sleeping and living rooms were gas fitted and had baths with hot and cold water. Planters from the delta flocked there after the harvest and enjoyed lavish entertainment.

Mobilians had mixed emotions as the secessionist movement swept the South. They feared war would disrupt the cotton trade and throw the local economy into chaos, which it did.

Mobilians enlisted and there were camps and fortifications nearby. The city, however, was not threatened until the summer of 1864. Until then, many Mobilians must have followed with interest the activities of Admiral Raphael Semmes, a Marylander who had moved to Mobile in the 1840s. Semmes's ship, the *Alabama,* terrorized the high seas and sank 69 Union vessels.

The war finally closed in on August 5, 1864, when the Union's Rear Admiral David G. Farragut, aboard the flagship *Hartford,* ordered his 14 wooden ships and 4 ironclads to steam through the pass guarded by Fort Morgan and Fort Gaines.

His adversary, Confederate Admiral Franklin Buchanan, led a tiny fleet, consisting of the ironclad *Tennessee* and the wooden gunboats *Gaines, Morgan,* and *Selma.* Buchanan had been in command of the South's *Merrimac* when it fought the *Monitor* to a standstill at Hampton Roads in March of 1862—the world's first engagement of ironclads.

Carter C. Smith's epilogue for *Two Naval Journals at the Battle of Mobile Bay* gives his salute to the encounter: "There was the drama of the defending Confederate squadron, outgunned more than six to one, bringing the attack to the Federal armada. There was great seamanship—and classic snafus. There was high heroism and chivalry. There was in the end a full-blown mythology—about who did and said what—almost before the smoke had cleared."

Fourteen of Farragut's ships steamed through the channel lashed together in pairs. The *Brooklyn* came to an abrupt halt, arresting the advance of the entire fleet while the guns of the fort played on it and the *Hartford*. Farragut watched as the *Tecumseh*, the lead ship, sank—the apparent victim of a floating mine, known as a torpedo.

Whether Farragut's order "Damn the torpedoes! Full speed ahead!" are his words or apocryphal ones remains a matter of historical debate. Local historian Jack Friend speculates the admiral "probably uttered his orders in a more orderly manner."

Soon after entering the harbor, the Union ships captured the *Selma* and disabled the *Gaines*. The *Gaines* sought refuge under the guns of Fort Morgan. The *Morgan* escaped.

Thus the *Tennessee* was left to defy the Union fleet. The Union vessels commenced to ram their adversary. During the battle the Union's *Lackawanna* missed the *Tennessee* and rammed her own flagship *Hartford*. The *Hartford* soon got clear and was ready to ram the *Tennessee* again when the Confederate ship struck her colors and ran up the white flag.

Farragut won the Battle of Mobile Bay, but the city remained a Confederate stronghold until the spring of 1865.

In March 1865, a force of 45,000 men was amassed against Mobile through a campaign along the Eastern Shore. It consisted of three commands—General Gordon Granger's Thirteenth Corps with 13,200 troops; A. J. Smith's Sixteenth Corps with 16,000 troops, plus 3,000 engineers, artillery, and cavalry; and Frederick Steele's column with 13,200 troops. Steele's command was sent to cut the railroad from Mobile to Montgomery.

Marching along the Eastern Shore, Smith and Granger's troops bore down on Spanish Fort and lay siege on March 27. The Union outnumbered the Confederates by more than three to one. Both sides ran out of ammunition, and the fighting stalled.

By April 4 the Union garrison was restocked and mounted an attack. The following day Confederate General Gibson telegraphed Major General D. H. Maury in Mobile a plea for reinforcements: "Enemy sweeps my flanks with heavy batteries, and presses on at all points . . . . My line is extended now to the water and in it. My men are worked all the time, and I don't believe I can possibly do the work necessary in the dense flats on the flanks . . . ."

The plea was unheeded, and while several hundred of his men covered him, Gibson and the rest of the garrison fled. The Union army moved on to Blakeley, where it united with Steele's forces.

The Confederacy fell April 9, 1865, with Robert E. Lee's surrender at Appomattox, but fighting continued north of Spanish Fort at Blakeley that afternoon. After a five-hour battle, the Confederates surrendered in what was probably the last charge of the war.

Mobile, left with a garrison of 5,000, was too weak to defend itself against an army with 10 times as many men. It surrendered April 12.

Unlike many Southern cities, Mobile was intact at the war's end. Ironically, the worst disaster in the city's history struck about six weeks later when a powder magazine near the waterfront at Lipscomb and Commerce streets exploded. The explosion rocked the city the afternoon of May 25 and ripped away an entire district within a 34-block area. About 500 to 600 people were killed according to newspaper accounts of the time.

An actual count of the dead has never been determined, for a south wind whipped up an inferno that consumed everything in its path. Because Mobile was a center of trade, many who did not call Mobile home doubtlessly lost their lives and were unaccounted for.

Julius Becker, foreman for the ordinance department, was on horseback at the corner of Government and Water streets when the blast occurred. In testimony at the court of inquiry he reported: "I first felt the concussion and shaking of the ground at the same time saw shells explode high in the air and heard the report like a long, heavy clap of thunder very loud. Then saw a dark smoke and thick flame of fire. I went towards the [cotton] press and within about a block and a half of it, but could not go nearer as shells commenced exploding all along. I saw that the warehouse was exploded and that the presses about were destroyed." Becker further testified that the blaze was so intense that he could not go near the location for eight days.

The magazine that exploded was a 180 by 160-foot building that was being used to store munitions captured from the Confederate forces. Two days before the disaster, a train with 30 tons of gunpowder captured in Gainesville had arrived, and about half of that was in the building at the time of the explosion, according to testimony from Brevet

After the War of 1812, settlers flooded into the state looking for land to grow cotton. As the cotton trade flourished, so did the city. Photo by Ric Moore.

Captain William S. Beebee, the 24-year-old ordinance officer in charge at the time. In addition, the building already held 200 tons of explosives.

Testimony after the explosion seemed to indicate that carelessness was to blame for the disaster. Two boxes filled with ammunition had been broken earlier in the day. Percussion shells that would explode with the snap of a thin wire appeared to be among the ordinance.

Becker testified the workers were handling their delicate job cavalierly. "The men were dropping the boxes and rolling them end over end from one side of the warehouse to the other," he said.

First the port's blockade and then the blast left Mobile's economy in a shambles. Reconstruction was difficult. At least 2 were killed and 20 wounded in a riot on May 14, 1867, after an incendiary speech given by William "Pig Iron" Kelley, a Pennsylvania congressman whose staunch defense of tariffs on iron imports had given him his nickname. The press reported that about 300 bodies were found at various locations around town, but Sarah Woolfolk Wiggins in a footnote for an article in *The Alabama Review* (January 1970) says reports immediately after the incident exaggerated the number killed.

Mobile languished for most of the rest of the century, but with time, the city recuperated. The cotton economy was eventually replaced with a timber economy, and the city flourished once more.

When electricity was introduced in the 1880s, it brought fundamental changes to the city. Carriages had to compete with the new electric trolley car service that replaced the horse-drawn cars in 1893. The city gradually developed suburbs along the streetcar lines and, with the introduction of the electric elevator, a skyline, shortly after the turn of the century.

Many Mobilians spent the summer months at summer cottages or in one of several hotels on the Eastern Shore. The best known was The Grand Hotel in Point Clear. Ferry boats such as the *Bay Queen*, the *Annie*, and the *James A. Carney* carried passengers and freight back and forth on a regular schedule, weather and tides permitting. The bay boats provided the only nonrail link to the two shores until the causeway was completed in 1927. Pilings along the Eastern Shore where the bay boats once docked stand as the last vestiges of the period. In Daphne alone, pilings from the Shonts Wharf, Belrose Wharf, Howard's Wharf, Dryer Wharf, and the Daphne Wharf mark the era.

Entry of the United States into World War I in 1918 stimulated the port's shipyards. The Alabama Dry Dock and Shipbuilding Company trained some 4,000 workers and built three steel-hulled minesweepers, two wooden-hulled steamers, and two seagoing barges for the war effort. In all, at least a half dozen shipyards from the Mobile area sprang into action. But, the shipyards' World War I contributions were to be but a dress rehearsal for the country's second entry into the world theater.

Mobile's economy flourished in the 1920s. As historians Melton McLaurin and Michael Thomason noted in *Mobile, The Life and Times of a Great Southern City*: "The emergence of the automobile as an inexpensive, reliable means of family transportation led to the development of the tourist industry of suburban Mobile. While the city relied heavily on its water-borne commerce, industries noted its reserves of water, cheap labor, and raw materials, as well as its excellent transportation facilities . . . . Bank deposits rose markedly, wholesale and retail trade prospered, and industrial employment rose."

Mobilians continued to recognize the importance of education. To alleviate crowding at Barton Academy, Murphy High School, a handsome Spanish Renaissance structure, was opened in 1926. Construction was made possible by a Mobile County bond issue passed by voters during the 1922-1923 academic year.

Mobile weathered the Depression better than some.

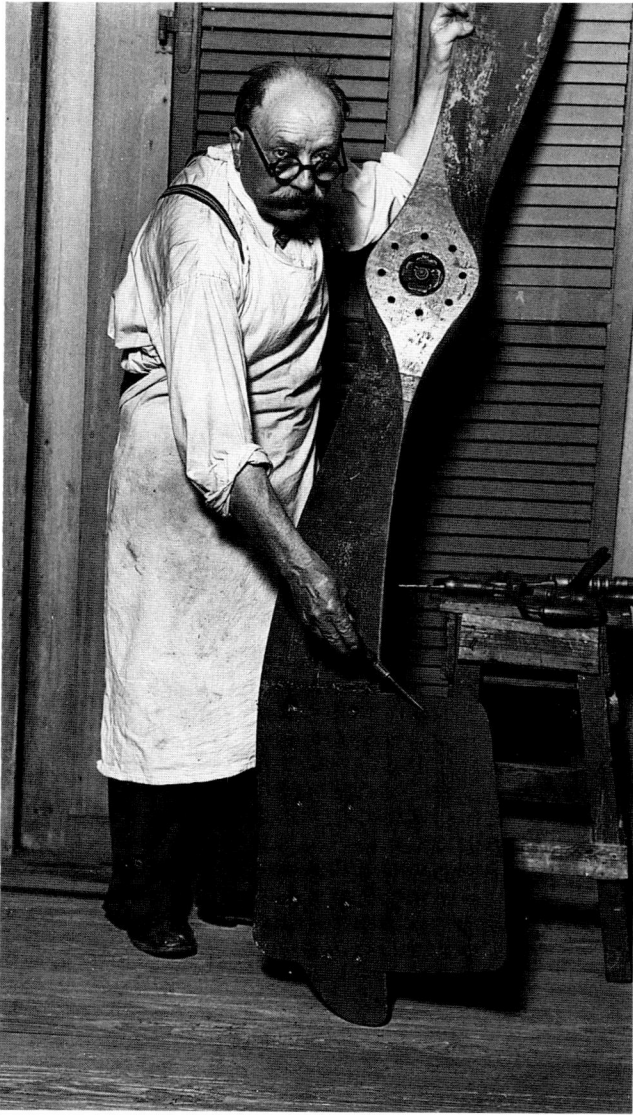

John Fowler pursued aviation long before the Wright brothers achieved their famous flight in 1903. Photo courtesy of the University of South Alabama Archives.

Carriages had to compete with the new electric trolley car service that replaced the horse-drawn cars in 1893. Photo courtesy of the Erik Overbey Collection, University of South Alabama Archives.

According to historians McLaurin and Thomason, Mobile escaped economic disaster because of its commercial rather than manufacturing base: "Many industrial positions, such as those in shipbuilding and repair and the railroad shops, were directly related to commerce. In comparison to Birmingham, with its industrialized economy founded on iron and steel production and goods manufactured from the two metals, Mobile breezed through the Depression."

Among other things, an announcement in 1939 that Brookley Field would be built south of the city, signaled that the city was on the brink of a new era.

Unlike any other event in the city's history, World War II converted the port from a sleepy Southern town into a bustling metropolis. Between 1940 and 1944, the

No other event in the city's history had an impact on Mobile like World War II. Once a sleepy Southern town, Mobile became a bustling metropolis. Recognized as the nation's fastest growing wartime city, Mobile glittered night and day, building, manufacturing, and shipping for the war effort. Photo courtesy of the ADDSCO Collection, University of South Alabama Archives.

metropolitan area's population boomed from 114,906 to 201,369. An article in the December 27, 1947, *Mobile Press Register* recalled that the city had been the nation's fastest growing wartime city.

The Second World War licked at the shores of Mobile and Baldwin Counties. A decked headline in the May 24, 1942, *Mobile Press Register* screamed: "Mystery Torpedoes Set Ships Aflame in Gulf; 57 lose lives in sinking of 2 more vessels; New Type Weapon Used for First Time in Submarine War; Mobilian Listed Among Victims of Disaster; Captain Says New Weapon 'Set Heavens Afire' as Sub Blasted his Ship."

Mobilian Bernard Fave died in the attack with the new weapon known as an incendiary torpedo. Home owners along the bayfront and Gulf Coast darkened their windows at night to prevent detection by the enemy. Some Gulf Shores residents still remember finding bits of wreckage and goods along the shore.

The Alabama Dry Dock and Shipbuilding Company, Gulf Shipbuilding Corporation at Chickasaw, and the Waterman Repair Division recruited thousands of willing, but unskilled, men and women into their ranks. At the peak of its activity, the Alabama Dry Dock and Shipbuilding Company counted 36,000 employees on its payroll. By 1943 Brookley Field had nearly 17,000 in its civilian workforce—a number amounting to Mobile's entire labor force three years earlier.

On the homefront, the war brought not only jobs to Mobile, but social upheaval also. Despite local resistance, women and blacks found jobs that had never been available to them before.

The housing shortage soon became critical. From 1941 to 1944, the population in the metropolitan area increased about 75 percent, while the supply of family housing increased less than a third.

Fuel and tire rationing further accentuated the need for workers to live in the city close to their jobs. By February 1943 Mobile's rationing board had declared special gasoline allotments would not be issued even for funerals.

Men worked in shifts and slept in shifts in what were known as "hot beds." To combat the housing shortage, a yellow, green, and red domestic propaganda leaflet showing a serviceman in jungle fatigues urged housewives to do their part: "The fight is ours. Mobile housekeepers must hold the line until new houses can be

After the outbreak of World War II, women and blacks found jobs that had never been available to them before. Photo courtesy of the University of South Alabama Archives.

built. You may not want to house a stranger in your home. Neither Do Our Men Want to Work, Fight and Suffer in Foreign Lands. You'll find American workers much more desirable than an Axis overlord. Ask any Frenchman!"

When peace was declared, housing became plentiful and the city had to readjust. But the war had fueled the city's economy, and the letdown was not fully felt for years. The thousands of rural residents who had come to work in Mobile wanted to remain in the cosmopolitan city they had come to call home.

By the end of the war, Mobile had emerged as a modern city. Perhaps Mobile's greatest strength in this age has been that of its leaders and their willingness to address the city's problems.

The natural beauty and plentiful resources that once attracted the early explorers continue to attract newcomers today. The cotton brokers, merchants, river pilots, and maritime traders who once walked the streets of DeTonti Square have been replaced with their modern-day counterparts. While Mobile remains a Southern city with a genial atmosphere and special charm, the Port City's heritage has given it a global perspective with international ties. Today it is a city with a pleasant blend of Old South charm and New South progressiveness. ⚜

From 1941 to 1944, the population of metropolitan Mobile grew about 75 percent, while housing increased less than a third. To combat the housing shortage, a propaganda leaflet showing a serviceman in jungle fatigues urged housewives to do their part: "The fight is ours. Mobile housekeepers must hold the line until new houses can be built. You may not want to house a stranger in your home. Neither Do Our Men Want to Work, Fight and Suffer in Foreign Lands. You'll find American workers much more desirable than an Axis overlord. Ask any Frenchman!" Photo by Ric Moore.

Chapter 2
DOWNTOWN
A second Golden Age.

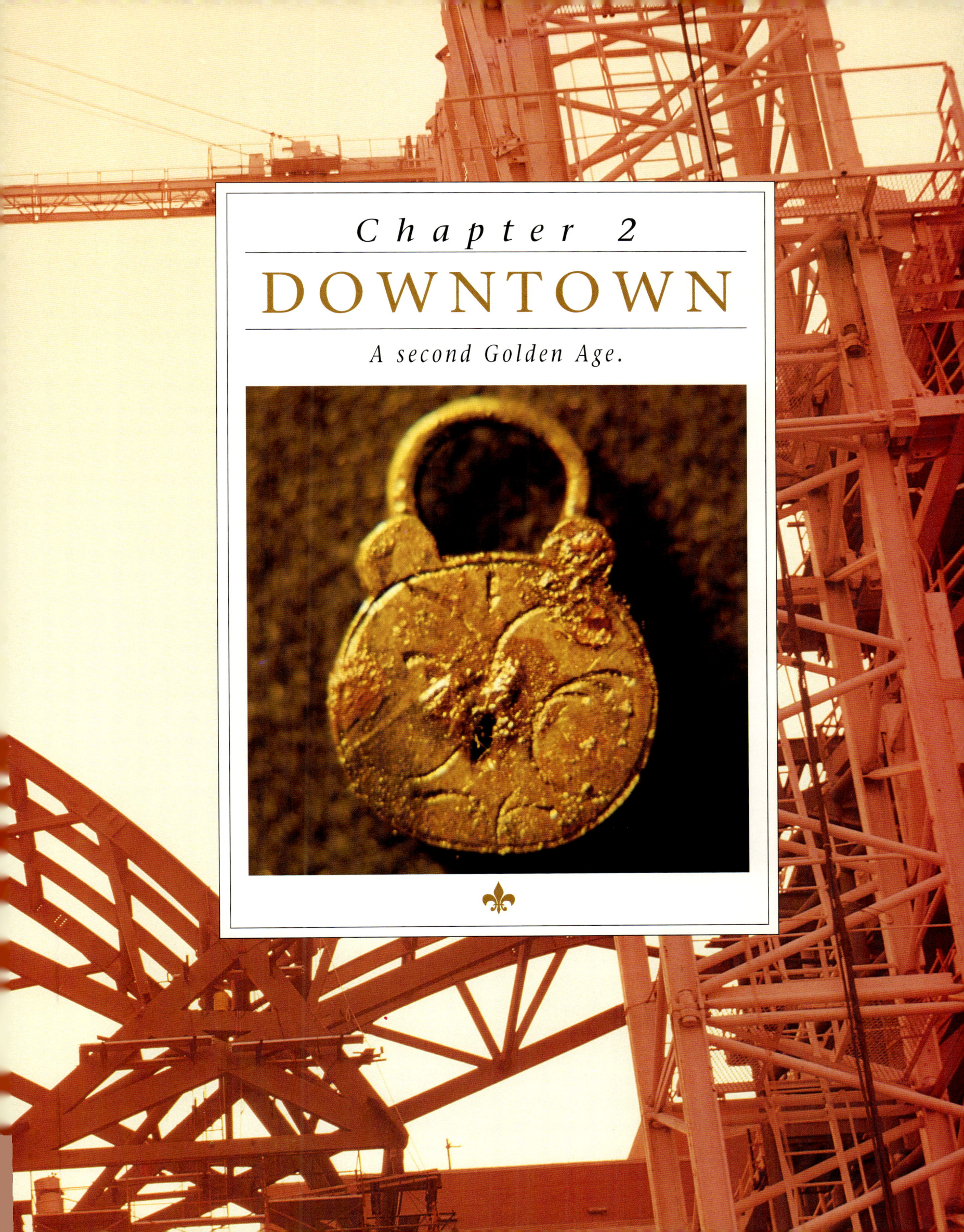

On the previous page
Mobile Government Plaza stands on a two-and-a-half-acre site where the Greyhound Bus Station and a parking lot once stood. The area was once considered the outer limits of colonial Mobile. Photo by Steve Goraum.

On the previous page, inset
Like a giant time capsule, the acres of asphalt at the Mobile Government Plaza construction site preserved and concealed artifacts from bygone eras. One of the most remarkable finds was this Indian locket which dates back to the 1700s. The locket is believed to have been traded with the French during the annual Indian "congresses." Photo by Greg Spies.

A wondrous canopy of trees covers Mobile, and because of that, Mobile has long been known to airline pilots as "the city under the trees." Photo by Ric Moore.

From all appearances downtown Mobile has entered a second Golden Age. Not since antebellum times when cotton was king have spirits been so high. Freshly painted, tidy shops and offices line the streets, while cultural events at Bienville Square keep downtown sidewalks crowded.

As recently as the 1960s critics called downtown Mobile "dingy" and the cultural and artistic scene "lacking." The criticism stung. Mobile began to address its problems. And though the city made great strides, it would take nearly three decades before the downward trend in the run-down area near the waterfront could be reversed.

The Historic Mobile Preservation Society, a group that was organized in the 1930s, and other civic groups set the stage for the area's revitalization by inspiring pride in the city's heritage. The Mobile Arts Council ensured the expansion and the survival of the arts. With the community awakened to the possibilities, the city took the initiative.

The Mobile Historic Development Commission, the city office charged with preserving the community's heritage, set ambitious goals. It wanted to overhaul two areas in the city that had fallen on hard times. A booklet called "An Outline of How Preservation of Mobile's

Traditional Architecture and Development of Mobile's Historic Districts Can Create a Multi-Million Dollar Industry" noted that a quarter of those vacationing by car take an interest in historic development.

Elegant historic districts such as Church Street East and DeTonti Square were redeveloped and used as residences or professional office space. The Mobile Civic Center with its rounded dome was perhaps the most notable change to the city's skyline. It provided a much needed auditorium and concert hall when it opened in 1964. Mobile's tallest downtown structure, the 33-story First National Bank Building (now AmSouth Bank), was completed in 1966. Fort Condé, reconstructed as part of the city's contribution to the bicentennial celebration, became the downtown visitors' center.

Hurricane Frederic ripped through in September 1979 and caused considerable damage. It was the first hurricane of any magnitude to hit the city since 1926. The eye of Frederic crossed Dauphin Island about 10 P.M. September 12. Peak wind gusts registered at 145 miles per hour. At 2 A.M. the following morning, the eye passed just west of Mobile. Total damage in Alabama, Florida, and Mississippi came to about $2 billion. Mobile County sustained nearly a billion dollars in damage—the greatest share by far. Many historic downtown structures were damaged. Mobile spent the rest of the year and the early 1980s cleaning up and rebuilding.

In the first half of the 1980s, private developers took the initiative with several structures on Government Street, one of the city's major thoroughfares. The Mobile Area Chamber of Commerce moved into a new building in 1981. In 1983 the Riverview Plaza was completed and is now known as the Adams Mark Hotel. In the same year, The LaClede Hotel, erected in 1855 and converted to a hotel in 1871, was given a face-lift. It now offers prime downtown office space. Another landmark, the Admiral Semmes Hotel, dating from 1940, reopened in 1984 as a luxury hotel. The hotel, which had been serving as a retirement home until Hurricane Frederic forced the residents' eviction, had housed the likes of First Lady Eleanor Roosevelt and Roy Rogers when it first served as a hotel.

Downtown, however, remained quiet, and many of the newly redone offices remained unoccupied until the early 1990s. In 1990, Mobile, under the leadership of Mayor Mike Dow, recommitted itself to revitalizing the inner city. A new organization, the Mobile Downtown Redevelopment Commission, was created in June 1990 to stimulate development through public/private partnerships.

In January of 1992 this group submitted a proposal known as "The String of Pearls" as a catalyst for down-

Another big project on the scale of the Convention Center and Mobile Government Plaza is the Exploreum Museum of Discovery with an Omnimax Theatre and a Spitz Planetarium. A fish-eye projection with a 180-degree unbroken image within a dome makes Omnimax audiences part of the action. Photo courtesy of Starboard Theatres Ltd.

town revitalization. Three pearls in "The String of Pearls" were soon part of the necklace. By the mid-1990s, funding for a $10-million Exploreum Museum of Discovery with an Omnimax Theatre and a Spitz Planetarium was secured through the cooperative efforts of the city, state, and county, as well as through local foundations, and private corporations. A fish-eye projection with a 180-degree unbroken image within a dome makes Omnimax audiences part of the action. Plans for another pearl gleamed as a three-acre riverfront park south of the Convention Center gained a $1.95-million federal grant in August 1993.

Though all the "pearls" in "The String of Pearls" were not immediately realized, that effort, plus numerous ongoing financial incentives developed to encourage owners of historic property to rehabilitate their buildings, created a stir. Speculation from casino interests that casino gambling would soon be legalized further fueled interest in the area.

The chief stimulus, however, was the decision to put the Mobile Convention Center at a downtown site. It had taken years to make the decision, and some would say that Mayor Authur Outlaw lost his bid for reelection over the fight.

Once the decision was made, jackhammers pounded, dust flew, and workers in yellow hard hats seemed to rule the I-beams in the upper reaches of buildings under construction as well as the streets down below. The former 212-room Sheraton underwent a $7-million renovation to become the Holiday Inn Downtown. The

Port City Brewery opened on Dauphin Street after a fire razed plans for housing it in the German Relief Hall. The Fine Arts Museum of the South opened FAMOS Downtown, a satellite gallery in the Cathedral Square Arts District. In addition, new nightclubs and restaurants opened each week.

As these projects got under way, the Downtown Redevelopment Commission sought developers and financing for other components of the necklace. In the meantime, downtown hummed with activity.

For the first time in about a decade, a private investor decided to lay out funds to construct a new building in downtown. McAleer-Rogers-Willard, Inc. took on the $2-million project—a two-story 40,000-square-foot building on Saint Francis Street near Bienville Square. It was completed in 1994 and leased to the General Services Administration for the Corps of Engineers. Most investors until that time were interested in renovation projects or low-risk projects with a heavy public-sector partnership.

Mobile municipal and county projects completed in the first half of the 1990s included a $19-million metro jail that could accommodate 480 inmates and a $58-million city-county complex known as Mobile Government Plaza. A six-story Mobile County Parking Garage with 532 parking spaces was built at a cost of $4.8 million to service the new complex.

The design for the Mobile Government Plaza boasted a twenty-first century architectural style. The winning design was selected from 195 entries submitted by architectural firms from throughout the world. A gigantic cascading atrium with scissored bow trusses supports the vaulted roof. The atrium joins a ten-story administrative office building with a nine-story court building. The judiciary building holds 22 courts, and each court, with the exception of the ceremonial court, is two stories high. The building's facade and interior of rosa porrino granite were imported from Spain.

The complex stands on the two-and-a-half-acre site where the Greyhound Bus Station and a wasteland of parking lots once stood. But before that, before cars and buses were ever invented, and indeed when the entire population of the city was measured in hundreds rather than thousands, the block stood on the outer limits of colonial Mobile.

Like a giant bank vault, the acres of asphalt, which became the complex site, preserved and concealed artifacts from bygone eras. From this chance time capsule, an archeological team uncovered more than a quarter of a million artifacts, enough for a revolving exhibit in the basement of the new building. The excavators unearthed clues showing that a public area, military quarters, and an Indian village once stood at the site.

The most remarkable find was a coin which is believed to date to 1670. The coin, bearing the imprint of Louis XIV of France on one side and a rose bush on the other, may be one of only three to have been minted.

Looking from Mobile Government Plaza toward the waterfront, one can't help but notice the Mobile Convention Center, which was undoubtedly the key to the renewed interest in downtown.

Like an exquisite multifaceted diamond, the $52-million Mobile Convention Center with its many glistening windows studs the waterfront. More than 45,000 square feet of windows afford panoramic views of the bustling harbor and Mobile skyline. Atop the convention center's patinated green roof soars a 13-story airy white spire representing a lighthouse in honor of Mobile's maritime heritage. The 317,000-square-foot building completed in September 1993 contains an exhibit hall, 16 meeting rooms, a 14,700-square-foot grand ballroom, an elegant lobby, and outdoor river terraces affording spectacular views of the waterfront. A graceful crosswalk over Water Street links the convention center to a high-rise parking lot and provides a romantic promenade for those attending social events at the center.

Promoters predicted the opening of the convention center would prove to be a once-in-a-generation event for Mobilians. Indeed, a black-tie affair that gave a preview to those willing to pay $100 per ticket drew 840 people.

Those attending the event, known as the River Rhapsody Gala, were entertained with a lavish cocktail reception followed by dinner and dessert. Four 300-pound blocks of ice that had been transformed into glistening ice sculptures graced the tables. And the Port City Symphony, classical and jazz ensembles, the Mobile Ballet, and the Mobile Opera entertained the crowd throughout the evening.

When the doors were thrown open to the general public on the following Saturday, 35,000 arrived. Planners had expected a crowd of 14,000, but the center accommodated the additional visitors with ease.

Before the doors ever opened, conventions, trade shows, and social events were booked years in advance for the world-class center whose special drawing card is its location on the waterfront with its constant activity. "Landlocked Midwesterners are taken by that," noted the president of the Mobile Convention and Visitors' Bureau, a private nonprofit group that contracts with the city to market and service the convention center business. Like the "landlocked Midwesterners," conventioneers from around the world are attracted to the romance of the seaport city.

During the mid to late 1800s cast iron was all the rage. Much of it was sold as scrap metal during World War II. The intricate balconies, fences, fountains, and lampposts that remain, combined with the majestic oaks and semitropical climate, lend the city a romantic ambience. Photo by Ric Moore.

The new convention center rolled a strike in snaring the American Bowling Congress for a visit shortly after it opened. About 95,000 bowlers and spectators visited between February and June 1994. And since they attended over a five-month period, it put less of a strain on the hotels. Planners were gleeful. "It's like a 1,200-delegate convention seven days a week for five months straight," said the head of the Mobile Convention and Visitors' Bureau.

For Mobile, the trickle-down effect, or "induced development potential" as it is known, would generate as much as $93 million in new construction and increased use of hotels, restaurants, and stores over time, according to a 1990 feasibility study produced by Economics Research Associates of Los Angeles, California. Indeed, hotels, restaurants, retail shops, and construction sites spawned as a result of the Convention Center, and the ongoing efforts to revitalize downtown opened hundreds of jobs.

With the gem in place, the city needed a setting to showcase it so conventioneers would have a place to go after convening for the day. The city adopted an urban design plan for downtown. Plans were made to upgrade the area bordered by Saint Francis Street to the north, Government Street to the south, Dearborn Street to the west, and Water Street to the east. Under the plan, street lamps replaced overhead lighting systems, and trees lined new brushed concrete sidewalks with flagstone borders and granite curbing.

During the spring of 1992, the Mobile City Council adopted two new ordinances that had far-reaching effects on the look of Mobile's historic districts. The Heritage Tree Ordinance, sponsored by the Mobile Tree Commission, gave protection to oaks (excluding water oaks and scrub oaks), hickories, sycamores, yellow poplars, sweet gums, magnolias, and cypress trees. Trees eight inches or more in diameter at four-and-a-half feet above the ground could not be cut without a review. An amended sign ordinance strengthened the city's power to regulate signage in historic districts.

As much as anything, the restoration of the fountain at Bienville Square in 1994 was a symbol of the return of downtown as a vital part of the Mobile community. The square had been a frequent site during the late 1880s for public musical programs sponsored by the Athelstan Club, an elite society of business and professional men. In 1905 the square had been a platform for President Theodore Roosevelt, whose Panama Canal project had aroused the hopes of Mobile businessmen. When thousands of Mobilians raucously celebrated the signing of the armistice on November 11, 1918, the day culminated in a giant rally at the square. And for years the square had been a place to congregate on New Year's Eve. But the park had fallen into disuse.

The restoration of the fountain at Bienville Square in 1994 was a symbol of the return of downtown as a vital part of the Mobile community. The square, once a frequent site during the late 1880s for public musical programs and New Year's Eve celebrations, had fallen into disuse. Photo by Ric Moore.

One can't help but notice the Mobile Convention Center, which was undoubtedly the key to the renewed interest in downtown. Like an exquisite multifaceted diamond, the Convention Center with its many glistening windows studs the waterfront. Photo by Ric Moore.

Those who dared walk by it skittered past like startled pigeons.

The square began its transition into a public park in 1824 when the United States Congress transferred a large plot of land to the city. The city acquired additional land, and in the 1850s the park gained a cast-iron fence, benches, and walkways. The fountain was installed in 1890 in honor of Dr. George A. Ketchum. Ketchum's company, Bienville Water Works, had constructed a 10-million-gallon reservoir on Moffat Road and brought running water to the city.

After more than a hundred years of service, the fountain was listing and had fallen into disrepair. Robinson Iron of Alexander City carefully sandblasted, primed, painted, and restored missing pieces of the fountain so it could serve once more as a focal point for the small, but much-loved, square.

The work was part of a larger Bienville Square improvement project. A horse trough identified through historical pictures as the one used at Bienville Square was rescued from the auction block and returned to its original home. The city was able to install 30 benches that were replicas of the existing 11 benches, thanks to the efforts of the Main Street Mobile manager who traced the patterns to a Mississippi foundry. Even the trash receptacles placed along Dauphin Street in June of 1992 reflect the Bienville Square theme. The iron units (with a liner for easy collection) carry the simple motif of the fence that encircles the square's fountain.

While Bienville Square was being restored to its old charm, funds were being raised to create a performing arts park three blocks southwest of it in the Cathedral Square Arts District, a 14-block area anchored on its east boundary by the University of South Alabama's Saenger Theatre for the Performing Arts and to the west by the historic No. 5 Fire Station. A design for the proposed square was created to accent the magnificent facade of the Cathedral of the Immaculate Conception. The plan reflected the basilica floor plan with its traditional nave, apse, and portico. Details of the plan showed a semicircular fountain at one end that could be covered and used as a stage, while the sunken area in the park's center would provide seating for the audience. Four columns designed as free-form sculptural pieces at the opposite end of the park would create a second stage, according to the plan. At the end of 1993, a campaign got under way to sell 10,000 inscribed bricks for the entranceway to help finance the project.

Downtown revitalization was a profound success story, as the area has become a mecca for the tourist trade generated by the new convention center and a retreat for workers on their lunch breaks. A number of financial incentive programs administered by Main Street Mobile and the Mobile Historic Development Commission made the revitalization of those areas possible. The Facade Program and Code Compliance programs offered loans of up to $10,000 each. Under the Facade Program, loans could be converted to grants if the property owner retained the title for five years. The Matching Grant Fund offered grants for facade renovations and roof repairs up to half of the project's total cost with a maximum award of $6,000. In 1992 alone, 19 separate buildings were aided through the programs.

Other programs helped preserve historically significant property throughout the city. Taxpayers who properly rehabilitated property listed on the National Register of Historic Places for commercial purposes were offered a 20 percent tax credit for all rehabilitation costs. The Mobile Revolving Fund for Historic Properties helped save endangered historic buildings from demolition by purchasing the buildings and reselling them to people willing and able to restore them.

Another effort helped those shopping for architecturally significant buildings identify what was on the market. The "Endangered Properties List" highlighted structures that were threatened through vacancy, deterioration, neglect, or commercial intrusion. Well-known properties such as the Battle House and the former YMCA, as well as lesser-known, but significant properties, were listed.

Perhaps one of the best barometers of an inner city's health, aside from the number of buildings being built and renovated, is the strength of its arts and cultural community. Structurally, downtown was back on its feet, but it wasn't until people returned to the sidewalks that it regained its pulse. Arts institutions and organizations, as well as corporate sponsors, took the lead in drawing people to the city's center and have also taken a key role in the overall development of downtown Mobile.

When the glittering renovation of the historic Saenger Theatre was completed in 1993, Symphony Concerts of Mobile went the extra mile to attract audiences, which may have been deterred by memories of what had been a seedy, crime-ridden neighborhood. It provided a shuttle service from west Mobile, Spring Hill, and the Loop area, extra security throughout the Saenger area on concert nights, and escorts to walk concertgoers to their cars. The August 1993 issue of *High Notes*, the newsletter for Symphony Concerts of Mobile, noted "the deserted downtown streets you knew five years ago have been replaced with the lively nightlife of bars and restaurants, creating a much safer environment for concertgoers."

*This nineteenth-century stained glass window depicts the Annunciation when the angel appeared to Mary to tell her that she would be the mother of Jesus. It is one of many such windows surrounding the Cathedral of the Immaculate Conception in downtown Mobile. The Catholic archbishop resides in Mobile, making it the See City for the archdiocese.
Photo by Ric Moore.*

A Gulf Coast Treasure

Outdoor events such as First Night Mobile introduce people to the arts and to Mobile's new downtown. First Night Mobile caps the year with a city-wide New Year's Eve Celebration. Photo courtesy of First Night Mobile.

Arts activities downtown created a constant promenade of people, which in turn promoted safer streets, contributed to the revitalization of businesses, and sparked life in the area, a Mobile Area Chamber of Commerce spokesman noted. "It's not just people's presence which determines the area's viability, however. It's the level of pride they bring with them and the sense that downtown is where they go to relax, enjoy, and meet their neighbors and friends."

As it turned out, the place that first breathed life back into the area had been a favorite haunt of Mobilians years ago: Bienville Square. Brown Bag in Bienville, sponsored by radio station 92 WZEW and Altus Bank, was inaugurated in 1985. The concerts, continued under the radio station's sponsorship, are a popular event on Wednesdays from April through October.

In the late 1980s and early 1990s, the arts community began playing to wider audiences as a number of downtown events joined the Brown Bag in Bienville series. Initiated in 1993, the Tuesdays at Twelve series, an ongoing program held at FAMOS Downtown and sponsored in part by the Mobile Public Library, invited people to spend their lunch hours in the area through a variety of activities such as walking tours, slide shows, lectures, and book signings. The Sunday Concerts series entertained crowds at various parks in downtown and throughout the city.

Outdoor events such as September Celebration, Sundays in the Square, and First Night Mobile captured even wider audiences and not only introduced more people to the arts, but they also introduced more people to the new downtown.

The oldest of those three events, September Celebration, initiated in 1987 by the Mobile Area Chamber of Commerce, offers a marathon of arts, entertainment, and cultural activities. The celebration grew like wildfire. In 1991 the city took over the project and presented 41 events in 10 days to choose from, while the 1993 celebration sponsored by the city's new Office of Special Events packed 81 events

A fireworks finale signals the beginning of the New Year and the end of First Night Mobile's success. Photo by Dave Hamby.

into 18 days. Whether you would like to listen to a symphony under the stars or try your hand at chalk art, the celebration has something for everyone.

During October the entertainment continues with the Sundays in the Square series. When the annual Do Dah Day Parade, featuring more than 300 costumed pets and their owners, ends at Cathedral Square, the Port City Symphony is likely to greet the Mobile SPCA-sponsored event with "The Baby Elephant Walk." And when Halloween rolls around, concertgoers are likely to hear such crowd pleasers as "Ghostbusters" and a suite from *Phantom of the Opera*.

First Night Mobile caps the year with a city-wide New Year's Eve Celebration. The event, which has its own board of directors, is sponsored by a coalition of groups, including the Mobile Arts Council, Main Street Mobile, the Office of Special Events City of Mobile, and corporate sponsors. A button costing a nominal fee admits the wearer to this alcohol-free street party focusing on the arts. Much of downtown—indoors and out—turns into a stage for this evening of art and entertainment. Dancers, musicians, puppeteers, storytellers, magicians, sculptors, and actors take over bank lobbies, storefronts, parks, and sidewalks. A fireworks finale signals the beginning of the New Year and the end of the event. Sponsors of the event proudly note that almost any promotion about downtown revitalization now includes a mention of First Night Mobile's success. ⚜

Chapter 3
PEOPLE

Men and women who have made their mark.

On the previous page, Perhaps living in a big city that considers itself a small town has certain advantages. Photo by Ric Moore.

On the previous page, inset Left-fielder Billy Williams, a perennial All-Star for the Chicago Cubs, was inducted into the Baseball Hall of Fame in 1987. He is one of four area players so honored. Photo courtesy of the National Baseball Library & Archives, Cooperstown, New York.

Somehow Mobilians tend to forget that Mobile has larger-than-life heroes. But there they are. Baseball's top home-run hitter of all time. A pop star who hit platinum. A doctor whose work stands second only to Pasteur's in importance . . . they have all called Mobile home.

Perhaps living in a big city that considers itself a small town has certain advantages. It's a place where children can spend countless hours playing red light, and catching lightning bugs, and giving shrill whoops that call friends together. It's a place where crickets send children home with an evening serenade. And it's a place where people like to share each other's company and tell stories.

It's hard to say what all this has to do with becoming an adult and making one's way in life. But those who have experienced it know it is important.

"It was a great place to grow up," recalls Judy Culbreth, editor-in-chief of *Working Mother* magazine. "I had a lot of freedom in Mobile growing up. I was a big tomboy." The freedom that a Mobile childhood provided "made me have a lot of courage," she says.

Freedom, strength, creativity, respectfulness, and a sense of place are qualities Mobile seems to champion. It is also a climate that supports a wonderful literary tradition. "I think that Southerners are natural storytellers. There is an appreciation of storytelling. A lot of us grew up with our grandparents telling stories to us," says highly popular mystery and romance writer Carolyn Haines (alias Caroline Burnes). Says Pulitzer nominee Winston Groom, "In cities like Mobile there is a tradition of storytelling that sometimes surpasses anything found in newer cities. I grew up in a tradition of storytelling whether at a hunting camp or at my grandparents' house."

"The people," recalls home-run king Hank Aaron, "were very close, so I had a great time growing up in Mobile." Aaron's inner strength gained during those growing-up years, nurtured by strong family ties as much as his batting ability, enabled him to go on to greatness. "I grew up with parents who had values and appreciated other people's values."

Aaron lives and works in Atlanta now, but he still comes back. "I love Mobile. . . . It's a place where I go back to see my parents to just break bread now and then."

❖

"Being born in Mobile was my first break, and moving to Toulminville was the second."
Hank Aaron
I Had a Hammer

In a state where football is a passion, Mobile stands out as a tiny enclave of baseball greatness. And while the roster is salted with a few great white players, the talent and number of its black players make Mobile unique.

Hank Aaron, who with his 715th home run on April 8, 1974, toppled Babe Ruth's reign as home-run king, is

During the late days of his campaign to break Babe Ruth's home-run record, Hank Aaron became frustrated with all the media attention. He was quoted as saying, "When it's over, I'm going home to Mobile and fish for a long time." Photo courtesy of the National Baseball Library & Archives, Cooperstown, New York.

the city's favorite son. During his 23-year major league career, he racked up more batting records than any other player in the game's history, including lifetime records of 755 home runs and 2,297 runs batted in. But Aaron is only one of four Mobilians enshrined in Cooperstown's Hall of Fame.

Mobile and its suburbs also spawned outfielder Willie McCovey, left fielder Billy Williams of Whistler, and pitcher Satchel Paige. Mobilian Ozzie Smith, "The Wizard of Ahs," is a sure bet to join them. In 1991 he won his thirteenth consecutive Gold Glove; by the end of 1992, he had amassed 542 stolen bases.

Together Aaron, McCovey, Williams, Paige, and Smith are the makings of an indomitable team. But then you can add Mobilians Amos Otis, a five-time All Star with the best career fielding average among center fielders; Tommie Agee of Whistler, a two-time Gold Glover who won the American League Rookie of the Year Award in 1966; and Cleon Jones of Plateau, whose batting average of .340 in 1969 was the best in the New York Mets' history. Aaron's brother, Tommie, played regularly as a rookie, managed in the minors, and coached for the Braves until dying of leukemia in 1984.

Hank Aaron broached the subject of why the area had such fertile ball fields in his autobiography, *I Had a Hammer*. "There are all kinds of theories on why Mobile turned out so many good ballplayers in my generation, but I believe that Carver Park had as much to do with it as anything. As soon as the park was built, the city started a black recreational league that pulled teams from every black neighborhood in town. The league was formal enough to count for something and informal enough to leave us to our own devices. The result was that neighborhood teams were always challenging each other, and the rivalries were pretty hot. . . ."

Unfettered by formal coaching, Aaron developed a style all his own. He was a cross-handed batter. Though he hit from the right side, he grasped the bat with his left hand above his right.

And he never swung like the other home-run hitters. Most transferred their weight from their back foot into the ball. Aaron put his weight on his front foot and lashed out at the last second. In his autobiography Aaron explained how swatting at bottle caps with a broom affected his style: "If you've ever tried to hit a bottle cap, you know that you can't sit back on your haunches. The way one of those things will dip and float, you've got to jump out and get it, and that's the way I always hit a baseball."

Aaron softly chuckled when he was asked about that story. The bottle cap practice helped him with timing, coordination, and keeping his eye on the ball, he said.

Satchel Paige offered six rules for staying young:
1. *Avoid fried meats, which angry up the blood.*
2. *If your stomach disputes you, lie down and pacify it with cool thoughts.*
3. *Keep the juices flowing by jangling around gently as you move.*
4. *Go very light on the vices, such as carrying on in society. The social ramble ain't restful.*
5. *Avoid running at all times.*
6. *Don't look back. Something might be gaining on you. Photo courtesy of the National Baseball Library & Archives, Cooperstown, New York.*

Those who don't know Aaron might wonder why he would say being born in Mobile was his first break. Aaron says he was free of the distractions that a bigger city might have thrown in his way. "If I had been born in New York City, I would have been focused in another direction," Aaron says. Moreover, Mobile was a place where his greatness could be discovered.

Ed Scott, a former Negro League player who managed Aaron with the Mobile Black Bears and scouted him for the Indianapolis Clowns, remembers well the day he found Aaron. The Scotts had no television, no air conditioning, and it was too hot to sit around the house. His wife was skeptical when he told her he was going to see what he could find on the ball field.

What he found was Hank Aaron. There was just a bunch of kids playing softball. Aaron was hitting off a 90-mph fastball. "I said, 'Gee look at those wrists,'" recalls Scott, who was attending an opening reception at the Fine Arts Museum of the South for an exhibition commemorating the Negro leagues.

Judsen "Judy" Culbreth, editor-in-chief of Working Mother *magazine, says that growing up in Mobile had its advantages. "I think growing up in Mobile made me very practical. I think it gave me a broader perspective." Ms. Culbreth is shown here with her children, Brett Culbreth Mosely and Charles Boykin Mosely. Photo courtesy of* Working Mother.

Scott, who still lives in Mobile, remembers Aaron's response when he asked the youngster if he would like to play with the Black Bears, a semi-pro team.

"He said, 'Will you get me a suit?'"

"I said, 'Yeah, I'll get you a suit,'" Scott said.

But the team played on Sundays, and it was made up mostly of men. That didn't sit well with Aaron's mother. Scott made several trips to the Aaron home to plead his case. But when Scott approached, Aaron would hide and his mother would put Scott off.

"She'd say, 'I won't let him go today, but I'll let him go sometime,'" Scott said.

One day, to Scott's surprise, Aaron trotted out on the field. "First time he got up there he didn't hit it over the fence, but he liked to hit it through a wall."

The day Aaron got on the train in Mobile to join the Indianapolis Clowns in Winston-Salem, North Carolina, Scott handed him an envelope addressed to Bunny Downs, the team's business manager. Scott knew a green kid barely 18 years old would have a hard time.

"I said, 'Bunny, forget everything about this kid. Just watch his bat.'"

Soon he got a note back. "A great find," it said.

As Aaron approached Babe Ruth's record, he endured pressure so intense a lesser man might have shelved his bat. Fame, hate mail, and death threats ensued. During those harried days, he once told reporters, "When it's over, I'm going home to Mobile and fish for a long time."

Today, Aaron is corporate vice president of community relations for the Atlanta-based Turner Broadcasting System, Inc. As senior vice president and assistant to the president of the TBS-owned Atlanta Braves, he has helped develop the talent of many outstanding players. In addition, he serves as vice president of business development for The Airport Channel, the service of Turner Private Networks, Inc. that provides customized news and information programming at airports around the United States.

Leave it to Beaver fails to reflect the life of today's families, says a magazine editor who should know.

Judsen "Judy" Culbreth, editor-in-chief of *Working Mother* magazine and a native of Mobile, says only about 12 percent of all families these days have a father who is the breadwinner and a stay-at-home mom.

"A couple of things have fueled women going back into the work force. Today it takes two 1990 paychecks to equal one 1950 paycheck," says Culbreth. "The second thing that has fueled it is more women are graduating from college, and they are making better grades than men even in math and science."

Working Mother magazine produces numerous surveys. In 1993 it highlighted the 10 best states for child care. In 1994 it published a comprehensive state-by-state look at child care. On an annual basis it publishes a list of the 100 best companies for working mothers.

"It's been very interesting because we have been in the news a lot," Culbreth says. Reporters use the magazine as a source for such issues as The Family and Medical Leave Bill, pay equity, and child care.

Culbreth was the former executive editor of *Redbook* before joining *Working Mother* magazine in 1988. She is a 1968 graduate of Mobile's Murphy High School and a 1972 graduate of the University of South Alabama. As one of ten college students to win a contest sponsored by *Glamour* magazine, she was awarded a trip to New York and Europe. The award launched her on her career.

"I realized two things—that I wanted to live in New York and I wanted to work for a magazine." Now that she has met both goals she muses that growing up in Mobile had its advantages. "I think growing up in Mobile made me very practical. I think it gave me a broader perspective. I'm not just connected to the Northeast."

Then there's Jim Busby—president, chief executive officer, and chairman of the board of QMS. High risks and great promise have characterized the young company, which investors still call a good buy.

Give him three cherries for the bar code—that little device that hastens shoppers through the grocery store checkout lines. Busby had a hard time convincing a banker to lend him $10,000 to finance the idea. In the 15 years since the company was established in 1977, sales have shot up to $260 million.

The bar code idea crystallized when Scott Paper Company needed labels with lettering of varying sizes—some had to be large enough to be read by a forklift driver on the other side of the warehouse and small enough to contain the shipping and ordering information that would only be read up close.

Busby was able to modify a computer printer so it could produce letters of different sizes on the same line. With complicated instructions and several passes of the paper through the printer, other computers could be made to produce the same results. But Busby's idea simplified the instructions and required only one pass of the paper.

The company has gone on to pioneer many other products, including color laser printers.

The Mobile area was also home to another inventor whose gadgets may be more familiar than his name. Miller Reese Hutchison (1876-1944), chief engineer for Thomas A. Edison Laboratories, owned more than 600 patents.

The Montrose native, who went to Mobile schools and was an 1892 graduate of Spring Hill College, invented the Dictograph (a bugging device for telephones) and the Klaxon (the electric horn that sounded the familiar "ooo-gah" for antique cars). He fitted England's Queen Alexandra with a hearing aid called an Acousticon. Mark Twain once chided Hutchison for

Jim Busby of QMS was able to modify a computer printer so it could produce letters of different sizes on the same line. His company has gone on to pioneer many other products, including color laser printers. Photo by Ric Moore.

Miller Reese Hutchison, whose gadgets may be more familiar than his name, was chief engineer for Thomas A. Edison Laboratories. He owned more than 600 patents. Photo courtesy of the Erik Overbey Collection, University of South Alabama Archives.

deliberately inventing the Klaxon to deafen people so he could sell them Acousticons.

Hutchison also invented the Moto Vita, a device that checks the efficiency of internal combustion engines. He developed the device after his son was killed in an airplane crash.

Hutchison translated at banquets and public affairs for Edison, who was nearly deaf, by tapping out messages in Morse code on Edison's knee.

The work of a Toulminville native who stamped out yellow fever and brought malaria under control in Panama through his sanitation efforts had a far-reaching impact, but was especially meaningful at home.

The work of Dr. William C. Gorgas had a far-reaching impact, but was especially meaningful at home. Gorgas led the successful effort to clear Panama of yellow fever- and malaria-carrying mosquitoes. His work led to the opening of the Panama Canal and thus thrust open Mobile's doors to international trade in a way it had never experienced before. Photo courtesy of Alabama Department of Archives and History.

Mobilian Jimmy Buffett, known for such songs as "Cheeseburger in Paradise" and "Son of a Son of a Sailor," is a 1964 graduate of Mobile's McGill Institute. He has been known to pop into local bars such as Judge Roy Bean's to play a few tunes. Photo by Elizabeth Zeschin.

Dr. William C. Gorgas's work led to the opening of the Panama Canal in 1914 and thrust open Mobile's doors to international trade in a way it had never experienced before. Moreover, yellow fever had been a disease that felled armies and did not bypass civilians or Mobile.

For years building the Panama Canal had been an elusive goal. The French had tried, but failed miserably. They lost 22,819 workers from disease within nine years, and at all times at least one-third of their workers were sick.

"Doctor Gorgas was one of the few men who recognized that, if we were to ever have a Panama Canal, the real problem was going to be the extermination of . . . mosquitoes—it was going to be sanitation first and then steam shovels," observed Charles F. Kettering, vice president and directing head of General Motors Research Laboratories.

Yellow fever struck coastal cities at least as far north as Boston. Mobilians sought refuge in the country when it hit the city.

A report in the September 12, 1839, *New Orleans Daily Picayune* described Mobile's plight: "A Memorandum on the margin of the *Chronicle* says that the deaths on Saturday were 13, and on Sunday they were 15—total deaths in eight days, 129 . . . The population of Mobile at the present time does not exceed 3,000. No business is being transacted. The banks are open but two hours in the day. The offices and stores are nearly all closed, and the business haunts present a most gloomy and desolate appearance."

Prior to 1900 doctors debated yellow fever's cause and cure. It was generally believed that it was caused by a "miasma" prevalent in the night air in low, swampy areas.

Mobile Dr. Josiah C. Nott, the physician attending Gorgas's birth, published a paper as early as 1848 challenging the commonly held belief that yellow fever was transmitted through a "miasma" and suggested that some microorganism or an insect was the vector. The theory gained no acceptance.

Later in the century Cuban epidemiologist Dr. Carlos Juan Finlay told an 1881 meeting of the Academy of Sciences of Havana that a certain species of a mosquito known as stegomyia (later renamed Aedes Aegypti) was the disease-carrying culprit.

The mosquito theory continued to be an object of discussion. Mobile doctor Sam Hodgson, son of the *Mobile Register's* editor, along with another doctor and Gorgas met on a Pensacola porch to discuss the idea in the mid-1890s. A 15-year-old Nicholas H. Holmes, who later became a widely known Mobile architect, recalled that conversation in a September 19, 1954, *Mobile Press Register* article. Holmes said he believed Gorgas "first got the idea of a connection of the mosquito with yellow fever at that time."

As a young architect, Holmes became ill while working on the Panama Canal. While hospitalized, Holmes met Gorgas and asked him whether he remembered the conversation. Gorgas reportedly replied, "Yes, Samuel was right."

While United States Army bacteriologist Dr. Walter Reed is commonly given credit for making the mosquito-to-yellow fever connection, Gorgas developed the plan for eradicating Aedes Aegypti and the malarial mosquito, Anopheles—2 of more than 800 species of mosquitoes.

Gorgas learned that for yellow fever to be transmitted, the female had to bite a patient within the first few days of illness. He also learned that the virus had to incubate in the mosquito at least 12 days before it could be transmitted to another person. In addition, he found that the mosquito was a weak flier. Most importantly, he learned the mosquito would only lay its eggs in a man-made vessel containing fresh water.

After clearing Havana of yellow fever and malaria, Gorgas continued his work in Panama. There he found the French hospital had unwittingly provided a perfect

On the previous page Eugene Walter worked with Federico Fellini and acted in many of his films. Photo by Ric Moore.

breeding ground for the mosquitoes. The hospital beds' legs were set in cups of water to protect patients from ants. In addition, several thousand earthenware rings filled with water for tropical plants provided a place where the mosquito larvae could flourish.

Gorgas was born in the home of his grandfather, John Gayle, former governor of Alabama (1831-1835), later a Congressman and a United States judge. The home was in Toulminville on Saint Stephen's Road. Gorgas died in London July 4, 1920, and was interred in Arlington National Cemetery.

Mobilian Jimmy Buffett's career took off in 1977 with *Changes in Latitude*, which climbed both pop and country charts. The album went platinum by year's end. "Margaritaville," a single from the album, went gold by year's end. He won over concert and radio audiences with such songs as "Cheeseburger in Paradise," "Come Monday," "Pencil Thin Mustache," "A Pirate Looks at Forty," and "Son of a Son of a Sailor."

The singer turned to writing and hit the top again. *Tales from Margaritaville* stayed on the *New York Times'* best-seller list for 27 weeks. *Where is Joe Merchant?* stayed on the *New York Times'* best-seller list for 23 weeks and took the number one spot on the list.

Buffett is a 1964 graduate of Mobile's McGill Institute. He attended Auburn before entering the University of Southern Mississippi to study journalism. Buffett's parents live in Daphne, and he has been known to pop into local bars such as Judge Roy Bean's to play a few tunes.

Eugene Walter has been described by *Alabama* magazine as an "Expatriate, novelist, artist, songwriter, actor, translator, gourmet cook, [who] spends his days in a small house in Mobile that is more like the littered landscape of a mind than a dwelling."

Walter spent 30 years in Europe, 5 in Paris, and 25 in Rome. He has worked with Federico Fellini, and he estimates he has acted in about a hundred movies. When Fellini frustrated his attempts for an interview, Walter made up one that Fellini later quoted from extensively when interviewed by the *New York Times*.

Walter is a prize-winning stage designer for more than 60 stage productions in the New York area. He also won the O. Henry citation for "I Love You Batty Sisters." His 1954 novel *The Untidy Pilgrim* won a Lippincott Prize. He earned a Sewanee-Rockefeller Fellowship for *Monkey Poems*. He once took his own traveling marionette show to schools and prisons along the Gulf Coast.

Walter, a Mobile native, attended Spring Hill College, University of Alabama (Mobile extension), Museum of Modern Art (New York City), New York University, New School for Social Research, Alliance Francaise, Institut Brittanique de la Sorbonne, and Instituto Dante Alighieri. He was the founder and first manager of the Mobile Symphony Orchestra.

Syndicated Washington Post *columnist Colman McCarthy was the Mobile City Golf Champion in 1958 and 1959. Photo courtesy of Colman McCarthy.*

People who recall local golf legends still remember Colman McCarthy, better known today as a syndicated columnist for the *Washington Post*. McCarthy was the Mobile City Golf Champion in 1958 and 1959 and earned the title at the Mobile Municipal Golf Course (now known as the Azalea City Golf Club).

Says Mobilian and golf aficionado Joe Teague, "I'm surprised that he is a syndicated columnist. He was so blooming good. He was unreal."

McCarthy will cite the high quality of the Spring Hill College faculty as one of the reasons he attended the school. But his off-the-cuff answer is, "Eighteen reasons. It had a beautiful golf course."

> ## "They could as logically have called Robert E. Lee a bandit as myself a pirate. . . ."
> **Admiral Raphael Semmes**
> *Memoirs of Service Afloat*

Viewed as a pirate by Union forces, Rear Admiral Raphael Semmes commanded the seas with the

Alabama. His ship was the most famous of the 20 Confederate cruisers to prey on Union merchant ships and whalers during the Civil War.

The fleet destroyed 257 Union vessels and forced more than 700 other Union ships to travel under foreign flags to avoid attack. The *Alabama* itself roamed the globe and sank 69 vessels. Semmes's daring won the imagination of those at home and abroad. He was the only officer on either side to be both a rear admiral and a brigadier general.

Besides the *Sumter*, the *Alabama* was the first steamer to be fitted as a warship. It could carry 350 tons of coal—enough for an 18-days' supply of fuel. However, the boat was a fine sailing vessel as well. Semmes's strategy was simple. Using the ship's sail power instead of its fuel, he could avoid detection by remaining at sea for long periods of time.

Semmes's escapades were finally curtailed when the *Kearsarge* sank the *Alabama* off the coast of Cherbourg, France, on June 19, 1864. The Union captain had hung all his ship's spare anchor cable over the midship section. Semmes failed to detect the makeshift armor because it had been encased with boards so that the ship looked like any other wooden vessel. In his *Memoirs of Service Afloat* Semmes complained bitterly: "It was the same thing, as if two men were to go out to fight a duel, and one of them, unknown to the other, were to put a shirt of mail under his outer garment."

Semmes evaded capture by leaping off the *Alabama* as it was sinking. The *Deerhound*, one of several vessels gathered to view the duel, plucked him out of the water. Because it was a neutral English vessel, Semmes slipped through his enemies' fingers once more, much to their chagrin.

Semmes served out the remainder of the war as commander of the tiny Confederate fleet on the James River below Richmond, Virginia.

Semmes was born September 27, 1809, in Charles County, Maryland. He was orphaned at an early age and reared by relatives in Georgetown. At 16, he joined the United States Navy. During a furlough, he studied law and was admitted to the bar in 1834.

His legal training proved propitious. He not only outmaneuvered his enemies at sea, but he also eloquently outmaneuvered them in the courtroom. After the war had ended, the Navy Department attempted and failed to indict him. During that period he was imprisoned for several months.

While serving in the Navy, Semmes was stationed at Pensacola. He bought a plantation in Alabama on the Perdido River, where he established his family in 1842. In 1849 they moved to Mobile.

After the war Mobilians elected him to the office of probate judge, but the federal government barred him from the position. Semmes practiced law in Mobile and lived at 802 Government Street. The home was bought for him in 1871 through subscription by his admirers. The two-story brick structure with intricate iron balconies now serves as a chapel for the First Baptist Church. A bronze statue at Royal and Government Streets commemorates him.

Semmes died in Point Clear August 30, 1877. He is buried in Catholic Cemetery in Mobile. ⚜

Rear Admiral Raphael Semmes's daring won the imagination of those at home and abroad. After moving to Mobile in 1849, Mobilians elected him to the office of probate judge, but the federal government barred him from the position. This bronze statue at Royal and Government Streets commemorates his life and the love the city had for him. Photo by Ric Moore.

To Name a Few . . .

Some were famous. Others were infamous. Some were born here; others were educated here or won fame here. Still others decided to settle here and call Mobile home. Here are a few of the many people who have made a mark on Mobile.

BUSINESS

Bill Bayley—Invented West Indies salad and fried crab claws. He and his wife, Ethel, owned and operated the highly touted Bayley's Restaurant at Cedar Point and Fowl River Roads in southern Mobile County.

Robert J. Fitzpatrick—Former president of Euro Disneyland. A 1963 graduate of Spring Hill College.

H. Taylor Morrissette (1931-1990)—President Colonial Sugar Company. Mobile native. Graduate of Gulf Coast Military Academy. A 1953 graduate of Spring Hill College.

Ed Roberts (1898-1964)—Industrialist and philanthropist. Succeeded John B. Waterman as head of Waterman Steamship Corporation. Under Roberts, the company flourished and by World War II it was the largest privately owned steamship line in the nation. Founded Southern Industries in 1946. Was director of and provided trust funds for University Military School and Mobile Infirmary Association. Named first recipient of Mobile's Man-of-the-Year Award in 1948. Attended University Military School. Mobile native.

John Barnett Waterman (1865-1937)—Shipping magnate. Organized and became president of the Mobile, Miami, and Gulf Steamship Company, known as the Waterman Line. An affiliate, Gulf Shipbuilding Corp., produced ships during World War II.

HEROES & OUTLAWS

Frank Boykin (1885-1964)—Timber and oil baron who managed hunting lands that helped replenish deer population. Flamboyant United States representative for Mobile known for saying "Everything's made for love." Political career spanned 27 years. The Birmingham News described him as "the politician who rewarded his district with extensive benefits while at the same time enriching his own portfolio." Self-made, self-educated, and worth more than half a billion when he died.

"Black Bart" Chamberlain—Former Mobilian now living in Switzerland who is hounded by federal government for more than $27.5 million. Was tried for evading price controls United States government had imposed in response to 1973 Arab oil embargo. Chamberlain was charged with shipping Citronelle oil to Bahamas and selling it back to the federal government for the higher imported oil price.

Timber and oil baron Frank Boykin was a United States Representative for Mobile. His political career spanned 27 years. He is pictured on the first row between a young girl and a woman holding roses. Photo courtesy of the University of South Alabama Archives.

MEDIA

Mary (Vaultz) Battles—First black television camerawoman in the United States. A 1968 graduate of Central High School. Mobile native.

Dot Moore—Local radio and television personality who has been on the air continuously for more than 30 years. Over a 15-year-period, she taped celebrity interviews three times a year for NBC. Hosted the "Dot Moore Show" among other programs. Narrated the Mardi Gras parade for Channel 10 since 1967. The Mobilian graduated from Murphy High School.

PUBLIC SERVICE

Rosemary Barkett—First woman Supreme Court justice in Florida; she became the chief justice. A 1967 graduate of Spring Hill College.

Ann Bedsole—First woman to be elected to the Alabama Senate. Elected to Senate District 34 in 1987.

Walter D. Bellingrath—Entrepreneur and philanthropist who moved to Mobile and gave the area one of the nation's most beautiful gardens, which opened to the public in 1932. Bellingrath and his brother William secured the right to bottle and merchandise a little-known soft drink called Coca-Cola in Mobile and Montgomery. Walter Bellingrath also invested in the Waterman Line and turpentine.

Alva E. Smith Vanderbilt Belmont (1853-1933)—Women's suffrage leader. Served as president of the National Suffrage Committee in New York. Her home in Washington, D.C., became headquarters for the National Women's Party and the World Woman's Party for Equal Rights. Mobilian.

Jeremiah Denton—Former United States senator from Alabama. Earned the Douglas MacArthur Meritorious Service Award. Vietnam prisoner of war who first alerted United States of the plight of American prisoners by blinking in Morse code on a widely televised newscast that POWs were being tortured. Won the Silver Star, Bronze Star, Air Medal, and Purple Heart. Attended Spring Hill College in 1942-1943. Mobile native. Awarded degrees from Spring Hill College in 1946 and 1986.

The Reverend Louis J. Eisele (1912-1988)—Known as "Father Earthquake." The nationally renowned seismologist was the first to record the March 2, 1964, Alaskan quake that killed 114 people and measured 8.5 on the Richter scale. Taught at Spring Hill College and operated the school's seismographic station for more than 40 years.

The Reverend Albert Sidney Foley (1912-1990)—Civil rights activist who worked with the Reverend Martin Luther King Jr. and fought the Ku Klux Klan. Was instrumental in preventing violence and boycotts from spreading to Mobile in late 1950s and early 1960s. Was also recognized for his work showing failure of system to adequately alert residents in the path of hurricanes. Taught at Spring Hill College.

Alexis Herman—As President Bill Clinton's public liaison director, the former Mobilian briefs Clinton and plans his social schedule. She is the highest ranking Alabamian working in the Clinton administration and has an office in the West Wing one floor above the Oval Office.

Linda Schele—Helped break Mayan code. Former University of South Alabama art teacher (1968-1980) became captivated by the mystery of the Palenque ruins after a trip to Mexico. During a 1973 conference it took a mere two-and-a-half hours for her and two others to decipher the hieroglyphics containing the history of Palenque from the beginning of the seventh century to its fall around the late eighth century.

ARTS & ENTERTAINMENT

Milton Brown—Songwriter. Wrote Eddie Rabbit hit "Every Which Way But Loose" for the 1978 Clint Eastwood movie by the same name. Song won the American Movie Award for "Best Movie Song," earned a Grammy nomination, a Country Music Association "Song of the Year Award," and was a People's Choice finalist. Artists who have recorded his songs include Jimmy Buffett, Merv Griffin, Loretta Lynn, the Nitty Gritty Dirt Band, Randy Travis, Anne Murray, the Little River Band, Tanya Tucker, Tom Jones, Kenny Rogers, and Maureen McGovern. Mobile native.

William Edward Campbell *(1893-1954)*—Wrote The Bad Seed, The Looking Glass, *and* Company K *under the pseudonym William March. Also immensely gifted and prolific writer of short fiction. Became vice president of Waterman Steamship Corporation. Mobile native.*

Ernest F. Fenollosa *(1853-1908)—A key figure in struggle to prevent wholesale destruction of Japan's cultural heritage. Commodore Matthew Perry opened the door to Japan in the mid-1800s. The pieces Fenollosa saved from an orgy of foreignism that swept Japan form the core of the Oriental collection at the Boston Museum, where he was curator. Married Mary McNeil of Mobile, a writer and poet. Couple had a country home called Kobinata at Spring Hill.*

Winston Groom—*Nominated for the Pulitzer Prize for* Conversations with the Enemy, *a nonfiction account of a Vietnam POW, which he wrote with Duncan Spencer. Also wrote* Shrouds of Glory, *(nonfiction) and the novels* Better Times than These, Gone the Sun, Only, *and* Forrest Gump. *Paramount Pictures turned* Forrest Gump, *the story of a 6-foot, 6-inch, 240-pound idiot savant, into a movie starring Tom Hanks and Sally Field. Earned "Best Fiction Award" from the Southern Library Association for* As Summers Die, *which was turned into a movie starring Bette Davis, Jamie Lee Curtis, and Scott Glenn. Vietnam veteran. Worked for the* Washington Star *for almost 10 years before leaving to become a novelist. Graduated from University Military School in 1961. Mobilian. Lives in Point Clear.*

John Hafner—*Three-time Fulbright Award winner. A 1960 graduate of Spring Hill College. Teaches at Spring Hill College. A Mobile resident who was raised in Daphne.*

Carolyn Haines—*Prolific mystery and romance writer. Has written more than 10 novels. Writes primarily for Harlequin Intrigue under the pseudonym Caroline Burnes. Author of the "Familiar" series, the adventures of a cat who has a penchant for solving crime. Also wrote* Summer of the Redeemers, *published by Dutton. Works in the University of South Alabama's Public Relations Department. Lives in Semmes.*

Beryl Henderson—*Opera star. His many performances include Baron Scarpia in* Tosca *with the New York City Opera National Company; Dancairo in* Carmen *with the New York Grand Opera; and Bartolo in* The Marriage of Figaro *with the Bronx Opera. Graduate of Davidson High School. Was a member of the Mobile Opera Chorus and Mobile Opera Workshop. Mobile native.*

Jay Higginbotham—*Author of 15 books. Works have been translated into 17 languages.* Old Mobile Fort Louis de la Louisiane, 1702-1711 *received five literary awards. Mobilian. City of Mobile archivist.*

Octavia Walton Le Vert *(1810-1877)*—*Headed the Mobile intelligentsia and social circles during mid-1800s. Her acquaintances included Henry Clay, President Millard Fillmore, Congressman David Crockett, Edgar Allen Poe, and Washington Irving. She had audiences with Pope Pius I and Queen Victoria of England. Her book* Souvenirs of Travel, *published in 1857, captivated readers with stories of travel in Europe.*

Julian Lee "Judy" Rayford *(1908-1980)*—*Writer, sculptor, folk chanter. Mobile eccentric who constantly startled those around him. Librarian recalls he would leave his fox terrier, Rosie, in the middle of the reference desk at Mobile Public Library while he did his research. "She's not a dog. She's my niece," he would say. A woman who was to take a private sculpturing lesson in her back yard recalls he chanted so loudly he could be "heard to the State Docks." While a student in Mobile schools, two of his poems were accepted by* American Mercury, *which was edited by H. L. Mencken. Wrote* Cottonmouth, The First Christmas Dinner, Child of the Snapping Turtle, *and a Mardi Gras history called* Chasin' the Devil Round a Stump.

Maryln Schwartz—*Author of* A Southern Belle Primer (or Why Princess Margaret Will Never Be a Kappa Kappa Gamma) *and* New Times in the Old South (or Why Scarlett's in Therapy and Tara's Going Condo). *Worked for the* Mobile Press Register *before joining the* Dallas Morning News. *Mobile native.*

Augusta Evans Wilson *(1835-1909)*—*With earnings in her lifetime of more than $100,000, she was the first successful female author in America. Her first novel,* Inez, a Tale of the Alamo, *was completed when she was 15; her last,* Devota, *was published two years before her death. Her novels included* Beulah, Infelice, Macaria, St. Elmo, Vashti, At the Mercy of Tiberius, *and* The Speckled Bird. *Derided at times for her flowery style, she nevertheless enjoyed immense popularity. Lived in Mobile.*

S P O R T S

Lauretta Freeman—*A la Bo Jackson, this Mobilian is a dual-sport athlete from Auburn University. The hot-shot basketball player and world-class high jumper capped her high school career at Williamson by winning the state high jump championship for three straight years and the state triple jump championship. As a high school senior, she won the Gatorade Track Athlete of the Year award. Became professional basketball player for Spain after graduating from Auburn in 1993. A 1989 graduate of Williamson High School.*

Paul Morphy *(1837-1884)*—*International chess champion 1858-1859. An 1854 graduate of Spring Hill College.*

Eddie Stanky—*Played with the Boston Braves, Chicago Cubs, Brooklyn Dodgers, and New York Giants. Appeared in the 1947, 1948, and 1951 World Series and played in four All-Star games. Left position as manager of the Chicago White Soxs to coach the University of South Alabama Jaguars. Under Stanky, Jaguars compiled a 14-year record of 488-193 at South Alabama from 1969-1979 and 1981-1983. Five of his clubs advanced to the NCAA Tournament. Won Sun Belt Conference titles in 1981 and 1983. Has homes in Mobile and Baldwin Counties.* ⚜

"In cities like Mobile there is a tradition of storytelling that sometimes surpasses anything found in newer cities," says author Winston Groom. Photo by Ric Moore.

John Hafner, a three-time Fulbright Award winner, now teaches at Spring Hill College. Photo courtesy of Spring Hill College.

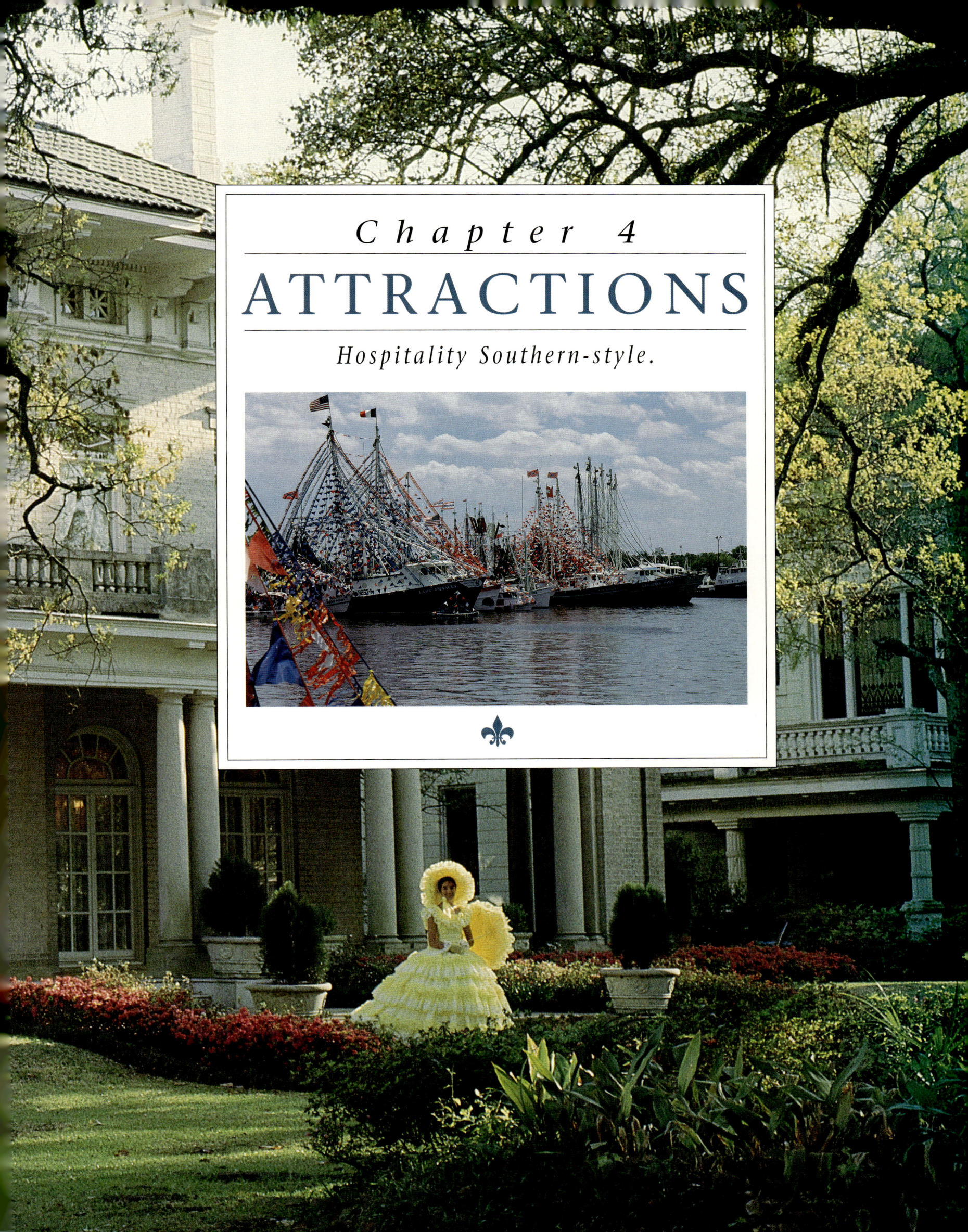

Chapter 4
ATTRACTIONS
Hospitality Southern-style.

A Gulf Coast Treasure

Mobile has four distinctive seasons—a spring whose frilly pink azaleas dazzle; a summer whose endless sunny days are punctuated by cooling thundershowers; an autumn autographed by golden hickories and scarlet Chinese tallows; and a snow-free winter whose nippy days are followed by warm ones.

Live oaks arching over wide boulevards and neighborhood streets provide a shady canopy to stroll under. The stately boughs support gray, beard-like Spanish moss, an air plant of the pineapple family, and immortalis moss, a fern that springs to life whenever a heavy rain freshens the city.

Beyond the oaks, thick-bladed Saint Augustine grass lawns sprawl in front of pillared mansions, raised Gulf Coast cottages, and dwellings with lacy ironwork balconies. Mobile's many beautiful architectural styles represent the city's rich and varied heritage. Seven distinctive historic districts tell the story. They are Oakleigh Garden District, DeTonti Square, Leinkauf, Ashland Place, Church Street East, Old Dauphin Way, and Lower Dauphin Street Commercial.

Traditional tourist attractions such as Bellingrath Gardens, Battleship *USS Alabama*, and Mobile Greyhound Park are complemented by a small, but vibrant, arts community that draws on national and international as well as local talent. Performers find audiences enthusiastic and supportive.

"The artistic climate is very surprising," a leader in the arts community says. It is through the gifted direction of people such as Winthrop Corey that the arts community has come to life. Under Corey's direction, timeless ballet classics such as *Swan Lake*, *The Nutcracker*, and *Romeo and Juliet* have captivated Mobile audiences over the years.

Corey has been a principal dancer with the Royal Winnipeg Ballet and the National Ballet of Canada. He is a summer faculty member of the Joffrey School in New York. His performances opposite Rudolph Nureyev in José Limon's *The Moor's Pavane* were hailed as "excellent in every way" by *The New York Times* and "chillingly effective" by *Time*.

Mobile symphony-goers enjoy the sounds of the Port City Symphony and the Mobile Symphonic Pops Band.

Timeless ballet classics such as *Cinderella* have captivated Mobile audiences over the years. Photo by Ric Moore.

On the previous page
The Azalea Festival is always a sure sign of spring. The delicate flowers turn the city's lawns and streets into a blaze of color for weeks. Photo by Ric Moore.

On the previous page, inset
On the third Sunday in May, shrimpers and fishermen sail to Bayou La Batre for the Blessing of the Fleet. Photo by Ric Moore.

The DeTonti Square Historic District, once the homeplace to the city's most prominent families, is a nine-block area named for Henri de Tonti, an early French explorer of the Gulf Coast region. After experiencing a general decline, the district is now emerging as a revitalized area with both restoration and new construction. Photo by Ric Moore.

The Port City Symphony is often joined by nationally and internationally acclaimed guests such as Ukrainian pianist Mykola Suk or Russian-born violin sensation Oleh Krysa. Other guests to the Mobile stage have included the Warsaw Concerto, the Slovak Sinfonietta, and the Louisiana Philharmonic.

The Mobile Symphonic Pops Band, formed in 1977 as a lasting symbol of Mobile's bicentennial celebration, is an all-volunteer group of 85 to 110 Mobile-area musicians from all walks of life. It plays at various locations, but its StarBright Concert series in Langan Park at the performing arts pavilion are particularly popular.

Now that the USA-Saenger Theatre has been renovated, the symphony has a new home. Since the lavish

Built in 1927 as a movie palace, the Saenger Theatre offered many Mobilians their first taste of the talkies. Now owned by the University of South Alabama, the theater has been lovingly restored and stages some of the city's finest live performances. Photos by Ric Moore.

movie palace has returned to her glory days, a visit makes for a romantic evening. Plush red velvet seats, intricate facades, and glittering gold trim set the mood.

Celebrating its golden anniversary with the 1995-1996 season, Mobile Opera, which one writer described as "a maturing diva whose voice is reaching its height of richness," might better be described as a grand dame. In recent years Mobile Opera has delighted audiences with *L'Elisir d'Amore (Elixer of Love)*, *Tosca*, and *Carmen* with imported professional principals.

Throw in a half dozen community theaters, and those looking for an evening of entertainment need go no further than Mobile.

While many communities boast a healthy interest in the arts, few of Mobile's size offer such high quality entertainment at such affordable prices. A 1989 survey of Mobile concert-goers found "an overwhelming majority (90 percent) indicated that concert tickets were 'priced right.'" Mobile Opera's most expensive seats are about a quarter of the median price of tickets bought elsewhere in the nation.

For those with a taste for the visual arts, The Fine Arts Museum of the South at Langan Park holds a permanent collection of more than 4,500 works spanning 2,000 years of culture. The highlight of the collection is a body of American nineteenth-century landscape paintings by Albert Bierstadt, Jasper Francis Cropsey, Asher B. Durand, John Frederick Kensett, John Henry Twachtman, and Thomas Moran.

European artists, however, are also represented. For example, Impressionist Pierre Auguste Renoir's *Roses* holds a place in the collection as well as Adolphe Bouguereau's *Young Girl Holding a Pink Gladiolus*. Though not as familiar to us today as Renoir, Bouguereau's paintings were so popular with Americans in the 1870s that a retrospective of his work planned in Paris for 1878 had to be cancelled because so few of his paintings were available in Europe.

FAMOS Downtown, a satellite gallery, displays art from the museum's permanent collection as well as local work in a Best of Mobile Show sponsored by the museum.

The Exploreum Museum of Discovery offers "hands-on" encounters that stimulate the curiosity of youngsters and delight adults. Visitors can whisper a message that can be heard 50 feet away or discover the secrets of ancient engineers by building a gravity-defying block arch or watch as the earth's movement "draws" a picture.

Though Mobile is a leader in the New South, it is a city steeped in tradition, and of that Mobilians are justifiably proud. Its many small history museums sprinkled throughout the city hold artifacts from throughout the ages.

Fort Condé is a good starting place. The partially reconstructed 1700s French Fort is the city's official welcome center and has information about the museums and other attractions.

The Museum of the City of Mobile holds 10 vintage carriages, exquisite silver produced by local silversmiths, and a carefully hand-stitched flag that flew over the *USS Oneida* when it took part in the Battle of Mobile Bay. Intricately designed Mardi Gras gowns and capes depict Mardi Gras royalty. A full-sized replica of the *Hunley*, a Confederate submarine credited with initiating submarine warfare, may be found at the museum as well.

Carlen House, a farmhouse built in 1842 in the style of a raised Gulf Coast "Creole Cottage," contains a wide assortment of artifacts reflecting the 81 years during which it was occupied. The style was designed to accommodate the weather. The dwelling was built on brick piers that protected it from floods that inundated the area. High ceilings and a central hall cooled and ventilated the house during the hot summer months. Recessed front and rear porches provided shade.

Other homes open to the public are the Richards DAR House, the Conde-Charlotte House, Oakleigh, and the Bragg-Mitchell Mansion.

The Eichold-Heustis Medical Museum of the South holds a curious assortment of artifacts reflecting 200 years of medical history. The museum is billed as a display of "the obsolete and the proven, the primitive and the innovative, the bizarre and the commonplace—all of which contributed to today's practice of medicine."

The Phoenix Fire Museum, housed in Fire Company No. 8, recalls Mobile's fiery past, a time when insurance companies offered rewards to the first fire company to extinguish any fire that burned a structure under their coverage. This practice occasionally resulted in fights breaking out between rival fire companies. Horse-drawn fire engines with steam boilers to pump water, fire plugs, and fire boxes document the struggle to douse the flames that posed a constant threat to the city during its early years.

Mobile's most visited attraction is a floating museum. The Battleship *USS Alabama* stands as a monument to World War II and Korean War veterans and is a favorite stopping place for tourists who want to inspect a battleship from stem to stern. Transferred to the Pacific Fleet in late 1943, the ship provided cover for amphibious assault forces and defended the carriers with intensive anti-aircraft fire.

"The story goes the admirals loved to have her," said director of marketing and public relations for the *USS Alabama*. "She was the hero of the Pacific."

Known as the "Mighty A," her anti-aircraft guns downed 22 Japanese planes. During the battle of the Philippine Sea, the *Alabama's* radar was the first to

Once home to a 2,500-man crew during World War II, the Battleship USS Alabama was known for her magnificent presence in the Pacific and fearlessly sailing in wartime waters. Today she stands as a monument to World War II and Korean War veterans and is a favorite stopping place for tourists who want to inspect a battleship from stem to stern. Photo below by Ric Moore. Photo left by Dave Hamby.

Divine nature and a single philanthropist gave Mobile Bellingrath Gardens, which in 1918 was just a fishing camp known as "Bellecamp." By 1932 the camp had evolved into a floral wonderland and magnificent private estate. Photo by Dave Hamby.

detect enemy bombers. As a result, American fighters and fleet gunners shot down 476 enemy planes.

The ship was also dubbed the "Lucky A." Though the *Alabama* saw 37 months of active duty during World War II, she never suffered any significant damage and none of her crew was killed in enemy attacks, though she was in nine battles earning her nine battle stars.

After the war, the ship was mothballed near Seattle, Washington, and was to be scrapped, but Alabamians launched a fund-raising drive to bring her home. Alabama school children raised almost $100,000, mostly in nickels, dimes, and quarters, while a corporate fund-raising campaign raised most of the rest of the $1 million needed to tow her here and to construct the 100-acre park where she is berthed.

The ship entered Mobile Bay in September 1964 after a three-month, 5,600-mile tow through the Panama Canal—still the longest ton-per-mile tow in history.

Visitors may also view as many as 18 vintage and rare aircraft and tour the *USS Drum*, a World War II submarine that sank 15 ships and earned 12 battle stars for her service.

Saving the "Lucky A" has been lucky for Alabama. More than 9 million visitors have clambered over her decks to inspect firsthand what it must have been like to be one of her crew. Though the admission and parking income barely pay for the ship's upkeep, the attraction has generated about $57.2 million in tourism dollars for the local community from the time it opened in January 1965 through September 1993.

While it was man's skill that built the battleship, it was divine nature and a single philanthropist who gave us the setting for Bellingrath Gardens.

Located 20 miles south of Mobile in Theodore off Interstate 10, Bellingrath Gardens offers a tranquil place to collect one's thoughts and is one of the nation's most beautiful gardens. Miles of footpaths wind through 65 acres of natural and landscaped areas dedicated to the gardens that are within the 900-acre Bellingrath estate. The garden remains open 365 days of the year.

Spring may seem the obvious time to visit a garden, but northern visitors will find the late fall and winter months breathtakingly beautiful. With an average annual temperature of 67.4 degrees, Mobile's growing season never ends.

At a time when most trees in northern climes stand bare unless adorned with snow, evergreens such as live oaks, water oaks, magnolias, waxmyrtles, yaupons, and red cedars provide a backdrop for one of Bellingrath's showiest seasons—the garden sports the second largest chrysanthemum display in the world. In October, the bronze, copper, gold, lavender, wine, and white flowers usher in fall and signal the end of summer.

By November, mum's the word. More than 60,000 chrysanthemum plants—many of them of the cascading variety—peak in what the garden bills as a Chrysanthemum Extravaganza. Sprays of color cascade from nearly every wall and bridge at Bellingrath and from the iron lacework balconies of the 15-room Bellingrath home. Topiaries in such forms as baskets, butterflies, and peacocks also grace the garden.

In December, 6,000 poinsettias announce the Christmas season. Though associated with Christmas, they are a tropical plant and, providing there's no cold snap, suited to a southern Christmas. Camellias with their dark green foliage and red, white, pink, or peppermint blooms also herald the season.

Horticulturally, the month of March titillates the senses. It begins with the shyness of a first kiss, and by mid-March it is bursting forth.

Noted gardener Jean Hersey once said, "In gardening, one's staunchest ally is the natural lust for life each plant has, that strong current which surges through everything that grows." And so it is at Bellingrath when late winter and early spring bring forth a showy array of azaleas preceded by one of the largest bulb displays this side of Holland.

By summer, the mood changes to a tropical one as allamanda, roses, salvia, hibiscus, and other blooms burst forth and linger until the first frost or earlier removal.

After some time at Bellingrath, you may want to visit the nearby Mobile Greyhound Park.

Ask a racing aficionado about the "dogs," and you will kindly be informed that a greyhound is not a dog. "You send a 'dog' out to fetch the paper in the morning. A greyhound races." And do they! Watch carefully or you may miss their sprint.

Bets placed. A hush descends on the crowd. They're off! Eight lithe, finely tuned athletes burst from their starting boxes. Red, blue, white, green, yellow, and multi-colored blankets blur together. Lighter than hoof-

"You send a 'dog' out to fetch the paper in the morning. A greyhound races." And do they! Watch carefully or you may miss their sprint. Photo by Ric Moore.

One of the nation's major post-season game is played at Ladd Memorial Stadium each January when outstanding college seniors from coast to coast meet in the Delchamps' Senior Bowl. Known as the "birthplace of NFL Legends," the Senior Bowl has played a pivotal role in the careers of hundreds of outstanding collegiate players. Photo by Ric Moore.

beats, 32 greyhound paws drum the track. Breathing, panting, straining, they hurtle around the bend. Heaving chests. Heaving haunches. Sand flies. Greyhounds fly. And then it is over.

As of September 1993, the track record for the three-eighth mile race was 37.26 seconds set in 1986; the record for the five-sixteenth mile race was 30.4 seconds set in 1988.

Of course, a good bet will draw a crowd anywhere. But a good rivalry between two athletes will draw a crowd too. When the two top greyhounds in the country were slated to race at the park, it drew a capacity crowd of 4,500. Clem Zwack Kennel's Charlie G won the contest over K's Clown by five lengths. That was back in 1975. "They only met in one race, but fans from time to time still talk about it," a racing director said.

In 1993 tension mounted once again as a blue brindle named JJ Blue Dancer closed in and eclipsed the record of another Mobile dog named Ski's Gallo. Ski's Gallo, a nationally recognized winner, had set

The temperate climate no doubt helps to account for the success of the golf industry on the Gulf Coast. Fairways are open year round. Photo by Ric Moore.

America's Junior Miss recognizes outstanding college-bound young women from around the nation. Talent, fitness, poise, and scholastic achievement all play a part in determining whom the judges will recognize. Photo by Dave Hamby.

records in Mobile when he scored 15 wins in a row and 52 for the season. In 1993, JJ Blue Dancer struck that record by winning 18 races in a row and 57 for the season.

Still another greyhound, Cancer Crusader, made his mark by coming in seventh. According to *Ripley's Believe It or Not*, Cancer Crusader was the seventh dog in the seventh race run at Mobile Greyhound Park on the seventh day of the seventh month of 1977. He weighed 77 pounds.

The top local greyhound event is the $20,000 added purse Port City Puppy Classic, usually held on the first Saturday of August. The event brings together the top-running puppies that have had their first official start in racing that year in Mobile.

Two events focus the national spotlight on Mobile each year— the Senior Bowl and America's Junior Miss.

America's Junior Miss recognizes outstanding college-bound young women from around the nation. For some, the program will help finance their education and launch their careers. During the program the judges award $81,000 to the top contestants. Nationally, more than $6 million in scholarships and other awards is given through local competitions.

Talent, fitness, and poise all play a part in determining whom the judges will recognize. Scholastic achievement also plays an important role in deciding who will represent their state at the contest. In 1993, for example, 12 were ranked number one in their class; 5 were ranked number two, and 42 of the 50 contestants were in the top 10 percent. All were in the top quarter or better.

With the Delchamps' Senior Bowl, Mobile's Ladd Memorial Stadium hosts one of the most important competitions around for career-hungry collegiate football players. While Mobile has no professional or college football teams, the city has the largest stadium on the Gulf Coast from Tampa to New Orleans and the third largest stadium in the state.

During the second or third weekend in January, the facility showcases the nation's finest college athletes

and top pro prospects. At the end of the 1993 season an impressive 73 percent of all Senior Bowl participants had been selected in the first five rounds of the NFL within the past 10 years.

Known as the "birthplace of NFL Legends," the Senior Bowl has played a pivotal role in the careers of hundreds of outstanding collegiate players, including such NFL greats as Walter Payton, Joe Namath, Steve Largent, Bubba Smith, and "Mean" Joe Greene.

The stadium is also home to the Gulf Coast Classic and the Alabama versus Mississippi High School All-Star Game. Some of the fiercest competitions, however, occur on Friday nights when local high school teams take over the turf. Six Mobile high schools call it their home stadium.

Baseball, tennis, and softball claim a faithful following in the Mobile area as well.

Eddie Stanky Field has hosted numerous Sun Belt Conference Tournaments and is home of the Mobile BayShark's professional, class AA baseball club. Other events have included the 1982 Babe Ruth World Series for ages 13 to 15, which attracted 45,000 spectators.

Whether you are a natural athlete or not, whether you hook, slice, or turn red on the green, you can find a golf course suited to your abilities within driving distance (so to speak).

Though greens continue to be built, demand for the sometimes frustrating, ever popular, sport does not seem to be sated. More than 20 public and 3 private

A Gulf Coast Treasure

Fishing tournaments draw more than 2,000 participants, and for a good reason—the fishing is incredible. Photo by Ric Moore.

Alabama's sugary white beaches are the number one tourist destination in the state. Photo by Ric Moore.

Marked by soft Gulf breezes and genuine smiles of welcome, the resort area offers captivating contrasts. Visitors are drawn by the sheer beauty of the outdoors, the temperate climate, historic landmarks, scrumptious seafood, Mardi Gras madness, and island getaways—but mostly, they are lured by the sun. Photo by Dave Hamby.

Thousands of runners compete each year in the Azalea Trail Run, which draws some of the finest athletes from around the world. Photo by Ric Moore.

Birdwatchers flock to the Dauphin Island Audubon Bird Sanctuary each spring and fall. Photo courtesy of Faulkner State Community College.

courses in Baldwin and Mobile Counties compete for the golf dollar.

Golf has become so popular along the Gulf Coast that in 1991 *Bayside Loafer* publisher Don Faggard launched a new entertainment magazine focusing solely on the sport. By 1993 he was distributing 200,000 copies of the free publication, which offers discounts at participating courses.

In 1992 he launched another venture—customized golf get-aways. Given the golfer's budget and time constraints, the company arranges everything from tee times to accommodations. Within a year about 2,500 golfers had participated for 10,000 rounds of golf.

The temperate climate no doubt helps to account for the success of the golf industry and the success of Mobile's local players. A May 16, 1993, article in the *Mobile Press Register* pointed out that Mobile schools had won 14 state championships. By comparison, Montgomery had won 8, Tuscaloosa 6, Birmingham 4, and Gadsden and Dothan each 3.

Gulf Coast fairways are open year round. Players in cities slightly north of Mobile find their greens closed part of the year, while those playing south of Mobile find the summer heat insufferable.

The Fine Arts Museum of the South is an internationally recognized cultural center recognized for its exhibits and acquisitions which span over two thousand years—from 2,000 paintings, sculptures, and porcelains to folk art such as quilts. Photo courtesy of FAMOS.

What's unique about Mobile County is not that it has so many courses, but that it is so reasonable. The median weekend rates for Mobile and Mobile County's public courses came to $21.60 for the cart and green fee in the spring of 1993—a rate surrounding areas found hard to beat. In fact those median rates were about 23 percent less than the Southeast as a whole and 37 percent less than the rates in the Northeast.

The quality of Mobile courses is driven by severe competition. A world-class course completed in 1992, the Magnolia Grove Golf Complex is part of the statewide Robert Trent Jones Trail. Magnolia Grove features 54 holes that will challenge even the best players.

But other courses are worthy of note. Early in its history, Mobile's Azalea City Golf Club saw such notables as Arnold Palmer, Fuzzy Zoeller, and Billy Casper tread its greens. Once named by *Golf Digest* as one of the 36 best public golf courses in the nation, the club has hosted four PGA tour events. Dramatic renovations at Azalea City have brought it above par once more.

Other options for those who want to swing into action in the Mobile area are Bay Oaks Golf Club, Citronelle Municipal Golf Club, Gulf Pines Golf Course, Isle Dauphine Golf Course, The Linksman Golf Club of Mobile, and Pine Hills Golf Club. The Country Club of Mobile and Skyline Country Club add private courses to the list.

Although pundits like to call it the Alabama "Golf" Coast, the area is rightfully known as the Alabama Gulf Coast. Alabama's sugary white beaches are the number one tourist destination in the state. Nearby Baldwin County's 32-mile stretch of Gulf sand offers a state park and a mixture of condominiums and beachfront cottages, while Dauphin Island in Mobile County offers a less hurried pace.

"We are an island community. We don't even have one red light on Dauphin Island," the park director noted in the early 1990s. A bridge built in 1953 links the island to Mobile County, and a ferry links it to Baldwin County. The slender, 18-mile isle is home to retirees and to fishermen whose families were among the area's first settlers.

The island hosts seven fishing rodeos, the Dauphin Island Race, and a special weekend each month associated with historic Fort Gaines. The regatta is billed as the largest one-day race in the nation. Competition on the regatta weekend is fierce.

The fishing tournaments draw more than 2,000 participants, and for a good reason—the fishing is incredible. Anglers in the 1993 Deep Sea Fishing Rodeo, for example, broke six records by reeling in a 13.72-pound sheephead, a 56.24-pound black drum, a 4.36-pound vermillion snapper, a 10-pound trigger fish, a 153.5-pound tarpon, and a 7.8-pound gafftopsail catfish.

Birders flock to the island during the spring and fall. The Dauphin Island Audubon Bird Sanctuary is the last stop for many migrating species before they begin their flights across the Gulf of Mexico to the Yucatan Peninsula and Central and South America. ⚜

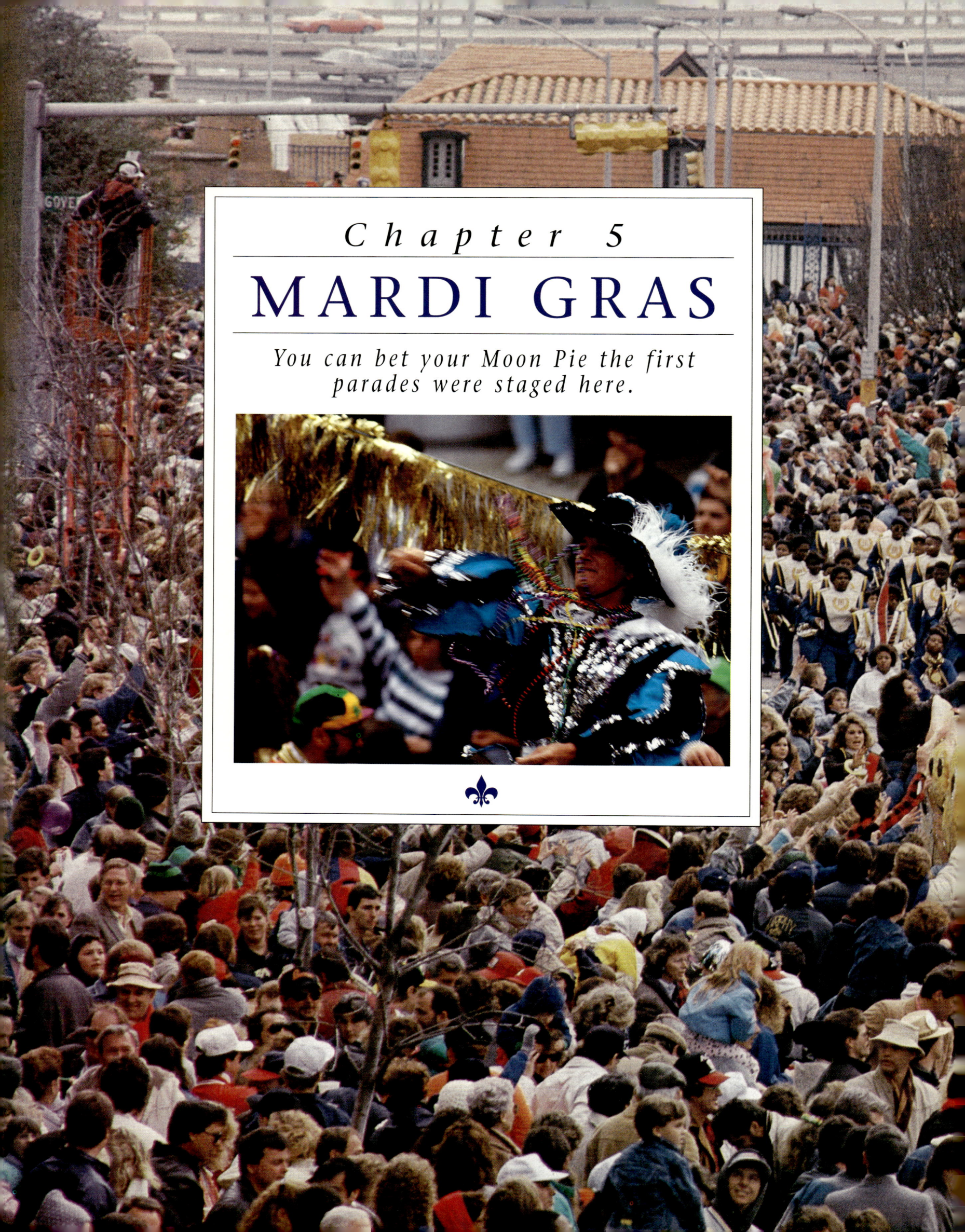

Chapter 5
MARDI GRAS

You can bet your Moon Pie the first parades were staged here.

Dressed as Chief Slacabamorinico, Joe Cain revived Mardi Gras after the Civil War. Only three other people have played the part since then: Julian Lee Rayford, Red Foster, and Wayne Dean. In 1967 Rayford decided that the proper place for Joe Cain's remains was beside his parents in the Church Street Graveyard. On February 5, 1967, the people of Old Mobile marched behind the famed Excelsior Band during the first Joe Cain Processional to the cemetery. Soon it was discovered that his family's plot was in another part of the cemetery, so Cain was moved again. Cain is one of the few people ever to be buried three times. His spirit lives on. A monument at the grave site says: "Here lies Old Joe Cain, the heart and soul of Mardi Gras in Mobile." Photo courtesy of the University of South Alabama Archives.

On the previous page
For the two weeks preceding Lent, the rules governing adult behavior are suspended, as young and old scramble for goodies. Photo by Ric Moore.

On the previous page, inset
Costumed revelers riding floats shower crowds with Moon Pies, doubloons, beads, and saltwater taffy. Photo by Ric Moore.

In those days preceding Ash Wednesday one might as well forget about trying to conduct business as usual in the Port City. For the two weeks before Lent, traffic comes to a halt as costumed revelers riding floats shower crowds with Moon Pies, doubloons, beads, and saltwater taffy. For a short time, the rules governing adult behavior are suspended, as young and old scramble for the goodies.

New Orleans may be more widely known for its Mardi Gras celebration, but the Crescent City's modern-day festivities owe a debt to members of Mobile's mystic societies, who a few years before the Civil War shared their knowledge of how to stage a Mardi Gras.

On the other hand, Mobilians must admit that it was probably a few Frenchmen on Louisiana soil who celebrated Fat Tuesday March 3, 1699, at which time Mardi Gras Bayou on the lower Mississippi was named. Mobile's celebration began in 1703, a year after the city was founded at Twenty-Seven Mile Bluff, and probably consisted of singing, eating, and drinking on Fat Tuesday, the day before the Lenten fasting began.

The mystic societies seem to have their origin in Mobile, which is known as "The Mother of Mystics." Mobile's early mystic societies, however, had their roots in New Year's Eve as well as Twelfth Night celebrations instituted during the Spanish occupation and later became associated with Mardi Gras.

Mardi Gras, a French word meaning "Fat Tuesday," was a day of feasting preceding Lent. Lent, a period of fasting and penitence in preparation for Easter, begins on Ash Wednesday and lasts 40 weekdays to Easter. Since Easter occurs on the first Sunday after the first full moon after the spring equinox, a date that also varies, the date for Lent and therefore the date for the culmination of Mardi Gras activities varies. The date usually falls sometime in February.

There are a number of versions of how Mobile's festivities began. The history of the modern celebrations probably dates to 1830 or 1831. A group, gathered for a dinner party on a New Year's Eve, roused the town with rakes, hoes, and cowbells that they raided from a hardware store. The rabble rousers, led by Michael Krafft, a handsome one-eyed cotton broker, serenaded Mobile Mayor John Stocking, who invited them in.

At first the group called themselves "The Midnight Revellers." Later it renamed itself "The Cowbellion de Rakin Society" in honor of the implements used in the impromptu parade. For the first 10 years, the group marched and was accompanied by a few horse-drawn vehicles. In 1840 it initiated a parade with floats having the theme "Heathen Gods and Goddesses."

In 1842 some of the younger members formed a new mystic group. Most of the men in the group marked, weighed, and sampled cotton. In their occupa-

The Order of Myths' emblem of Folly chasing Death around the broken column of life and flogging him with gourd-like pig bladders is synonymous with Mardi Gras to many Mobilians. Some say the broken column represents the broken hopes of the Confederacy, while Folly's triumph over Death represents the unbroken courage and spirit of the South. Photo by Ric Moore.

The Excelsior Band has been leading the Order of Myths for more than a hundred years. The group plays Dixieland jazz, show tunes, and standards from the 1940s and 1950s. Photo by Ric Moore.

tion they were known as "strikers," so the new group was known as the "Strikers Independent Society." The Strikers stopped parading in 1881, but they continue to hold balls. Traditionally, invitations are hand-delivered on Christmas morning.

An undated clipping preserved in a scrapbook at the Museum of Mobile gives an account of how Mobile's Mardi Gras was introduced to New Orleans and how it was reintroduced after the Civil War to Mobile. The account is signed by Joseph S. Cain, the man credited with reviving Mobile's celebration after the Civil War. Cain held a variety of positions, including county coroner, clerk of the old Southern Market, and cotton broker.

The story goes that Cain first took to the streets of Mobile in 1866 in an attempt to lift the spirits of the defeated city, which had been a Confederate stronghold until the end of the war. Cain's get-up as Chickasaw Indian Chief Slacabamorinico poked fun at the Union, for the Chickasaws had never been defeated. Cain's account follows:

"In 1845, which was the first year of the writer's mystic career, the Cowbellions, the Calfbellions, composed entirely of butchers, the Strikers Society, the T.D.S. Society, the Indescribables, [sic] composed of Firemen, constituted the New Year's Eve Parade. In 1857 . . . one of the Strikers Society moved from Mobile to New Orleans and inaugurated Mardi Gras in that city. I have had repeated inquiries as to the manner in which I introduced Mardi Gras to Mobile. It was thus: In 1806 [sic 1866] Washington Fire Company No. 8, of Mobile, of which I was a member, attended the Annual Parade of the New Orleans Fire Department, as the guests of Perseverance Fire Co. No. 13. In that year Mardi Gras occurred on the 5th of March, the day after the parade of the Fire Department. I appeared on the streets of New Orleans on that day in Mardi Gras costume, and was the special care of No. 13. My experience on that occasion was so pleasant that I determined on my return home, that Mobile should have its own Mardi Gras celebration, and so announced in the *Mobile Daily Tribune* of that period. In 1867 the L.C. [Lost Cause] Minstrels, organized by myself, made their first parade and created an immense excitement. From that time to the present the number of mystic societies has increased wonderfully, and the Mobile Carnival has become a feature in our city, that for beauty of design and conception defies any other city in our broad land. This is written as a general reply to innumerable inquiries."

In the 1960s, the bodies of Cain and his wife, Elizabeth, were removed from a cemetery in Bayou La Batre in south Mobile County and reinterred in the Church Street Graveyard in downtown Mobile. The bodies were transferred at the insistence of Julian Lee "Judy" Rayford, a sculptor, poet, author, and folklorist who had a fascination with Mardi Gras. For several years those attending the Joe Cain Procession staged picnics at the graveyard, but some of the grave sites were damaged with all the merrymaking, and the event was moved elsewhere.

Mobile's black community takes pride in presenting the Mammoth Parade. This float honors the many black baseball players from the Mobile area. Photo by Ric Moore.

Cain's counterpart prior to the Civil War, Michael Krafft, who died in Pascagoula, Mississippi, in 1839, was also reinterred in Mobile. His final resting place is Magnolia Cemetery. One may see the emblems of the Cowbellions, the rakes, hoes, bells, and a cow in relief on his marble monument. (The Resurrection Cowbellion de Rakin Society, formed in 1989, stages an escapade and ball on New Year's Eve and meets again at Krafft's grave on his birthday to read an original poem in tribute.)

As time went on, Mobile's Mardi Gras celebration became more elaborate. By 1895 the Mobile City Directory listed 20 mystic societies.

The Order of Myths opened a new era, which caused the main mystic celebration to move from New Year's Eve to Mardi Gras. Organized in 1867, the group is Mobile's oldest parading society. An article in the February 26, 1868, *Mobile Daily Register* correctly predicted the historic significance of the event: "Yesterday was a new era in the mythical, mystical, poetic, romantic, and artistic history of Mobile. The mystic societies of New Year's Eve have long since become celebrated, but the last day of the Carnival had heretofore been unnoted in our local calendar. The 'Order of Myths' have changed all this, and henceforward, no doubt, Mardi-Gras will be

Everyone wants a piece of the action. Photo by Ric Moore.

looked forward to with an anxiety as eager as that which attends upon New Year's Eve."

The Order of Myths' emblem of Folly chasing Death around the broken column of life and flogging him with gourd-like pig bladders is synonymous with Mardi Gras to many Mobilians. Some say the broken column represents the broken hopes of the Confederacy, while Folly's triumph over Death represents the unbroken courage and spirit of the South.

The Excelsior Band has been leading the Order of Myths for more than a hundred years. The all-black band was formed on the corner of Selma and Scott Streets on November 23, 1883, by John A. Pope to commemorate the birth of his son. The son, John C. Pope, became the leader of the band in 1902 at the age of 19. The group plays Dixieland jazz, show tunes, and standards from the 1940s and 1950s.

Dating from 1869, the Infant Mystics, so named because of the youth of its founding members, evolved from the older H.S.S. and first paraded under the new name in 1874. The first parade featured a calcium light, one of the new headlights from the Mobile and Ohio Railroad brought to town from Whistler, a suburb of Mobile, by a special train the day of the parade. The idea was imported from New Orleans. A cat serves as the main feature on the society's emblem float.

The Knights of Revelry, organized in 1874, is famed for its serio-comic parades and was the first society to parade during the day. At times the group has had an uncanny ability to foretell the future. Floats in 1895 and 1909 depicted fantasy trips to the moon. The emblem has changed over time. Currently Folly dances in a champagne glass on the emblem float.

The Comic Cowboys, which was founded in 1884, with Dave Levi as organizer, are said to hail from Wragg Swamp. Springdale Plaza and Bel Air Mall, one of Mobile's busiest shopping areas, stands on the site today. The Cowboys are known for their lampoons. Their motto is "without malice," and their emblem is a cowboy/jester hat with horns, which sits atop a cowbell. Each year a burlesque queen, "Little Eva," reigns over the parade waving "her" scepter, a plumber's friend, to the crowd.

The Krewe of Columbus, a Catholic society formed by the Knights of Columbus, first paraded in 1922. The parade's theme was the "History and Trials of Columbus." The 1934 parade was to have the theme "A Tragedy in the Heavens." A tragedy from the heavens indeed befell the parade, which was rained out and had to be postponed until the following year. The Krewe was reorganized in 1937, and its membership broadened to include non-Catholics. The new organization was referred to as the Crewe of Columbus. The newspaper reported that the society used tractors instead of mules in the 1941 parade.

Other parading organizations soon followed those already mentioned. They include the Mystic Stripers Society, Mystics of Time, Maids of Mirth, Order of Polka Dots, Order of Athena, Order of Inca, Joe Cain Society, Conde Cavaliers, Pharaohs, Mammoth, Mystics of Children, Krewe of Marry Mates, and Order of LaShe's. The Mobile Mystics are the newest of the parading societies. Other parading societies have sprung up in Prichard, Tillman's Corner, and Fairhope.

The first carnival association was formed in 1872. Daniel E. Huger was selected as the mythical Emperor of Joy to reign over the celebration the following year.

In 1894, the first black mystic society, the Order of Doves (OOD), held its first ball. Miss Florina Nicholas, attired in pink silk, was acknowledged belle of the ball. The OOD went out of existence in 1914. A new group called the Original Utopia Club was organized in that year. The group still exists.

In 1938 A. S. May, founder and president of the Knights of May Zulu Club, presented a two-float parade down the streets of Mobile. Winston A. Allen was named "King Tuttle," and Ruby Morgan was named his queen.

The Colored Carnival Association of Mobile (now known as the Mobile Area Mardi Gras Association) named its first king and queen in 1940. They were Alex Herman and Aliene Jenkins. To this day, the black king is known as "Elexis." The first mayor, now known as a grand marshall, was Samuel Besteda.

The monarchs of Mardi Gras rule for the four days preceding Ash Wednesday. The white king and queen are chosen by the Mobile Carnival Association. The reigning monarchs are usually third or fourth generation Mobilians, and someone in their families has usually been a former king or queen or has been in a Mardi Gras Court. Their families must have contributed time and money to the Carnival Association. The queen is chosen by the Carnival Association from debutantes that are presented at the Camellia Ball held in November, and the debutantes that are not selected become her court. Members of the association's board nominate candidates and decide by consensus who will reign.

The Mobile Area Mardi Gras Association has a similar selection process, with a few important differences. Those wishing to serve as a MAMGA king or queen must submit a biography to the board. The board takes a vote from that pool of candidates.

The royal couples share a similar mythology. Each king arrives on a royal yacht from the Isle of Joy over a sea of lemonade and lands in Mobile. Each receives

King Elexis I arrives on a royal yacht from the Isle of Joy over a sea of lemonade and lands in Mobile. He receives keys to the city and rules until midnight on Fat Tuesday. Photo by Ric Moore.

On the following page The reigning monarchs of Mardi Gras are usually third or fourth generation Mobilians, and someone in their families has usually been a former king or queen or has been in a Mardi Gras Court. Photo by Ric Moore.

keys to the city and rules until midnight on Fat Tuesday.

The coronation that follows is lavish, with exacting attention paid to the smallest details. Heralds, military escorts, and knights promenade before the arrival of their king to the Mobile Civic Center arena, which for a short time is transformed into a throne room. The king arrives, promenades, and introduces her majesty, who is escorted by military escorts and surrounded by ladies of the court.

The royal couples' costumes are expensive and elaborate. To serve as a king or queen costs from $10,000 to $25,000. Expensive materials such as velvet, ermine, and satin studded with rhinestones or seed pearls adorn the royal robes, befitting true royalty.

Taking on the royal role can be a weighty responsibility, as 1981's Queen Laurie Taylor learned. *Queens of Mobile Mardi Gras 1893-1986* recalls: "Petite Queen Laurie, who is 5-feet-4 1/2 inches tall had some difficulty pulling her train, which is six yards long and two yards wide with an 18-inch deep border of ermine at the base. The train and gown, which glittered with stones and rhinestone banding, weighs 60 pounds."

Anyone can attend the coronation for the price of a ticket, but the most highly attended events, the parades, are free. The floats form a tableau, a living scene, whose theme is continued at masked balls held by the mystic societies. In earlier times and still today, the tableau draws heavily from history, literature, and cultural events. Newspaper accounts from the 1800s gave elaborate accounts of each tableau.

Beads and Moon Pies were the favorite catches in 1994, according to a *Mobile Register*-University of South Alabama poll. Overall, the poll showed 26 percent preferred beads, 23 percent preferred Moon Pies, 11 percent preferred doubloons, and 5 percent preferred cups. Serpentine and candy were each favored by 1 percent of the paradegoers. The poll also showed those in the 40-plus age group preferred Moon Pies, while those in the under-40 age group preferred beads.

In an attempt to make Mardi Gras safer, hard objects were banned in 1969. Boxed items such as Cracker Jacks, rubber balls, and other potential missiles could no longer be thrown.

Moon Pies got a boost when Cracker Jacks were outlawed. Nevertheless, the graham cracker-type cookie with a marshmallow center covered with chocolate, vanilla, or banana can cause a bruise if lobbed hard enough. Death by Moon Pie, however, is more likely to occur by gorging on too many at one sitting. While counterfeits exist, the real articles are made in a Chattanooga, Tennessee, bakery and were trademarked in 1919.

Unlike New Orleans' celebration, which has captured the imagination of the nation, Mobile's celebration continues to be a community affair thrown by Mobilians for Mobilians. Photo by Ric Moore.

Concern for safety goes way back. A February 27, 1900, article in the *Mobile Register* reported the early problems with confetti: "Confetti throwing was introduced into the Mobile carnival for the first time yesterday, and it had not been in vogue very long before some person threw a handful into the face of the daughter of one of the carnival visitors and was promptly knocked down by the father of the young woman."

"Three ladies, into whose faces some young man had thrown handfuls of the stuff, complained bitterly to Chief of Police Soost of such conduct."

"Chief Soost saw at once that if he did not do something to nip the practice in the bud, there would be a repetition of the morning knock-down, and knowing that some man would resent such an act toward ladies in their charge with a shot from a pistol instead of a blow from the fist, he issued an order to the police force to bring in any person caught throwing confetti in the faces or on the clothing of ladies and charge the offender with disorderly conduct."

Over the years, Mardi Gras has been racially segregated by custom, though the arrivals by yacht, balls, and coronations are similar. In 1993 barriers began to fall as the city opened its Mardi Gras season with the first truly integrated ball. For the first time in its 300-year history, the royalty of both carnival groups met. When the monarchs met, bowed, and waved their scepters in salutation, the crowd of more than 1,000 applauded. The ball, held at the Mobile Civic Center on November 13, was held in association with the Quebec Winter Carnival. Organizers were anxious about how everybody would mix, but by 11 P.M. the dance floor was crowded with couples, black and white, line dancing and doing the "electric slide."

Organizers were quick to point out that the Mobile International Carnival Ball was not an attempt to integrate the mystic societies, but rather an occasion to recognize the economic benefit to the city that Mardi Gras generates, which is an estimated $25 million or more a year. All but 10 of the city's 68 mystic societies were on hand to receive medallions from Mayor Mike Dow. Visitors from Guadalajara, Mexico, and Quebec City attended the event. The Quebec City delegation brought Bonhomme, the snowman mascot of their carnival.

The royal Mobile couples met again on February 8, 1994, at the Mardi Gras du Carnaval Ball in Quebec City. The international debut held at the Loewe Le Concorde was televised live on Quebec's largest French-language station.

Another integrated function occurred about two months after the first such event, as the Head Start

Policy Council threw a ball at the Greater Gulf States Fairgrounds to raise funds for Head Start centers that had been damaged by a summer storm.

Almost every demographic segment is or has been represented by Mobile's mystic societies. Unlike New Orlean's celebration, which has captured the imagination of the nation, Mobile's celebration continues to be a community affair thrown by Mobilians for Mobilians. Since the establishment of Le Krewe de Bienville in 1961, some without connections have been offered the chance to see a genuine Mobile Mardi Gras ball, because the group sells tickets and promotes itself through literature left at local hotels. New groups such as The New Mobilians and the Krewe of Out-of-Towners also give those new to the area a chance to join the fun. ⚜

The trick to making a good Moon Pie catcher has to do with finding a container deep enough so they won't bounce out and big enough so it is an easy target. Inverted umbrellas and laundry baskets also suffice. Moon Pies got a boost when boxed items such as Cracker Jacks were outlawed, but the cookie can cause a bruise if lobbed hard enough. Photo by Ric Moore.

Chapter 6
THE DELTA
A natural gem.

Against an azure sky, a raft of white pelicans riding a warm air current circles an invisible spire in ever tighter circles before heading back to the more open bay.

A sudden plunk and water swirls as some nameless creature zigzags beneath the surface.

An alligator slides down a mud bank.

A flock of startled ducks makes a thunderous noise as wings beat air.

Migrating monarch butterflies congregate to fold and unfold their wings as they pause in preparation for their trip to Mexico.

A lone heron stands statuesque before moving slowly on to stalk an unwary minnow.

This is the Mobile-Tensaw Delta, a vast wilderness whose southern end lies within minutes of downtown Mobile by way of Bankhead Tunnel.

This natural treasure boasts a wide variety of holdings. Altogether, the delta harbors 115 species of freshwater fish, 119 species of reptiles and amphibians, and at least 300 species of birds. Nine kinds of wetlands have been identified in the delta. Untold numbers of Civil War and Indian artifacts, some dating from A.D. 1250, are buried there.

The delta and neighboring area harbor some mammoth specimens from the plant kingdom. On the west side of the delta in Saraland stands a live oak with a girth of 31 feet. On the delta's east side grows a bald cypress measuring 131 feet high and 27 feet around. Both trees have benefited from the rich, delta soil, which traces its history to Mississippi, northern Alabama, and Georgia as well as the rich Alabama Black Belt.

A number of endangered and threatened species inhabit or visit the Mobile-Tensaw Delta. The bald eagle nests there. The Alabama red-bellied turtle is found exclusively in the Mobile-Tensaw Delta and was chosen as the state reptile in 1990. Both are endangered. Sturgeon reproduce in the rivers. The Gulf sturgeon is threatened and the Alabama sturgeon (whose existence as a distinct species is in dispute) was proposed for the endangered list as of early 1994.

On the previous page
Deep lush forests, mysterious Indian mounds, and some of the best fishing are just a few features of this sportsmen's paradise. Photo by Dave Hamby.

On the previous page, inset
The alligator reigns as undisputed King of the Delta. Though they seem log-like as they bask in the sun, they can obtain speeds in short bursts of up to 20 miles per hour and are able to down a small deer. They may grow to 16 feet long in exceptional cases, but the largest ones in the delta are generally 11 to 12 feet in length and weigh 450 to 550 pounds. Photo by Ric Moore.

A monarch butterfly pauses from a journey that may cover 2,000 miles in its trek from Canada and the northern United States to California, Florida, and Mexico. It is the only species to make the two-way migration. Other species, which are dependent upon the vegetation found only in wetlands, will rarely leave the swamp. Photo by Ric Moore.

The presence of ospreys, bellwethers of a pristine environment, indicates conditions are improving. Kamikaze-like, these fish hawks plunge after their prey at speeds that would kill a lesser bird.

A pair near Chickasaw has chosen a precarious roost above the marsh on a high-voltage pylon. Osprey nests have been reported to weigh as much as half a ton. A clutch that an Alabama Game and Fish Division officer had been watching fell into the water. But like Moses in the bulrushes, the birds floated along unhurt because the nest acted as a raft.

The delta's duck population has dropped drastically over the years as the result of drought, loss of wetlands, and creation of a refuge in the northern part of the state. In the 1950s the duck population blackened the sky and numbered in the tens of thousands; in the 1990s it numbered in the thousands.

Still, the delta supports a wide variety of ducks. Dabbling duck species include wood ducks, mallards, teal, mottled ducks, northern shovelers, gadwalls, American widgeons, and pintails. Diving ducks include ring-necked ducks, ruddy ducks, buffleheads, redheads, canvasbacks, and lesser scaups. Large numbers of American coots winter in the lower portion of the delta.

Of course the alligator reigns as undisputed King of the Delta. They are prolific. About 150,000 to 200,000 call the delta home. An alligator nuisance control agent removed 24 of the reptiles ranging from 5 to 11 feet in length from the Eastern Shore during one busy week in 1991. In 1967 the United States Fish and Wildlife

Service classified the alligator as an endangered species, but by 1977 the alligator population had increased so much that the reptiles were reclassified as threatened. Alligators bear a similar appearance to their Florida cousin, the American Crocodile, an endangered species that could be devastated if hunting were permitted. For that reason, alligators are afforded special protection because of the similarity.

Alligators, though they seem log-like as they bask in the sun, can obtain speeds in short bursts of up to 20 miles per hour and are able to down a small deer. They may grow to 16 feet long in exceptional cases, but the largest ones in the delta are generally 11 to 12 feet in length and weigh 450 to 550 pounds.

A maze of waterways laces this immense wetland and wildlife paradise, which consists of about 250,000 acres of flood plain swamps and marshes. The total average flow of the Mobile and Tensaw rivers comes to 39.3 billion gallons a day and ultimately flows into Mobile Bay. In comparison to the other United States rivers, the volume discharged ranks fourth after the Mississippi, Yukon, and Columbia Rivers. This discharge dumps more than 4 million tons of sediment a year into the bay.

The watershed ranks as the sixth largest in the nation and spans more than two-thirds of Alabama, plus portions of neighboring Mississippi, Tennessee, and Georgia. A report from the Marine Environmental Sciences Consortium at Dauphin Island notes Chesapeake Bay is about 10 times the area of Mobile Bay, 3 times the average depth, but has only 1.5 times the drainage area, so the volume of the water in Mobile Bay is comparatively small, while the water coming in is about the same as in Chesapeake Bay.

The delta arises from the waters of five major rivers that meander throughout the state: the Coosa and the Tallapoosa, which form the Alabama; the Black Warrior; and the Tombigbee.

About 30 miles north of Battleship Memorial Parkway, the Tombigbee and Alabama Rivers join, flow south for 5 miles, and then divide into the Mobile and Tensaw Rivers. The waters of the Mobile and Tensaw Rivers form the heart of the Mobile-Tensaw Delta.

In the rich bottomlands formed by the delta grow stands of oak, gum, and cypress. Wood ducks, turkeys, freshwater game fish, and white-tailed deer prosper in this area, which is less flood-prone. Here, too, is where the timber industry conducts much of its logging activities.

Further south, toward Interstate 65 and beyond, bald cypress and water tupelo predominate in a hauntingly beautiful deep alluvial swamp. Low, depressed areas in the flood plain catch water, thus keeping this area flooded for prolonged periods. Over thousands of

The Mobile-Tensaw Delta harbors at least 300 species of birds. Photo by Ric Moore.

The Alabama red-bellied turtle is found exclusively in the Mobile-Tensaw Delta and was chosen as the state reptile in 1990. Photo by Ric Moore.

Duck populations have dropped drastically over the years as the result of drought, loss of wetlands, and creation of a refuge in the northern part of the state. Still, the delta supports a wide variety of ducks. Photo courtesy of Faulkner State Community College.

years, rivers overflowed their banks and deposited sediment to create a natural levee. Deep shade and heavy rainfall inhibit most undergrowth.

This almost impenetrable swamp gives way in the southern half of the delta to more diverse growth and defines the boundary between animals that frequent freshwater and saltwater habitats.

Bald cypress and water tupelo thrive, but so do such species as blackgum, red maple, green ash, and swamp cottonwood. Shade-tolerant species such as Virginia willow, swamp palmetto, and panic grass grow under this canopy. And where the sun pierces through openings in the canopy, grow plants that occur predominantly in the adjacent marshes—plants with names like arrow arum, pickerelweed, and golden club.

Locked in the heart of this area of the delta between the Middle and Tensaw Rivers are 16 Bottle Creek Indian mounds believed to date back to at least A.D. 1250. The site is located on Mound Island, about 30 miles northeast of Mobile in Baldwin County.

A kind of Venice in the swamp, the mounds are accessible only by boat and are believed to have been the home of a boat-oriented culture. A canal, possibly used for transportation, is associated with the mounds. Houses were perched on smaller mounds. Larger mounds—one rises some 55 feet in the center—supported the chief's home and a temple.

The people who first lived here were agrarian and had priests and hereditary chiefs. They are part of the Pensacola culture, a subculture of the Mississippian Indian culture that dominated the Southeast.

The location was at a cultural crossroads. North-south river routes and a major east-west trail gave the people who lived here control of important trade routes. High land suitable for developing commerce and trade routes is associated with either side of the Mobile-Tensaw Delta. By contrast, the Mississippi overflows its banks during rainy months and floods the surrounding low-lying areas. For this reason the Mobile-Tensaw Delta was more hospitable than the Mississippi Delta and could support inhabitants—a kind of Mesopotamia of the Southeast, says one student of the area.

Clues to the nature of this culture have been unearthed by the Gulf Coast Survey, a program of the Alabama Museum of Natural History, University of Alabama. Excavations in the early 1990s of the middens, the garbage heaps, indicated the Indians ate clams, fish, deer, corn, and hickory nuts. The most significant find was a rectangular bowl with step-like sides. The bowl is similar to the "prayer bowls" found in the Southwest, where they are associated with important ceremonial functions.

By the time the French arrived, the area appeared to be vacant, but recent excavations indicate that the island continued to be inhabited into the 1700s. These may have been descendants of the ancient Bottle Creek tribe or of the Mabilians (translated as "Mobilians" by R. G. McWilliams in *Iberville's Gulf Journals*), an important tribe contacted by the de Soto expedition.

Pierre Le Moyne d'Iberville described the site when he made his third expedition to the New World in 1702 to relocate Fort Biloxi, the French capital of Louisiana, to a location on Twenty-Seven-Mile Bluff just north of present-day Mobile. In his March 4, 1702, journal he reported: "My brother [Bienville] came back this evening. He had observed several sites formerly occupied by Indians, which war with the Conchaque [a name that applied to several Choctaw towns] and the Alibamons [members of the Creek confederacy] has made them abandon."

"Most of these settlements are on islands, this river being full of them for 13 leagues. [Bienville] got an Indian to show him the place where their gods are, about which all the neighboring nations make such a fuss and to which the Mobilians used to come and offer sacrifices. The Indians claim that a person cannot touch them without dying on the spot and that they came down from the sky. A gun had to be given the

The Mobile-Tensaw Delta is a treasure prized by sportsmen, boaters, lumbermen, photographers, researchers, scientists, and all those who value nature and its vast array of surprises. Photo by Ric Moore.

Indian who showed where they were; he did not get closer to them than 10 steps away, and with his back turned. It took a search to locate them on a little hill among the canes, near an old village that is destroyed, on one of these islands...."

Iberville postulated the "gods"—images of a man, a woman, a child, a bear, and an owl—could have been made by a member of de Soto's expedition.

While the mysteries of the Bottle Creek Indians remain locked in the delta, busy causeways further south that carry thousands of cars each day may be a marvel to archaeologists exploring this area a thousand years hence.

Here at the southernmost end of the delta, Interstate 10 (Jubilee Parkway) and U.S. Highway 90 (Battleship Memorial Parkway) run almost parallel and link Mobile County to Baldwin County. As traffic speeds past, a seemingly endless flat expanse of shallows interrupted by rushes and mudflats mirror the ever-changing sky.

This area at the head of the bay where saltwater meets fresh forms a nursery. Around 90 percent of the Gulf's commercially harvested seafood spends at least part of its life in such a nursery. Shrimp, for example, the mainstay of the seafood industry, spawn in the Gulf, but must migrate to an estuary to spend part of their life cycle. Likewise, the larvae of blue crabs hatch in the Gulf, but must mature in an estuary. The area at the head of the bay is one of several estuaries associated with Mobile Bay. (Others are found at Weeks Bay in Baldwin County and Bayou La Batre in Mobile County.)

Special conditions create this nursery upon which so much depends. Protected from the effects of wave action, shrimp and crab larvae develop, clams set, and plants root. Tiny plankton and nutrients remain suspended in the quiet waters of the upper bay. Light penetrates the shallows, fostering growth of bottom plants and tidal flat organisms, while the fresh water, shallows, grass beds, and intertidal marshes keep predators at bay.

The interlocking web of life is complex. Feed and be fed upon—it's an unmerciful rule of nature. From the tiniest microscopic organism on up the ladder to the largest marine fishes and even to man, a loss in any rung can mean the collapse of an entire ecosystem. The continental shelf teems with sea life that feeds on marine fish and organisms that spend a part of their life cycle in an estuary. For that reason, scientists believe that most marine life in the Gulf of Mexico is ultimately dependent upon estuaries.

Around 23 million pounds of finfish and shellfish, valued at about $36 million, are landed annually in Alabama waters according to the Auburn University Marine Extension-Research Center. Both by weight and

Tended only by Mother Nature, this showy swamp flower heralds spring in the delta. Photo by Linda Clements.

dollar value, shrimp are the most important catch. Of the total catch, that delicacy accounts for 14.8 million pounds and is valued at $32.7 million.

Jubilees, a little-studied phenomenon that occur on the Eastern Shore, underscore the richness and diversity of sea life found in the bay's waters. Periodically during the mid-to-late summer, crabs, flounder, shrimp, and other sea life congregate along the shore at night or in the twilight hours when an east breeze brings a slight chill to the air and makes the water still as glass. Scientists believe a combination of events deplete the water of oxygen, causing sea life to amass along the shore. Usually, after only a few hours, this unique set of conditions dissipates, and the seafood bonanza returns to the depths. Naturally, when a jubilee occurs, neighbor calls neighbor and people grab their scoop nets, gigs, wash tubs, and kerosene floundering lights to catch the fish, crabs, and shrimp, which are sluggish and easy to collect. During a large jubilee, sea life carpets the sandy bottom, and it is possible to catch tubfuls of crabs and dozens of flounder.

Besides their important role as a nursery, estuaries can temporarily store flood waters, reducing the threat of flood damage.

While the interplay of rivers, tide, wind, and mixing of salt with fresh water gently purify the water flowing through the delta and bay each day, once in a generation or so Mother Nature cleans house in a more forceful way. One of the few positive effects noted by scientists after Hurricane Frederic came through in 1979 was that the bay had been cleansed of man-made pollutants—many of which were deposited long before there was any recognition that they could be harmful to man or to the environment.

The story of how the delta was formed begins about 21,000 years ago during the peak of the Wisconsin Ice Age. An ice cap more than 10,000 feet thick covered Canada. As the Ice Age peaked, the ice cap grew larger and absorbed enough water from the oceans to cause the sea level to drop such that the coast was 60 miles to the south of the present coast. When the sea level dropped, the rivers' courses steepened, causing the rivers to gouge deep valleys as they raced to the sea. The river that surged through this area cut the Mobile River Valley and created the bluff along the Eastern Shore.

The lower delta stretches like an endless prairie under an ever-changing sky, while the upper delta has a canopy so dense sunlight rarely pierces it. A maze of waterways laces this immense wetland and wildlife paradise, which consists of about 250,000 acres of flood plain swamps and marshes. Photo by Adrian Hoff.

A pelican rides an air current before he dives for a fish. Photo by Ric Moore.

When the ice cap to the north began melting sometime between 15,000 to 18,000 years ago, the sea level rose and flooded the Mobile River Valley, the area which would later become Mobile Bay. The Mobile River system widened and slowly snaked its way back and forth as it deposited sediment, thus forming today's delta.

Much of the delta is accessible only by boat, and then only by an experienced navigator who knows the delta. This relative inaccessibility has not protected the delta from the advances of man. Some 35 percent of the delta's brackish and salt marshlands, or about 6,680 acres, were lost within the 25-year period between 1955 to 1979.

In recent years, groups representing the seemingly conflicting interests of industry, the state and federal government, and sportsmen have joined forces to preserve the delta for future generations. In October 1988, the United States Fish and Wildlife Service, the Alabama Game and Fish Division, Scott Paper Company, and the Coastal Land Trust agreed to work together to improve the habitat for waterfowl that winter in the region.

The delta project is part of one of the largest wildlife restoration projects ever attempted. The ambitious goal of the North American Waterfowl Management Plan, a joint effort of the United States and Canadian governments, is designed to restore continental waterfowl populations to historical levels by the year 2000.

Duck counts across the nation and in the delta showed the number of ducks had fallen precipitously. Droughts in the United States and Canada, together with loss of habitat, were blamed.

The Coastal Land Trust, consisting of a group of area businessmen, most of whom are also sportsmen, has raised money and bought more than 20,000 acres of privately owned land in the delta since the organization was founded in 1984. The Trust then sells this land to the state or federal government and uses the money to buy more land. As part of the project, Scott Paper Company has designated 67,850 acres and the Alabama Department of Natural Resources has designated 27,000 acres for special management programs. The terms of the agreement are renegotiated every five years.

Such is the Mobile-Tensaw Delta. It was a treasure prized by early American Indians more than 700 years ago; it is a treasure prized today by sportsmen, boaters, lumbermen, photographers, researchers, scientists, and all those who value nature and its vast array of surprises. ⚜

A seemingly endless flat expanse of shallows interrupted by rushes and mudflats, where saltwater meets fresh, forms a nursery. Around 90 percent of the Gulf's commercially harvested seafood spends at least part of its life in such a nursery. Shrimp, for example, the mainstay of the seafood industry, spawn in the Gulf, but must migrate to an estuary to spend part of their life cycle. Around 23 million pounds of finfish and shellfish, valued at about $36 million, are landed annually in Alabama. Photo by Ric Moore.

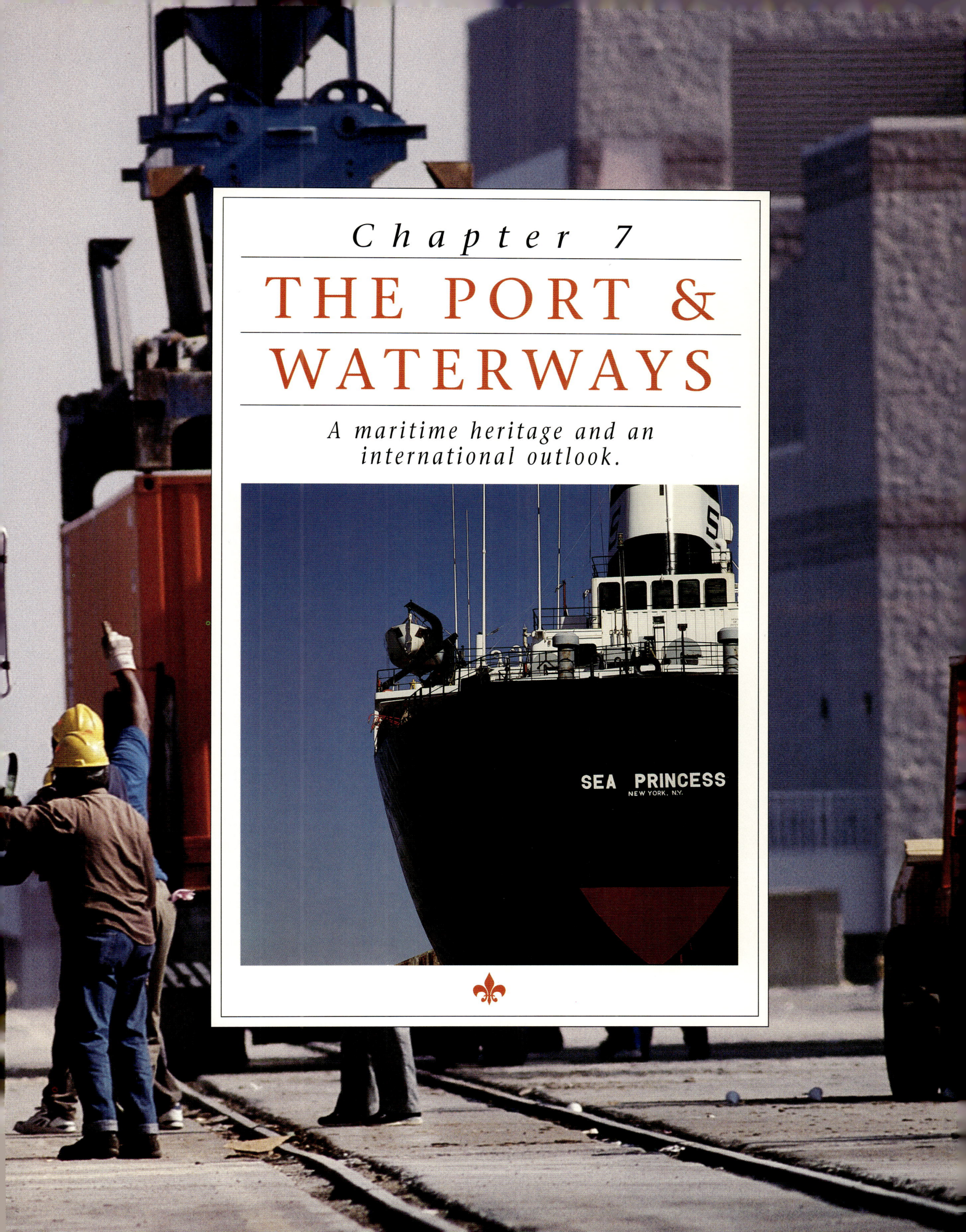

Chapter 7
THE PORT & WATERWAYS

A maritime heritage and an international outlook.

A Gulf Coast Treasure

Four major railroads, Burlington Northern, CSX Transportation, Illinois Central, and Norfolk Southern have direct lines to Mobile, and the Alabama State Docks has its own rail system with 70 miles of track. Photo by Ric Moore.

On the previous page
Both nature and man have worked to create the highly productive harbor, which is among the foremost in the nation. Photo by Ric Moore.

On the previous page, inset
Founded as one of America's first seaports, the city of Mobile is testimony to a thriving maritime economy; and its vital network of rivers linked to the nation's heartland by the Tennessee-Tombigbee Waterway is more important than ever. Photo by Ric Moore.

Late at night a giant freighter sailing up the Mobile Ship Channel slides past the twinkling lights of the western shore. Viewed from across the bay, the lights look like a glittering necklace. A full moon hangs like a copper penny above the city. As times passes, a fog rolls in. Then, when most people are asleep, the deep groan of a foghorn breaks the stillness—a reminder that commerce carries on day and night from the Port of Mobile.

The shipping industry has been a vital part of this city since it was founded. The port's history is filled with romance, adventure, and curious twists.

Today's deep-draft ocean-going juggernauts viewed from the docks make even the city's skyscrapers appear small. Huge cranes tower where the masts of wooden sailing vessels once rose.

A visit to an older warehouse on property belonging to the Alabama State Docks helps document the changes that have come about through automation. At one time, men worked shoulder-to-shoulder here, shoving, hauling, and carrying cargo in and out of the warehouses. In those days horsepower meant pulled by a horse. As if to emphasize the fact, an old doorway big enough for a man, a mule, and a cart takes on diminutive proportions next to a new doorway big enough for a semi-truck—one of more than 52,000 a year that will visit the Alabama State Docks General Cargo Warehouses. The jagged edge where bricks have been dislodged to enlarge a doorway leading outside seems to further underscore the importance of large-scale machinery in today's shipping operations.

The Alabama State Docks' modern-day bulk handling operation also differs from bygone times. Bulk cargoes, in contrast to general cargoes, consist of commodities such as coal that can be handled continuously, by way of pipes, chutes, conveyor belts, and other such devices. Here again, automation made a difference. The miles of modern conveyor belts that mark the skyline look like giant roller coasters and can handle as much as 7,500 tons of coal per hour.

One thing that hasn't changed is the port's commitment to international trade. The Center for International Trade and Commerce (CITC), created in 1980, matches Alabama manufacturers and agricultural producers instantaneously with trade leads from throughout the world. This service, sponsored by the Alabama State Docks and the University of South Alabama, is provided free.

As of 1993 the leading export nations for the port were Canada, followed by Japan, and then Mexico. In 1990 Mexico held the number 17 spot, but jumped to number 3 in 1992. The North American Free Trade Agreement (NAFTA), which went into effect January 1, 1994, further thrust open the door to trade, and a knowledgeable source familiar with the port predicted at the time that Mexico would soon surpass Japan as an exports market.

The Port of Mobile's international outlook is reflected through its many business and informal ties throughout the world. The consulates of 15 nations are represented at the port. Twelve customhouse brokers are available to inspect foreign flag ships. The port's broad outlook and international influence extend to the community.

Mobile has nearly a dozen sister cities in countries throughout the world. Havana, Cuba; Kosice, Slovak; Malaga, Spain; and Rostov-on-Don, Russia, are some of those represented. The sister city programs promote friendship and an international exchange of ideas. The city's International Festival, established in the early 1980s, represented 50 different countries in 1993.

Exports exceed imports by nearly two-to-one at this port. Among the port's chief export items are general merchandise, grain, coal, crude petroleum, and forest products. But it is this last item in its many forms that has carved Mobile a niche in the world shipping market. By 1992, 52 percent of all forest products that moved through Gulf Coast ports moved through Mobile. New Orleans, the second largest mover of forest products along the Gulf Coast, handled 10 percent of that product.

The Alabama State Docks' 360,000-square-foot Forest Products Terminal at Pier C, dedicated in 1992, is the largest waterfront forest products warehouse in the world.

The "South C" Forest Products Terminal looks like a pantry in a well-scrubbed kitchen. The State Docks' housekeepers buff and scrub the specially coated floors until they are gleaming. At any given moment, someone riding a washer-scrubber machine (it looks like a power lawn mower) will dash through.

Viewed from the far end of the forest products terminal, forklifts with their reflections shimmering in the shiny floors appear to be miniature children's toys. The white packages they carry seem to be sugar cubes. The building's immense size creates this illusion—the terminal is so large, six football games could be played simultaneously within it.

As many as three vessels at a time can berth at the terminal. In one swoop, a crane can lift a load off the flatbed of a truck. A covered, lighted platform allows rail loading and unloading to continue day or night, rain or shine. Forty rail cars can be handled at a time, and as many as 80 to 100 cars can be handled during an eight-hour shift.

Introduction of new industries—a $400-million newsprint plant and a $700-million wood pulp mill at Claiborne, as well as other regional industry expansions—demanded that the State Docks take the initiative to build the forest products terminal so the docks could efficiently handle the growing demands placed on it.

Both nature and man have worked to create the highly productive harbor, which is among the foremost in the nation. But for sailors entering Mobile Bay, it still looks much as it did when early explorers charted its waters.

On either side of the mouth, the headlands cup gracefully inward. To the west lies Cedar Point. To the east lies a long sandy spit of land covered with pine, oak, and waxmyrtle. The arm of land now known as Fort Morgan Peninsula conceals most of the bay's mouth from view. Behind it lies a deep basin used as a harbor by early ships.

Barrier islands thinly clad with pines and palmetto form a protective chain along the coast from Mobile west to the Mississippi. Cedar Point and Fort Morgan Peninsula almost embrace the eastern-most island known as Dauphin Island, which guards the bay's entrance.

The Port of Mobile lies near the head of the bay on Mobile River. The bay itself is relatively large and shallow with an overall area of nearly 400 square miles and an average natural depth of 9 to 10 feet. It is about 30 miles long and varies in width from 8 miles at the northern end to 20 miles at the southern end.

John Barnett Waterman set out to establish his own line after World War I. The Waterman Line continued to expand after the founder's death in 1937 and became the nation's largest privately-owned shipping line. Photo courtesy of the University of South Alabama Archives.

Malcom McLean made sweeping changes to the shipping industry when he moved to Mobile and developed containerized shipping. Though McLean's corporate headquarters are now in New York, a number of Mobilians have ridden on his wave of success. According to an April 16, 1979, Business Week *article: "With no formal corporate organization, he runs each new venture by drawing from a pool of loyal Mobile associates, many of whom have become millionaires through their McLean connection." Photo courtesy of Malcom McLean.*

It was soon recognized that the harbor must be improved to compete with other ports. Since 1826 the U.S. Corps of Engineers has repeatedly dredged the channels deeper and wider to keep pace with the growth of the port and the size of the vessels using it.

The Mobile Ship Channel is dredged to a depth of 40 to 45 feet. Dredging to the existing dimensions was completed in 1965. Since the original appropriation of $10,000 in 1826, a total of about $249 million was spent through fiscal year 1992 on improvements in Mobile Harbor: $96 million for new work and about $153 million for maintenance, including about $5 million in emergency dredging due to Hurricane Frederic in 1979. Theodore Ship Channel cost $53 million in federal funds.

Between 1895 and 1915, a series of 17 locks and dams were built between Mobile and Birmingham to accommodate steamboat traffic. The dams were later raised to deepen the channels for barges.

Today Alabama has one of the most extensive inland water systems in the United States with more than 1,500 miles of navigable routes. Located along those waterways are 10 inland docks belonging to the Alabama State Docks. Most of them have grain elevators and are strategically located on the Chattahoochee, Tennessee, Alabama, and Warrior-Tombigbee River systems. Many are equipped with warehouses, conveyor systems, and storage tanks, and all have concrete docks with mooring dolphins.

Four major railroads, Burlington Northern, CSX Transportation, Illinois Central, and Norfolk Southern have direct lines to Mobile. In addition, the Alabama State Docks has its own rail system with 70 miles of track.

The port's strategic location guarantees its success. Only 33 miles from the open waters of the Gulf of Mexico, the Port of Mobile is closer than any other Gulf port to routes leading to the East Coast, South America, the Far East, and Europe. The Gulf Intracoastal Waterway, which extends more than 1,300 miles along the Gulf Coast, traverses the lower end of Mobile Bay. Within the waterway's minimum 9- to 12-foot depth and 125-foot width, barges move more tonnage than on the Saint Lawrence Seaway. The Tennessee-Tombigbee Waterway, opened in 1985, links Mobile to America's breadbasket and the industrial East. The "Tenn-Tom" threw open more than 16,000 miles of inland waterways to the port and gave it a direct link to Chicago and Pittsburgh.

The average annual commerce in Mobile Harbor for the five-year period from 1989 to 1993 was 36.6 million tons. In 1993 commerce reached a total of 37 million tons.

While the Alabama State Docks has contributed significantly to the port, private industry has flourished and today is responsible for moving more than half of the port's tonnage. A glance through the Port Directory found in the back of each issue of *Port of Mobile* magazine, a publication of the Alabama State Docks, attests to the numerous enterprises that have grown up around the port. For example, the December 1993 issue listed 6 bunkering services, 11 grain merchants, 58 truck lines, 25 ship chandlers, 13 shipbuilding and repair companies, 9 stevedoring companies, 16 towing companies, and 24 steamship agencies and lines.

The port is home to some industry giants. Bender Shipbuilding & Repair Co., Inc., a family-owned business, is one of the world's largest builders of steel-hull vessels and has converted more vessels to new uses than any other American shipyard. Its facilities stretch along a mile of Mobile's waterfront.

Ryan-Walsh, a marine cargo handling company, was formed a couple of years after the Civil War and has corporate headquarters in Mobile. The company's core activity is stevedoring—providing the supervisory personnel and equipment needed to load and unload shallow-draft and deep-water vessels. The company operates in more than two dozen ports in coastal and riverside cities throughout the United States. In 1993 Ryan-Walsh began international operations with the formation of EMESCA/Ryan-Walsh, S.A., a joint venture operating in Puerto Cabello, Venezuela. It also has sales offices in London and Tokyo. The company moves virtually all types of cargo—forest products, containers, steel, coal, grain, and so on.

What is believed to be the world's largest grapple bucket is found in Mobile and belongs to Mobile-based stevedoring giant Cooper/T. Smith. With its giant claws, the bucket can handle 400 tons of steel scrap an hour. The company operates on all three United States coasts and says it ranks as one of the top scrap iron handlers in the world.

Sometimes it's a fast-moving risk-taker with a small company and a good idea that has the most potential for having an impact on the port. Among the most famous of these is John Barnett Waterman, a Louisiana native who moved to Mobile in 1902.

After being tutored in the trade by working for some major steamship lines, Waterman set out to establish his own line after World War I. He obtained financial backing and lobbied Alabama senator and presidential candidate Oscar Underwood to secure shipping assignments from the United States Shipping Board, an agency created during the war to coordinate shipping. He was able to secure only a single vessel, but went forward with his plans.

Waterman's company thrived. In the mid-1920s he created the Mobile, Miami, and Gulf Steamship Company, which, combined with the Mobile Oceanic Line, made up the Waterman holdings. Under the inspired direction of industrialist and entrepreneur E. A. Roberts, the Waterman Line continued to expand after the founder's death in 1937 and became the nation's largest privately-owned shipping line.

Mobile's Win Thurber is a modern-day shipping magnate with a story similar to Waterman's. Winchester Steamship Agency, a company with a staff of two founded in 1980 by Thurber, was so successful that Ryan-Walsh bought it out shortly after it was founded, and Thurber was made senior executive of Southern Steamship Agency, a subsidiary of Ryan-Walsh. In turn, Thurber and two other investors bought Southern Steamship Agency from Ryan-Walsh in 1985. Southern Steamship Agency became a part of the Thurber Company. Its staff of 2 had grown into an organization employing more than 250 locally and more than 1,300 throughout North America. In 1990 Inchcape Shipping Services and Marketing Group, a British company that boasts it is the largest shipping agency network in the world, bought the company.

The shipping business was forever changed in the 1950s by the advent of containerization. The father of that invention was a Mobile resident.

Malcom McLean, a native of Maxton, North Carolina, who moved to the Mobile area in 1955, began with one truck during the Depression. His Winston-Salem, North Carolina, -based McLean Trucking Company became one of the largest in the industry before selling out for $6 million in 1955. Reinvesting that money, McLean revolutionized freight transportation by putting cargo in standardized containers that could move by truck, railroad car, or ship. When McLean moved to Mobile, he bought Pan Atlantic Steamship Co. from Waterman Steamship Corporation for $7 million and four months later, using borrowed funds, bought the rest of Waterman for $42 million.

In 1960 McLean changed the name of Pan Atlantic to Sea-Land Service, Inc. Sea-Land became the foundation for his containerization brainchild. McLean built Sea-

McDuffie Terminal, the largest coal facility on the United States Gulf, is the only terminal in the nation offering both rail and barge access. Photo by Ric Moore.

Steamboats such as the Cypress *pushed cotton upriver from Mobile. Photo courtesy of the Erik Overbey Collection, University of South Alabama Archives.*

To counteract a decline in grain handling, the State Docks began an aggressive marketing program that stemmed the decline and may go down in history as the best idea since sliced bread. Photo by Ric Moore.

Land into the largest shipping company in the world before selling it in 1969 for $160 million in preferred stock to R. J. Reynolds Industries, Inc. These days the boxcar-like containers move most of the nation's dry cargo.

The port's modern history is necessarily intertwined with the history of the Alabama State Docks—a state-owned and operated enterprise that has served as an economic catalyst for the port.

In 1915 state legislator Harry T. Hartwell, who had helped develop one of the port's largest private docks, introduced a bill to create a State Harbor Commission to oversee construction of the State Docks at Mobile. World War I intervened, and the effort was temporarily abandoned. The war also guaranteed that the Alabama State Docks would be built.

Even before the United States entered World War I, it brought great prosperity to the port, as Europe demanded materials to support the war. In 1914 work began on a modern shipyard north of Mobile at Chickasabogue. As the war was pending, the Alabama Dry Docks and Shipbuilding Company (ADDSCO) was created and produced seven ships for the war effort. Starting with $600,000, its sales and services approached $1 billion by the time the shipyard reached its 50th birthday. In all, half a dozen Mobile shipyards repaired or built ships during the First World War.

In 1919, a year after the war ended, the federal government encouraged states and municipalities with harbors or navigable waterways to build at least one public terminal. Local business and political leaders seeking to strengthen Mobile's economy were receptive to the idea. Two historians, Melton McLaurin and Michael Thomason, authors of *Mobile, The Life and Times of a Great Southern City,* sum up the thinking of the time: "Specifically designed to better facilitate the Birmingham trade and to lure additional commerce from the Midwest through Mobile, the State Docks were also viewed by Mobilians as a magnet that would draw national industries to the Port City. The community's leadership hoped that while breathing new life into Mobile's commercial economy, the docks would simultaneously help to achieve their second objective—a broader economic base."

The Alabama Constitution, however, prohibited state funding of internal improvements and had to be amended before the state docks proposal could be initiated. Since the railroads operated their docks at a loss as a way to lure business, they were unsupportive of the proposal that would authorize a state-run competitor.

Alabama voters rejected an amendment in 1920 that would have cleared the way for a state-run docks. At least one authority credits the railroad interests with undermining that initial attempt to amend the Alabama Constitution. The railroads, according to a 1922 survey of the port, owned 15 of the 32 piers and wharves operating at the time. When voters were given a second chance in 1922, they passed the amendment overwhelmingly.

A three-man State Docks Commission was established to oversee the project. It authorized a $10-million bond issue to construct the State Docks and called General William Sibert out of retirement. Sibert, a native Alabamian, was highly regarded for his work on the Panama Canal.

It took two years to procure the land, move the L&N Railroad, and change the yards of Southern and M&O in such a way as to make available the site for the State Docks.

Sibert turned 540 acres of miry land into the most modern docks facility in the world. The first ship to dock was the *Edgar F. Luckenbach,* which unloaded 750 tons of sugar in May 1927 while the docks were still under construction. Officials dedicated the docks June 25, 1928.

Work on the project was started during Governor William Woodward Brandon's administration. In a tribute to Brandon held in December 1926, close to the end of his term, Sibert commended Brandon and predicted the importance of the port. Carolyn Brandon Greene's *Brandon, Sibert and the Alabama State Docks, 1923-1928* quotes Sibert as saying: "This port is going to be of more and more importance to the people of Alabama as generations go by.... The proximity of Alabama to the sea will be of immense importance to the site in its coming struggle for foreign trade, and if this is coupled with an economically and non-politically run port, many new markets for products of Alabama will be opened in every quarter of the globe."

Over the years the State Docks has expanded numerous times. Even through the Great Depression, it expanded and handled significant amounts of cargo. For most of its years, the State Docks has been self-sustaining and has reinvested its "profits" into its facilities.

World War II had a dramatic impact not only on the State Docks, but also on Mobile's shipyards. The shipyards produced 192 vessels during the war, or about one ship a week. By 1943 the Alabama Dry Dock and Shipbuilding Company and Gulf Shipbuilding employed 40,000 people.

The former ADDSCO site at Pinto Island on the Mobile River's east bank again saw a frenzy of activity when it became apparent that the United States would be involved in Operation Desert Storm. Atlantic Marine (which leased and finally bought the site in 1992) was commissioned to repair six Sealift ships—military cargo vessels. The company announced 400 job openings in 1991, thereby doubling its workforce and becoming Mobile's hottest employer.

Layoffs were a certainty after the brief foray into the Middle East, but were slight when compared to the restructuring that occurred after World War II. In a December 27, 1947, *Mobile Press Register* article, Chamber of Commerce President E. Roy Albright noted that 6,750 people in search of work had registered with the local United States Employment Service.

As the community moved from a wartime to a peacetime economy, however, activity along the waterfront that had been held back by the war grew and expanded. Tonnage reports at the Alabama State Docks rose from 1.7 million tons in 1939 to 2.7 million tons in 1945. In 1947 the tonnage moved by the Docks swelled to 4 million tons and never returned to prewar levels.

The private sector also moved forward during the postwar years. Albright's 1947 report recalled: "Several important new steamship services have been given to Mobile during the past year, including new services to the west coast of South America by the Chilean Line, new operation to Cuba by the Sewanee Fruit & Steamship Co., and the inauguration of new service to several additional Atlantic ports in the operation of the Pan Atlantic Steamship Co. The Waterman Steamship Corporation has constantly expanded its operations and is now operating more than one hundred ocean-going vessels."

The Waterman Steamship Corporation marked its confidence in Mobile's postwar future by beginning construction in 1947 of the 18-story Waterman office building.

The Alabama State Docks continued to expand after World War II ended. In the mid-1950s, addition of a modern grain elevator brought trade from the Midwest's breadbasket. During the 1960s, The International Trade Center was built. In addition, a bulk liquid plant and warehouses were constructed, the bulk materials handling plant was expanded, and the grain elevator was improved. To accommodate new industry, 3,000 acres were acquired in Theodore Industrial Park. In 1975 McDuffie Terminal Bulk Coal Plant, the largest such plant of its kind on the United States Gulf and the second-largest in the nation, was completed. A $45-million bond issue approved in 1975 enabled further expansions.

A study of the docks for the years 1984, 1985, and 1986 by the University of South Alabama's Center for Business and Economic Research pointed out that the jobs of 59,000 people in Alabama depended either directly or indirectly upon the Alabama State Docks and that it generated $1.3 billion in wages and $72.5 million in state taxes annually.

Mother Nature, political upheaval on the international front, and some hefty investments by key industries across the state made the late 1980s volatile years for the State Docks. However, private industry took the initiative, and overall the Port of Mobile saw some of its most productive years ever as the decade of the 1990s began to unfold. For the first time, the total combined annual tonnages for the State Docks and private industry hit the 40-million-ton mark.

The port won business during the Drought of '88, which brought the worst dry spell in America since the days of the Dust Bowl. As a result, the Mississippi River fell to its lowest levels since records were first kept in 1872, and its barge traffic came to a halt. The good news for the Port of Mobile was that the 234-mile-long Tennessee-Tombigbee Waterway was unaffected and remained open as the only viable barge route between the nation's interior and the United States Gulf. A record 10 million tons of cargo were transported along the waterway.

The Russian grain embargo and United States crop failure due to disease crushed the grain market in the late 1980s. In fiscal year 1987, the Alabama State Docks' grain elevator handled 101 million bushels of grain. By the following year the amount handled plummeted to 21 million bushels. By fiscal year 1992, the docks handled only 9.6 million bushels. To counteract the trend, the State Docks began an aggressive marketing program that stemmed the decline and may go down in history as the best idea since sliced bread.

"Boutique marketing" resulted in an almost 300 percent increase in grain handled by the docks in 1993 over the previous year. Under the "boutique" approach, the State Docks' grain marketing service aggressively sought to attract smaller customers and offer them personal service for their special needs. Such simple ideas as sending barley malt in bulk carriers instead of by container ships generated so great a savings that it convinced one customer to export through the State Docks instead of elsewhere.

In 1990 voters approved a $20-million bond issue designated for capital improvements at the State Docks and for improving the ship channel at the Port of Bayou La Batre. Blakeley Terminal, a 153,000-square-foot warehouse on Blakeley Island on the east side of Mobile River, opened. And the Mobile Ship Channel from McDuffie Coal Terminal to the seabuoy was dredged 5 feet deeper, making it 45 feet deep. The deeper channel enabled colliers to carry an additional 18,000 to 20,000 tons of coal.

McDuffie Terminal, the largest coal facility on the United States Gulf and the only one in the nation offering both rail and barge access, faced fierce competition as the international coal market softened. However, during one busy week in 1992, the facility exported more than 400,000 tons of coal on eight ships—enough to supply electricity to Mobile County residences for four and a half months. In all, the tonnage for the year amounted to 7.3 million tons—enough to supply the county's homes with power for 19 years.

Another big story on the Mobile waterfront during the early 1990s was the opening and then the closure of Naval Station Mobile. Lobbyists had sought to win the facility for the state since the mid-1980s. The $77-million installation, which was home to four Navy frigates, had been open less than a year when it was announced in March 1993 that it and 31 other major bases were targeted for closure. Upon its return to the State Docks, which was the original landowner, the Mobile Homeport Reuse Committee began looking for new ways to make use of the base.

Mobile's many assets and the former naval station's attractive site drew numerous inquiries from prospective tenants. The decision on who would occupy the site remained in limbo as this book went to press.

The story of Mobile's waterfront cannot be complete without a mention of the Mobile Convention Center. This $52-million gem, which opened in September 1993, pays tribute to the city's maritime heritage. From the vantage point of the convention center's terrace, tourists and long-time residents can watch as ships from around the world glide by. At the same time, sailors now have a landmark that will forever be associated with the vibrant Port of Mobile. ⚜

The Coast Guard has district offices in Mobile. The polar unit, which conducts scientific research, is stationed here, but most people associate the Coast Guard with the kind of rescue functions shown in this drill. Photo by Ric Moore.

Here, a Coast Guard cutter discharges giant jets in a watery display that could extinguish a fire at sea. Photo by Ric Moore.

Chapter 8
MOBILE ON THE MOVE
Industrial muscle. High-tech capabilities.

> ❧
> "I believed, until now, that all cities in America had decayed into crammed concrete jungles, but Mobile sparked a growing hope about cities that I had never had before."
> **Peter Jenkins**
> *A Walk Across America*

On the previous page
Singapore Aerospace's first major United States investment was the largest economic announcement for the Mobile area since World War II and brought hundreds of jobs to the community. Photo by Ric Moore.

On the previous page, inset
**Sometimes the team effort and expert knowledge of the area that a small, local company can provide win that company business and respect. Such was the case with Jordan Pile Driving, which repaired the railroad trestle within eight days after a barge rammed a bridge on September 22, 1993, causing the worst wreck in Amtrak history.
Photo courtesy of Jordan Pile Driving.**

Cars rush through the tunnels as Mobile awakens. The clock on the *Mobile Press Register* building shows it's time to get moving. The harbor bustles with business. Mobile is on the move.

Mobile's population topped the 200,000 mark, growing faster than the state as a whole in 1992, according to figures released by the United States Census Bureau.

During the late 1980s and early 1990s Mobile became a "hot" place in the Sunbelt to open or expand a business. In fact, in the 1980s, Mobile's economic base expanded faster than in any other period since World War II, while Mobile's metropolitan area population grew 7.5 percent.

Among the significant announcements during this period was the decision by Sears Telecatalog Center to settle here. The center, which opened in 1988, changed its mission and its name after the company's catalog folded. It reopened in 1993 as Sears TeleCenter, a product service center. Thus when customers call a toll-free number to order parts or service for their Sears weedeater, lawnmower, or washing machine, they may hear a soft, southern, Mobile accent. The company employs 1,000 to 2,000 part-time workers, depending on the season.

Another significant job provider is Atlantic Marine, a shipbuilding and repair company that moved to Mobile from Jacksonville, Florida, in 1989. It employs about 800 people.

Mobile Aerospace Engineering, Inc., Singapore Aerospace's first major United States investment, was the largest economic announcement for the Mobile area since World War II and brought hundreds of jobs to the area after it announced in 1990 that it would locate here.

In the same year, World Omni Financial Corp. announced plans to consolidate services of nine existing southeastern branches into a single $3-million facility in Mobile. Within 14 months, the automotive financier announced plans to expand and had more than 450 employees on its payroll.

Established companies also reported gains as the 90s unfolded. Among those who scored a whopping success was Bender Shipbuilding & Repair Co., which in 1991 signed the largest contract in its 72-year history. Under the $50-million contract, Bender agreed to build four vessels for Marine Spill Response Corp., an organization created by those in the oil and petroleum industry to fight catastrophic oil spills in United States waters.

In that same year, Huls America, Inc., a German chemical manufacturer, broke ground for a new $100-million plant.

In 1992 the state became one of the top 10 producers of natural gas in the nation, and that did not include Exxon's production, which went on-line in 1993. Exxon's take increased the state's offshore gas production by about 70 percent and was expected to nudge the state's ranking up a notch.

Small business, the engine of economic growth, has a growing niche in Mobile too. In Mobile County, 95 percent of all businesses are classified as "small," and they create close to 65 percent of the jobs in the area.

Leaders in the public and private sectors have collaborated to create an environment for the success of small businesses. Entrepreneurs who are ready to launch a company can get a boost through the Business Innovation Center. The center provides office space and support services so new businesses can get off the ground.

Mobile Commerce Park, a newly established full-service light industrial/business park with a campus-like setting—the first of its kind in the Mobile area—gives businesses everything they need to prosper.

Mobile County consistently leads the state in the number of new businesses and expansions or capital investments announced each year. Between 1985 and 1993, 43,000 net new jobs were created in the Mobile MSA, according to Alabama State Employment Service statistics. In all, 160 new businesses and industries and

Small business, the engine of economic growth, has a niche in Mobile too. Whether it's a carwash that suds up an automobile to make it sparkle or a laundry that cleans suits, small family-owned businesses add the personal touch that make a community worth living in. In Mobile County, 95 percent of all businesses are classified as "small," and they create close to 65 percent of the jobs in the area. Three years after it opened in 1985, Bebo's Car Wash cleaned up $2.5 million a year, had a staff of almost 100, and washed more cars than any competitor in the Southeast. Photo by Ric Moore.

Filmmakers have discovered Mobile. In 1993 alone, more than $1.7 million worth of projects were filmed here, including feature films, television specials, music videos, commercials, documentaries, and industrial projects. Photo by Ric Moore.

The $66-million Cochrane/Africa Town U.S.A. Bridge links Mobile to Prichard, Mobile County's second largest incorporated area. The span is the state's only cable-stay bridge. Photo by Dave Hamby.

The Mobile industrial base is one of the strongest in the Southeast. Paper mills, ship-building and aviation builders, chemical plants, the lumber industry, computer hardware and software production, textiles, and seafood processing illustrate the diversity of Mobile's industry.

Plentiful raw materials such as natural gas, water, and timber and a friendly business climate make Mobile a choice location for many kinds of businesses and commerce.

Professional services, distribution and transportation, government, and retail and wholesale trade are all strong sectors in the Mobile economy.

Major industrial sites include Mobile River Industrial Park, Theodore Industrial District, and Brookley Complex.

Corporate offices, research companies, and light industry have a place at Mobile Commerce Park.

A fair climate, plentiful water, and beautiful surroundings give this area a natural advantage that many kinds of jobs depend on.

Mobile's historic sites and the nearby Gulf beaches make the area a destination for tourists year round. Visitors to Alabama's coastal region spend almost $100 million annually.

Many of those living in Bayou La Batre in southern Mobile County bank on commercial fishing for a living. Overall, 23 million pounds of seafood valued at $36 million are landed in Alabama waters each year.

Bountiful rainfall and a coast warmed by the Gulf Stream give Alabama's two coastal counties an extended growing season and a well-diversified agricultural economy. The nursery business and the cattle industry are the top agribusinesses in Mobile County. One of the nation's largest wholesale nursery businesses, Flowerwood Nursery, Inc. has roots here. Vast pine forests provide timber for Mobile's paper mills.

Mobile's two largest employers are the Mobile County Public School System and the University of South Alabama/USA Medical facilities. The county schools and the university complex each employs more than 5,000 employees. Following them in the number on their payrolls are Scott Paper Company and Mobile Infirmary. Other major employers are Ciba-Geigy Corp., the City of Mobile, the County of Mobile, Delchamps Food Stores, Gayfers Department Store, International Paper Company, Providence Hospital, Saad Enterprises, Sears TeleCenter, and Springhill Memorial Hospital.

Some important agencies of the federal government have district headquarters in Mobile. Both the United States Coast Guard and the U.S. Corps of Engineers are major employers.

Cliff Lambert is a successful independent consultant who was the project manager for the Mobile Government Plaza. Photo by Ric Moore.

489 expansions of existing industries were announced during that period. Those announcements represented a capital investment of $4 billion and 15,427 new jobs and reflect only those businesses from which the Mobile Area Chamber of Commerce received reports.

Part of the reason for the local economy's upturn had to do with an aggressive $3.8 million five-year marketing campaign begun in 1986 that attracted the attention of corporate decision makers throughout the world.

The campaign, spearheaded by the Mobile Area Chamber of Commerce and produced by Mobile's Townsend, Barney & Patrick Advertising, Inc., was recognized by the Atlanta-based *Site Selection* magazine as one of the ten best in the world five out of the last six years. *Site Selection* is an international trade magazine whose readership principally consists of corporate real estate executives representing major corporations.

The campaign spread the word about Mobile through such publications as the *Wall Street Journal*, *Business Week*, *Fortune*, *Entrepreneur*, and *INC.* as well as through a direct mail campaign to nearly 2,000 executives.

The success of the "Tell the World" campaign is told in numbers. In the year before the campaign was initiated, 14 companies visited Mobile; while the campaign was on, the city averaged 85 visits a year.

From 1986 to 1990, the Mobile Area Chamber of Commerce received 63,662 requests for general information on the Mobile area. Of those, 4,169 interested businesses called back for more in-depth information. This led to 449 visits by prospective companies to Mobile.

Award-winning marketing materials promoted Mobile worldwide in English, Japanese, German, French, Chinese, and Korean. A Japanese Saturday School was established in 1987 to induce Japanese businessmen to bring their families here and invest in Mobile.

The "Tell the World" campaign was followed by the "Show Business Mobile" program, a $3-million, four-year economic development plan that reemphasized Mobile's many assets.

Those assets include low operating costs, a highly skilled and capable workforce, state support for employment training programs, and a low cost of living. Mobile's location in the Central Time Zone ensures "just in time" parts delivery and non-stop service across the United States.

In 1994 a third fund-raising campaign, called "Mobile in Motion," was launched for economic development. This campaign would carry the community's efforts to attract new business and industry and help small businesses through 1999.

In Mobile, businesses small or large that use components for their products from the world market don't have to compete at a disadvantage with their foreign counterparts. A portion of the Brookley Complex, a former military base, was designated a foreign-trade zone in 1983. The zone enables companies to manufacture and store products without customs duties or other taxes until the product leaves the zone for U.S. consumption. Duties are paid on the end product, not the component parts, thus resulting in a substantial savings for the company producing the product.

Businesses have a capable workforce to draw from. More than half a dozen colleges and universities provide a pool of educated workers and graduates, ensuring high-caliber recruiting opportunities. Employees who wish to improve themselves have a wide variety of evening courses from which to choose.

Though salaries are lower here, employees enjoy a higher standard of living than might be expected because money goes farther. The April 1994 issue of *U.S. News and World Report* named Mobile 10th out of 100 top housing markets nationwide. The Port City had the most inexpensive homes of the top 10, yet homeowners had enjoyed a 7.7 percent appreciation rate in the value of their homes from 1991 to 1994. *Money* magazine's 1994 retirement guide ranked neighboring Baldwin County's Fairhope as the number two retirement spot in the nation. The rural setting of Baldwin County with the cosmopolitan advantages of Mobile have also made Fairhope a favorite place for artists and writers to settle.

Though Mobile may be one of Alabama's fastest growing cities, it is still one of the easiest to get around in. Bus, train, plane, or car—gridlock is not a problem for travelers or commuters. A modest, but efficient, airport where no one gets lost makes flying a pleasure. Six commercial and three freight airlines serve the Mobile Regional Airport. Passengers who prefer ground travel can take Amtrak.

Most Mobilians still associate cloverleafs with good luck rather than with pretzel-like intersections. Slow, steady growth for most of Mobile's history has ensured that most of the city is laid out in a grid. Drivers, therefore, find Mobile an easy city to negotiate. Parking at the major shopping areas in west Mobile is free.

Awe-inspiring spans and tunnels tie the city to the surrounding area. The $80-million Cochrane/Africa Town U.S.A. Bridge links Mobile to Prichard, Mobile County's second largest incorporated area. Twin tunnels, the Causeway and Bayway, link Mobile County to neighboring Baldwin County, part of Mobile's primary retail trade area and the state's fastest growing county as of 1991.

A sound infrastructure makes Mobile an attractive place for business and industry too. A network of barge and towing lines, air transport companies, railways, and trucking companies connects Alabama's seaport with North America. Two of the nation's major interstates intersect in Mobile—Interstate 65 terminates in Chicago, and Interstate 10 stretches from Los Angeles to Jacksonville, Florida. In addition to its commercial airport, a second airport at Brookley Complex can handle large-scale aircraft.

Mobilians enjoy this vibrant city's status as a seaport and industrial center. But more than that, they enjoy its gracious way of life and its grace, charm, and beauty. It is a city whose citizens expect an even more prosperous future. ⚜

Around 23 million pounds of finfish and shellfish, valued at about $36 million, are landed annually in Alabama waters, making the commercial fishing industry a mainstay of Mobile's economy. Photo by Ric Moore.

Chapter 9

HEALTH & EDUCATION

Mobile's two biggest employers help keep mind and body in shape.

The Alabama Institute for Deaf and Blind Mobile Regional Center offers support for parents of newborns, helps elderly people losing their sight or hearing, and reaches out to sensory-impaired people of all ages in between. Photo by Ric Moore.

On the previous page
Mobile area schools prepare students for careers in the sciences as well as in traditional fields. *Photo by Ric Moore.*

On the previous page, inset
A special moment between a new father and his child is captured forever. *Photo by Ric Moore.*

Good health and a good education for our children, ourselves, when it comes down to basics—these are among the things we want and need most.

Mobile led the state as one of the first to establish a four-year college (1830), the first to establish a public school system (1836), and the first to establish a modern medical college (1859). Though the medical college was transferred to Tuscaloosa in 1920, it wasn't until 1944 that another four-year college opened in Birmingham. Today, Mobile is home to one of the state's two medical schools.

Mobile is also home to one of the state's five state-supported centers for adults and youngsters who have sensory impairments. The Alabama Institute for Deaf and Blind Mobile Regional Center offers support for parents of newborns, helps elderly people losing their sight or hearing, and reaches out to sensory-impaired people of all ages in between. Murals brighten the walls in this cheery environment where it's hard to repress a smile as the fingers of a little girl dance like a sunbeam on water as she signs to her instructor.

The Mobile County Public School System and the University of South Alabama/USA Medical facilities are

the area's largest employers. More than 5,000 are employed by the school system, and a like number are employed by the university and its medical complex.

Hospitals, clinics, and nursing homes sprinkled throughout the community attend to the varying needs of couples seeking to have their first child or the long-term needs of the elderly. Mobile is Alabama's second largest hospital market and draws patients from as far north as Monroeville and from communities along the Mississippi and Florida Gulf Coasts.

Mobile Infirmary, the single largest hospital in the Mobile area, is the largest private not-for-profit hospital in Alabama and is second in size only to the University of Alabama Hospital in Birmingham. Mobile Infirmary's sprawling complex at its Springhill Avenue location offers virtually every form of care, with the exception of organ transplants.

Providence Hospital, founded by the Daughters of Charity in 1854, stresses its staff's dedication to treating each patient as a unique individual with medical, emotional, and spiritual needs. The hospital moved in 1987 to a new location in west Mobile. The ultra-modern building housing the hospital features a skywalk connecting the hospital to an office plaza. The complex overlooks a lake surrounded by beautifully landscaped grounds. The hospital was the first in the state to offer stereotactic radiosurgery, a new technique that allows treatment of brain tumors or lesions without traditional surgery.

Springhill Memorial Hospital, the area's only for-profit general hospital, was founded in 1975. Areas of strength include urology, pediatrics, surgery, and women's care. The hospital is the only area hospital offering lithotripsy, an advanced non-invasive treatment of kidney stones.

With four hospitals at three locations, the University of South Alabama has the region's most extensive health care system. Making up the system are the USA Medical Center, USA Knollwood Park Hospital, USA Doctors Hospital, and USA Knollwood Park Long-Term Care Hospital. In its first two decades, the university's medical school has trained more than a thousand doctors. The university's nursing program is among the seven largest in the nation.

The University of South Alabama Hospitals' system has distinguished itself during its short history. The hospitals treat more than 22,000 patients annually. More than 4,000 babies are delivered each year,

SouthFlite USA, a helicopter staffed with specially trained paramedics and nurses, zips patients to a hospital. In 1993 alone, SouthFlite transported 355 patients. Photo by Ric Moore.

employing the region's only neonatal intensive care unit. In times of crisis, SouthFlite USA, a helicopter staffed with specially trained paramedics and nurses, zips patients to a hospital. In 1993 alone, SouthFlite transported 355 patients.

USA's research community has made significant contributions toward a healthier way of life. In 1990 researchers at the USA Cancer Center discovered a certain protein involved in the body's iron metabolism and named it Mobileferrin in honor of the city where it was discovered. USA's Comprehensive Sickle Cell Center is among the nation's leading centers combating sickle cell anemia. In 1992 alone, researchers conducted research projects ranging from cancer to heart disease and attracted more than $11.5 million in grants.

The Franklin Memorial Primary Health Center was established in 1975 to provide quality health care in the Davis Avenue community. The center was named after Dr. James Alexander Franklin Sr., a physician and scholar who unselfishly assisted Mobile's black community for many years. The center has gained a reputation for providing quality health care to those in need regardless of their ability to pay. Each of its physicians is on the staff at the University of South Alabama Medical Center.

Many health services are available for free or at a nominal cost through the Mobile County Health Department. More than 65,500 vaccinations were administered during 37,000 patient visits in 1992 alone.

Good health is fundamental to our well being, but so is the opportunity to pursue intellectual challenges in an academic setting.

Mobile has the oldest and largest public school system in the state of Alabama. Barton Academy, completed in 1836, houses the administrative offices of the Mobile County Public School System. The building was shared with private schools until 1852 to help defray costs. Today, Mobile's private and public schools offer a quality education for all who pursue it.

Mobile takes particular pride in being the home of the state-supported Alabama School of Mathematics and Science. There, talented junior and senior high school students from throughout the state can develop their college-level skills while obtaining a high school diploma. The school opened its doors in 1991 and offers a superior tuition-free educational opportunity.

Mobile also takes pride in the seven magnet schools operated by the Mobile County Public School System. The schools offer enhanced programs in specific areas. For example, students at LeFlore High School of Advanced Studies/Communication & Arts learn that

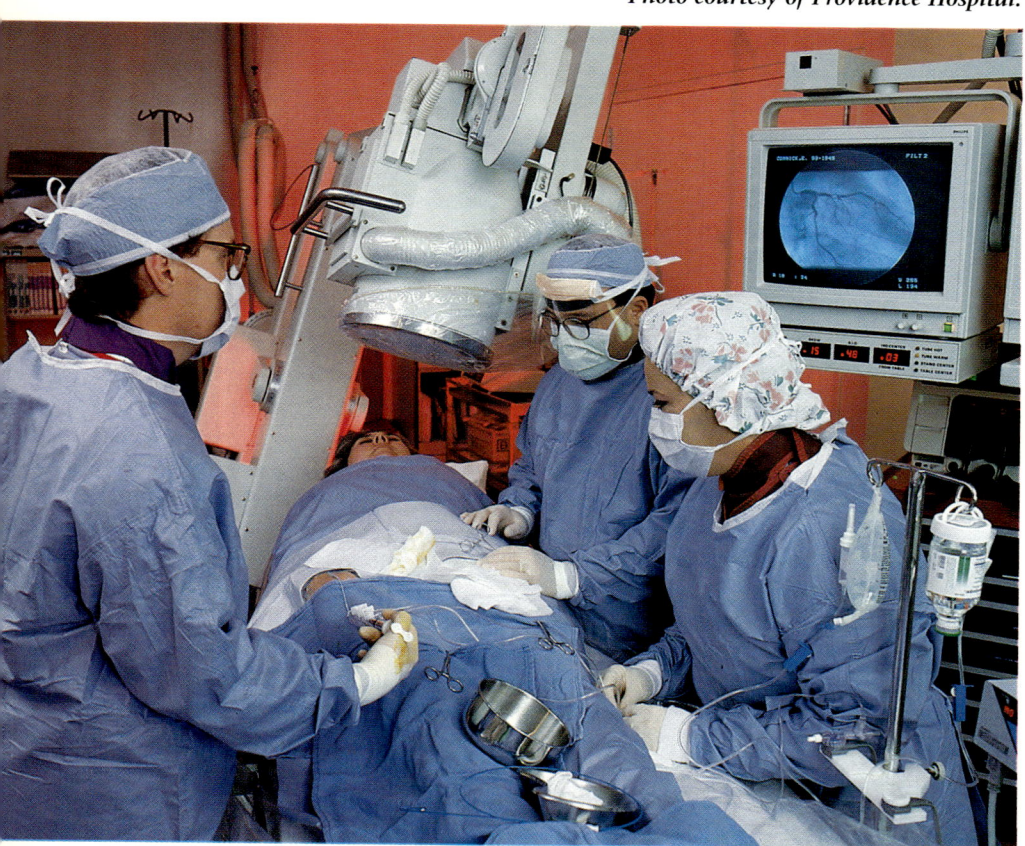

Mobilians are committed to assuring the best health care possible in what is rapidly becoming a "hospital town." Photo courtesy of Providence Hospital.

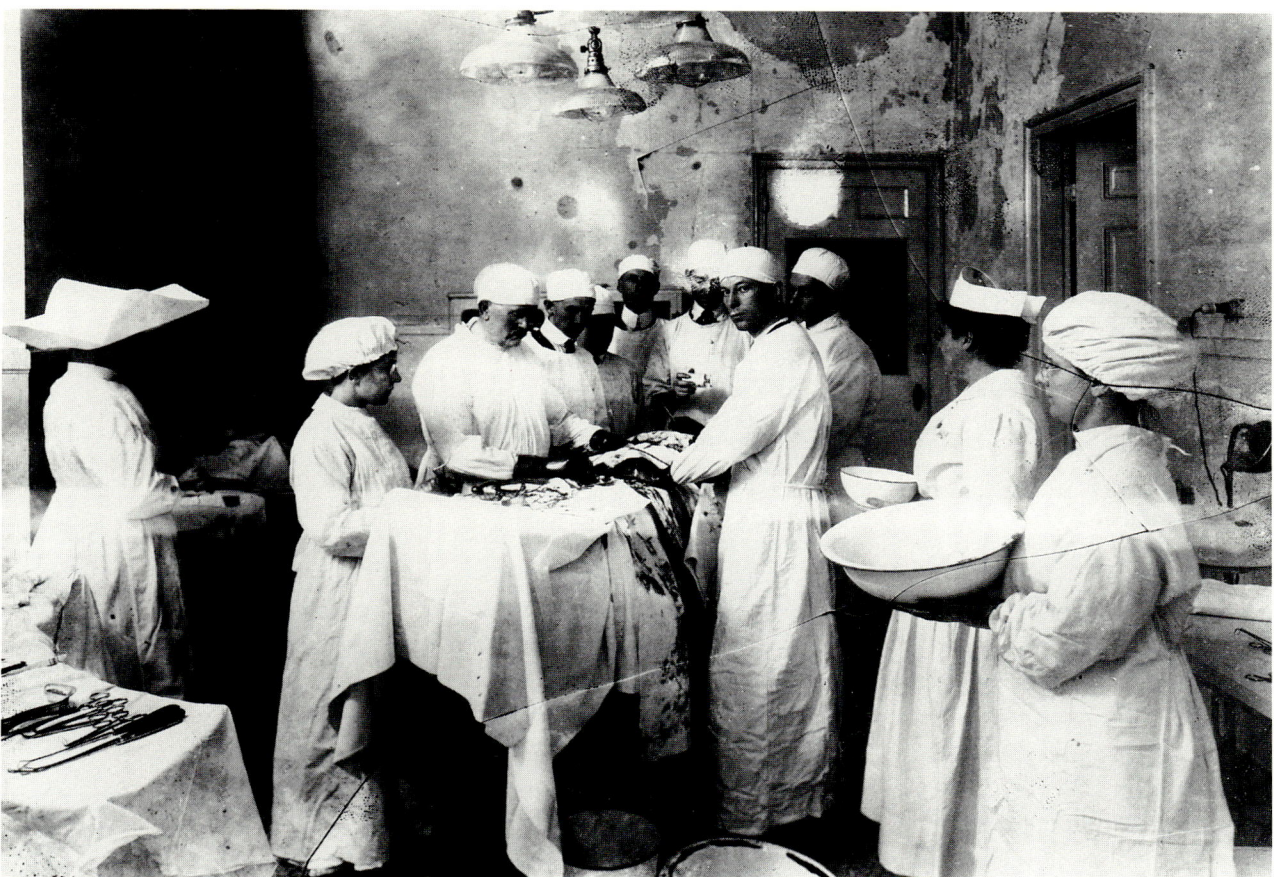

Mobile was Alabama's first medical center. The county's medical society is more than 150 years old. In this 1915 photograph, surgeons perform a procedure at City Hospital. Photo courtesy of Erik Overbey Collection, University of South Alabama Archives.

the camera never blinks as they focus on mastering how to operate a TV camera. The school draws on talent from the local Alabama Public Television affiliate and has access to a studio and equipment on a par with the local television stations.

In another magnet program, third graders at Old Shell Road School for Creative & Performing Arts, in conjunction with the Kids Creating Opera program of Mobile Opera, Inc., delighted audiences with *Why Mosquitoes Buzz in People's Ears*. The libretto, based on an African folk tale, was crafted in language arts classes, and the melodic lines were written in music classes. The project received a boost from the International Paper Company Foundation and QMS, who underwrote the effort.

Locally and nationally, parents, educators, and leaders both in government and the business community have come to realize that fundamental changes need to occur in the public school system to ensure an educated future for young people—and an educated work force for the industries of tomorrow. Leaders in Mobile's public schools have turned stumbling blocks into building blocks by seeking innovative solutions to problems. Much of this has been accomplished through a grass-roots community organization called Mobile 2000.

Through one program, Partners in Education, local public and private sector leaders are winning commu-

Research conducted in Mobile has made significant contributions toward a healthier way of life. Photo by Ric Moore.

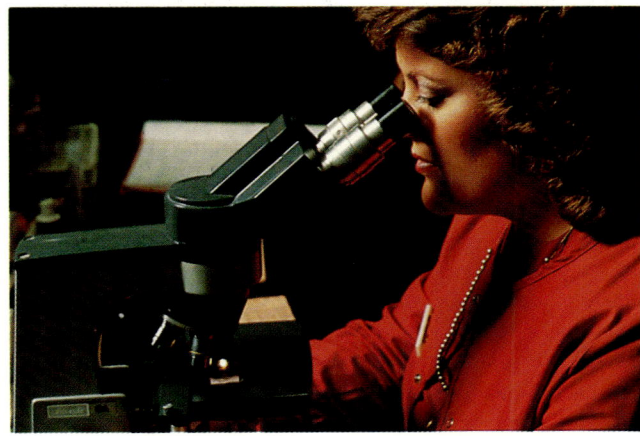

Spring Hill College's rare books collection harbors a third edition of Johnson's Dictionary, *dating from 1765; a copy of the first American edition of Hawthorne's* Blithedale Romance, *dated 1852; and at least two books published before 1500, as well as many other interesting volumes. Photo courtesy of Spring Hill College.*

nity support that will hopefully translate into broad-based citizen backing for local reforms. Hundreds of businesses and community organizations have been matched to the county's public schools through this program.

The partnership activities are as varied as the needs. When Theodore Middle School students heard from the manager at Waste Management of Alabama that they shouldn't bother to apply for a job collecting garbage if they didn't have a high school diploma, it raised a few eyebrows, until the speaker explained that a diploma indicates a person is able to set goals and is dependable.

Elsewhere, things began to add up for students at two elementary schools as employees from two local businesses lent a hand. Employees at South Central Bell help out at Westlawn Elementary, while McDonald's employees from the South Wilson Avenue and Saint Stephens Road locations help out at Fonvielle Elementary School.

These are just a few of the ways that businesses and organizations have helped students through the Partners in Education program. The program is designed to capitalize on local resources to strengthen academic instruction and to expose students to the working world and answer requests for special needs at the school level.

In turn, students have supported companies in such ways as coming to sing Christmas carols and contributing classroom assignments and artwork to generate goodwill and encourage a more personally involved community. School bands, choral ensembles, and Azalea Trail Maids enhance special events for partners. Schools publicize partnership activities and distribute information about the partner to the community.

Providing for the special needs of minority students with an aptitude for engineering and other math-related occupations is another challenge for the Mobile County Public School System, and through a special program the schools are doing just that. (A minority is defined as an American Indian, black, female, Puerto Rican, or Mexican American). The Southeastern Consortium for Minorities in Engineering (SECME) holds training workshops for teachers and identifies businesses willing to provide scholarships, technical assistance, or motivational speakers. SECME was formed in 1975 by the deans of engineering from six southeastern universities. As of 1993, 30 of the county's schools had participated in the program.

SECME competitions whet students' interest in engineering and allow them to apply design and construction skills. Designing a paper airplane or kite becomes a science. Figuring out the greatest distance you can drop an egg without breaking it becomes an "egg-xacting" experience. And building a better mousetrap car becomes a brainteaser to be solved. SECME students competing in this last competition have advanced to become winners at both state and national levels.

The Arts Coalition of Mobile, an ad-hoc group of area arts organizations, promotes putting the arts back into the classroom. The Coalition's 1992-1993 arts-in-education resource guide reminds educators: "It is more than coincidental that nationwide studies have shown that students in school arts programs have achieved higher averages in all subjects and develop academically more rapidly than others. Direct correlations between arts instruction and reading, spelling, and math skills underscore arts study as a decisive factor in a student's educational success."

Thanks to a wide variety of sponsors, students in the Mobile County Public School System are frequently offered a special opportunity to hear and see for themselves a variety of productions. In the past, the offerings have run the gamut.

The special programs available to students through the public school system are no substitute for hard work. These days students can't use the excuse, "It was too hard. I couldn't figure it out." Tutors staff a homework hotline Monday through Thursday evenings. The program, inaugurated in 1987, fields more than 10,000 calls a year. The kinds of questions students ask are analyzed so adjustments may be made to the curriculum.

The hard work pays off. Each year, the public school system produces about 10 National Merit Scholarship finalists. Graduating seniors win an average of $19 million in academic and athletic scholarships.

As of the 1993-1994 school year, the Mobile County Public School system served more than 67,000 students who attended 54 elementary, 20 middle, and 15 high schools. The district also operated one pre-kindergarten program, three special centers, and three vocational centers, as well as a 640-acre outdoor environmental studies center.

From its beginning until the mid-1850s, the Mobile Public School System shared its facilities with private schools. To this day, Mobile's many fine private and parochial schools remain an important ingredient in the educational choices available to students in the area.

A strong mix of institutes of higher education offers intellectual challenges and practical skills to students who wish to continue their education.

The University of South Alabama, which opened its doors in 1964, draws students from across the nation and around the world. With a student body of 12,000, and an average class size of 22, the university is small enough to offer its students personal attention, yet large enough to offer a wide range of educational experiences. The 1,200-acre rolling campus in west Mobile offers both graduate and undergraduate courses.

Situated on a knoll overlooking Mobile is the third oldest Jesuit college in the nation and the second oldest college in Alabama. Spring Hill College, founded in

The Mobile public school system's magnet schools attract some of the area's most talented students. Students at LeFlore High School of Advanced Studies/Communication & Arts learn that the camera never blinks as they focus on mastering how to operate a TV camera. Photo by Donald Berry, senior in the LeFlore High School of Communications & Arts.

Good health and a good education for our children are among the things we want and need most. Mobilians strive to provide these basics for every citizen. Photo by Ric Moore.

1830, is recognized as one of the top liberal arts colleges in the South by *U.S. News and World Report*. *USA Today* listed Spring Hill among the country's "choosiest" colleges, and *Barron's Profiles of American Colleges* listed the college in its "competitive" class.

This private Catholic college, which has an enrollment of about 1,400, has a long list of distinguished graduates. Among them are international chess champion Paul Morphy (1854); chief engineer for Thomas A. Edison Laboratories, Miller Reese Hutchison (1892); syndicated *Washington Post* columnist Colman McCarthy (1960); and the first woman to serve as a Florida Supreme Court justice, Rosemary Barkett (1967).

In 1948, a time when segregation was a way of life, the college administration declared the campus open to all races—not because it was a law, but just on principle.

From the rotunda within the administration building to the Gothic-style Saint Joseph's Chapel, to the oak alley leading to an antebellum home to the hilly golf course—this campus is steeped in tradition and natural beauty.

The University of Mobile, founded in 1961, is on a 765-acre suburban campus nestled in a wooded area of north Mobile County and has a student body of about 2,000. The independent Baptist comprehensive coed institution is known for its family atmosphere and small classes.

The University of Mobile has a history of commitment to a quality liberal arts and sciences education in the Christian tradition. It offers both graduate and undergraduate degrees. And its athletic program is consistently awarded the Thomas Howell Commissioner's Cup for the best overall athletic program in the Gulf Coast Athletic Conference.

Located near Chickasabogue Creek, which flows along the edge of the campus, is the school's Dwight Harrigan Forest Resources Center. This 124-acre environmental study center provides "a classroom beneath the trees" to further the study of Alabama's woodlands.

In addition to its four-year colleges, Mobile has close to a dozen vocational and technical schools that fulfill the needs of students who wish to acquire professional skills or strengthen their ability to compete in the workforce. With campuses scattered throughout the city, a better education is just a step away. Many cater to the special needs of working students through their part-time degree programs during the day and evenings, adult and continuing education programs, co-op programs, and internships.

Bishop State Community College, a state-supported two-year college, is one such institution that commits itself to making an education accessible to anyone who

McDonald's at both South Wilson and Saint Stephens Road are Partners in Education with Fonvielle Elementary School. Pat Marshall, McDonald's owner, pays high school and college students their regular wage to serve as tutors to help youngsters with their math and reading skills. Photo by Ric Moore.

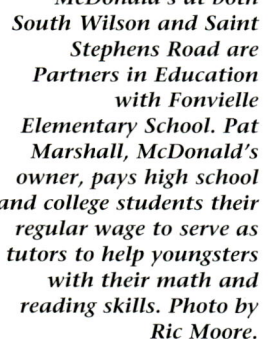

wants one. Whether one wants to become a medical technician or a teacher's aide, Bishop State has a program at one of its urban campuses designed for the special needs of students seeking an associate degree.

Mobile's intellectual life is not limited to its institutes of higher education. The city has several literary circles and professional societies dating from the 1800s. The Shakespeare Club, founded in 1897, selects its members who still meet regularly to study the plays of the Great Bard. The Medical Society of Mobile County, founded more than 150 years ago, is also still active. One of its founders, Dr. Josiah Nott, suggested yellow fever was spread by mosquitoes almost 50 years before the idea was generally accepted.

The Shakespeare Club and the Medical Society of Mobile County are just two more examples of the long-standing interest that Mobilians have had in the arts and sciences. That interest must translate into action as the city's leaders challenge its citizenry to provide for a better tomorrow for Mobile's most precious resource—its children. ⚜

Mobile takes particular pride in being the home of the state-supported Alabama School of Mathematics and Science. Photo by Steve Goraum.

The Alabama Aviation and Technical College, whose main campus is in Ozark, has a branch campus at the Brookley Complex. The college is the state's only aviation college and the only public two-year college in the Southeast whose primary mission is to prepare technicians for employment in the aviation industry. In 1989 the college further distinguished itself by becoming the first two-year college in the nation designated as an official Federal Aviation Administration Education Resource Center. Photo by Ric Moore.

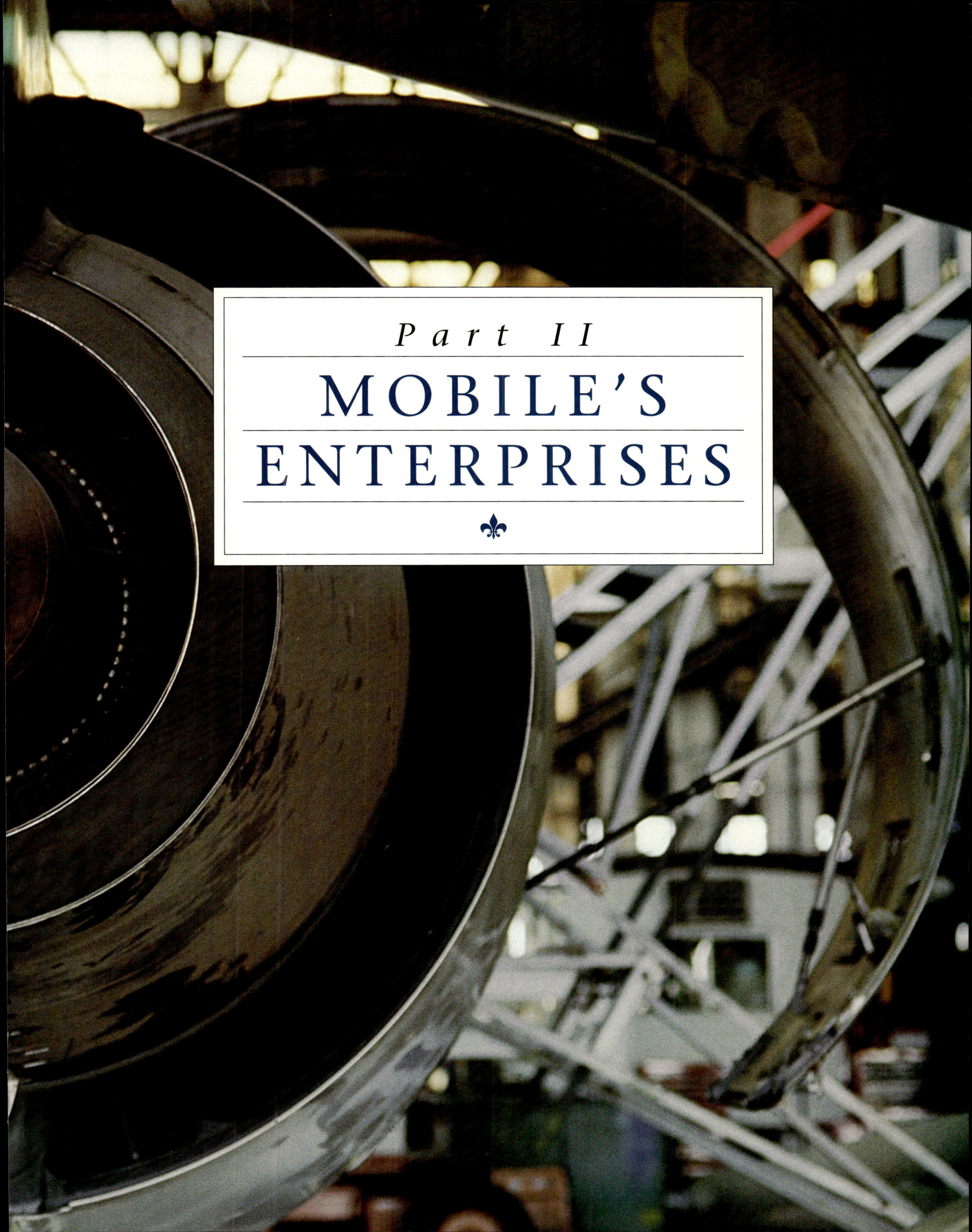
Part II
MOBILE'S ENTERPRISES

Chapter 10
NETWORKS

Mobile Gas
The Mobile Airport Authority
South Central Bell
WKRG-TV
Contel Cellular
WBLX AM and FM Radio Stations
ST&T, Inc.
Alabama Power Company

MOBILE GAS

Shown is corporate headquarters for Mobile Gas—Mobile's oldest corporate citizen.

Mobile's Oldest Corporate Citizen

Mobilians enjoy a unique lifestyle that goes beyond beautiful sunsets, our canopy of oaks, and rolling waves along the shores of Mobile Bay. Our community blends a rich heritage with a fresh vision of the future, keeping the best of the past and moving forward to make tomorrow even better.

Mobile Gas Service Corporation is proud of its long heritage and community partnership with Mobile. We're Mobile's oldest corporate citizen, pledged to providing good customer service, being involved in the community, working to help solve problems, and improving the environment for all.

Mobile has grown from a small city by the bay into a major seaport community. We've grown too—from a few hundred customers in 1836 to approximately 100,000 customers today.

It is truly a time for teaching, learning, and growing for all of us. Working with the Mobile Fire Department and the Safe Kids Committee, Mobile Gas helped develop a coloring book to teach children fire safety. This book is used as part of the Fire Safety program presented to thousands of students each year.

From Bayou La Batre to Axis, from Mobile Bay to Wilmer—we're serving the energy needs of families, businesses, and industries with clean, abundant natural gas that is produced in Mobile Bay and other areas of South Alabama.

Along with gas for homes and businesses, Mobile Gas sells and services major appliances, with branch offices for customer service, bill payment, and the sale

A Gulf Coast Treasure

of household appliances located in downtown Mobile, Prichard, Saraland, Bayou La Batre, and Theodore, Alabama. The company's corporate office, which also has a merchandise showroom, is located at 2828 Dauphin Street, Mobile, Alabama.

At Mobile Gas, customer service is all the things we do for the customer, from the moment we first make contact to the day we have totally serviced that customer's needs in a satisfactory manner. We view customer service as more than just being courteous; it's the only way to do business. It is the new standard by which our customers measure our performance.

Our community is on the move, and the area's abundant natural gas supply has helped fuel that growth. The discovery of natural gas in Mobile Bay is regarded as the most significant national energy find in the last 25 years. And Mobile Gas is in a position to tap the abundant energy reserves for the benefit of the entire community. Vast quantities of natural gas will help improve our environment. This discovery will keep natural gas costs low and improve the quality of life we want for our community and families.

Mobile Gas is a long-time supporter of education excellence in our schools. It is our duty to pass the mantle of education and progress to the next generation, and the benefits of education have never been more evident. Education is a cornerstone of growth.

Mobile Gas has grown side by side with Mobile. Through each decade, with every generation since 1836, it is our commitment to continue to provide service excellence to every customer, year after year. Our product is natural gas—the natural fuel of the nineties and beyond. ⚜

Natural gas production from Mobile Bay continues to grow, as natural gas from Exxon's production platform flows to Exxon's processing plant in the southern section of Mobile Gas's service area.

For over 155 years, Mobile Gas has made customer service its number one priority. Our customers are friends and neighbors.

123

THE MOBILE AIRPORT AUTHORITY

The Brookley Complex

The Brookley Complex, a dedicated all-freight airport and 1,700 acre industrial complex in Mobile, Alabama, is an outstanding multi-modal facility with immediate access to air, ground, rail, and water transportation. It is served by Interstate 10, which links the Atlantic Ocean to the Pacific, Interstate 65, which ties the Gulf of Mexico to Chicago, and two major railroads.

Serving airlines worldwide, Mobile Aerospace provides major inspection and maintenance services on commercial jet aircraft, and is a specialist facility for major modifications of narrow and wide-body aircraft, including Boeing 747s.

Brookley is a remarkable testimonial to the vision, determination, and commitment of the leadership of the City of Mobile and the Mobile Airport Authority. Brookley's success is extraordinary, rising from virtually nothing in 1969, when it was the largest military base closing in United States history, to where it now stands: home to over 100 diverse and growing businesses with more than 4,000 employees. Tenants and visitors enjoy Brookley's restaurants and beautiful bayfront golf course.

Brookley's freight-only aviation facilities include two runways (9,600 feet and 8,600 feet), an instrument landing system, a control tower, and three fixed-base operations. Brookley can accommodate aircraft ranging in size from the smallest private aircraft up to a Boeing 747 carrying a NASA Space Shuttle. On site are complete cargo handling services, frozen and perishable products processing and storage facilities, six aircraft hangars, convenient Customs and USDA Inspection services, and a Foreign Trade Zone. On-site aircraft rescue and fire fighting services are ready to respond to any emergency.

The Complex's eastern edge borders Mobile Bay with its deep-water channel leading to the Gulf of Mexico and the Alabama State Docks at the Port of Mobile. Brookley Complex companies ship overseas and throughout the United States through the Tennessee-Tombigbee Waterway, which connects to 16,000 miles of navigable waterways and ports in 23 states.

CSX, the nation's largest railroad, runs along the northwest side of the facility. Spur lines into the Complex connect Brookley with industrial and commercial markets throughout the United States.

Brookley has over four million square feet of industrial space, including warehousing, distribution, and light manufacturing facilities; and with 1,700 acres, businesses at Brookley have room to grow. The Complex's Foreign Trade Zone permits companies to manufacture, process, assemble, and store products without customs duties or other taxes. Brookley is served by a host of freight forwarders, customs house brokers, and trucking firms.

Brookley tenants include several world-class air freight and aviation-related firms, including Airborne Express, Teledyne Continental, and Mobile Aerospace Engineering. Teledyne Continental Motors chose Brookley for their international headquarters. A developer and manufacturer of aircraft engines, Teledyne built the engine that powered the Voyager Aircraft on its historic 1986 non-stop flight around the world. Mobile Aerospace serves airlines world wide, provides major inspection and maintenance services on commercial jet aircraft, and is a specialist facility for major modifications of narrow and wide-body aircraft, including Boeing 747s.

Located in the heart of one of the fastest growing economic regions of the country, the Complex is an ideal air freight gateway between Latin America and the United States. It offers convenient, low-cost, congestion-free, multi-modal air freight access to domestic

Airborne Express is one of several world-class air freight and aviation related firms who call the Brookley Complex home.

and international markets. It is closer to many major markets than other traditional gateways. In 1992 the region combining Alabama, Georgia, Mississippi, Tennessee, South Carolina, and Arkansas exported more than 38 million pounds of air freight to Latin America, while air freight imports from Latin America through Southeast United States' ports were over 614 million pounds.

Mobile's mild climate and its skilled, hard-working, and friendly people make it a first-rate place to work and live. Many firms are attracted by the Alabama Industrial Development and Training facility at the Complex, which recruits and trains prospective employees for new and expanding companies at Brookley and throughout the area.

Committed to keeping Brookley as one of the least costly airports in the Southeast United States, the Airport Authority has been able to hold its fees to some of the lowest in the region.

Built from the ashes of the largest military base closure in United States history, Brookley is now one of the most attractive industrial complexes in the nation. The Mobile Airport Authority has aggressive plans for the future, including expanding air freight—particularly with Latin America—attracting new air freight airlines, expanding aircraft maintenance services, and continuing to be a major economic force in the region.

Mobile Regional Airport

Mobile Regional Airport is 12 miles west of Brookley and serves a regional population of well over half a million. More than 800,000 travelers and many more thousands of greeters and well-wishers pass through this modern facility each year. Six commercial and three freight airlines serve the new $26 million passenger terminal with daily departures to many of the country's major hubs, as well as business and tourist centers. The airport is also home to a variety of growing general aviation and aviation service companies.

Passengers enjoy Mobile Regional Airport's restaurants, gift shops, convenient parking, children's play areas, and meeting rooms. They pass by exhibits showcasing selected local artists. Passengers can take a convenient limo or taxi into town, which is only eleven miles away. Often decorated in seasonal themes, the spacious airport reflects what is special and unique about the region—hospitality. Nowhere in the world are people welcomed more warmly, better treated, or greeted by more friendly faces than in Mobile.

As with Brookley, the Airport Authority has bold, long-term plans for the future, including a parallel runway to accommodate increasing traffic, and an international concourse for flights to Latin America.

The Mobile Airport is staffed with talented individuals determined to preserve and enhance Mobile's tradition of being the friendliest, most hospitable city in America. Quality passenger service is Officer Jimmy Jones' goal as he helps a young traveler find her way.

The Mobile Airport Authority is made up of diverse and talented individuals from public and private sectors. The Authority's mission is to be a self-sustaining economic force in the region, to attract new businesses, create new jobs, and provide quality passenger and freight air service at competitive fares.

Twenty years ago Brookley was a recently closed military base, and the Mobile Regional Airport was in an outdated terminal building. Today Brookley is a thriving and vital industrial complex and aviation center, poised to become a primary air freight gateway to Latin America. The Mobile Regional Airport is a modern and highly efficient facility prepared to become an important international airport on the Gulf Coast.

While the Mobile Airport Authority is committed to an aggressive long-term development plan, it remains determined to preserve and enhance Mobile's tradition of being the friendliest, most hospitable city in America. ⚜

Nowhere in the world are people welcomed more warmly, better treated, or greeted by more friendly faces than in Mobile.

SOUTH CENTRAL BELL

Light cascades through an array of fiber optic strands similar to those being installed for existing telecommunications and futuristic services by South Central Bell in Mobile. The hair-thin strands of glass can handle about 24,000 phone calls simultaneously.

Bringing People and Information Together

Early in 1879 *The Daily Register* carried a story regarding Mobilian A. C. Danner, who had just returned from a European business trip. In Europe he attended a lecture in which Alexander Graham Bell told of his latest invention.

Danner was so impressed that he ordered two of Bell's "miracle inventions," and when the telephones arrived he connected them with about 100 feet of wire between his office and shipping shed. Everyone was amazed, especially those who were skeptical about something as magical as human voices traveling over wire.

By late 1879 the newspaper reported that Danner's "intercom" system had been expanded to a telephone exchange. Businesses anxious to begin taking telephone orders for their services and products quickly joined the new telephone exchange. Soon after, a list of 43 customers in the Mobile Telephone Exchange was published in the paper, and Mobile embarked on a new era.

"Since Mobile had the first telephone exchange in Alabama, we've got quite a long history in this city. I'm proud to say, we also have a tradition of excellence," says South Central Bell District Manager Charles Nicholson.

Danner's simple "intercom" was the forerunner of today's complex telecommunications network provided to the Mobile area by South Central Bell, a subsidiary of BellSouth Telecommunications, Inc., headquartered in Atlanta and Birmingham.

"Mobile has, for its size, one of the most modern telephone systems in the Southeast," says Nicholson.

In the Greater Mobile area alone, South Central Bell employs more than 500 dedicated and experienced personnel who provide the very latest in telecommunications services for almost 235,000 valued customers.

South Central Bell continues to aggressively deploy fiber optic cable in the Mobile area. Through fiber optic technology, information is transformed into laser-generated light pulses and carried with great speed through micro-thin, spun-glass fibers.

Such fibers, formed into cable no thicker than a crayon, are capable of carrying more than a million conversations simultaneously at a speed several hundred times faster than transmissions over the traditional copper wires.

Fiber optic systems offer noiseless, error-free voice and data transmission with fewer service problems. It's also becoming more economical than copper wire in an increasing variety of applications.

According to Nicholson, "We are well positioned in Mobile with the latest in technology, equipment, and facilities. The telecommunications industry is changing daily and we have the technology in Mobile to meet the needs the future will bring. All Mobile central offices are electronic and the majority of them are digital. That is significant because we are able to give highly-technical businesses exactly what they are asking for in telecommunications services."

Testimony to South Central Bell's stated mission of "bringing people and information together" is the thousands of messages sent daily across Alabama through more than 82,000 miles of fiber optic cable and 22,750,000 miles of traditional telephone lines and microwave towers.

A leader in the deployment of electronic switching and fiber optics, South Central Bell has spent in excess of $3.7 billion on the Alabama network since 1982, bringing the Information Age to its Mobile customers. Plans are to spend more than $849 million on its network during the next three years. Approximately $742 million is set to expand and enhance advanced technologies.

South Central Bell enjoys a well-deserved reputation as an exemplary corporate citizen, supporting a multitude of local organizations. "At South Central Bell, we have a real commitment to education, and we work hard to be involved in the community," says Nicholson.

A researcher from Bellcore, the research lab of the regional Bell telephone companies, examines an experimental neuro-electronic microchip, the world's first microchip that can learn by example. The chip is based on neutral network concepts where electronic circuits model the neurons and synapses of the human brain and can solve a problem 100,000 times faster than a software program.

A Gulf Coast Treasure

Albert Ward, a South Central Bell cable splicing technician in Mobile, prepares fiber optic cable for installation. South Central Bell continues to aggressively deploy fiber optic cable throughout the area. The company's telecommunications network has more than 82,000 miles of fiber optic cable in Alabama and plans to spend more than $849 million over the next three years to assure Alabamians access to the most up-to-date telecommunications service available.

South Central Bell has instituted several programs to encourage employees to support their favorite educational, cultural, or civic organizations, either with monetary gifts or gifts of time and effort.

Significant is South Central Bell's "Matching Gifts Program," in which employees are encouraged to support Mobile's higher education and cultural organizations.

Another important program is South Central Bell's "Volunteer Services Grants Program," through which employees can apply for a company grant for any non-profit organization to which they donate a significant amount of their free time.

Although Alabamians can boast of one of the nation's most advanced Information Age telecommunications networks, just when we think there's nothing new to be done, another marvel of advanced telecommunications technology appears. The possibilities for enticing new services are limitless.

Nicholson says, "The technology is changing so fast that in a few years you won't recognize the telephone business. Tomorrow the telephone is going to be an instrument that you talk over, send data and faxes over, that you receive entertainment over. It's going to be a multimedia piece of equipment."

South Central Bell's Integrated Services Digital Network (ISDN) allows simultaneous transmission of data, voice, and video over one digital telephone line, giving customers high-speed transmission, greater flexibility, and accuracy in their communications systems.

Today the technology exists to provide a host of interactive services ranging from home shopping and entertainment, to distance learning for schools, to highly sophisticated medical services such as remote imaging.

Customers using Touch-Tone phones are able to access personalized audio information and services, or they may use their computer terminal to obtain personalized information and services.

For example, a student using a computer in one school writes a paper, and his assigned partner across town in another school edits it on his own computer. Or a real estate prospect sits in an office in one city and, with the aid of a computer, "walks" through a parade of homes in another city.

Customers can "let their fingers do the walking through the yellow pages" by using a voice or video version of The Real Yellow Pages®. They will locate a business, order a pizza, check a list of downtown hotels, or shop directly from home, using an "electronic mall."

The manner in which we work will change. Public network services will link our homes, schools, and offices, thereby expanding our traditional concepts of working offices.

There are other changes, too. Private citizens will easily connect to and exchange information with on-line government services, libraries, or classrooms. Doctors will be able to monitor health signs from home-bound patients, home-security systems will be monitored, and the police or fire department will be apprised of any unique situation involving your home or family. Indeed the future of telecommunications is exciting.

Today's advanced telecommunications infrastructure aids in the expansion of established businesses and the recruitment of new ones. This results in new jobs for Mobilians and an improved quality of life for all, the private citizen as well as those involved in the corporate arena.

South Central Bell has come a long way in the last 100 years. It has evolved from Danner's "intercom" and the days when the telephone repairman rode a bicycle to today's unimaginable telecommunications technologies. But one thing remains constant, and that is South Central Bell's commitment to excellence in service to the Mobile community.

South Central Bell is right on line in their mission of "bringing people and information together" and of having their "mission accomplished." ⚜

South Central Bell is committed to meaningful involvement in education. Through a well-educated workforce, Mobile will be able to meet the challenges of the future.

WKRG-TV

Mobility is the ability to move, to change, to respond. It's also the dominant trait of tomorrow's telecommunication superhighway. And it's everywhere at WKRG-TV.

Begun almost 50 years ago by a young architect named Kenneth R. Giddens, WKRG-TV remains today the only locally owned major media in Mobile. The Giddens family continues to steer their company through dramatically changing times in the broadcast industry. The result is a diverse company that operates the CBS television affiliate, the largest teleproduction facility on the Gulf coast, and the regional satellite uplink for CBS News. But the focus is a singular one of responding to the needs of the community and the customer.

This ability to marry service to the community with business acumen is the WKRG-TV trademark. It reflects a compassion for people and a passion for success. It is

the driving force behind a company that will not only survive the communications revolution at hand, but will also remember the traditions of simpler times long after the year 2000.

WKRG-TV's mobility has made it what it is today. It's place in Mobile's history is dynamic and changing. But the constant is a sense of place, of having roots. It is a home town awareness that only WKRG-TV can bring to the table, as a leader toward a new Mobile. ⚜

A Gulf Coast Treasure

CONTEL CELLULAR

Contel Cellular has met the needs of its customers by providing wireless communications service since 1985 in Mobile and Baldwin Counties and 1988 in Santa Rosa and Escambia Counties. Contel has grown to six retail stores with three service and installation facilities in the four-county area. The new Gulf Coast Area office based in Mobile was recently established to provide market-specific programs and support services closer to the customer. The company's subscriber and employee growth has been phenomenal. Presently, Contel employs over 125 people, which represents a 50-percent increase since 1993 in customer and network support.

Annette Jacobs, area vice president, Gulf Coast, stated: "Solutions are part of our sales process. Our commercial account executives provide consultative wireless business service, while our retail sales associates meet the needs of busy consumers. Both distribution channels match a customer's cellular uses to the appropriate equipment and monthly rate plan."

Contel Cellular continues to invest in the Gulf Coast network system, improving the quality handheld service. This investment extends to network linkage with other cellular service carriers in neighboring Gulf Coast markets.

Contel Cellular offers numerous community services by responding quickly to local disasters, such as the recent Amtrak train wreck in the north Mobile River Delta. Contel was contacted by Emergency Management Personnel and immediately provided 25 loaner cellular telephones and free service for all federal, Amtrak, and local officials who coordinated rescue and clean-up efforts. Contel responded again with loaner telephones when the landline telephone facili-

Contel Cellular has met the needs of its customers by providing wireless communications service since 1985 in Mobile and Baldwin Counties.

ties on Dauphin Island, 30 miles south of Mobile, suffered a lightning strike, severing communications for island residents.

Contel Cellular is active in the Mobile Area Chamber of Commerce, Mobile County Home Builders Association, Eastern Shore Chamber of Commerce, Pensacola Chamber of Commerce, Pensacola Jazz Fest, and the Delchamps' Senior Bowl, as well as many other community activities.

Contel Cellular provides cellular services in 32 metropolitan markets in the United States. The company is a limited partner in 27 additional metropolitan markets and has ownership interests in 64 rural service areas. Based on total-market population of POPs, Contel Cellular is the sixth largest cellular telecommunications company in the United States, with interests in cellular systems representing 24.2 million POPs.

Contel Cellular is a publicly traded company, of which 90 percent of the outstanding shares are owned by GTE Corporation.

Contel Cellular continues to invest in the Gulf Coast network system, improving the quality handheld service. This investment extends to network linkage with other cellular service carriers in neighboring Gulf Coast markets.

WBLX AM AND FM RADIO STATIONS

No other radio station along the Gulf Coast has achieved the same standard of market presence and positioning as has WBLX FM–"The BEAT of the BAY." Since 1974, 93BLX has consistently been identified as one of the most successful radio stations in the country according to various rating sources, including ARBITRON, industry trade magazines *Billboard* and *Radio & Records*, the *National Association of Broadcasters*, the *Radio Advertising Bureau*, as well as *Jim Duncan's Radio Revenue Analysis* and *Miller, Kaplan, Araise*, and *Company Market Revenue Report*.

WBLX FM thrilled Mobile's black community on May 17, 1974, when it began broadcasting its 25,000 watt Urban Contemporary music format from downtown Mobile's 11-story Van Antwerp Building. In 1976 WBLX moved atop the 34-story First National Bank Building and increased its power to 63,000 watts. In 1984, WBLX initiated the "regional FM radio" concept, broadcasting from an 1,800 foot tower in Baldwin County, Alabama, and increasing its power to 100,000 watts. These modifications improved WBLX's signal coverage to include 25 counties across three states along the Gulf Coast.

On October 31, 1990, April Broadcasting, Inc. purchased WBLX AM/FM as flagship stations of the emerging broadcast company. April was created by Jon Smith and Phil Giordano, two former ABC executives with over 25 years of experience in the broadcasting business. After analyzing over one hundred potential acquisitions in their first year of operation, April Broadcasting, Inc. chose to make its initial investment in Mobile because it recognized the strength of the radio stations and Mobile's cultural diversity and vibrant economic growth potential. Giordano said, "WBLX will compare to any of the best radio stations anywhere in the country. We are pleased and fortunate to be a part of such wonderful communities and successful operations."

WBLX's success is a coveted achievement in the highly competitive media business, where only one in four radio stations are profitable. Target marketing, consumer confidence, and customer service in radio means satisfying your listening audience and your advertisers, according to Vice President and General Manager David Clark. "Target marketing means product knowledge, and WBLX is the eyes, ears, and the voice of Mobile's black communities. WBLX provides consumer confidence and customer service by being Mobile business community's conduit to the black community, and the most immediately identifiable advertising response in Mobile! That is why our advertiser turnover is among the lowest in the country."

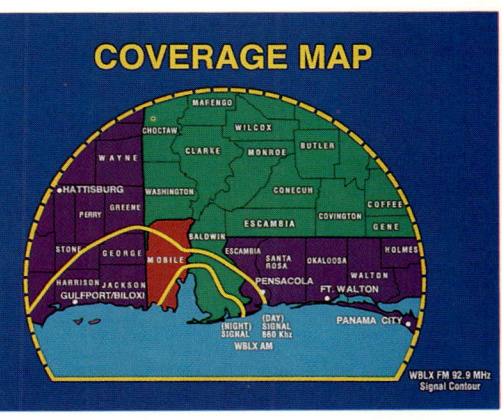

Mobile, Alabama, the 99th ranked Metropolitan Statistical Area by total population, is the 26th ranked Black M.S.A. African-Americans today are a powerful consumer group and are three times more likely to purchase goods and services advertised on radio than television or newspaper. Clark says, "Using national averages as a guide, Mobile's black population spends nearly $1 billion of its annual disposable income—almost 30 percent of Mobile's total retail sales—making WBLX's audience a dynamic economic force. We tell business, industry, and government we can improve their sales, increase profits, and improve public image. We believe it, we mean it, we do it all the time because WBLX WORKS!"

Being attentive to issues important to our audience means taking a pro-active leadership role throughout the general community—public and private sector, retail and industry—and WBLX does just that with station campaigns like providing book covers to the Mobile County Public School System, "Say NO to Drugs," "STOP the Violence," "School is COOL," and involvement in civic association activities like The Boys' and Girls' Clubs, Mobile 2000, Sickle Cell Disease Association, Downtown Redevelopment, and Town Meetings. By proudly serving black community interests and advertiser needs, WBLX serves Mobile!

In 1984, WBLX initiated the "regional FM radio" concept, broadcasting from an 1,800 foot tower in Baldwin County, Alabama, and increasing its power to 100,000 watts. These modifications improved WBLX's signal coverage to include 25 counties across three states along the Gulf Coast.

WBLX's success is a coveted achievement in the highly competitive media business.

ST&T, INC.

In 1985 when AT&T and South Central Bell divested, a small group of their employees recognized the effects the downsizing would have on the communication needs of business customers. The group, which was accustomed to solving customers' needs and providing technical solutions to problems, decided this was the opportune time to go into business for themselves and thus founded Mobile-based ST&T, Inc.

At this time the telecommunication industry was undergoing tremendous change and growth, and ST&T met this challenge by offering a level of service not met by other companies. The company's steady growth is directly connected to its philosophy of becoming involved in whatever capacity and remaining involved until the customers' needs are met to their complete satisfaction.

This success has been possible because of ST&T's employees' intense desire to provide a high level of service, whether to the small entrepreneurial company or to the major corporation.

Today ST&T's four offices, Mobile, Pensacola, Montgomery, and Jackson, Mississippi, boasts of over 5,000 satisfied customers requiring varied levels of service and products. In recent years, ST&T's use of state-of-the-art technologies and products supporting digital transmission has caused the company's customer base to increase tremendously. In evidence, one customer, the United States Navy, had ST&T install their fiber optic service, one of the first such installations in the area.

ST&T has become the Mobile area's premier multi-vendor in the telecommunication industry. The company's extensive variety of products and services, ranging from the small key system to the 10,000-line PBX, will accommodate customer requirements. Peripherals such as automated attendant, call accounting, and voice mail are also offered. New technology needs are met with computer cabling and fiber optic networks designed and installed by ST&T's engineering and technical personnel.

The first major cabling site for the firm was the building of the new Providence Hospital in 1987, which doubled the size of ST&T's operation. During this installation, ST&T designed and produced a product for integrating cable with computers, a process other companies said couldn't be done. As a result, ST&T emerged as a leader in the telecommunication field.

ST&T president Joe Jefferson says, "This tenacity on the part of our employees has resulted in our being a major player from a service stand-point, assisting businesses on a consulting basis with integrity and honesty to supply solutions and fill the void created by divestiture of national companies."

He adds, "Our people here are our greatest assets. Our employees are carefully selected, and most are seasoned experts of the telecommunication field with an attribute of longevity and sincere dedication to customer service."

In 1987 ST&T was selected to become an authorized sales representative for South Central Bell, based upon the firm's reputation for integrity and high rate of customer satisfaction, the company's financial stability, past sales performance, marketing and technical expertise, and the size and experience of their marketing force.

ST&T's mission statement has not changed. *"ST&T, a leading telecommunications company, provides quality products and skilled technical services for our customers through a single point of contact."*

"Focusing on these concepts will insure continuous operation while promoting personal growth for ST&T's employees and support for the Mobile community, both today and tomorrow." ❧

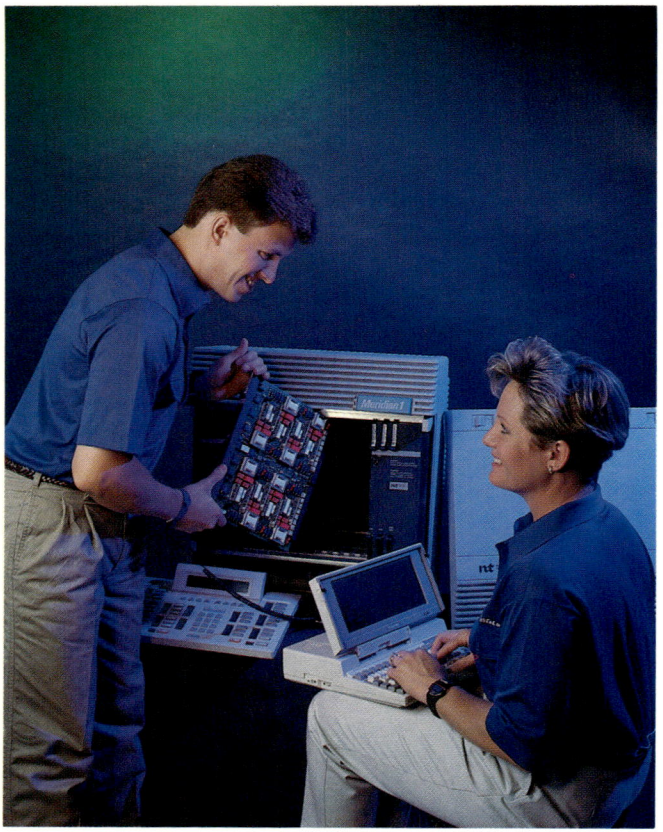

ST&T's certified technicians provide continuous analysis and support for every business system.

Expedient on-site response continues as the primary focus for ST&T and is a major contributing factor in the company's steady growth.

Alabama Power's commitments to communities it serves shows through its Teacher Corps program, in which 750 employees volunteer their time in the schools teaching students on a variety of subjects, including electrical safety.

ALABAMA POWER COMPANY

The energy to make Alabama better

In 1906 ours was a country of oil lamps, candles, gas lights, and coal-burning stoves. Many parts of the country were in the midst of the Industrial Revolution; the South lagged behind, dependent on its lien-crop, tenant-farm system.

That year, Captain William Patrick Lay, his son Earl, and their attorney, Oliver Hood, incorporated Alabama Power Company. Lay, a Gadsden steamboat captain, dreamed of harnessing the water power of the state's river system.

Even by that early year, however, electricity was not totally unheard-of in Alabama. Small generators were developed in cities around the state in the late 1800s, initially to power street lights. Electric street cars and appliances began making their way into Alabamians' lives.

Visionaries like Lay saw great waters going to waste, power which was capable of the industrial development of the state. However, Lay's vision lacked money. Several years after starting the company, he met James Mitchell, a pioneer in hydroelectricity, who was seeking a place to build an electric industry from its foundation. Mitchell found it in Alabama. Along with Montgomery attorney Thomas Martin, Lay and Mitchell began to consolidate separate groups with claims along Alabama rivers.

These visionaries saw the completion of Lock 12, now Lay Dam, and the first steam plant at Gadsden. Transmission lines were run to a number of cities and towns, proving to early skeptics that electric power was a reality, not a dream.

Some years before Alabama Power was formed, the Electric Lighting Company of Mobile was serving the city with electricity. Several years later, the Mobile Light and Railroad Company was formed and ran in competition to the Electric Lighting Company of Mobile. In 1906—the same year Alabama Power was created—H. M. Byllesby and Company of Chicago purchased the Electric Lighting Company and the lighting end of the Mobile Light and Railroad Company and operated the new company as Mobile Electric Company.

Another company also had a presence in Mobile. Gulf Electric Company owned a steam plant in Mobile built in 1912 that was located behind the existing Alabama Power Company office on Saint Joseph Street. In 1921, Gulf Electric Company began leasing a steam plant in Chickasaw from Chickasaw Shipbuilding and Car Company. In 1925, Gulf Electric Company purchased Mobile Electric Company, and in 1927, Alabama Power purchased Gulf Electric. Alabama Power bought the Chickasaw steam plant in 1939 as the site for a new plant. One generating unit—built in 1951—still operates part of the year. A much larger steam plant was later built along the banks of the Mobile River north of the city near Bucks. Named the James M. Barry Electric Generating Plant, its first unit began generating electricity in 1954.

Today, Alabama Power Company is one of five operating utilities of The Southern Company and directly serves 1,018 communities in 56 of Alabama's 67 counties. Alabama Power's fourteen hydroelectric plants, six coal-fueled plants, one oil/gas plant, and one nuclear plant provide electricity for 1.2 million customers in the southern two-thirds of the state.

Electricity in Alabama continues to be a bargain with Alabama Power's prices among the lowest in the United States. Alabama Power Company has, for the past decade, seen its prices rise by less than one-tenth that of inflation.

Alabama Power is strongly committed to the communities which it serves with electricity by supporting education, economic development, charitable and civic causes, and providing energy assistance to those in need.

As the twenty-first century approaches, Alabama Power Company plans to continue its legacy of service to the state and provide its customers with reliable electricity at a reasonable price. Alabama Power wants to continue to provide the energy to make Alabama better. ✤

Alabama Power began assisting in the economic development of the state in the 1920s, and still continues this effort today. The company operates the Alabama Resource Centers, which are high-tech, one-stop economic development information centers that help the busy business executive see the entire state by computers and videos.

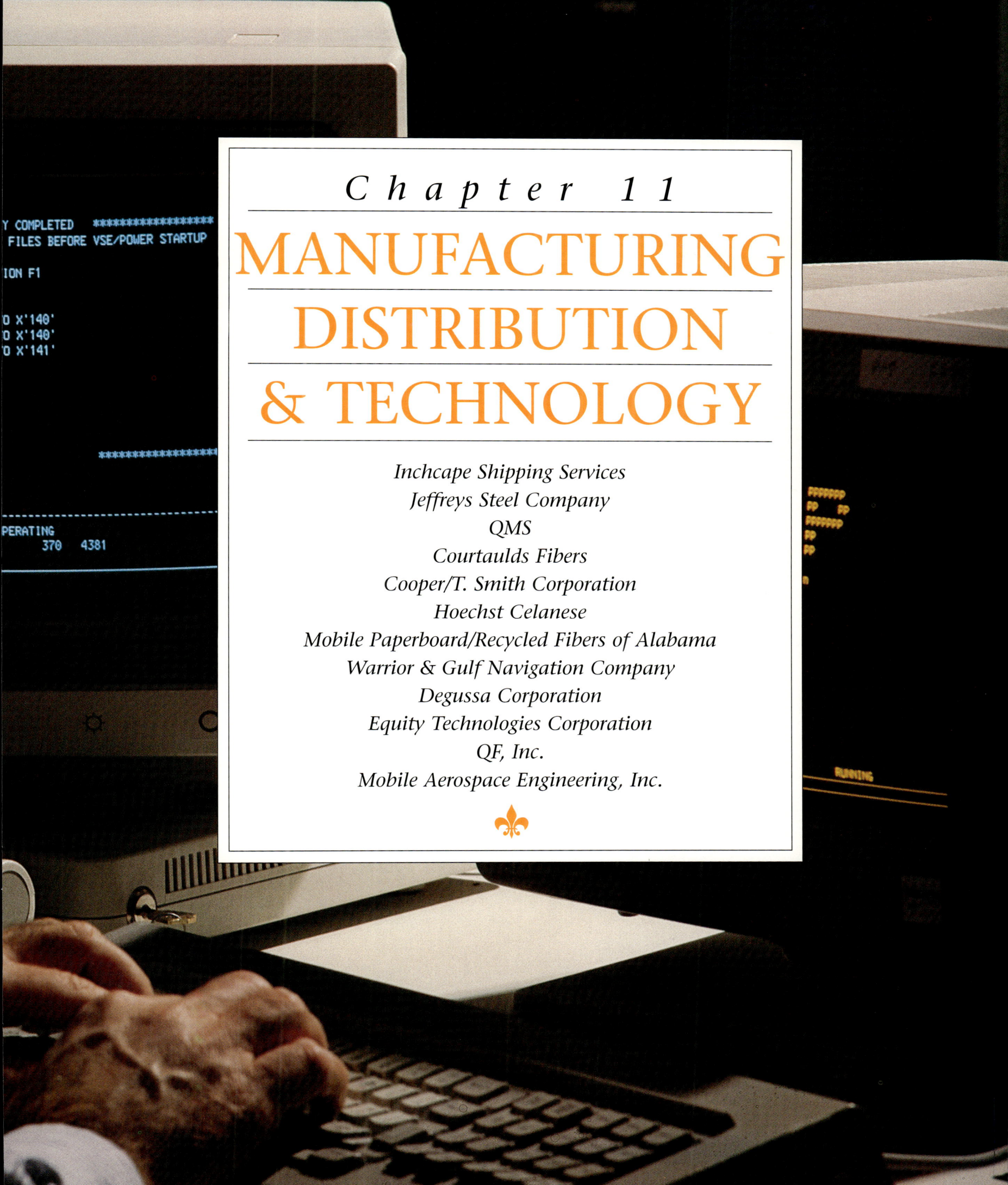

Chapter 11

MANUFACTURING DISTRIBUTION & TECHNOLOGY

Inchcape Shipping Services
Jeffreys Steel Company
QMS
Courtaulds Fibers
Cooper/T. Smith Corporation
Hoechst Celanese
Mobile Paperboard/Recycled Fibers of Alabama
Warrior & Gulf Navigation Company
Degussa Corporation
Equity Technologies Corporation
QF, Inc.
Mobile Aerospace Engineering, Inc.

INCHCAPE SHIPPING SERVICES

Phileas Fogg did it in 80. Win Thurber can do it in 30, usually less. Jules Verne created Phileas Fogg to be the hero of his popular novel, *Around the World in 80 Days*. Mr. Fogg was imagined to be a resourceful but quirky Englishman who wagers 4,000 pounds that he can go around the world in 80 days.

Phileas Fogg may have been quirky, but he knew when to wager and when to pass. He would have passed if pressed to bet as to who was the fastest globe-trotter, he or Win Thurber—a real-life hero of the executive sort whose character is a fascinating mix of Southern charm, a flair for adventure, and shrewd business intuition.

Win Thurber travels further in one month than most people do in a lifetime. In the span of 30 days, he might circle the world a time or two, cross the Atlantic once or twice, and commute a number of times between New York and his home in Alabama, sandwiching at least one trip to the west coast in between commutes.

Phileas Fogg traveled the world for adventure. Win travels the world for business. As he explains, "The guy who goes and gets it done personally is the guy who gets the business!"

Win handles all the Americas' (North, Central, and South) operations for Inchcape Shipping Services, the largest shipping agency network in the world, with operations in more than 80 countries around the world.

Inchcape is a service organization which enjoys a worldwide reputation for its substantial financial strength, its presence in the world's fastest-growing markets, and its inspired and motivated management and staff, which is committed to the many manufacturers and customers who share in Inchcape's expertise.

Inchcape is a dedicated and tailored organization. It is divided into three global business streams—motors, marketing, and services. Each of these divisions is made up of international businesses. These businesses all focus on what they do best, then aim to do it better than anyone else in the world.

Inchcape's vision is global, but its service is personal. The company recognizes that they serve as intermediaries in other people's industries. Inchcape has no product to sell other than its expertise and personal service.

Win Thurber is part of Inchcape's "personal touch." He has been with Inchcape since 1990, when the international corporation purchased his company, Southern Steamship Agency, and placed him in charge of Inchcape's North American operations. Thurber explains: "Inchcape's marketing resources are excellent. They have representatives all over the world. The contacts that used to be handled once a year, can now be handled daily because the company has personnel in place to take care of whatever problem arises. Inchcape has good management and a planning department that helps its satellite operations analyze situations and make good decisions."

Inchcape's Americas' operations are headquartered in Mobile, Alabama, for particular reasons. Mobile is home to three universities whose graduates comprise a skilled, knowledgeable, and dedicated workforce from which Inchcape can hire. Mobile also offers an extremely attractive cost of doing business. Mr. Thurber adds, "Mobile is my hometown and the place I choose to live

Inchcape Shipping Services, the largest shipping agency network in the world, with operations in more than 80 countries around the world, enjoys a worldwide reputation for its substantial financial strength, its presence in the world's fastest-growing markets, and its inspired and motivated management and staff.

with my wife and help-mate, Kathy, and our three children."

Win Thurber earned his stripes, so to speak, in the shipping industry by working for two major United States' carriers, Sea-Land and Sea-Train. At Sea-Land he had the rare opportunity to work for Malcolm McLean, whose purchase of the Waterman Steamship Company of Mobile led to the construction of the first container ship in the world. Today, Mr. McLean is recognized as the father of containerization. Win served in a number of domestic positions at Sea-Land before being named as Sea-Land's Western European Marketing Manager.

At Sea-Train he first served as the company's European vice president and then as its United States executive vice president and general manager.

In 1980 Thurber founded his own shipping services company. He nurtured his company from a two-person office into the largest agency of its kind in the United States. Its principals represented a kaleidoscope of nationalities who hailed from "sea to shining sea."

Early in 1980, Ryan Walsh Stevedoring offered not only to buy Win's company but also asked Win to oversee Southern Steamship Agency's operations. It was an offer he could not refuse.

In an interesting turn of events, Win and two investors purchased Southern Steamship Agency from Ryan-Walsh in 1985. The company enjoyed considerable growth, expanding from an initial staff of two—Thurber and a secretary named Rachel—into an organization employing more than 250 locally and over 1,300 throughout North America . . . and Rachel, now an executive assistant and liner coordinator worldwide.

Rachel, who had 16 years' experience in the shipping industry before coming to work for Mr. Thurber, candidly describes her first 11 years working for an ingenious, sometimes eccentric, corporate hero: "It's been one heck of a ride. I've never been bored in my job, and Mr. Thurber never ceases to fascinate me with his enthusiasm, remarkable memory and knowledge, and his people skills. He's incredible."

Inchcape's purchase of Southern Steamship merged the best in the United States with the best in the world, and the results were understandably extraordinary.

The purchase added to Inchcape's operations in the Far East, Southeast Asia, Europe, and the Middle East and provided the final link needed to complete the company's universal network of trade services. The acquisition also provided Inchcape with a significant list of new clients, while establishing its presence in both the United States and Canada.

Building upon its rich heritage, which dates back to the mid-1800s and the beginning of modern international commerce, Inchcape Shipping Services faces the future poised and ready to become the number one source for customer service, customer satisfaction, and franchise performance in the world, while providing the highest level of performance for both Inchcape principals and their customers.

The story of Phileas Fogg and his daring trip around the world has a happy ending. Mr. Fogg wins the wager . . . and a wife.

Win Thurber smiles as he rubs his chin and ponders his story's ending. He shakes his head and laughs, "Well, I've already got Kathy . . . but the story is just now getting good. It's a long way from over."

The future promises continued growth and success for Inchcape Shipping Services. Helping to bring this promise to fruition is the talented and dedicated staff of Mobile's National Inchcape Headquarters.

Mr. Thurber adds a personal strategy for continued success: "You only need two things in life to succeed: one is to work hard and the other is to be damn lucky." ⚜

Win Thurber travels further in one month than most people do in a lifetime. In the span of 30 days, he might circle the world a time or two, cross the Atlantic once or twice, and commute a number of times between New York and his home in Alabama.

Jeffreys' outstanding achievements can be attributed to their ability to satisfy the needs of their valued customers. The Linde CM 95 allows Jeffreys to custom design any pattern to meet exact client specifications. Using templets or computer generated programs, this pattern burning machine can burn any special design or configuration.

Offering an experienced staff of trained professionals, Jeffreys uses the most current technology to enhance processing capabilities. Smart-Cam allows Jeffreys to draw the design based on customer specifications. Once a design is drawn, it is down-loaded to the various burning machines for processing.

JEFFREYS STEEL COMPANY

The Mobile-Gulf Coast area, long known for its expert marine craftsmanship, gave entrepreneur Leon Jeffreys an idea over 25 years ago. If someone could establish a company which could provide the industry with a consistent supply of quality and tailored steel, a successful, profitable relationship could be forged between the two.

Thus in 1967 Jeffreys Steel Company, Inc. was born. Fortune did not come at once. Jeffreys started small, with only five employees, 11,000 square feet of warehousing space, and 20,000 square feet of outside storage. But with Jeffreys' knowledge of shipbuilding and construction, as well as his strong connections with suppliers and mills in Alabama, the company grew steadily until today it is among the leading steel service centers in the Southeast.

Headquartered in Mobile, Jeffreys Steel now employs over 150 people and offers over 275,000 square feet of warehouse space. In addition, the company has aggressively expanded into new markets and now operates seven service centers with an extra 200 employees.

From the beginning, Jeffreys Steel's philosophy has been "to provide a high level of service in the sale and delivery of steel plates, shapes, custom processing, and value-added services which will satisfy our customers' requirements and improve their level of performance."

Dependable customer service has remained the cornerstone of Jeffreys Steel, and this philosophy has enabled the company to grow, while adapting to Mobile's changing industrial base. Because of such a high level of customer satisfaction and loyalty, Jeffreys has been able to expand into Louisiana, Mississippi, Florida, and other Alabama locations.

Jeffreys Steel is not a steel mill; it's a steel service center, a business which buys a finished product from a mill and then resells it to the middle man or direct to the end user. Jeffreys' state-of-the-art descaling equipment allows customers to purchase stock steel and have it completely custom processed, all at one location.

Toby Jeffreys, president and CEO, says: "We are able to take a standard stock piece of steel and blast it, paint it, burn it, form it, bend it, roll it, do anything that they [customers] need. These processed pieces are similar to pieces of a jigsaw puzzle, so all the customer has to do when he gets it on their yard is to weld it up and do the finishing touches. In other words, they complete their puzzle."

This capability makes Jeffreys unique among other service centers. Currently, the company is heavy into the industries of gaming boats, oil supply boats, fishing boats, barges, as well as the chemical industry, providing for these customers services which no other service center in the Southeast can offer.

The company is uniquely qualified to meet the needs of the coastal region's construction and marine industries, providing precision workmanship in an economical and timely manner, all under one roof.

An up-and-coming industry which is new to the Mobile area is the movie business. Mobile is well on its way to becoming "Hollywood South" with local filming of movies such as *Close Encounters of the Third Kind* and *Under Siege*, for which Jeffreys Steel supplied materials.

Jeffreys' main product is carbon steel, which is stocked in approximately 350 sizes and shapes. They also "buy out" materials they do not ordinarily carry in stock in an inventory totaling over 37,000 tons. Once customers' orders are pulled or worked, about 90 percent of such orders are loaded and shipped on Jeffreys' own transportation fleet.

The fleet consists of more than 45 over-the-road tractors, over 90 trailers which measure 40 feet to 60 feet in length, and local short trucks in which to ship their orders to over 6,000 customers serviced from their eight service centers.

Using plasma to burn steel, Jeffreys can process to specification at a faster and more efficient rate.

Jeffreys' Pangborn Descaling Machine uses high pressure shot blasting to remove mill scale from the metal. Immediately after blasting, the metal is treated with a primer to prevent rusting.

opportunity for the young employees to practice communication skills, exchange and implement ideas, and learn the over-all concepts of a successful team. Their experienced people offer the knowledge of how the company came to be successful and stable. The end result is not just a "job," but a family "career" at Jeffreys Steel.

Jeffreys' family of employees are actively involved in the Mobile community, donating their time, efforts, and talents to various charities and civic organizations. The company, an active member of the Mobile Area Chamber of Commerce, supports Habitat for Humanity, the Senior Bowl, the Mobile Symphony, Sales and Marketing, and America's Junior Miss.

During 1993 Jeffreys' sales totaled over $50 million in their sales territory, which includes nine southeastern states: Alabama, Arkansas, Florida, Georgia, Kentucky, Louisiana, Mississippi, South Carolina, and Tennessee.

In the summer of 1993, Jeffreys purchased Port Everglades Steel Corporation (PESCO) Service Center Division located in Fort Lauderdale and Tampa, all inventory and accounts receivables, and its two facilities. The purchase of PESCO, which had been in business since 1953, significantly enhanced Jeffreys' ability to serve key customers in this area.

Recently, Jeffreys Steel had the unique opportunity to be featured on the Discovery Channel's *U.S.A. Corporate Profiles* series, which was designed to distinguish business excellence in different regions of the country. The company was highlighted on the national cable television network during the "Pride of the South" episode.

Jeffreys says, on a strong, positive note: "We feel extremely blessed and are very thankful that we have been given the opportunities and successes we have had and are excited, as well as optimistic, about our future in the Mobile-Gulf Coast area and the future of the Southeast."

Besides carbon and steel shapes and plates, Jeffreys also provides "Custom Processing Services," or "Value-Added Services," which means they take the carbon steel shapes and actually "add value" to them. In other words, they can reshape the piece, either cut the length, roll it into a radius, shot blast it, paint it, or punch or drill holes in it. It just depends on what the customer's needs are at this time.

To keep in step with the latest technologies, Jeffreys is constantly installing new equipment such as plasma burning machines, shot blast machines, press brakes, shears, structural and plate rolls, and other types of equipment which will enable them to remain on the "service" edge of their industry.

Jeffreys prides itself on maintaining "partnerships" with their customers. That is, they dedicate themselves to working hard, offering competitive pricing, remaining customer and industry-knowledgeable, and by keeping the customer's success and profits in the forefront.

There are all-important basic principles which have made Jeffreys Steel the progressive, successful, and financially stable company it is. By maintaining a sufficient in-house steel inventory, establishing proper purchasing relations, and monitoring credit and financial conditions, they have been able to remain ahead of the competition.

According to Jeffreys, their employees actually own stock in the company's retirement and profit-sharing plans. He says: "Each of these employees has the ability to control cost, make suggestions, implement ideas, and improve our level of service to the customer. We do not have one or two owners; we have over 350 owners, and this arrangement has created a positive effect on company growth. Employees now own 19 percent of the company and eventually will own 30 percent."

The workforce at Jeffreys is a mixed bag; there are the "young," and then there are the "experienced." The company has "Quality Teams," which provide an

A Gulf Coast Treasure

QMS

It all started when a light bulb exploded in Jim Busby's head as he drove home one dark evening and nearly sent him careening into the ditch alongside Old Shell Road. "I know how to make it work!" he exclaimed to himself.

Jim's startling revelation led to the creation of a circuit board that could add "brains" to an electronic printer. It was also the beginning of QMS, today's world leader in the design and production of intelligent printers.

Mr. Busby, president and CEO of QMS, explains: "QMS is all about making technology useful to mankind. Everything that we do here at QMS is computer based, and most relates to software. We don't make hardware. Instead, we make hardware smart."

Headquartered in Mobile, Alabama, QMS maintain sales and support operations in 68 countries and provides QMS-certified service to over 230 worldwide loca-

Headquartered in Mobile, Alabama, QMS maintains sales and support operations in 68 countries and provides QMS-certified service to over 230 worldwide locations.

tions. International offices are located in Canada, Europe, Australia/New Zealand, Japan, and Southeast Asia. More than 50 percent of QMS business is conducted overseas. QMS Japan is the fastest growing part of QMS's overseas business, as evidenced by the $3,014 million in sales posted by QMS Japan in April of 1994.

"The mission of QMS has always been to seek out and win over customers for life," Busby reveals. The corporation has carried out its mission by remaining the world leader in printer technology. QMS consistently proves its ability to increase the quality and performance of its products through its innovative technology while decreasing the cost to the customer.

QMS has introduced many new products into the market of smart, nonimpact print systems with the presentation of a prototype Lasergrafix printer, which was appropriately sized and priced for office use.

The QMS SmartWriter followed. Then QMS made industry history when it introduced its KISS (keep it smart and simple) at an unheard-of price of less than $2,000. KISS resolution and quality were able to duplicate that of the most expensive impact printer. It operated at two to four times the speed of the printers it emulated, and it did so noiselessly. Once again, QMS had successfully cut corners without reducing quality.

QMS produced the first laser printer to feature artificial intelligence: the PS-410 was a desktop-size laser printer with built-in ESP (emulation sensing processing) technology, developed by QMS, that eliminated the need for users to specify the language desired for their documents.

QMS continued to amaze and delight the industry with such revolutionary creations as the ColorScript Laser 1000—the first color laser desktop printer which provided high quality color and monochrome printing in a single device. The ColorScript Laser 1000 provided low cost per page, making it an affordable printing solution for general business use. The printer also contained QMS Crown Technology, which made it compatible with numerous other computer environments.

QMS Crown Technology is simply defined as a modular open-ended document processing and printing technology that transforms electronic data into documents more efficiently and productively than any competitive technology. Crown's multi-tasking capabili-

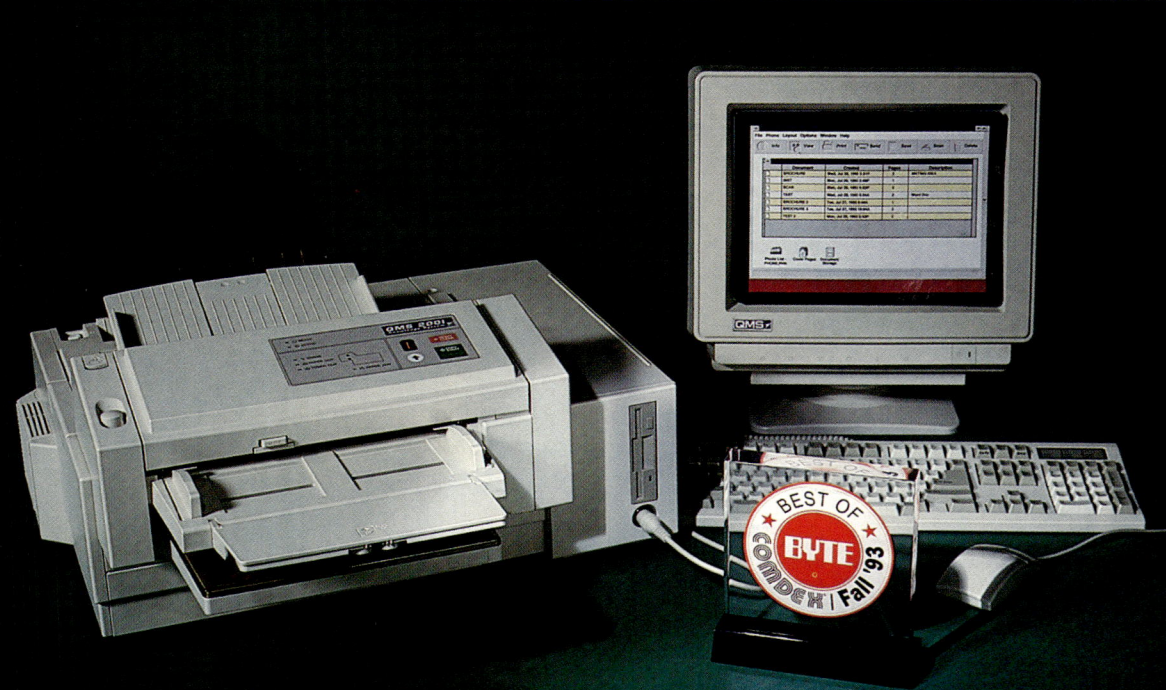

Every day is exciting at QMS. New products and technology are introduced regularly.

ty is one of its most fascinating features and allows Crown printers the unique advantage of being able to compile, process, and print different documents at the same time. The result is a host computer that is able to devote more time to performing computer tasks while its printer is able to handle a wider variety of printing tasks quickly and precisely.

QMS has also set a remarkable first in software—for example, the QMS Knowledge System (also known as TAKO). This system is a software-based expandable desktop office system. It is the first of a new generation of integrated office systems developed by QMS. Future options will include voice, telephone, audio, video, and network connectivity. QMS and its Knowledge System effectively bridge the gap between paper-based information and electronic communications in one fell swoop.

The TAKO—which is Japanese for octopus—is an example of the Knowledge System in action. The name is appropriate for this system, for the TAKO—in one neat unit—performs many functions. The TAKO office system is a combination of fax, printer, copier, scanner, and computer. It is able to process and handle documents, store documents without the use of paper, hold faxes and print them only if told to do so, and scan 20 pages at a time. The TAKO is the forerunner of a multimedia all-in-one PC and is reasonably priced.

When Jim Busby discusses the TAKO, his face beams and he exclaims, "Isn't that neat!" Busby's enthusiasm and fascination with his work never diminish. He has always loved tinkering with electronics. He admits, "I didn't have a grand plan when I formed QMS. I came from a poor background. Success to me meant owning a three-bedroom brick home. All I wanted to do was own a little business that would give me a measure of independence."

Busby started QMS in 1977 in his 10' x 10' bedroom as a part-time business. He was already working full time as an electrical engineer at a local paper plant and was going to night school to get his master's in business.

Jim Busby has never forgotten his humble heritage and is committed to giving back to the community which has provided him with so much. Education is one of his top priorities and QMS frequently donates computers to local schools and funds a variety of scholarships as well.

QMS is particularly sensitive to the needs of small businesses in the Mobile area, and QMS does whatever it can to support their growth. In 1993 QMS was recognized as a business who best supported minority businesses in Mobile.

Protecting the environment is another concern of Busby. He is proud that his company is one of the cleanest manufacturers in Mobile. Some QMS printers are energy star-compliant, meaning that they conserve power and energy. Energy star-compliant printers actually shut themselves off when not in use and go into a sleep mode until they are needed. Another new mode of print conserves the toner used in printing by using less toner on rough drafts. The company is looking into recycling cartridges and printers as well.

Every day is exciting at QMS. New products and technology are introduced regularly. CAE—computer aided engineering—enables huge sheets of paper to be printed with high resolution. This technology is able to print 1,200 dots per inch, as opposed to 60 in older systems. It can also print 1,440,000 per square inch instead of 4,000.

The QMS Hammerhead line of printers is fast, economical, and fitted with more features and functionality, including the capability of performing as many as 100 million different operations per second.

QMS greets the future with great enthusiasm. The company remains committed to developing products that anticipate market needs and incorporate emerging technologies to provide customers with the best combination of features, functions, reliability, and value available anywhere.

QMS consistently proves its ability to increase the quality and performance of its products through its innovative technology while decreasing the cost to the customer.

QMS remains committed to developing products that anticipate market needs and incorporate emerging technologies to provide customers with the best combination of features, functions, and value reliability available anywhere.

COURTAULDS FIBERS

Courtaulds' fibers are sold to numerous companies for use in the production of personal hygiene products, static-free laundry softeners, adhesive bandages, clothing, drapery, and computer diskette liners.

Few companies can boast of roots reaching back almost 300 years, but Mobile's Courtaulds Fibers Inc. is an exception. The largest manufacturer of rayon in the United States, Courtaulds expanded from Great Britain to this country at the turn of the century and by 1952 had built a facility in Axis, just 20 miles north of Mobile.

Today Courtaulds' fibers are sold to other companies that manufacture their own products, such as clothing, drapery, personal hygiene products, static-free laundry softeners, computer diskette liners, and adhesive bandages.

The process used to manufacture rayon was developed by Courtaulds almost 100 years ago. It begins with trees and ends with a substance similar to cotton.

Courtaulds' rayon is 90 percent cellulose derived from trees and 10 percent water. About 90 percent of the wood pulp comes from tree farms, where specially chosen species are grown from seedlings to maturity in 7 to 10 years.

Products made from rayon, when properly disposed of, break down completely into carbon dioxide and water. The cycle from tree to fiber and back again to the tree encompasses only 10 to 15 years, with trees constantly being replanted.

The company provides an annual payroll of over $39 million, which represents only a fraction of the direct economic impact Courtaulds has on the Mobile area. During a one-year period their total contribution to the local economy is about $181 million. The company has been very effective in providing employees with a steady, respectable living.

Employees repay this respect with enormous loyalty. Some of the 500 plus workers have been with Courtaulds for up to 40 years, with many representing the second generation of family employees.

In 1992 Courtaulds built its $100 million Tencel plant. The Tencel fiber's acceptance in the market place prompted the company just a year later to announce a $134 million expansion which will double the plant's production capabilities.

Courtaulds recognizes these workers in many ways. For the last 11 years the company has planted a tree, along the entrance roadway to the plant honoring each employee celebrating 25 years with the company. A plaque with the employee's name is placed at the base of each tree.

Courtaulds is a significant, but quiet contributor to the community and is very proud of being a "Partner in Education" with Mobile County's Adopt-A-School program.

This commitment to the Mobile area continued in 1992 when Courtaulds built its $100 million Tencel plant to manufacture the newest man-made cellulosic fiber.

Tencel is used in making apparel, home furnishings, and non-woven materials. It's biodegradable and environmentally friendly, since its major raw material, wood pulp, is obtained from managed tree farms. The manufacturing process is based on a solvent spinning technique in which all of the solvent is recycled. This process, developed in England, took Courtaulds 10 years and $100 million to bring to commercial scale.

Alone or blended with other fibers such as wool, cotton, or linen, Tencel is as drapeable as silk, soft as cashmere, and comfortable as the finest cotton.

Tencel has found a particular niche in the high fashion clothing industry. International fashion designers such as Calvin Klein and Girbaud have incorporated the fiber into their fashion lines. Tencel is strong, easily dyes into bright colors, and can be made machine washable.

As evidence of Tencel's immediate acceptance in the market place, the company announced a $134 million expansion of the facility just over a year after it opened, more than doubling the plant's production capabilities.

Courtaulds is very proud of its Mobile location and feels the right chemistry is here for the future. With its history, economic impact, and fibers found in a wide array of products, the company is truly interwoven in the very fabric of our community. ⚜

COOPER/T. SMITH CORPORATION

Cooper/T. Smith Corporation is one of America's oldest and largest stevedoring firms. The company is headquartered in Mobile, Alabama, and has offices in 38 ports and owns 37 satellite companies.

The roots of Cooper/T. Smith's stevedoring history run deep, reaching back to 1840 and Terrence J. Smith, a plucky Irish immigrant who created T. Smith & Sons, the strongest stevedoring and tugboat company in the United States Gulf.

While Terrence Smith was developing his business in New Orleans, an industrious Scotsman named Angus Cooper was launching his own stevedoring enterprise in Mobile, Alabama. This was the beginning of three generations of strong, steady growth in a multifaceted maritime service company.

In 1983, T. Smith & Sons and Cooper Stevedoring Company merged to form Cooper/T. Smith Corporation, the parent company for a multitude of service companies that support the all-encompassing maritime organization and the only national stevedoring company in Mobile that is still locally owned.

Today the company is headed by sole owners Angus R. Cooper II, Chairman, and David J. Cooper, President.

Angus and David Cooper credit little of their success to heredity and most to the demanding requirements laid down by both their father and grandfather, who enforced a "roll up your sleeves" approach to stevedoring.

"In the summers during high school and college, David and I did every imaginable job on the docks," Angus Cooper II recalls then continues, "Our management style is hands-on. We believe in being out on the cranes and the tugboats learning about things for ourselves."

David smiles and adds, "Our father felt it was important for us to work every long, dirty, painful job the company had. It was a great way to learn about the business—all first-hand. We learned what to expect—both from our equipment and our people—and we learned what the customer expects too."

Angus Cooper Sr., 13th child of an Alabama homesteader, founded Cooper Stevedoring with only one account. In his day, deals were signed and sealed with a handshake and workers were paid as they worked in silver dollars. Cargo consisted of bagged goods, lumber, cotton, sugar, and pineapples. Workers moved cargo with short hooks that acted as extensions of their arms, while sturdy hand trucks or dollies transported this cargo to winches. It's no wonder that Angus Cooper Sr. was the first stevedore to introduce the use of manual lift trucks.

Today Cooper/T. Smith has grown from a small enterprise into a progressive, innovative, and multi-port business employing thousands nationwide. Longshoremen are now hired from union halls and are paid by check with complete cargo records kept by computers.

In 1966 the company built floating cranes. These cranes are the workhorses of the business and are used for heavy lifts and mid-stream operations. Industrial innovation such as this has established Cooper/T. Smith as one of the major stevedoring operations in the world. Floating cranes, floating grain elevators, gantries, forklifts, front-end loaders, tractors, and other waterfront equipment are Cooper trademarks.

The company also has 37 affiliate corporations. These related enterprises include warehousing, insurance, terminal operations, barge fleeting, push-boat operations, and floating terminals.

This vast and complex organization has earned international respect for its efficiency and expertise in working ships' cargo at both ocean ports and on United States inland waterways. This respect is maintained by the leadership of Angus and David Cooper and their proven ability, imagination, attachment to the waterfront, and "hard hat" determination which has built Cooper/T. Smith into a major player in the worldwide maritime industry.

The vast and complex organization of Cooper/T. Smith has earned international respect for its "hard hat" determination which has built the company into a major player in the worldwide maritime industry.

HOECHST CELANESE

In a word, Hoechst Celanese represents quality. Quality inspires Hoechst Celanese to provide a safe working environment for its employees, one that encourages each employee to strive for continual improvement, innovation, and creativity in all aspects of the business.

The Bucks plant is an environmentally responsible multiproduct manufacturing site that returns millions of dollars to the Mobile economy.

Quality is essential to effective communication in the workplace at Hoechst Celanese in order to assure customers that their expectations will be met and surpassed.

Hoechst Celanese is the 5th largest chemical company in the United States and the 77th largest U.S. company in the Fortune 100 listing. The parent company, Hoechst AG, based in Germany, is the 31st largest industrial company in the world with annual sales approaching $20 billion.

The Hoechst Celanese facility in Bucks, Alabama, is part of the Specialty Chemicals Group of Hoechst Celanese Corporation. It manufactures chemicals used in agriculture, textiles, pulp and paper, and other specialty applications. The plant's workforce includes 160 employees and 50 contract personnel.

At the Bucks plant, quality assurance is customer-driven. Processes are continually improved to meet changing needs and expectations.

The Bucks site began operations in 1970 with the opening of a plant to make sodium bisulfite, used in manufacturing acrylic fibers. In 1972 the facility's sodium hydrosulfite operation came on stream. Sodium hydrosulfite is used by the textile industry for fabric cleaning and bleaching processes, and by the clay industry to aid in the production of high-quality paper used on the covers of such magazines as *Sports Illustrated.* Sodium hydrosulfite and sodium bisulfite are combined by paper mills to brighten newsprint such as that on which the *Mobile Press Register* is printed.

By 1982 two amines units were in operation. These multi-product plants produce a variety of alkyl amines which are used by other chemical manufacturers to make herbicides, insecticides, and pharmaceuticals. For example, Monsanto uses our isopropylamine to manufacture Roundup®, a familiar aid in weed control, and diethylamine is used to manufacture DEET-100, the active ingredient in such products as Off!®, Cutter®, and other insect repellents.

Sulfur dioxide production at the Bucks Plant began in 1978. Plant workers boast, "We make the best SO_2 in the country." Most of this product is used to make sodium hydrosulfite at the Bucks and other Hoechst Celanese locations. A significant amount, however, is used by textile, pulp and paper, waste treatment, plastics, and wine fermentation industries.

A joint venture formed at the Bucks location in 1985 between IB Chemical Co. and Mitsubishi Kasei produces isobutylidene diurea, a slow-release specialty fertilizer used on golf courses, turf farms, and in agriculture.

Hoechst Celanese's Corporate vision is to be a leader in its targeted markets, a preferred employer in its industry, recognizing that people are its most valuable asset.

The Bucks plant and its employees contribute annually to the United Way, as well as provide scholarships to local high school and college students. The plant is an active Partner in Education with Robert E. Lee Elementary School, encouraging student excellence in academics, attendance, school pride, and self-esteem.

The Hoechst Celanese Bucks location is one of several chemical manufacturers in north Mobile located in the LeMoyne Industrial Park (LIP). These LIP companies have formed a Community Advisory Panel that includes company representatives and area residents. This group meets regularly to discuss environmental issues and chemical safety.

Hoechst Celanese is an active member of the Chemical Manufacturers Association and fully supports that group's concerted efforts to reduce emissions and protect the environment. Voluntary Hoechst Celanese actions in these areas have earned the company a respected—and continually improving—position in the top quartile of the CMA membership in safety performance. ⚜

MOBILE PAPERBOARD/ RECYCLED FIBERS OF ALABAMA

Founded in 1918, Mobile Paperboard Corporation is the oldest paper mill in Alabama. Known then as Gulf Paper Mills, the company began operations under the one-year guidance of President D. H. Greene until 1919 when J. M. Walsh became the new president, and the chipboard mill operated successfully until 1923, when it was destroyed by fire.

The new mill, Mobile Paper Mills, Inc., was built in 1924 on the east side of Three Mile Creek and began operations in 1925, using equipment from the old mill. In 1931 as the nation sank into the Great Depression, the mill was temporarily shut down, only to reopen in 1932. Over the years the mill changed hands while continuing to upgrade and modernize.

In 1984 the Newark Group bought the mill, and the name was changed to Mobile Paperboard Corporation. Improvements continued, with the most noteworthy addition being the construction of the #2 paper machine in 1989. This machine, teamed with the existing #1 paper machine, produces a combined total of 400 tons of quality paperboard per day, requiring about 12,000 tons of recovered waste paper per month for raw material.

The Newark Group's expertise dates back to 1893, when one of their mills was granted the first patent to manufacture boxboard from old newspapers. Today the Newark Group is a 100 percent recycled paperboard manufacturing and converting company with 12 mills located across the nation. These mills operate 18 paper machines making nearly one million tons per year of various paperboards from recovered waste paper.

Mobile Paperboard's 200 employees keep the plant operating 24 hours per day, seven days per week. The mill remains a reliable and consistent producer of high-quality recycled paperboard, which is converted into products for the agriculture, furniture, and publishing industries. Manufactured also are tube cores and partition inserts for packaging.

The company's converting divisions use a portion of the mill's production to make paperboard products useful to other manufacturers, with the balance being sold on the open market to a variety of industries.

The Newark Group also owns Recycled Fibers of Alabama, which is the buying arm for Mobile Paperboard. From its offices located in Mobile's Brookley Complex, it purchases secondary fibers according to Mobile Paperboard Mill's specified requirements.

Depending on these requirements, the grades of purchased paper usually consist of old newspapers, old corrugated containers, box cuttings, and office mix papers.

The Mobile plant collects, sorts, grades, and packs over 60 different grades of wastepaper from retail stores, grocery stores, municipalities, and other public facilities that generate large amounts of wastepaper.

The Recycled Fibers Division purchases and sells over 2 million tons of wastepaper per year, which translates into over 10 percent of all wastepaper collected for recycling in the nation.

The Mobile facility is one of three packing plants in a division, with the Southeast regional office located in Atlanta, Georgia. This office serves as a brokerage office and sales service office for the plants.

In a society becoming ever more conscious of the value of recycling for the sake of a clean environment, the Newark Group's Mobile Paperboard Corporation and Recycled Fibers of Alabama maintain places of importance.

Each of these companies is dedicated to continuous improvement, encouragement of new ideas, experimentation, and change, while remaining a responsible corporate citizen within the Mobile community. ⚜

Mobile Paperboard's #2 paper machine began production September 1989. The eight cylinder, 110 inch trim machine is capable of over 200 tons per day of paperboard production.

WARRIOR & GULF NAVIGATION COMPANY

Today Warrior & Gulf Navigation Company, with its large, versatile fleet of modern and efficient water carriers, hardly resembles the original fleet used when the company was formed in 1940. The company began service with 31 barges, a harbor tug, and 3 vessels, one of which was a stern wheeler.

Warrior & Gulf now owns and operates 23 modern towboats with horsepower ranging from 1,800 to 2,200 and over 260 open and covered barges.

When the Gulf Intracoastal Waterway between New Orleans and Galveston was completed in 1945, standards for tug and barge movements between Mobile and Texas ports changed. For the first time, river towboats and barges were able to move west from Mobile to Texas ports. While the company continually grew, Warrior & Gulf's barges moved goods from Port Birmingham, which was and remains the largest river port in the Birmingham area, to Mobile, New Orleans, and then to Houston.

Warrior & Gulf remains a major factor in Intracoastal Waterway shipping. They continue barging many commodities, particularly ferro alloys, pig iron, scrap, bauxite, steel products, coke, magnetite, and several other cargoes, which usually originate in the New Orleans area. Using the Intracoastal Waterway from New Orleans to Port Birmingham continues to show savings for shippers over competing rail and truck lines.

Since the 1984 opening of the Tennessee-Tombigbee Waterway, with its lock and dam system, more and more cargoes have moved through the system's 16,000 miles of navigable inland waters. Currently operating primarily on Alabama's Black Warrior, Tombigbee, and Tenn-Tom River systems, Warrior & Gulf is able to interline with other carriers, making it possible to ship to virtually any port located on the nation's navigable waterways.

Mobile River Terminal, a wholly-owned Warrior & Gulf Navigation Company subsidiary, operates a modern bulk-handling facility at the Port of Mobile, providing customers with efficient and economical means of transferring bulk cargoes directly on and off ocean-going vessels, river barges, rail, or storage. Well-trained employees operate the terminal's modern ship unloader and conveyer system.

Warrior & Gulf's state-of-the-art Mobile Bay Wood Chip Center is located on the Theodore ship channel, 24 nautical miles up the Mobile Bay ship channel. With its 800 foot dock length and a depth of 40 feet, the facility is one of the most sophisticated of its kind.

During any 24-hour operational day, the Wood Chip Center is capable of loading, for export, 24,000 net tons of wood chips and unloading a barge into storage every two hours. Wood chips are carried by belt conveyers to a ship where a jet slinger, which achieves maximum compaction, stows them in the vessel's hatch.

Over the years river tonnage increases have placed added emphasis on Warrior & Gulf's terminals. Adolph N. Ojard, Warrior & Gulf's president, says: "Our long history and reputation for providing top notch barge transportation services is enhanced by our ability to offer 'one stop shopping' to our customers. We provide ancillary logistical services such as loading and unloading services for bulk ocean going vessels as well as for barges at Mobile River Terminal and storage and transfer services to truck, rail, and barge at Port Birmingham."

Executive offices and operational headquarters of Warrior & Gulf Navigation Company are located in Chickasaw, Port of Mobile. With the use of a central computer system, headquarters is able to identify and keep track of all the company's floating equipment. Such a system allows them to rapidly retrieve any information which will expedite the efficient movement of all company water carriers and let their customers know the status of their company's cargoes' movements. The Chickasaw facility is also a full maintenance depot for towboats and barges.

Warrior & Gulf Navigation Company continues to provide the most economical, efficient, safe, and high-quality services possible. They constantly modernize their fleet, facilities, and equipment, allowing maximum usage of the Intracoastal, Warrior, Tombigbee, and Tenn-Tom Waterway systems.

(right) Warrior & Gulf operates a large versatile fleet of water transportation equipment.

(left) The Mobile River Terminal, located at the Port of Mobile, is equipped with a modern ship unloader and an efficient conveyer system.

Degussa Corporation's Mobile plant has always believed in establishing open, direct, and honest communication with its neighbors. The old adage "Seeing is believing" is the basis for Degussa's open invitation, "We can tell you about our operation . . . but why not come and let us show you?"

Degussa Corporation is the major United States subsidiary of parent company Degussa AG based in Frankfurt, Germany. It began construction in the Theodore Industrial Park in 1973.

Mobile was the location of choice made by a site selection team that scrutinized 16 potential plant sites. The team was looking for a location that provided a strong labor force, a variety of transportation opportunities, access to natural resources, and tax and incentive structures. Mobile met all these requirements plus one—an overwhelming desire to welcome Degussa as a corporate citizen of Mobile.

Degussa, in turn, promised to invest $200 million into Mobile's economy and staff its plant by drawing solely from the local labor market. Well, the plant did not live up to its promise. It exceeded it.

Mr. Charles Story, vice president of governmental and public affairs concedes, "Degussa is never satisfied at just meeting the standards. We choose to surpass them."

And surpass they did. Degussa has invested over $600 million into the Mobile economy and employs 854. All employees have been recruited from within a 50-mile radius of Mobile. The educational opportunities that Degussa offers to all its personnel have been recognized as some of the best in the United States chemical industry.

Degussa's first two decades in Mobile witnessed phenomenal growth for the plant. Six plants were constructed to produce the primary products: Aerosil®, Methionine, Hydrogen Peroxide, Cyanuric Chloride, Quab®, and plant-wide utilities.

The Aerosil and Methionine plants were the first and, to date, the most successful plants built by Degussa.

Aerosil is Degussa's most versatile product, with more than 200 uses. Although its name may not be recognizable, its products are. This harmless, snow-white, feather-light powder extracted from silicon metal is found in paint, toothpaste, lipstick, ketchup, table salt, insulation, and many more familiar products.

Methionine is primarily used as an additive to chicken feed to improve production. Degussa has been noted for its consistently high levels of methionine purity, which are attributed to Degussa's quality improvement process. As the only plant in the United States manufacturing DL-Methionine, the facility manufactures over 80 million pounds of this amino acid annually.

DEGUSSA CORPORATION

The Hydrogen Peroxide plant has been an exciting expansion for one of Degussa's fastest growing products. The plant is world class, state-of-the-art, and computer operated. The production of Hydrogen Peroxide is a clean process which produces a positive environmental product that is used daily in waste and environmental treatments.

One of Degussa's most effective growth products is three-chloro-two-hydroxypropyl trimethyl ammonium chloride, or you can call it Quab as most choose to do. Quab is used in a variety of applications from paper making and textiles to cosmetics.

Degussa is particularly proud of its state-of-the-art waste water management treatment plant that it developed in conjunction with NASA. This plant utilizes an artificial marsh environment called a rockreed filter. This filter provides tertiary (third) treatment of waste water. Waste water is first treated chemically, then run through a holding pond, and finally allowed to flow over the artificial marsh, where the roots of the marsh plants skim the water of all remaining pollutants.

"Are we matching the quality of water in Mobile Bay with this program," asks Mr. Story? Statistics answer, "No, you're exceeding it."

Degussa's future looks promising. The company is already spending 25 percent of its capital investment on environmental and recycling equipment and has devoted considerable acreage to waste management facilities. The public can look forward to Degussa's continued commitment to protecting the environment.

Mr. Story predicts, "Degussa has established a facility that is well-positioned to grow and fully expects to grow." The Degussa of tomorrow will include more plants producing more products through state-of-the-art technology. ⚜

Degussa has invested over $600 million into the Mobile economy and employs 854 people who have been recruited from within a 50-mile radius of Mobile.

(Left to right) Judy Stephenson, Robert Stanley, Reginald Croshon, Chip McNeill, and (center) Cathy Anderson-Giles—the Equity Technologies' management staff—consider the ability to learn and the desire to work crucial to becoming a successful ET team member.

EQUITY TECHNOLOGIES CORPORATION

No waiting. No worrying. No problems. "Proving these promises can be a reality, when it comes to telecommunications service, is the nucleus of our success," Cathy Anderson-Giles explains enthusiastically.

It's a success story that began when Cathy and her business partner (and husband), Al Giles, started Business Communications Distributors (BCD). BCD was established to sell new and refurbished AT&T telecommunications equipment. After BCD expanded from its base in Mobile to Birmingham, Atlanta, and New Orleans, the need for high-quality electronics service led the Giles to join forces with Wayne Anderson, John Burlew, and Randy Stone to form Equity Technologies (ET).

Equity Technologies is a service-only business that offers its clients service from four major divisions—deinstallation, customer site service, electronic repair, and refurbishing. "Deinstallation," Ms. Anderson-Giles explains, "is industry jargon, which simply means the reverse of installation. Our first major customer for this division was, and still is, AT&T Credit Corporation."

Deinstall services are provided by more than 2,000 ET certified telecommunications technicians throughout North America. These experienced technicians remove equipment, conduct an on-site audit for verification, and determine if any equipment or parts are missing. "Our Deinstall Division then arranges transport of the telephone system, facsimile equipment, computers, or data equipment into Mobile," continues Ms. Anderson-Giles. Because accuracy is crucial, another audit is conducted at the Mobile facility. Only then is the complete report sent to the client so the equipment can be sold and the client's equity value recovered.

"The most frequent manner of disposing of large blocks of equipment for our clients is a bid package delivered to potential buyers. A current project, when complete, will allow us to offer clients the option of having ET handle the entire bid procedure, from researching markets to putting bid lists together and sending them out for bid," Cathy states.

The newest division at ET, Customer Site Service, involves wiring and repair of telephone equipment at the customer's site of business. The Electronic Repair Division, ET's first endeavor, oversees testing and repair of telephone, facsimile, printer, modem, computer, and other equipment that interacts with a telecommunications network. All ET repair technicians are certified for board-level repair in at least two types of equipment. The Refurbishing Division handles the process of bringing electronic instruments to a like-new cosmetic appearance. Cathy adds, "We package the serviced equipment in individual boxes or in bulk packaging for sale in larger lots." The serviced units are either returned immediately to the client or stored in ET's warehouse facility for shipment on demand.

Cathy insists that the real secret to ET's success is its skilled, dedicated, and enthusiastic personnel. "A team of ET employees representing each division, nonmanagement as well as management, is responsible for deciding when to add personnel and whom to add. We can teach the job skills needed for employment with us, so our teams look at the ability to learn and the desire to work—those things that can't be taught but are crucial to becoming a successful team member."

Also contributing to ET's success is a state-of-the-art computer system, which has been developed on-site. The system tracks, monitors, and reports on equipment and service so clients have the efficiency and security of instant access to information about their equipment at all times. "We're in a fiduciary relationship with our clients, so it's important for us to always know the exact status of any piece of equipment we're handling. Trust is crucial in our relationship with our clients, and our computer system is crucial to creating the climate of trust."

The future for Equity Technologies is bright. Utilizing technological advances in combination with a superior database and unsurpassed expertise, the company plans to expand its services in all areas. Cathy adds confidently, "By staying on the cutting edge of technology and entering international markets, each of us at ET will be able to make our personal and professional dreams a reality."

All ET repair technicians are certified for board-level repair in at least two types of equipment. Electronics technician Ken Trammell services a client's telephone system.

QF, INC.

In 1981 Fishking Processors, Inc. of Los Angeles, California, purchased the Quality Foods shrimp processing plant in Bayou La Batre, Alabama, a historic fishing and shrimping community nestled on the southwest edge of Mobile Bay.

Founded in 1955, Fishking was the company which introduced premium shrimp coated with light, airy textured Japanese-style breading to the American public. Fishking's "Mrs. Friday's" brand fast became the premier line of quality breaded seafood products in North America.

Fishking originally purchased Quality Foods in order to supply the parent company with an additional source of raw materials from the Gulf Coast, but changing market conditions and increased consumer demands found QF, Inc. manufacturing their own line of ready-to-fry breaded seafood products under the "Gulf Mex" label. Of the many diverse seafood processors located in Bayou La Batre, QF remains the only company coating seafood products with batters and breadings, many of which are produced in Fishking's own Los Angeles bakery.

Shrimp remains the mainstay of QF's product line, having processed over 150 million shrimp in 1993. Besides Gulf Coast shrimp, QF searches the oceans of the world for the finest raw shrimp available.

The philosophy on which Fishking's founder, Masashi Kawaguchi, based his business is still very much a part of QF's operating philosophy. The insistence on excellence starts with the use of only the freshest and finest quality raw materials. Each shipment of raw material is checked for quality in house prior to processing.

The shrimp are then carefully peeled and deveined and delicately coated with just enough batter and breading so the taste and appearance of the shrimp meat can be enjoyed and appreciated.

Employees carefully hand-pack each shrimp, and every package is weighed to ensure that customers get exact portion control and net weight. The boxes of breaded shrimp are rushed to blast freezers where they are quickly frozen at minus 40 degrees to lock in the flavor.

A full-time staff of Quality Control technicians monitors each step in the production process by continually testing products to ensure that standards of excellence are met. To further assure premium quality, the plant is under "voluntary" United States Department of Commerce inspection.

QF is able to identify their products as being "U.S. Department of Commerce, Packed under Federal Inspection," which means that the enclosed fishery product has been inspected, statistically sampled, and found to be of good quality. Many of QF's products are labeled with the Grade A Shield. This mark is given only to top quality products.

In the mid-1980s, QF began looking at alternative seafood sources to augment its extensive line of breaded shrimp products. Squid, or calamari, was the answer. QF coats their popular calamari rings and steak strips with delicious Italian herb and Romano cheese-flavored bread crumbs.

The finest in raw materials from around the world, coupled with an unequaled eye to detail in every aspect of quality manufacturing, has made "Gulf Mex" one of the most respected labels in the industry. "Gulf Mex" brand products—shrimp, calamari, and scallops—are proudly served by some of the finest restaurants and industry feeders in North America.

QF, Inc. presently provides year-round employment to approximately 200 residents of Mobile County. By maintaining a vigorous research and development program, QF, Inc. continues to look forward to an expansion of its production with the addition of new products and extension of its distribution channels. ⚜

QF, Inc. manufactures a wide range of gourmet breaded seafood items.

Heavy maintenance checks and aging aircraft modifications take place inside the hangars of MAE.

MOBILE AEROSPACE ENGINEERING, INC.

Mobile Aerospace Engineering, Inc. (MAE), was set up in September 1990 by Singapore Aerospace Ltd., an established aircraft engineering company operating in the Asia-Pacific region. As part of its strategy to diversify into commercial aircraft maintenance and to meet worldwide demands for third-party aircraft maintenance and modification work, Singapore Aerospace established MAE as the foothold in the United States to serve the North and South American market.

MAE, a Federal Aviation Administration (FAA)-approved Aircraft Repair Station, specializes in undertaking heavy maintenance, inspection, repair, refurbishment, and modification of narrow and wide-body aircraft ranging from Boeing B727, B737, B747, to McDonnell Douglas DC9/MD80, DC10, MD11, and Lockheed L1011.

MAE is strategically located at the Brookley Industrial Complex in Mobile on the southern coast of Alabama. Mobile was selected from among several other sites because there were two B747-size hangars readily available with ample land in the vicinity for future growth. The Brookley airfield also has a 9,600-foot runway complete with an Instrument Landing System (ILS). The warmer weather in the area also means greater flexibility to work all year round. In addition, the state and city governments offered several incentives, including the financing of the hangars' rehabilitation through industrial revenue bonds issued by the Mobile Airport Authority.

MAE's main facility consists of a two-B747 bay, 130,000-square-foot hangar, and 70,000 square feet of support shops and administrative offices. In its second and third years of operation, MAE added a 34,000-square-foot, dedicated aircraft wash/strip rack, another 200,000 square feet of hangar space, and additional new equipment to enhance its range of services. The maintenance hangars can easily accommodate four wide-body aircraft (up to B747) and eight narrow-body aircraft simultaneously.

Singapore Aerospace is comprised of a group of companies that together offer a unique and wide range of products and services, including heavy aircraft maintenance, structural modification and refurbishment, aircraft engine and aero-component overhaul and repair, aircraft and avionics system design and integration, and manufacture of aeroengine and aircraft parts and sub-assemblies. MAE brings along with it the reputation and commitment of Singapore Aerospace to provide its customers with quality, reliability, and service excellence.

Within the short span of its first three years of operation, MAE has emerged from its start-up status to establish itself as one of North America's leading third-party repair stations, despite the slow recovery in the airlines industry. Among its customers are airlines and chartered operators, freight carriers, and leasing companies.

The type of work MAE performs includes heavy maintenance inspection and checks, life-extension work on aging aircraft, corrosion prevention and control programs, major structural work and modification, passenger-to-freighter conversions, complete interior refurbishment or reconfiguration, avionics modifications and fleet standardization, and aircraft strip and paint.

Starting from scratch and growing steadily, MAE maintains a work force of about 450 technical, engineering, and administrative personnel, comprised mainly of licensed Airframe and Powerplant (A&P) aircraft mechanics.

MAE's business is selling labor. The company's success depends largely on the workforce producing quality and on-time maintenance services in an efficient manner. With its parent company in Singapore, MAE enjoys excellent continual support from the Singapore Aerospace group of companies, can draw on their skills and experience as required, and can count on sending some of its workforce to Singapore for on-the-job training and job enhancement.

Together with the Singapore Aerospace group, MAE is committed to meeting the long-term needs of the aviation industry and is continually strengthening its capabilities to remain at the forefront of the aerospace technologies. MAE has developed a work-force that is highly skilled, technically competent, and extremely motivated. The company takes special pride in maintaining the highest possible standard of quality, workmanship, and reliability that has won many satisfied customers. ⚜

Narrow and wide-body aircraft maintenance and modification have boosted MAE's reputation as the leading third-party repair station.

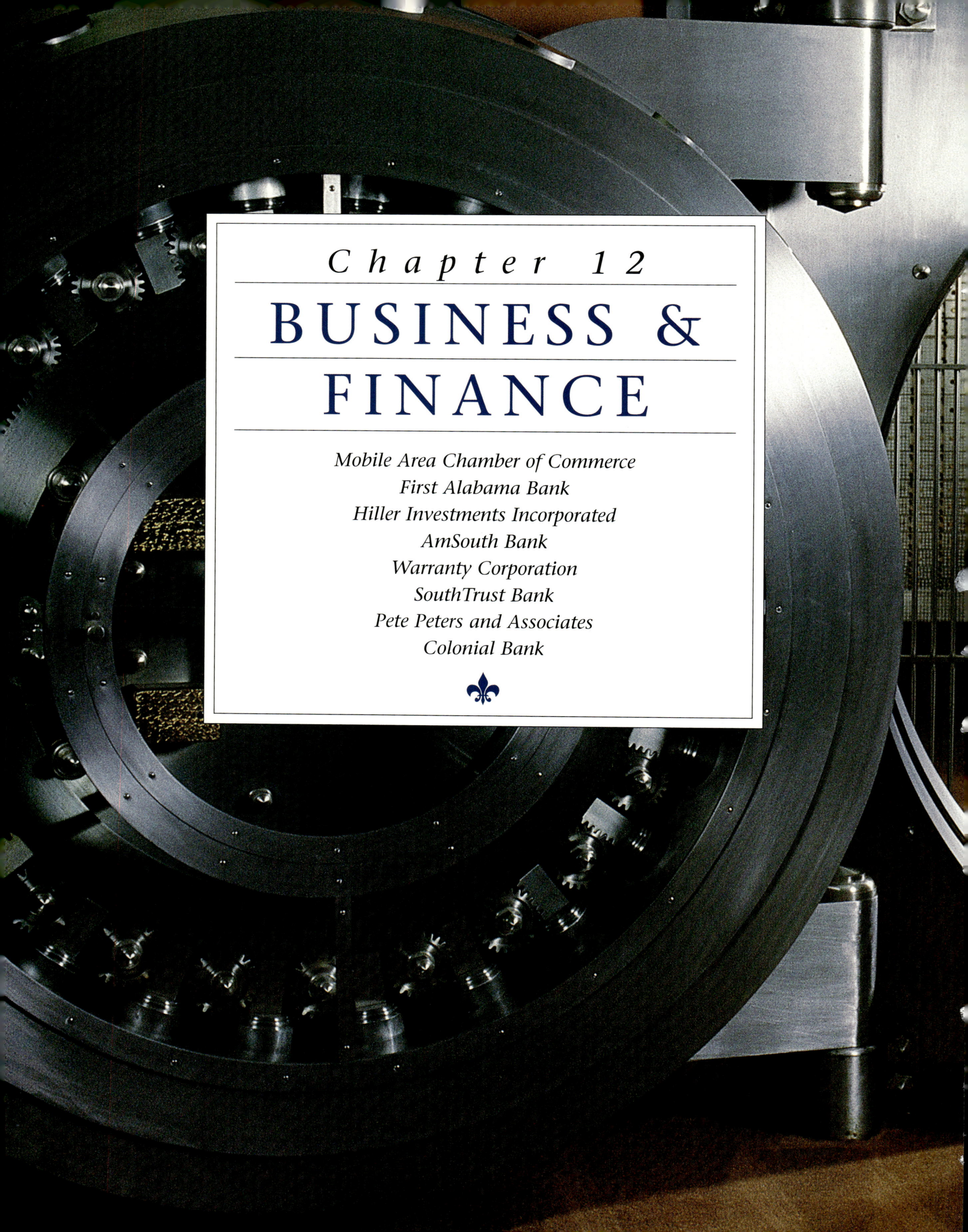

Chapter 12
BUSINESS & FINANCE

Mobile Area Chamber of Commerce
First Alabama Bank
Hiller Investments Incorporated
AmSouth Bank
Warranty Corporation
SouthTrust Bank
Pete Peters and Associates
Colonial Bank

MOBILE AREA CHAMBER OF COMMERCE

It seems appropriate that a historical city such as Mobile has a Chamber of Commerce equally as rich and steeped in history. Incorporated in 1836 under the name Mobile Commerce and Business League, the Mobile Area Chamber of Commerce was the first such business organization in the state of Alabama.

After changing its name using such titles as the Board of Trade and Maritime Exchange and Shipping Association, the organization was reincorporated in 1960 under its present name of the Mobile Area Chamber of Commerce and remains one of only 10 percent of chambers nationally which are accredited by the Chamber of Commerce of the United States in Washington, D.C.

Although its name may have been updated and the programs which it offers are constantly changing to meet the needs of the Mobile area business community, the foundation on which the Chamber was established remains steadfast. The Chamber's mission as a private business organization is "to serve as a progressive advocate for business needs [in order to] promote the Mobile area's economic well-being."

The Chamber's many activities can be categorized into three main focuses. First is "Economic Development and Job Creation," whereby the Chamber works to bring in new businesses while helping existing companies prosper and expand. It is the community's main source for assisting small business owners and managers, providing them vital counseling and information services.

The second focus area is "Governmental Affairs," by which all levels of government—local, state, and federal—are monitored and lobbied on issues affecting business.

Finally, "Community Improvement" focuses on improving Mobile's infrastructure and lifestyle. With a good quality of life, businesses will thrive and new businesses will be attracted here.

In today's global economy, Mobile remains a worldwide contender for new and expanding business and industry. More and more international firms are locating in the Mobile area. The Chamber's dynamic economic development marketing program "Mobile In Motion" is keeping this community in the international race for business locations. The Chamber has also established the World Trade Council to stimulate interest in the international trade arena and to offer support to local businesses interested in exporting.

As a participant in this international community, Mobile has taken advantage of successful sister-city relationships with over a dozen countries.

Such hard work and extraordinary vision has paid off for the Chamber. During the five-year period prior to 1994, membership increased by 32 percent to include over 2,500 members. The reason for this phenomenal growth is the variety of opportunities offered to Chamber members.

Small businesses (those with less than 50 employees) make up almost 90 percent of the Chamber's membership and are a real target for the organization's wealth of experience. Such companies benefit greatly from management counseling delivered by the Chamber's Senior Corps of Retired Executives (SCORE), who themselves have been successful in running small businesses. And the "Small Business Innovation Center" sponsored in part by the Chamber, offers special help for small businesses during their crucial first five years in operation.

Chamber members gain insight into marketing and research while "networking" with other Chamber businesses, to the benefit of everyone.

The Chamber allows members to be as active as they like. Active companies may choose to work on Chamber committees such as planning the Annual Meeting, working in legislative affairs, or helping select the "Small Business of the Month." There are numerous committees, so there's a place for every expertise and energy.

"Mobile's on the Grow," the Chamber's report on area growth and advancements, shows Mobile's economy shining with a steady, healthy glow. In 1993 Mobile ranked ninth on a list of overall employment growth in the Southeast and number two in service employment growth with more than 4,300 people added to the Mobile area workforce. During 1993 the Chamber reported 87 new and expanding companies, creating 1,725 new jobs, with capital investments of $483.7 million. This growth is expected to continue through the year 2000.

Site Selection magazine selected the Chamber's Economic Development Department as one of the top 10 such organizations in the United States in 1989, 1991, 1992, 1993, and 1994 and that department's senior vice president was elected as one of the 10 outstanding young developers in the country.

INC. magazine ranked Mobile 50th out of 192 cities as "Most Entrepreneurial Cities in America," *U.S. News and World Report* named Mobile 6th out of 100 top housing markets nationwide, and Mobile's small business program was recognized as one of the "nation's most innovative small business programs."

A Gulf Coast Treasure

Mobile Mayor Mike Dow says, "The Mobile Area Chamber of Commerce plays a vital, dynamic role in letting the world know what Mobile has to offer. The Chamber tirelessly spreads the word that Mobile is a great place to visit, a great place to do business, and a great place to live."

The success story of the Mobile Area Chamber of Commerce is not measured by numbers alone, and it did not occur by accident. It is the end result of many dedicated people working diligently for the overall benefit of private business and the community at large. ⚜

This painting by Judith Hempstead called Azaleas & Cast Iron was one of the winning art pieces in the Chamber's annual Pride Arts Competition. The competition features local art depicting sites and activities in the Mobile Bay area. The event is part of the Chamber's overall effort to promote community pride.

FIRST ALABAMA BANK

First Alabama Bank of Mobile traces its banking lineage back to 1901, when it opened for business in Mobile as Merchants National Bank with only three officers and two employees. Ernest Ladd Sr., one of the original tellers, would later serve as bank president, chairman of the board, and, for 25 years, as the bank's leader.

In 1981 Merchants National merged with First Alabama Bancshares, the state's first bank-holding company. Today, First Alabama Bancshares is known as Regions Financial Corporation, a $10 billion plus multi-bank holding company. Regions has offices in Alabama, Florida, Georgia, Tennessee, Louisiana, and South Carolina. The bank continues to operate in Alabama, however, as First Alabama Bank.

Probably even Ladd could not have envisioned such phenomenal change, but directly because of his dedicated community leadership, great things evolved for Mobile as well as for the bank.

When the time came for Mobile to build a football stadium, the drive was led by Merchants National, and, because of the bank, others gave financial support to the project. Today, each fall weekend, Ernest F. Ladd Memorial Stadium serves as the playing field for the Mobile area's high school football games. Besides being responsible for raising the money for the stadium's construction, Merchants National's J. Finley McRae, successor to Ladd, provided the leadership to found the Senior Bowl, held each January in Ladd Stadium, which features outstanding pro prospects from colleges and universities around the country.

First Alabama's automated teller machine network, The Right Place, allows customers 24-hour-a-day access to their accounts.

First Alabama operates from an impressive high-rise building constructed in 1929 in downtown Mobile. The bank occupies the entire block, with several connecting buildings.

Today, First Alabama operates from an impressive high-rise building which was constructed in 1929 in downtown Mobile. The bank occupies the entire block, with several connecting buildings.

State-of-the-art technology has allowed the bank to continue to concentrate on its first priority, the "customer." Dedicated bank employees use the very latest in banking technology, freeing them to serve their customers with that "personal" touch which has been, and will continue to be, important to the bank.

First Alabama's automated teller machine network, The Right Place, allows customers 24-hour-a-day access to their accounts. Alabama's shared ATM network, the Alert System, also allows customers to use over 300 Alert-member, automated teller machines throughout the state and other networks across the nation.

The bank services a wide clientele base, from the household checking account, to college student loans, from financial advice and loans for mom and pop enterprises, to intricate financial services for national and international corporations.

Consumer and corporate services are varied, including financial advice and investments, trust services, international services, industrial development, oil and gas services, forestry management, and cash management.

In December 1993 First Alabama Bank expanded its services with the acquisition of Secor Bank and its $2 billion deposits and locations in Alabama, Florida, and Louisiana.

"First Alabama Bank has a tradition to uphold," says Carl E. Jones Jr., Chairman and CEO in Mobile. "Since 1901 our service to the customer and community has been a commitment which we take most seriously."

HILLER INVESTMENTS INCORPORATED

In 1994 Hiller Investments Incorporated celebrates its 75th year in business. Herbert S. Hiller founded the business in 1919 in New Orleans, Louisiana, to design and provide fire protection equipment for commercial and shipyard customers. In the ensuing 75 years, the company has grown to include nine operations, including facilities located in Texas, Louisiana, Mississippi, Florida, Virginia, Alabama, and Singapore. The operations are involved in the manufacturing, distribution, installation, and service of products and systems used in both fire protection and specialty flooring.

Company headquarters was moved to Mobile in 1988 because of the city's more central Gulf Coast location and the greater opportunity for growth provided by the Mobile area.

One of the company's largest operations, Hiller Systems, Inc., is also located in Mobile and employs over 150 people. They supply fire protection and specialty flooring needs to marine, commercial, and industrial customers.

Fire protection systems include fire detection and alarms, automatic sprinklers, and other fire suppression systems involving non-toxic chemicals, inert gas, and foam systems, all to protect life, equipment, and other valuable assets. Hiller engineers work with architects, consulting engineers, and owners to develop the appropriate system for the hazard involved. For example, protection is provided for computer rooms, telephone switch gear areas, steam turbines, printing presses, restaurant grills, and oil production platforms. Cargo holds, electronic areas, and engine, pump, steering gear, and emergency generator rooms are protected on ships. Explosion suppression systems are provided for dust collectors, conveyors, and other process equipment. Hiller manufactures its own control systems, hose reels, and foam-dispensing stations used in fire protection.

Another growing market for the Hiller Companies is security systems. These systems can also be integrated into the fire alarm systems. Hiller designs and installs closed-circuit television monitoring, nurse call, card access, sound, and other communication systems. Protection is provided for commercial buildings, hospitals, nursing homes, industrial plants, and casinos.

Hiller's specialty flooring includes non-skid materials, antimicrobial systems, gym floors, waterproof systems, decorative epoxy, seamless, and chemical-resistant floors. Carpeting, tile, and reinforced wall systems are also installed. Hiller works with architects and owners to select the specialty flooring that meets the application requirements. Flooring systems are provided for decks, showers, and other areas for Navy and commercial ships. They specialize in the application of materials to meet United States Coast Guard and Navy Mil Spec requirements. In the commercial area, specialty flooring is installed in hospitals, nursing homes, grocery stores, warehouses, schools, casinos, and commercial office buildings.

Hiller Investments' management team (left to right) R. H. Evers, C. F. Robinson, L. D. Greenwood (owner and president), J. R. Copeland, and E. L. Savadra see a bright future as they expand the business base and look for new opportunities.

In both fire protection and specialty flooring, Hiller represents and distributes products from the leading manufacturers in their fields. They also service and maintain all systems sold with trained and experienced personnel. Hiller supplies and recharges portable fire extinguishers and provides other personal safety equipment such as fire-resistant clothing and gloves, air-breathing apparatus, masks, and other similar equipment. Inventories are maintained to assure prompt, effective service when needed.

Mobile's shipyards, key industrial plants, and a variety of commercial facilities number among Hiller's customers. The new Mobile Government Center is protected by a fire alarm system provided by Hiller Systems, and the Convention Center utilizes a Hiller-supplied closed-circuit television security system.

Hiller Investments Incorporated's president and owner, L. Duncan Greenwood, sees the company continuing to expand its business base as it looks for new opportunities on the Gulf Coast and other areas. ⚜

This 1860 building with its original cast iron facade is the home of Hiller Investments and is on the National Register of Historic Places.

A Gulf Coast Treasure

AMSOUTH BANK

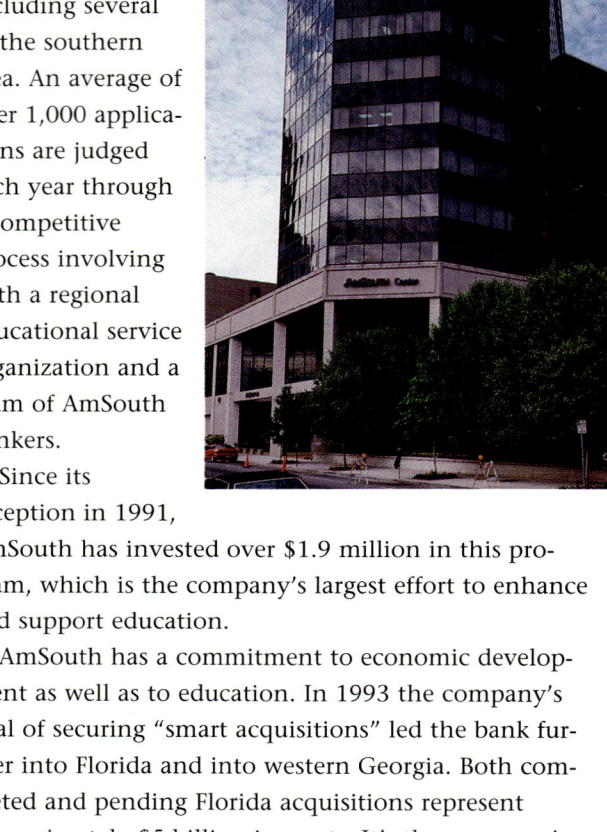

AmSouth Bank's rich heritage reaches back to 1872, when Swedish adventurer, sea captain, and businessman Charles Linn and six associates organized a bank in Birmingham. An on-going national depression and a cholera epidemic clouded the bank construction project, which some skeptics, because of the uncertainty of the times, called "Linn's Folly."

But Linn persevered and soon "Linn's Folly" became "Linn's Wisdom," and eventually Captain Linn's bank grew to become the lead bank of AmSouth Bancorporation with more than $12 billion in assets and over 240 banking offices in four states.

In 1983 banks in over 20 Alabama counties (some of which began operations as early as 1865) merged to form a statewide bank, AmSouth Bank, and in 1985 there was the largest bank merger in state history, AmSouth's merger with FirstGulf Bancorp, headquartered in Mobile. Now AmSouth's southern area, which includes Mobile and Baldwin Counties, has 24 operating offices.

John C. Hope III, executive vice president and southern area manager, attributes AmSouth's growth to the financial strength of the company due in large part to the bank's traditional approach to banking, the highly qualified personnel, and the variety of quality products and services available. "In Mobile we have had the privilege of servicing a community that reflects our commitment to tradition as well as our hopes for the future," he said. "Over the years, AmSouth has been able to combine the heritage of the past with current technologies to make AmSouth Bank one of the largest and strongest financial institutions in the Southeast."

One of AmSouth's goals is to support each local community in which it operates, while preserving that area's traditions. To this end, AmSouth continually pursues opportunities to support civic, cultural, charitable, and economic programs in each community it serves.

Of major significance is the AmSouth Fund for Educational Excellence, established to provide educators funding with which to develop and support innovative educational ideas in primary and secondary schools (K-12) and preschools. In 1992-1993 AmSouth awarded 80 grants, totaling $538,536, to Alabama and Florida schools, including several in the southern area. An average of over 1,000 applications are judged each year through a competitive process involving both a regional educational service organization and a team of AmSouth bankers.

Since its inception in 1991, AmSouth has invested over $1.9 million in this program, which is the company's largest effort to enhance and support education.

AmSouth has a commitment to economic development as well as to education. In 1993 the company's goal of securing "smart acquisitions" led the bank further into Florida and into western Georgia. Both completed and pending Florida acquisitions represent approximately $5 billion in assets. It's the company's belief that these acquisitions will prove a real asset to the AmSouth shareholder.

To AmSouth, quality banking "means offering the highest quality products and services and building quality banking relationships which last a lifetime." The company believes their relationship with their customers is just like any other relationship, the more you put in, the more you get in return.

With that goal in mind, AmSouth offers its customers discounts on loans and rebates on mortgages, discounts on telephone banking, bankcards, and various other quality services.

AmSouth quality comes in many different forms, such as checking, savings and investments, consumer credit services, trust services, commercial banking, and convenience services.

Besides serving the individual customer, AmSouth is dedicated to assisting local industry. Because of their $12 billion strength, AmSouth is able to provide major local industries' multimillion-dollar credit needs without going outside the Mobile area for additional financial backing.

Being progressive while remaining ever aware of their heritage and focusing on service to the individual, as well as to the large corporation, has enabled AmSouth to remain a real success story. "Linn's Folly" has truly evolved into "Linn's Wisdom," not only regionally, but also in AmSouth's southern area of Mobile and Baldwin Counties. ⚜

AmSouth's southern area includes Mobile and Baldwin Counties with 24 operating offices located throughout the area. Photograph by Ric Moore.

AmSouth combines the heritage of the past with current technologies to make the bank one of the largest and strongest financial institutions in the Southeast. Photograph by Ric Moore.

WARRANTY CORPORATION

Warranty Corporation was founded in early 1987. The company sells new and used car warranties via direct mail to customers who have purchased vehicles. In many cases, Warranty Corporation is the only available source for an extended warranty.

Warranty Corporation is well managed by experienced executives with successful backgrounds in insurance, law, and finance. The company began with five employees and was housed in a small, nondescript gray bungalow. After several years of phenomenal growth, which averaged 57 percent annually, the corporation is staffing to employ over 200 professionals and construct a 10,000 square-foot office complex in west Mobile.

Warranty Corporation's success is evidenced by its millions of dollars in annual warranty sales, the results of the more than three million advertisements mailed out each year. This has made Warranty Corporation one of the post office's largest regional customers—a customer who invests over one half million in postage a year.

Warranty Corporation is online with national data bases with access to all manufacturers' automobile histories, including recalls, manufacturers' repair bulletins, and individual model histories. This information is vital in determining whether a problem is covered by the manufacturer or if it is a mechanical failure for which the company is responsible. If it is a non-mechanical failure, Warranty Corporation still assists the client in cutting the cost of repair by helping to find the necessary parts at wholesale prices. Warranty is able to offer the lowest possible price on parts because it is able to buy in such great volume from wholesale warehouses.

The Warranty Corporation is assisted by an additional staff of over 200 certified field inspectors scattered throughout the nation who are hired by the company through a national inspection firm. These inspectors are all ASE certified mechanics who handle major claims by relaying pictures of the failed part or parts via computerized cameras and telephone modems to the Mobile office. Using this latest technology aids the company in resolving repairs in the fastest possible time.

A tour of the company's facility reveals that Warranty Corporation is completely self-sufficient and operates with an impressive arsenal of equipment. A refrigerated storage facility is necessary to store envelopes, which are purchased by the millions, in order to protect them from Mobile's damaging humidity.

The company's data processing department is responsible for insuring prompt customer service and responsive claim assistance. Computers file all contracts, access national telephone data bases to locate parts nationwide, log into national data bases to learn about various automotive recalls and manufacturers, and are able to read both mainframe computer tapes as well as PC environs.

Electronic duplicators utilize desktop publishing software to produce the corporation's printed material, while rows of lasers address outgoing mail to the tune of 5,000 letters per hour.

Warranty Corporation maintains substantial monetary reserves in the investment department of a major bank. The company has also invested substantial funds to establish a national trust to be used in case of a natural disaster or other catastrophes. The company's customers are assured of the financial strength backing each extended warranty.

Being such a unique business has attracted the attention of major automobile manufacturers, Lloyds of London, and other major insurance companies who wish to establish national programs through Warranty Corporation.

Personal service is of utmost importance in the way Warranty Corporation conducts business. Customers need to be able to talk to a live voice when they have a question or problem. Warranty customer service operators are indeed alive and friendly. One operator shares, "I'm always asked if I am a real person—and the customer is thrilled to discover that I really am." ⚜

Warranty Corporation is accustomed to handling millions of dollars in benefit requests. These requests are processed quickly and paid promptly.

Personal service is of utmost importance in the way Warranty Corporation conducts business. Customers need to be able to talk to a live voice when they have a question or problem, and Warranty Corporation customer service operators are trained to provide a high level of professional service.

SOUTHTRUST BANK

SouthTrust Bank of Mobile was established on April 1, 1965, under the name "Commercial Guaranty Bank." June 3, 1965, witnessed the official opening of the bank, and within two days, Commercial Guaranty had attracted more than $6 million in deposits. In 1973 CGB became part of a holding company, later to be named SouthTrust Corporation. In October, 1982 the name of the bank was changed to SouthTrust Bank of Mobile, which has since grown into one of the most successful and respected financial institutions in the Mobile region. SouthTrust Corporation is currently the largest bank holding company in the state of Alabama.

Robert Wilbanks, president and Frank Schmidt, chairman and CEO of SouthTrust Bank pose in front of a Fresco at the main office. Created by Albrizio, who spent more than two years creating his exquisite masterpieces, the project proved to be one of the largest and most ambitious artistic endeavors ever undertaken outside the field of outdoor sculpture. Shown is "Air" which represents man's efforts to conquer space. Painted in 1948, it is prophetic in that it envisioned outer space exploration more than a decade before the first manned orbital flight.

The SouthTrust system is unique in that it encourages all of its affiliate banks to operate as separate and autonomous entities, able to make all banking decisions through local management staffs and boards of directors. This system produces swift processing of all loans, which is considered important to both private and commercial customers.

"It's important to our customers to know that their business is being handled by people they know and trust," said Frank Schmidt, chairman and CEO of SouthTrust Bank of Mobile. "Because our board of directors and executive management is right here in Mobile, we have a partnership with the community. Our customers can feel secure knowing financial decisions which will affect them are made right here at home."

All SouthTrust Bank of Mobile offices are identical in physical structure and services offered. The main office, located in downtown Mobile at 61 Saint Joseph Street, however, breaks the mold and leaves visitors breathless. Upon entering the bank's lobby, visitors are met by the inspiring frescoes of artist Conrad Albrizio, whose work also graces Mobile's Civic Center and the Mobile County Courthouse.

Fresco is known for its endurance, and so is SouthTrust Bank of Mobile. The bank's hallmarks of success lie in its commitment to community banking, high standards of business conduct, the ability to operate above the standards for growth and profitability, and creative and energetic leadership from local directors, officers, and staff.

SouthTrust's Quality Service philosophy is the first of its kind in banking. The promise of satisfaction guaranteed assures customers that the bank will provide quality service, or it pays the customer in cash.

The bank guarantees courteous service; accurate handling of all transactions, from the correct spelling of names to the correct change for a cashed check; same-day response time to any customer question or problem; ATM availability; and promptness, which assures that no customer will wait in a lobby teller line for more than five minutes.

SouthTrust takes pride in being able to turn problems into positive and memorable experiences for its customers. The bank is willing to take that extra step or two, or three, or however many it takes to guarantee its customers' total satisfaction.

SouthTrust operates 13 offices, 2 remote drive-through facilities, 9 AnyTime Teller machines—7 of which are drive-through, an international business department, a trust department, and, rarely seen in the banking business today, a local customer service department.

"The people we serve are important to us," Schmidt said. "That's why our board is comprised of business men from every phase of life in Mobile. It is this influence that prompts our employees to become involved in serving the community."

SouthTrust Bank of Mobile expects its employees as well as its directors to be supportive of their community. The board annually reviews the list of the company's community involvement. This involvement is too numerous to list but includes a variety of business, educational, civic, church, sports, and leisure associations and charities.

"SouthTrust Bank of Mobile has been an important part of our community for many years, and we remain committed to helping serve the financial needs of Mobile residents," Schmidt said. "We are delighted that we can offer the advantages of a hometown bank backed by the resources of a major southeastern bank holding company." ⚜

Changes bring questions, and questions bring clients to Pete Peters and Associates. Questions like:

"Pete, I've been working with a stockbroker for five years. He's had some good recommendations, but overall my portfolio is worth less than I invested. What can I do?"—a nationally recognized management consultant.

"Pete, I know I need life insurance, but I don't want whole life; I just want term. Do you think I'm making a smart decision?"—a young cardiologist.

"Pete, I want to be fair to my employees, but I have no idea which benefits I should provide them. Do you?"—a successful business owner.

Pete listens thoughtfully then answers each question. He knows that professional money management found most often through mutual funds will strengthen a portfolio; the best type of insurance is the kind that will be there when needed, whether term or permanent; employees are a company's most valuable resource, and choosing appropriate benefits for them is crucial.

It's easy for Pete to put himself in his clients' shoes, because he has been operating his own business for about 15 years. Developing a lasting relationship means more to Pete than simply selling a product.

A Chartered Life Underwriter and Chartered Financial Consultant, he created Pete Peters and Associates to assist small business owners and professionals with their estate, financial, and insurance planning. Services include personal disability, health, and life insurance planning; college education funding; personal retirement planning; communicating and implementing employee and executive fringe benefits; and funding buy-sell agreements.

Pete Peters and Associates was one of the first independent life and health insurance agencies in the Mobile area. As an independent agent, he would have the freedom to shop the market for the products best suited to meet his clients' needs without obligation to an insurance or investment company's product line.

Sincerity, honesty, dedication, experience, and knowledge about the industry are qualities that have earned Pete and his company national recognition. The

After listening to Brad Beard's concerns, Pete makes recommendations regarding his business and personal financial planning. Photo by Steve Goraum.

PETE PETERS AND ASSOCIATES

recipient of national sales and quality awards, he has earned a life membership in the Million Dollar Round Table. Only three percent of the world's insurance agents become members of this prestigious table, and their membership is based upon their production. Pete has also been singled out as one of the Outstanding Young Men of America and as Mobile's Life Underwriter of the Year.

The mission of Pete Peters and Associates is to provide quality service and to assist clients in achieving financial security and economic success.

Financial planning is divided into four steps: setting goals, developing a plan to reach those goals, implementing the plan, and evaluating the plan's success. "Financial security requires a solid foundation, which is usually achieved by accumulating adequate cash reserve and adequate life, health, and disability insurance," Pete explains. "Personal savings, life insurance, and disability income coverage are crucial for a family's financial protection. We help our clients achieve this protection through savings, investments, college, retirement, and estate planning."

Business planning is also a large part of Pete's practice. Businesses define economic success in terms of profit. "My purpose is to help businesses maximize their greatest resource—their employees—by suggesting appropriate fringe benefits and effective ways of communicating the value of these benefits to their personnel. If possible, I like to explain the benefits face-to-face with each and every employee."

Pete's business planning also includes evaluating retirement plans, group life, disability, and dental insurance, funding buy-sell agreements, salary continuation plans, deferred compensation, and executive retirement plans.

Pete learned a long time ago to "never miss an opportunity to listen." He adds, "God gave us two ears and one mouth, and I try to use them accordingly. I will continue to listen to what my clients need, and I will continue to strive to meet those needs." ⚜

Pete responds to Larry Batchelor's questions pertaining to his estate and retirement planning at an early morning breakfast. Photo by Steve Goraum.

Whether building or buying a home, Colonial Bank helps by providing the security and convenience of dealing with one person and one bank for all lending needs. Colonial vice president E. J. Atkins and regional president and CEO Mike Fitzhugh tour a construction sight with local builders.

COLONIAL BANK

No other bank in Alabama is so uniquely capable of combining its statewide resources with hometown service as Colonial Bank. It provides incomparable service with more than 1,300 professional Colonial employees dedicated to ensuring customer satisfaction.

Colonial Bank is Mobile's hometown bank, offering service from bankers who share local values and understand that hometown perspective. These bankers are also highly motivated professionals with a personal stake in this community.

"The strength of our bank is derived from the relationship we develop with our customers," says Mike Fitzhugh, chief executive officer and president of The Colonial Bank of Mobile. "Without our customers we have little to sell. The reason we open our doors each business day is to help our customers grow. Being a relatively small bank gives us the opportunity to know our customers and to provide personal service."

Colonial Bank established its presence in Mobile over a decade ago. Today the company has expanded from one to eight locations serving the Mobile and Baldwin County areas. Continued growth and expansion describe this bank's future.

Although the Colonial Bank of Mobile is small in size, it is immense in capabilities. Its parent organization, The Colonial BancGroup, Inc. is a multi-state bank holding company headquartered in Montgomery with 92 offices in Alabama and 4 offices in southern Tennessee and total assets of over $2.7 billion.

Since its founding in 1981, Colonial BancGroup has distinguished itself by offering banking services in the state's largest markets, such as Birmingham, Huntsville, Montgomery, and Mobile. Colonial also plays a leadership role in dozens of smaller cities and towns across Alabama and Tennessee. And from its beginning, Colonial BancGroup's priorities have been to establish a statewide banking system while continuing to enhance the value of the company by increasing profits and maintaining a strong capital base.

At Colonial, each individual bank's competitive position is strengthened by a commitment to local management. Each bank is endowed with the authority to approve loans—large and small—at a local level. Additionally, Colonial's local board of directors is a diverse group of successful men and women chosen from a variety of backgrounds who provide support for Colonial's management team.

The Colonial Bank of Mobile participates in numerous community activities and organizations. Its primary community commitment, however, is public education and it proudly sponsors four schools. The bank has also committed millions of dollars towards the renaissance of downtown Mobile.

For the growing number of customers who welcome the personal service of a hometown bank, Colonial Bank offers a distinct variety of services to make banking easy and convenient. Colonial has a number of checking services that meet the needs of its customers, their families, and their businesses. Whether building or buying a home, planning for a dream vacation, starting a new business, or financing a child's education, Colonial Bank helps accomplish goals by providing the security and convenience of dealing with one person and one bank for all lending needs.

The people at Colonial Bank are working hard to build solid relationships with their customers. That's what Colonial means by "Good People, Great Service." ⚜

The Colonial Bank of Mobile's primary community commitment is public education. Colonial Bank regional president and CEO Mike Fitzhugh visits with the student council and principal William Lawrence of Council Traditional School.

Chapter 13
PROFESSIONS

Adams and Reese
Miller, Hamilton, Snider & Odom, L.L.C.
Johnstone, Adams, Bailey, Gordon and Harris
Lewis Communications, Inc.
Lyons, Pipes & Cook, P.C.
Gottlieb, Barnett, & Bridges Engineering Consultants
Sirote & Permutt, P.C.
Richardson, Daniell, Spear & Upton, P.C.

ADAMS AND REESE

Adams and Reese, Attorneys and Counselors at law, is a Gulf South law firm with offices in Mobile, New Orleans, Baton Rouge, Houston, and Washington, D.C. offering a full range of legal services. The firm's 150 attorneys, who have diverse styles, backgrounds, and personalities, practice in Alabama, Texas, Louisiana, Mississippi, Florida, Georgia, Washington, D.C., and several other states and jurisdictions.

Adams and Reese recognizes that a business's profitability, reputation, and mere existence depend on its success at avoiding legal entanglements as well as defending them. The firm's phenomenal growth is representative of their overwhelming desire to continue to meet the ever-changing and specialized needs of their clients.

Victor H. Lott Jr., a partner in Mobile, says: "The major difference between Adams and Reese and other firms in this area is that we have the resources of a 150-man firm, which is more than three times larger than any firm in this part of the state. So we bring a lot to bear with a small office." For example, Adams and Reese has the very latest in telecommunications and computer systems allowing instantaneous communications between offices, attorneys, and clients, ensuring the firm's services are responsive, uniform, and efficient.

Adams and Reese, as a full service law firm, is designed to tend to the needs of its diverse clientele. Their attorneys' practice areas include general and maritime litigation, pharmaceutical and medical device litigation, products liability, professional liability, health care law, governmental relations, labor and employment law, international law, customs law, environmental law, commercial law, real estate law, bankruptcy, oil and gas law, general corporate matters, tax, trust and estate planning, and the regulations of utilities and common carriers.

Adams and Reese is organized into specialized practice groups. Attorneys may be involved in as many as two or three practice groups by virtue of their expertise in diverse areas. For instance, the Commercial Litigation and Employment Law Practice Group provides counseling and representation to clients on commercial business ventures and employment issues.

The Environmental Law Practice Group advises and represents clients concerning environmental issues or state or federal environmental regulations. Many of the environmental lawyers at Adams and Reese have technical backgrounds in petroleum engineering, chemical engineering, and geology or have worked in the chemical or petroleum industries. Other lawyers in our Environmental Practice Group worked for regulatory agencies responsible for the enforcement of environmental regulations.

Mobile's proximity to the Gulf of Mexico, has made maritime law a special interest to this office. Along with New Orleans, Houston, and Baton Rouge, Mobile is a major center for shipping, towage, and offshore activity. Adams and Reese's Maritime Practice Group represents and counsels their clients on the substantive and procedural rules governing maritime liabilities. In-house seminars familiarize their clients with certain insurance programs, contractual allocation of risks (indemnification), safety programs and accident reporting, and investigation procedures.

Adams and Reese recognizes that American businesses are changing the ways in which they operate overseas. To meet these changes Adams and Reese formed its International Practice Group, which assists clients, both foreign and domestic, on matters concerning international business.

Other practice groups address products and professional liability and litigation, health care law, local, state, and federal governmental matters, real estate and commercial law, corporate, securities, tax and estate planning, among others.

Adams and Reese attorneys have outstanding reputations in litigation and general business law and offer clients their talents and resources for a full range of legal services.

Adams and Reese realizes their obligation, not only to the professional community, but also to the community at large. The firm encourages and supports participation of its attorneys and staff members in professional, cultural, and civic organizations.

Professionally, many of Adams and Reese's attorneys have served on local and state bar committees, and many have held executive-level positions in both the Alabama State Bar, the Mobile Bar Association, the Alabama Law Institute, the Alabama State Bar Foundation, the Alabama Defense Lawyers Association, the Defense Research Institute, and the International Association of Defense Counsel.

Concomitant with its role of providing quality legal services, Adams and Reese recognizes its responsibility to the community to be a good corporate citizen. Adams and Reese supports many local community and civic organizations. Firm members serve on numerous civic and community boards. The firm is also very active in supporting downtown redevelopment projects and special Mobile events such as the Senior Bowl.

A particular project which gives much satisfaction to Adams and Reese is a charitable program called H.U.G.S., which stands for Hope, Understanding, Giving, and Support. Not only does Adams and Reese support H.U.G.S. financially, but they also allocate attorney and staff service hours to further this program.

A large part of the H.U.G.S. work involves the partnership in education program. Adams and Reese has adopted Most Pure Heart of Mary School, the first Catholic school in Mobile to become a partner. Firm members have developed a close, direct relationship with the school staff and students by taking them on field trips, supporting reading projects, attending school parties and events, and participating in the school's Career Day. A special project is the sponsoring of a Christmas art contest, in which the winning artwork is used on the firm Christmas card each year.

In 1993 Adams and Reese, as a result of their work with H.U.G.S., proudly accepted the Award for Excellence in corporate community service. This prestigious award was presented by the Washington based Points of Light Foundation, a non-profit, non-partisan group organized to work towards solutions to social problems. Adams and Reese is the only law firm in the nation to receive the award.

The firm represents a number of major industries in the Mobile area, including chemical, steel, energy, timber, and maritime interests.

Adams and Reese is extremely proud of the work accomplished through the H.U.G.S. program. In addition to spreading hope and happiness to needy children, elderly, handicapped, and homeless people, they and their families experience the personal satisfaction and fulfillment that comes from serving the Mobile community.

The goal of Adams and Reese is to continue serving its long-standing clients in an efficient manner while reaching out for new clients in the industries and practice areas which have brought to the firm its full measure of success across the Gulf Coast and the nation. ⚜

No representation is made that the quality of the legal services to be performed is greater than the quality of the legal services performed by other lawyers.

MILLER, HAMILTON, SNIDER & ODOM, L.L.C.

Nestled beneath the spreading limbs of beautiful, moss-covered live oak trees on State Street, Miller, Hamilton, Snider & Odom, L.L.C. takes on the look and feel of old Mobile. Embraced by this antebellum setting, the ambiance of antiquity is an illusion. Housed within these beautifully restored structures are highly rated attorneys, the latest in computer processing and office technology, one of the most complete hard volume and computerized library systems in the state, and the highly skilled office and paralegal staff necessary to assist lawyers in their specialized areas.

Founded as an individual practice in 1977 by John C. H. Miller Jr., the past 17 years have seen the firm grow to over 27 attorneys. Keeping a finger on the pulse of the state, regional, and national change is vital for the proper representation of Miller, Hamilton, Snider & Odom's clients. In order to better maintain this vigil, the firm opened offices in Montgomery, Alabama, and Washington, D.C. The Montgomery office is staffed by three lawyers and their support personnel. This office deals predominately, but not exclusively, with state and regional-oriented issues. The predominant areas in which the Washington, D.C. office works are national, international, and environmental in scope.

Miller, Hamilton, Snider & Odom's list of partners reads like a list from "Who's Who" in the legal profession, with four of the firm's lawyers having executive level experience with financial regulatory agencies in the nation's capital. One of the firm's lawyers was director and chairman of the Federal Deposit Insurance Corporation, another served as chief of the Antitrust Division of the Alabama Attorney General's office, and still another served as legal advisor to the Governor of Alabama. Two of Miller, Hamilton, Snider & Odom's members are Rhodes Scholars.

In today's economic climate, the diversity of representing corporate and financial industry clients, as well as many individuals, has offered MHS&O the opportunity of continued growth and education. Eager to accept all challenges, MHS&O has taken advantage of these opportunities and used them to benefit their clients. MHS&O clientele includes banks, banking and savings and loan holding companies, savings and loan associations, estates, individual entrepreneurs, real estate developers and investors, health care providers, national resource and energy developers, commercial transportation firms, broadcasting corporations, tax exempt organizations, chemical manufacturers and construction, and architectural and engineering firms. This variety of clientele has led to lawyer specialization, which has greatly increased the areas of expertise held by the firm.

A client-oriented firm, Miller, Hamilton, Snider & Odom is a proponent of the "total quality" movement.

In today's economic climate, the diversity of representing corporate and financial industry clients, as well as many individuals, has offered Miller, Hamilton, Snider & Odom the opportunity of continued growth and education.

It is committed to constant communication, the utilization of sensible technology, and cost-effective client representation. MHS&O takes pride in maintaining three priorities: a "can do" attitude, "total quality service," and the ability to listen to their clients. The firm uses its creative resources to achieve positive results and has established a strong track record of success by subscribing to this philosophy.

The proactive stance exhibited in business is carried beyond the office and into the community by the entire firm. Community involvement is a way of life at MHS&O and extends from historic Mobile's renovation, education reform, and state growth through charitable involvements on an individual and firm level. MHS&O is proud of its people, working diligently to provide a kindred environment. The positive result of this caring attitude is increased team spirit, productivity, and the desire to excel.

The MHS&O member list boasts some very impressive individuals, with equally impressive credentials: John C. H. Miller Jr., Palmer C. Hamilton, Ronald A. Snider, Michael D. Waters, Bradley R. Byrne, George A. LeMaistre Jr., Lester M. Bridgeman, Louis T. Urbanczyk, Christopher G. Hume III, Richard A. Wright, M. Kathryn Knight, Matthew C. McDonald, Mark J. Tenhundfeld, Joseph R. Sullivan, Susan Russ Walker, A. Carson I. Nicolson, and (Of Counsel) Lewis G. Odom Jr. and George A. LeMaistre Sr. In its quest for excellence and diversity, MHS&O is continually expanding its family of lawyers. Currently there are 12 lawyers complementing the firm as associates.

Miller, Hamilton, Snider & Odom established its reputation in the banking and financial industry; however, economic changes in client needs have added a great deal of diversity to the firm. A partial list of areas

Miller, Hamilton, Snider & Odom is committed to constant communication, the utilization of sensible technology, and cost-effective client representation.

of concentration covered by this progressive family of lawyers includes antitrust law, aviation law, arbitration and mediation, banking law, banking regulatory law, bank organization and holding company formation, bankruptcy, business law, civil litigation, civil rights and litigation, commercial law, commercial and residential lending and loan closing, corporate law, creditor's rights, director's and officer's liability, financial institutions, employment law, general civil and insurance defense, government litigation, local government defense law, merger and acquisition, mortgage law, probate law, real property law, secured transportation law, securities law, taxation law, transportation law, and workers compensation law.

Miller, Hamilton, Snider & Odom is a forward-thinking, proactive law firm with the expertise necessary to serve and counsel its clientele anywhere in the nation. ⚜

No representation is made that the quality of the legal services to be performed is greater than the quality of the legal services performed by other lawyers.

JOHNSTONE, ADAMS, BAILEY, GORDON AND HARRIS

Founded in 1897, Johnstone Adams remains one of the oldest major law firms in Alabama and along the Gulf Coast. Their 25 attorneys represent regional, national, and international clients in all areas of law, with the exception of domestic relations and criminal matters.

With constant dedication over the last century, Johnstone Adams has developed a depth and experience that clients have come to expect. A long list of clients, many of whom have been represented by the firm for over 60 years, is confirmation of Johnstone Adams' success.

Johnstone Adams is a full-service law firm. With this in mind, attorneys regularly develop special knowledge and skill in more than one practice area.

Admiralty Law

Representation of steamship operators and marine underwriters has been a significant part of this firm's practice since its founding last century. Johnstone Adams represents nearly all American-flag steamship operators as well as London underwriters who insure the vast majority of the world's tonnage.

This practice involves the defense of injury and death claims, commercial disputes (including cargo and charterparty litigation and arbitration), vessel documentation and financing, and additional matters such as oil spills, immigrations, and customs problems.

Energy lawyers, former Alabama State Bar president Ben H. Harris Jr. and Alan Christian, are shown at a gas processing plant located in Mobile County.

Banking and Bankruptcy Law

Johnstone Adams has a thriving financial practice, representing lending institutions and federal agencies in-state and out-of-state. Johnstone Adams has represented one of Alabama's largest banks for many years.

The firm has experience with a wide range of banking issues, including the formation of bank holding companies, the acquisition of other banks, and defense against takeovers. The firm represents clients in litigation concerning loans, bankruptcies, and other regulatory matters.

Johnstone Adams also has expertise in the negotiation of terms and the drafting of legal documents for financial transactions such as real estate construction and permanent loans, asset-based loans, municipal and industrial bonds, and more.

In the field of bankruptcy, Johnstone Adams represents not only lenders, but also secured and unsecured creditors, and structures transactions to minimize risk. These transactions include workouts, collection matters, and foreclosures. The firm is also well-versed in claims concerning government agencies.

Business and Tax Law

In the field of corporate law and securities, Johnstone Adams provides a variety of legal services related to the formation, operation, and dissolution of businesses. The firm represents corporations, as both counsel and ligitator, in mergers, acquisitions, and takeovers.

Besides defending corporations against stockholder-derivative suits and other stockholder claims, the firm has counseled officers, directors, and stockholders on their rights and responsibilities.

Five of the attorneys at Johnstone Adams have advanced law degrees in taxation, assuring a high level of expertise, training, and experience in taxation matters.

The firm represents a broad spectrum of clients in both tax and business planning and in tax litigation. The firm provides comprehensive income and estate tax planning services in personal and business transactions, and assists employers in developing and implementing employee benefit plans in order to maximize tax advantages provided by such plans. It represents individuals and business clients in disputes with the Internal Revenue Service and state and local revenue departments in all tax areas, including the handling of audits, administrative appeals, and refund claims, as well as tax litigation in federal and state courts.

Energy Law

Energy law is another area of expertise at Johnstone Adams. Since the 1955 discovery of oil in Citronelle, Johnstone Adams has handled energy matters, particularly related to oil and gas. The firm counsels and liti-

Johnstone Adams is knowledgable and experienced in other areas of the law as well. For example, the firm offers a wide range of services in labor relations, civil rights, and employment law, governmental law, real estate development, and construction litigation.

Wade Perry and Watson Smith, listed as health care lawyers in Best Lawyers in America©, *inspect sophisticated diagnostic equipment at an area health care facility.*

Community Involvement

The attorneys at Johnstone Adams have enough time to serve their valued clients and to give back to the community. Johnstone Adams lawyers regularly volunteer as speakers for Continuing Legal Education Programs. Also, over the years Johnstone Adams lawyers have served as board members of numerous special community organizations and as president of a great many, including YWCA, Mobile Mental Health, Symphony Concerts of Mobile, the Opera Board, Mobile Area Council of Boy Scouts, the Family Counseling Center, Mobile Pre-School for the Sensory Impaired, Volunteer Mobile, WHIL Public Radio, and Boys' and Girls' Clubs of Mobile.

gates for energy lending institutions, title companies, and oil and gas operators, both major and independent.

The firm provides services in all areas of oil and gas regulation, guiding clients in real property acquisitions for refineries, helping clients to obtain various required permits, advising clients on the rules and regulations governing the industry, and representing clients in every aspect of oil and gas financing.

Health Care Law

Johnstone Adams has a thriving health care practice representing a myriad of health care providers in south Alabama and along the Gulf Coast. Johnstone Adams' clients include health care systems, general acute care hospitals, rehabilitation hospitals, professional corporations, and other health care providers as well as health maintenance organizations and preferred provider organizations.

Johnstone Adams advises health care providers on matters such as physician recruitment, physician contracting, medical staff credentialing, disciplinary hearings and bylaws, managed care contracting, certificate of need and health department laws and regulations, medical records issues, malpractice defense, private inurement and other tax issues, and a wide variety of other areas.

Other Practice Areas

General civil litigation, including insurance contract disputes and the torts of fraud and bad faith, has increased recently in Alabama. Johnstone Adams represents more than half of America's largest accident, health, and life insurance companies. Success breeds success, and Johnstone Adams attorneys consistently receive high marks from judges, clients, and other attorneys.

Indeed, Johnstone Adams offers the same tradition of excellence to its clients as it does to the community. Since 1897, Johnstone Adams has remained committed to the best possible legal service for our clients—in all matters—in any given practice area. ⚜

No representation is made that the quality of the legal services to be performed is greater than the quality of the legal services performed by other lawyers.

Mike Allen, an associate editor of American Maritime Cases©, *and Tom Rue, member, Maritime Law Association board of directors, are pictured in a familiar environment.*

LEWIS COMMUNICATIONS, INC.

Results are what Lewis Communications produces for its clients. Pictured are Larry D. Norris, president, Lewis Advertising/Birmingham, Inc.; John H. Lewis Jr., president and chairman of the board, Lewis Communications, Inc.; and Emil T. Graf III, president, Lewis Advertising/Mobile, Inc.

J. H. Lewis Advertising, Inc. was founded in 1951 by Jack H. Lewis. Mr. Lewis would no doubt be both surprised and excited with the metamorphosis his advertising agency has gone through since then.

Lewis Advertising, the small, local ad agency of the fifties is today Lewis Communications, Inc., a full-service, regional marketing communications firm with advertising offices in Mobile, Birmingham, and Nashville, as well as public relations and market research divisions based in Mobile which service all three offices. Clients represent a variety of products and services from all over the Southeast.

John H. Lewis Jr., CEO and president of Lewis Communications, smiles as he recalls his unexpected entrance into his father's business. "I graduated from college with a degree in Business Administration and planned to go into banking after the Army. The night before I was to leave for duty, Dad suggested that I try it with him when I returned. That was the first time he had ever suggested that I consider entering the family business. I cautiously agreed. That was in 1966, and I'm still here."

Mr. Lewis continues, "Our purpose at Lewis is to hire a talented staff whose mission is to produce an effective marketing communications product which assures our clients that their goals and objectives will be met and that they will enjoy the highest possible return on their marketing investment."

Lewis Communications and its talented staff's mission is to produce an effective marketing communications product which assures that clients will enjoy the highest possible return on their marketing investment.

To carry out this goal, Lewis Communications has developed a Benefits Testing Program which pinpoints the primary benefit the client's product or service offers to the marketplace—information that is crucial in the production of a successful advertising campaign.

Ironically, the ad is the last item that Lewis supplies its client. Larry Norris, president and CEO of Lewis Advertising/Birmingham, explains, "The 'creative' [ad] is the last thing we do at Lewis. This sets us apart from other creative shops. We don't work from a standard formula. It's hard to recognize a Lewis advertising product simply from its 'look.' We develop a personal strategy and plan for each client before developing their creative. That's what keeps Lewis Advertising's work unique and our business fun."

Results are what Lewis produces for its clients. These results are the outcome of extensive research into the client and his product or service. The knowledge gained from this intensive study enables Lewis to create an effective advertising concept.

Emil Graf, president and CEO of Lewis Advertising/Mobile, adds, "Our business is to grow business . . . and the variety of creativity offered by our firm is what keeps our work alive and growing."

Lewis Communications is a member of the American Association of Advertising Agencies and was one of only 700 agencies out of 10,000 to qualify for membership in this association. AAAA membership elevates Lewis Communications into an elite number of agencies responsible for creating, preparing, and placing more than 75 percent of all advertising produced in the United States.

Lewis is also a member of the International Federation of Advertising Agencies—an international network of non-competitive agencies providing information and help to member agencies and their clients around the world. IFAA member agencies collectively place over a billion dollars of advertising worldwide.

Many advertising messages reach their market. Lewis Communications realizes that the message has to go beyond reaching. It has to be heard. The goal at Lewis is to make its clients part of the elite minority whose advertising messages are remembered, rather than part of the majority forgotten. ⚜

LYONS, PIPES & COOK, P.C.

Founded in 1899 in Mobile, Alabama, today Lyons, Pipes & Cook is one of the leading law firms in the Gulf Coast market, serving clients with local, regional, national, and international interests. No matter how simple or complex the issue, the attorneys at Lyons, Pipes & Cook are guided by the principles of experience, judgment, service, value, and concern.

Experience includes representing most insurance carriers with operations in the Southeast, including successful litigation of the largest accidental death case in the state and assisting most of the nationally and locally operated oil and gas firms with exploration and production activities in the southeastern United States, including rapid resolution of local, state, and federal environmental issues.

The firm provides judgment that is built on both knowledge and experience, combined with the skill and courage to furnish objective counseling. Through sharing its knowledge and experience, Lyons, Pipes & Cook has enabled clients to structure the legal and financial framework for several thousand corporations and partnerships, including what has become both the largest and fastest growing steamship agency in the United States and to control the combined expenses of litigation and settlement in insurance and other defense matters by applying the ability to anticipate results.

The Lyons, Pipes & Cook attorneys and staff are supported with the resources, training, and systems to deliver on the firm's service promise ranging from state-of-the-art communications and information processing equipment to cost-control and billing management systems, an extensive legal library, and on-line legal database systems that insure current information.

Value is delivered by taking the initiative to analyze issues, frame strategies, find opportunities, and devise cost-cutting solutions while never losing sight of being a staunch advocate for a client. Focus on this principle has benefited numerous clients, including a major oil and gas producer who was able to avoid many costly regulatory delays during off-shore drilling and a manufacturer that saved $100,000 with a cost-cutting strategy for a real estate exchange.

Lyons, Pipes & Cook seeks out attorneys to whom concern comes naturally and then nurtures and rewards this talent. Focus on this principle is illustrated by the firm's involvement in community activities ranging from service as general counsel to the Mobile Area Chamber of Commerce and the Mobile Chamber Foundation and Executive Committee of the Alabama Wildlife Foundation, to participation in local, state, and national professional organizations, including President of the Mobile Bar Association, Chairman of the State of Alabama Disciplinary Commission, member of the Alabama State Bar Board of Examiners, and Chairman of the Admiralty and Maritime Law Committee of the Mobile Bar Association, and several other voluntary posts.

Through their focus on these principles, the firm of Lyons, Pipes & Cook delivers the added value to corporations, individuals, government, and private organizations that fuels the growth of their practice. ⚜

No representation is made that the quality of the legal services to be performed is greater than the quality of legal services performed by other lawyers.

Lyons, Pipes & Cook's offices are located at 2 North Royal Street in the downtown business district.

GOTTLIEB, BARNETT, & BRIDGES ENGINEERING CONSULTANTS

GBB specializes in port facility's development, such as the high-speed grain shipping facility shown here at the Alabama State Docks.

This company, originally founded in 1954 under the name of Ewin, Campbell, & Gottlieb, is owned and managed by Bob Barnett, Paul Bridges, and Stan Gottlieb. These engineers, along with their staff of mechanical, structural, and civil engineers, offer over 110 years of engineering experience.

GBB specializes in industrial and marine construction and services many ports in the Caribbean and along the East and Gulf Coasts of America. Much of the work designed by GBB for these clients is manufactured locally by Mobile firms.

The Gottlieb, Barnett, & Bridges of today consists of a staff of 16, after beginning operations in 1954 with a three-man team. The company services clients all over the world including port authorities, transportation companies, and equipment and industrial manufacturers.

Although the business is specialized, its projects run the gamut of variety—from the design and supervision of construction of the grain shipping facility at the Alabama State Docks to assisting in obtaining a huge traveling gantry crane from a project in the Netherlands, redesigning it for shipyard use, having it reconstructed, and placing it in operation at the Alabama Shipyard. The firm has also designed several maritime facilities for casino boats in inland locations along the river basins of the Midwest and South.

As an expert in the marine field, GBB has been particularly innovative in all aspects of design for the container industry since 1956.

Gottlieb, Barnett, & Bridges is known never to back down from a challenge. They accepted the opportunity to handle the innovative Diamondhead project, an idea conceived by Malcolm McLean—founder of containerization and Sea-Land Service, the country's largest container shipping line. The project's goal was to build finished condominium modules in a warehouse at Brookley Field before floating completed units by barge to various foundation sites. GBB's role was to design and construct all the special equipment and facilities necessary to bring this tedious task to fruition. These units can be seen today in Lake Forest, Sandestin, and Diamondhead resort, located between Bay Saint Louis and New Orleans.

Sea-Land Service, Inc. has been a client of Gottlieb, Barnett, & Bridges since containerization began in Mobile in 1956. GBB provides Sea-Land with both consulting and design services for the company's worldwide terminal facilities. GBB is responsible for the design and modification of Sea-Land's shipboard and dockside container handling equipment and the design of its container stowage and securing systems for its vessels.

GBB's experience in producing feasibility studies and primary designs, as well as final designs, material specifications, and supervision of facility construction, has secured jobs for the company that are not necessarily marine-related. For example, the firm has designed multi-million dollar plant expansions for Mobile-based chemical plants and structural designs for additions to a major Mobile hospital, as well as new schools, churches, and office buildings.

Projects have been studied, designed, modified, inspected, and erected for such clients as Sea-Land Service, Inc., the Ports of Mobile, Pensacola, Gulfport, Wilmington, New Orleans, Charleston, Houston, Port Everglades, Long Beach, Jamaica, and Trinidad, the United States Navy, NASA, Bender Shipbuilding, Atlantic Marine, and Alabama Shipyard, including the former Alabama Dry Docks & Shipbuilding Company. These projects include shipboard cranes, Goliath cranes, gantry cranes, derricks, transporters, container cranes, spreaders, polaris missile handling cranes, wharves, warehouses, and office buildings. Clients such as Kerr-McGee, Hess Oil, Texaco, Scott Paper Company, and Degussa Corporation appreciate GBB's skill in relating structural design to the entire facility.

Work done by this relatively small company has taken its engineers to over 35 foreign countries and 26 different states and territories of the United States. One of the advantages of a small company is that the owners actually do much of the engineering work themselves. The future of Gottlieb, Barnett, & Bridges foresees a slow, steady growth in the size of the company, and the company's outlook is bright. The number of projects in and around the Mobile area is increasing at an exciting pace, and GBB will play a prominent role in the growth of this area. ⚜

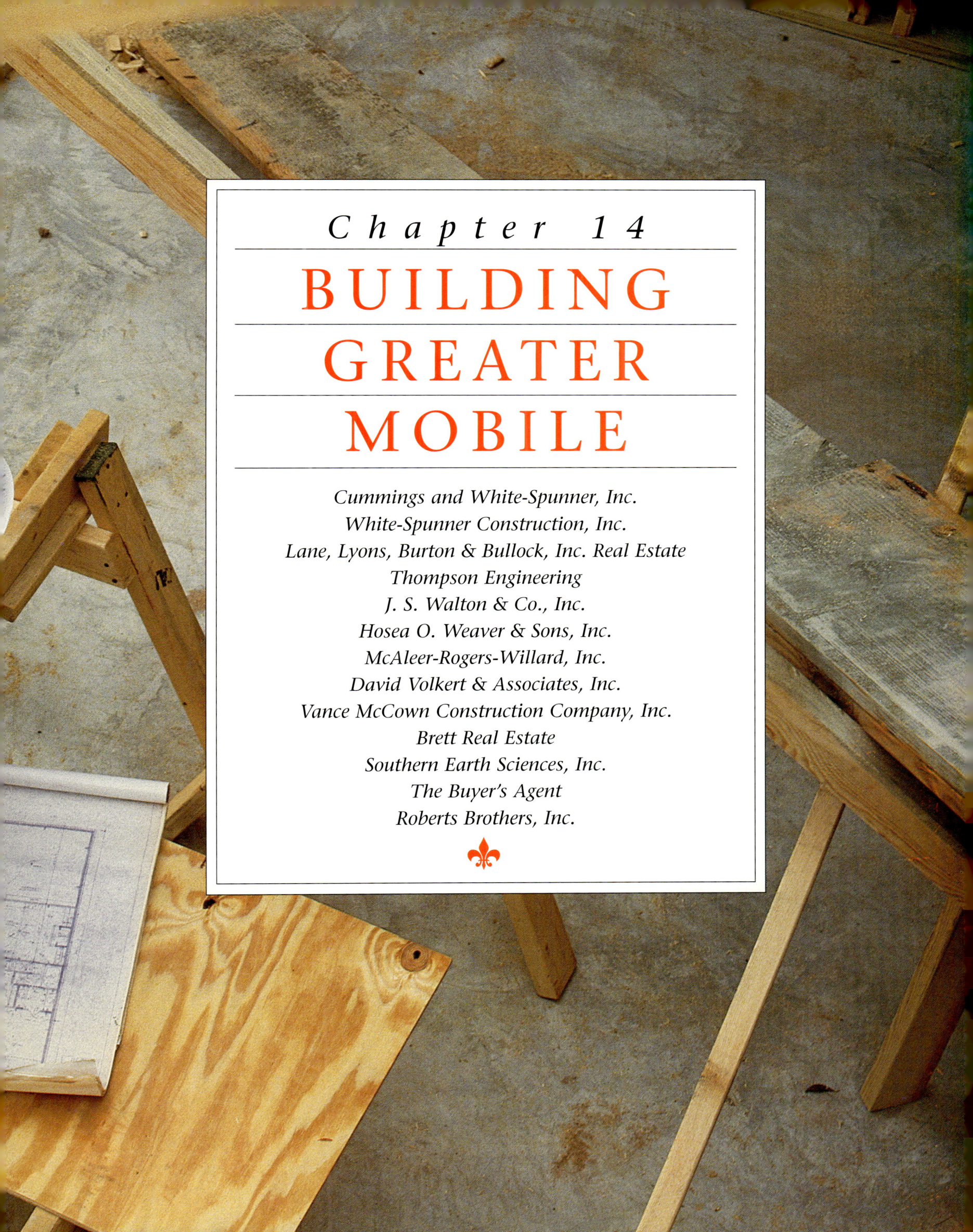

Chapter 14
BUILDING GREATER MOBILE

Cummings and White-Spunner, Inc.
White-Spunner Construction, Inc.
Lane, Lyons, Burton & Bullock, Inc. Real Estate
Thompson Engineering
J. S. Walton & Co., Inc.
Hosea O. Weaver & Sons, Inc.
McAleer-Rogers-Willard, Inc.
David Volkert & Associates, Inc.
Vance McCown Construction Company, Inc.
Brett Real Estate
Southern Earth Sciences, Inc.
The Buyer's Agent
Roberts Brothers, Inc.

CUMMINGS AND WHITE-SPUNNER, INC.

In 1954 Marl M. Cummings Jr. and Blacksher White-Spunner formed the original real estate firm of Cummings and White-Spunner. The partnership, which was incorporated in 1956, continued successful operations until the latter part of 1977. At that time, the corporation's principals divided the company, but continued to operate their separate commercial and residential real estate development and brokerage businesses.

Then, in April of 1990, a second generation of the two families, Marl M. Cummings III and Jay White-Spunner, who had been operating their fathers' firms, united in a merger, forming Cummings and White-Spunner, successor to the original real estate operation.

The second version has been the same as the first. The merger, with White-Spunner serving as company president and Cummings as senior vice president, has enjoyed its success because of what each principal brings to the firm. White-Spunner says, "I have more experience in development, and Marl has a great expertise in management."

Both the original company and the new one have been leaders in the development of commercial and residential real estate. For almost 40 years, the firms and their partners have been among Alabama's leading developers of land, regional and neighborhood shopping centers, office buildings, apartment complexes, single-family subdivisions, warehouses, and numerous mixed-use properties.

The numbers speak for themselves. The new Cummings and White-Spunner is currently responsible for the leasing and managing of 29 shopping centers, 6 office buildings, and 46 other properties, for a total of 2.2 million square feet. The firm's annual rental collections approach $15 million, and the annual sales volume has averaged $5 million over a five-year period. On a square footage basis, Cummings and White-Spunner is involved with approximately 70 percent of the retail space in the Mobile metropolitan area.

The company's long list for whom it has constructed stores or office buildings includes such industry leaders as Delchamps Food Stores, Gayfers, Morrison's, First Alabama Bank, Harco Drugs, Winn-Dixie Stores, and a host of others.

In 1993 the firm built two K-Marts in west Mobile, each encompassing 114,000 square feet, while the following year they constructed a Delchamps Food Store, which covers 58,000 square feet.

Cummings and White-Spunner has been a leading corporate citizen in its home community of Mobile. A great example is the firm's pro bono involvement with the Alabama School of Mathematics and Science, for which they were widely recognized. Additionally, for beautification efforts beyond the norm, Keep Mobile Beautiful has presented the company with its "Mayor's Award" for landscaping efforts at Ambassador Plaza. And the community recognition list goes on.

Cummings and White-Spunner has built its reputation brick by brick, building by building. From one generation to the next, excellence, expertise, and a heritage of community pride well position the company for the 90s and into the next century. ⚜

Cummings and White-Spunner has built its reputation brick by brick, building by building, guided under the leadership of (left to right) Jay White-Spunner and Marl Cummings.

WHITE-SPUNNER CONSTRUCTION, INC.

White-Spunner Construction, Inc. was founded in 1979 by John White-Spunner as a commercial contractor in the Mobile area. Since that time, with the help of dedicated company employees, White-Spunner Construction has become widely recognized for its ability to produce quality projects in a safe and timely manner.

In addition to Alabama, the company is licensed and performs work in over 20 states. This wide area of exposure allows for very competitive pricing in areas in which the company has extensive experience in commercial, industrial, and multi-family construction.

While producing both bid and negotiated projects, the company has maintained continuing contracts with highly respected clients such as Coca Cola Bottling Co., Home Depot USA, Delchamps, Publix Super Markets, Winn-Dixie, Exxon, Morrison's, South Central Bell, K-Mart, K.F.C., General Mills, Pep Boys, QMS, Charter Oak Outlet Malls, and various multi-family developments.

White-Spunner Construction, Inc. invests in ongoing education for all its employees and utilizes the latest in computer technology for estimating, accounting, and site designs. With over 5 million square feet of completed projects, the company is set to grow well into the future.

The company believes in community activity and supports numerous civic groups such as the YMCA, Mobile County Public Schools, various private schools, youth sports, Volunteers of America, American Cancer Society, local hospitals, and several wildlife organizations.

As an active member of the Mobile Area Chamber of Commerce, Associated Builders and Contractors, International Council of Shopping Centers, and Home Builders Association, the company remains highly involved while constantly improving in all aspects of construction.

All company jobs are contracted and built according to a schedule which is prepared by the project manager. He communicates with the owners, subcontractors, and suppliers and designs a schedule to satisfy everyone involved. This written schedule insures that everyone is conscious at all times of the progress-stage of the job. Such arrangements allow an overall understanding of the construction process and organization on a particular project.

All costs are kept current through the use of the company's computer system. At the time the project begins, the company's estimated costs are entered into the computer. As the job progresses, the actual day-to-day costs are entered and compared to the estimated costs. This process aids in keeping job costs under control.

Accident prevention is a primary goal of everyone at White-Spunner Construction. The company's safety program includes safety meetings and safety inspections which have led to the consistent completion of many accident-free projects.

Providing a drug-free job site is of utmost importance to the company, and all employees are required to take pre-employment drug screening and random drug tests.

White-Spunner inspires dedication and loyalty in its employees. Since the company's inception, there has been very little personnel turnover. The company is proud of its employees' long-term experience and their continuing participation in company profits.

Keeping the same dedicated employees, White-Spunner Construction, Inc. is able to consistently meet or exceed their clients' expectations. ⚜

Built in 1994, the 180,000 square foot Delchamps, K-Mart Shopping Center is one of over 50 shopping centers built by White-Spunner Construction, Inc.

White-Spunner Construction has become widely recognized for its ability to produce quality projects in a safe and timely manner such as the new Lenox Gates Apartments, with 228 luxury apartments.

LANE, LYONS, BURTON & BULLOCK, INC. REAL ESTATE

In medieval times churches displayed one red door which invited visitors to enter into a sanctuary of serenity, tranquillity, and peace of mind.

Lane, Lyons, Burton & Bullock, Inc. Real Estate has borrowed from this medieval tradition. A red front door invites clients to enter and enjoy the peace of mind that all their real estate needs will be met, both residential and commercial. They are also introduced to red-carpet treatment from owners Shirley Lane, Lucy Lyons, Beverly Burton, and Carolyn Bullock.

Lane, Lyons, Burton & Bullock, Inc. Real Estate was established in 1986, confirming that where there's a will and four determined women, there's success. The company is proud of its reputation of honesty, integrity, and fine homes.

The conception and birth of this company creates quite a scenario: Four women decide to form a real estate company. They all have experience and salesmanship; but none has a clue about running a business.

Lucy Lyons laughs as she remembers the day they were incorporated. "We found ourselves sitting on a curb beside a pay phone—incorporated with no place to go!" She adds, "At first we naively thought that 'we four' could handle all the selling and managing. Well, we now have 17 associates in the company!"

Today Lane, Lyons, Burton & Bullock has a secure address at 5418 Old Shell Road. The company's sales have increased each year with the average home sale placed at $150,000.

Some may wonder how four women can get along so well for eight years. "It works because we are all so different," explains Carolyn Bullock. "For example, I like all the legal stuff so I handle all the contracts, closings and such."

Lucy considers herself the token scrooge. "I'm careful with money so I decide where to spend it."

When situations get touchy, Shirley Lane's gentle way with words smooths any ruffled feathers. "I'm the peacemaker. I simply call upon my skills as a wife, mother, and school teacher."

Beverly Burton—a "Bev of all trades"—is described as imaginative, organized, mechanically inclined, and computer smart. Beverly admits, "I'll come up with this grandiose idea which stimulates the creative juices in my partners and inspires them to create an entirely different concept!"

These women consider their profession a privilege, not a pain. "This is so much fun. . . for work," says Lucy. "The amount of business that our company generates for its size is truly amazing. We have logged many twelve-hour days and seven-day weeks, which has landed all four of us in The Million Dollar Club."

Carolyn simply states, "Our work is definitely not drudgery." Speaking softly, Shirley adds, "The office is my home away from home. This profession is such a rewarding career, particularly for a woman."

Beverly interjects, "This is a people business, and we all love people. When a new family comes to Mobile, I practically move in with them until they are settled!"

When asked what the future holds for Lane, Lyons, Burton & Bullock, all four women respond, "We are looking forward to growing with the community and its needs . . . together!" ⚜

A red door invites clients to enjoy the peace of mind that all their real estate needs will be met with the help of owners Lucy Lyons, Beverly Burton, Carolyn Bullock, and Shirley Lane.

THOMPSON ENGINEERING

Since its inception in 1953, Thompson Engineering, a full-service applied science and engineering consulting firm has pursued an unrelenting commitment to excellence. The sustaining philosophy of the Thompson Engineering group is to provide their clients with the best service possible.

With main offices and laboratory in Mobile and field offices throughout the Southeast, the firm offers a range of engineering services unparalleled by any engineering organization, within the geographic regions served.

Their staff of over 100 employees consists of engineers, scientists, technicians, and support personnel, offering expert services in the fields of geotechnical, marine, and environmental engineering, hydrogeology, water resources, laboratory sciences, materials engineering testing, and construction inspection/management services.

Thompson's professional staff possesses a wide-ranged knowledge of environmental regulations affecting the potential acquisition/remediation of local waterfront and industrial facilities. With the ability to provide in-house resources in an integrated team project management approach, they are able to draw from their complement of professionals and state-of-the-art field and laboratory equipment to respond to the specialized requirements involved with environmental, geotechnical, and construction projects.

Directly because of Thompson's multi-disciplined corporate divisions, the firm is able to provide clients with cost-effective engineering solutions through the teaming of resources in geotechnical engineering, earth science, water resource/dredging, materials engineering/construction, environmental engineering/sciences, and forensic engineering. In appreciation for a job well done, Thompson Engineering received the United States Navy's Design Excellence Award for geotechnical services performed at Naval Station Mobile.

In an era of increasing concerns over environmental issues, Thompson's Environmental Services Division offers a multi-disciplinary, scientific expertise and a practical working knowledge of complex environmental regulatory processes.

Thompson's Hydrogeological Services Department is capable, through laboratory analyses and computer modeling, to develop practical solutions to problems related to contaminants released into the earth's soils and groundwater.

The company's Water Resources Division offers regulatory compliance and project planning services, as well as effective design solutions to construction challenges along coastal regions and inland river systems. Their staff excels in innovative designs and "Fast Track" project management under the most demanding conditions.

Thompson's Laboratory Division provides expert evaluation and testing of collected materials and data, enabling them to perform virtually any test associated within either the geotechnical or construction areas.

The company's Construction Materials Engineering and Testing Department serves commercial, industrial, and governmental areas. The Africatown-Cochrane Bridge across the Mobile River required a special concrete which was designed by Thompson.

One of the largest construction projects in the history of Mobile's downtown area, Mobile's $55 million Government Plaza, required vibration and dewatering studies to monitor the structural integrity of adjacent historic buildings. Thompson was able to manage and control this aspect of the project within this critical downtown area. Furthermore, Thompson's geotechnical engineers prepared a value engineered alternate for the difficult foundation system at the Complex, saving more than $1.5 million on the base bid approach.

The company also provided quality assurance services for the complex roof system at the newly constructed Mobile Convention Center.

All of Thompson's operations are equipped to maintain efficient communications with on-site or home office engineering systems and personnel required to provide results and evaluations needed for the project at hand.

Thompson Engineering has a great stake in the Mobile area. As a company, they are involved in many civic organizations such as the United Way, Junior Miss, Senior Bowl, and are supporters, through scholarships and gifts, of Spring Hill College, the University of Mobile, and the University of South Alabama.

They particularly take pride in their sponsorship of a Boy Scout Explorer Post, in which boys and girls ages 15 and older who are interested in mathematics and engineering are introduced to a well-rounded view as to just what exactly an engineer does.

Thompson Engineering has earned the respect of their community and the confidence of their many clients, and justly so. Through their wide array of services, they have demonstrated technical and administrative ability to provide immediate attention to a full spectrum of engineering tasks. ⚜

Thompson Engineering designed the special concrete material mixes needed to construct the Africatown-Cochrane Bridge across the Mobile River.

Thompson conducted vibration, dewatering and monitoring studies and value engineered a cost savings foundation design to accommodate the structural integrity of adjacent historic buildings while Mobile's $55 million Government Complex was under construction.

J. S. WALTON & CO., INC.

J. S. Walton & Co., Inc. was founded in Brandenburg, Kentucky, by John S. Walton Sr. in 1919. One of the firm's first jobs was building sidewalks in Princeton, Kentucky. Walton operated in Brandenburg until 1927, when he moved his operation to Gardner, Florida. There, his company built four bridges, including the old bridge over the Yellow River on Florida State Route Number 87. He then moved to Mobile, where the business remains today. The company holds "Contractor's License Number 31," making it one of the longest operating contracting companies in the state.

In 1945 Norman J. Walton Sr. and John S. Walton Jr. joined their father's firm, which throughout the years, has continued to perform extensive construction work in highway, heavy, and industrial areas.

In 1970 the third Walton generation was introduced into the firm when current president, Norman J. Walton Jr., joined the company. Norman is a past president of the Alabama Road Builders' Association, the Mobile County Road Builders' Association and the Mobile Section of Alabama General Contractors. He serves as national director of the Associated General Contractors of America, Inc.

In 1988 William R. Walton came to the firm and is serving as the company's secretary/treasurer as well as president of the Mobile County Roadbuilders Association.

J. S. Walton & Co. has completed numerous heavy and industrial construction projects, state and local resurfacing and drainage projects, and plant site developments in Mobile and surrounding areas.

The company has also been instrumental in the development of the transportation network for Mobile and Baldwin Counties, recently completing the widening of University Boulevard in front of the University of South Alabama in Mobile.

The firm also completed the site development for Naval Station Mobile at the Navy Homeport, Range Line Road in South Mobile County, a runway addition to Mobile's Bates Field Airport, rehabilitation of Mobile's Water Street, and the construction of U.S. 98 in Fairhope.

A great part of the company's success is attributed to the dedication and skill of its employees, some of whom have been with the firm for over 30 years.

In 1991 J. S. Walton & Co. became a partner in Mobile Asphalt Company, which concentrates on base and asphalt paving projects. The company's employees operate from asphalt plants located in Saraland, Bay Minette, and Leroy, Alabama, with an area of operations encompassing eight southwest Alabama counties: Mobile, Marengo, Escambia, Monroe, Washington, Clark, Choctaw, and Baldwin.

Besides being widely involved in the business community, J. S. Walton & Co. is an active participant in Mobile's civic arena. It is a member of the Mobile Area Chamber of Commerce and supporter of Mobile United, the Mobile Arts Council, Mobile Area Boy Scouts of America, and the Senior Bowl. Norman Walton also serves on the South Alabama Regional Planning Commission.

J. S. Walton & Co., Inc., a name synonymous with quality, stability, and safety throughout the Mobile area, has been a part of Mobile's past growth, an active part of the present, with a dedicated eye cast toward the future, remaining ever sensitive to the special construction needs of its many clients along the Gulf Coast. ❦

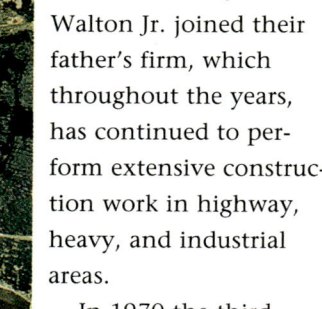

The site development for Naval Station Mobile shows the diversity in construction that J. S. Walton & Co., Inc. provides to the Mobile community.

J. S. Walton & Co., Inc. is active in the growth of downtown Mobile with such projects as Water Street Rehabilitation.

HOSEA O. WEAVER & SONS, INC.

Hosea O. Weaver started his company, now Hosea O. Weaver & Sons, in 1952. He climbed aboard an old bulldozer, settled into its rickety and unyielding seat, and began pushing dirt, building fish ponds, and clearing land for his customers.

Hosea's business grew and prospered because, "I paid attention to all the mistakes I saw my competitors making and then tried to eliminate them from my business. I made sure to provide my customers with quality service and quality products. That's how you get repeat business."

As the company grew, so did its services. Today Hosea Weaver & Sons is a full-service highway and industrial sitework contractor capable of performing a variety of services, including excavating, grading, concrete, installation of storm sewer, water, sanitary sewer, hot mix asphalt manufacturing, and asphalt laydown.

Hosea Weaver & Sons is respected for its dedication to detail. When preparing a project for completion, Weaver & Sons accepts responsibility for completing all phases of the project including monitoring subcontractors work with quality control, quality assurance, and even the guarantee that the grass will be thick, green, and growing.

Paul and Calvin Weaver have worked for their father for as long as each can remember. Mr. Weaver began to relinquish control of his company to his sons in 1973 and in 1985, Paul and Calvin Weaver completed their purchase of the company.

Weaver & Sons purchased its first hot mix asphalt plant on Schillingers Road in 1983. Three more plants followed and are located in Robertsdale, Theodore, and "all over the place," which describes Weaver's portable plant. The portable plant reduces customer construction costs by relocating crushing and asphalt plant operations directly to the work site.

Hosea Weaver & Sons' hot mix asphalt plant located in southern Mobile County is equipped with the materials and testing equipment necessary to maintain the high standards of the company.

Each of the four plants is equipped with the materials and testing equipment necessary to maintain the high standards of quality established by the company. The recycling of old roadway asphalt, a process conducted at all the plants, eliminates the necessity of disposing of the used asphalt and reduces the cost.

Hosea Weaver & Sons employs a local labor force of over 175, and most of Weaver's personnel have been with the company for over 15 years. Paul Weaver is proud to be able to say that "the majority of the money we spend is recycled back into the local economy which helps fuel our community's growth and development."

Employees are offered on-the-job training to help them pass the stringent state highway certification examinations which are required in order to receive the qualified technician rating needed on the job site.

Each crew represents a delicate balance between brawn and skilled technology. Laborers do the physical work, a qualified supervisor directs, and certified lab personnel test materials to make sure that they will produce the desired end product.

Hosea Weaver & Sons was the first in the area to invest in a roadway milling machine, which removes old asphalt, commonly known as "Rap."

The job that positioned Hosea Weaver & Sons at the top of their profession in the region was the $30 million renovation of Interstate 10 from the George Wallace Tunnel to Interstate 65 in 1990. Weaver's commitment was $12 million. The project consisted of additional lanes inside and out, removing the old concrete roadway, and replacing it with new asphalt. This project was different in that the old concrete roadway was chopped, crushed, sized, and recycled back into the new asphalt mix making Hosea Weaver & Sons the first area contractor to recycle concrete into asphalt.

Paul Weaver has two special recipes. One mixes limestone, granite, gravel, sand, and liquid asphalt to create asphalt. The other blends vision, determination, skill, honesty, and quality to produce success. ⚜

Hosea Weaver & Sons is respected for its dedication to detail. (left to right) Hosea O. Weaver, Paul Weaver, and Calvin Weaver accept the responsibility for completing all phases of the project.

McALEER-ROGERS-WILLARD, INC.

Guy McAleer, Mike Rogers, and Steve Willard, owners of McAleer-Rogers-Willard, Inc. enjoy an impressive commercial construction business. The recently completed AmSouth Bank is added to a long list of satisfied clients. Photo by Ashley Inge.

McAleer-Rogers-Willard, Inc. was formed in 1992 as a general contracting firm. The company experienced immediate success due not only to the quality and professionalism of its work, but also to the compatibility of the talents represented by its owners, Guy McAleer, Mike Rogers, and Steve Willard.

Guy McAleer is able to offer the company his experience in real estate which enables him to assist clients in locating a construction site, as well as informing that client what preliminaries are necessary to prepare a site for construction. Mike Rogers and Steve Willard have degrees in building construction. Mike Rogers specializes in commercial and industrial construction, while Steve Willard's expertise is in retail and restaurant construction.

Today, McAleer-Rogers-Willard, Inc. is highly respected in the construction industry and enjoys an impressive commercial construction business both in Mobile and in surrounding states. McAleer-Rogers-Willard, Inc. has supervised and constructed a variety of projects running the gamut from medical clinics to a vault manufacturing plant to schools, banks, churches, offices, and numerous renovations.

The U.S. Army Corp of Engineers and the United States Probation Office are located in downtown Mobile at 201 Saint Michael Street—a McAleer-Rogers-Willard, Inc. building. Photo by Ashley Inge.

The company's entrance into the restaurant business has proven challenging, but profitable. Working for Pizza Hut, Checkers, Hardee's, and Krystal restaurants is fast and technically demanding. It is crucial for the contractor to be familiar with all the specialized aspects of this business. These jobs have specific timetables, which can be as tight as 30 days from contract to opening day. The superintendents employed by McAleer-Rogers-Willard, Inc. who oversee each of these jobs are seasoned supervisors with an average of 25 years of construction experience.

McAleer-Rogers-Willard, Inc. is a quality-oriented company which strives for success by simply pleasing its clients. All three owners agree: "We want to make our clients happy. We may not always be the lowest price, but we are always the most dependable."

Mike Rogers adds: "The contract between McAleer-Rogers-Willard, Inc. and its clients represents a business relationship that guarantees quality craftsmanship and no surprises. We have established ourselves as honest people who do what is right. We do not want the reputation as a company who makes money on unexpected changes not listed on the bid sheet."

Guy, Mike, and Steve enjoy what they do and work well together. Their compatibility and mutual respect have resulted in a steady growth in sales and tremendous success for the company. Mike Rogers admits, however, that their goal is to be a successful mid-size contractor, so that they will be able to continue to pay personal attention to detail while maintaining their high quality of craftsmanship.

Guy, Mike, and Steve realize that without their employees their company would never have gotten off its pilings. "Our employees are our most important asset, and we show our appreciation for their talent and loyalty by providing health insurance, profit sharing, and financial support for work-related education."

Safety is another important issue at McAleer-Rogers-Willard, Inc. All three owners agree: "We lose respect for those who refuse to follow safety rules. The company, therefore, sees to it that safety rules are top priority at all times!"

Mike concludes by emphasizing: "McAleer-Rogers-Willard, Inc. has a reputation for being honest people who do what's right. It's usually apparent what is the right thing to do, which many times is not the most profitable choice. One of our major concerns is maintaining our reputation of being a quality and honest contractor. After all, we plan on being around for a long time."

DAVID VOLKERT & ASSOCIATES, INC.

Mobile is the home base for a world-class engineering and architectural firm—David Volkert & Associates, Inc. Ranking in the top one percent of the more than 28,000 engineering firms in the United States, Volkert brings 70 years of experience to the design of projects for its clients.

Founded in 1925 in New Orleans, the firm was acquired by David G. Volkert, P.E., in 1954 and renamed David Volkert & Associates in 1963. Today the employee-owned organization is governed by a board of directors with Mr. Volkert serving as chairman of the board and T. Keith King, P.E., as president and chief executive officer.

Volkert's success story is one of innovative planning and design, stable growth, and client satisfaction. Day by day, the firm continues to compile an impressive record in the design of bridges, highways, port improvements, material-handling facilities, airports, utilities, stadiums, subways, site developments, environmental services, and buildings for educational, commercial, industrial, and military use.

The firm's 10 offices, located throughout the Southeast and the Eastern Seaboard, employ more than 350 professionals, including experienced engineers, architects, planners, and environmental specialists supported by a full-service team of surveyors, drafters, construction inspectors, financial analysts, computer specialists, CADD operators, specification writers, and cost estimators.

Volkert Environmental Group, Inc., a subsidiary of David Volkert & Associates, Inc., has a staff of certified professionals and support personnel cross-trained in various environmental disciplines. They possess the experience and technical expertise required to complete environmental projects within the guidelines set by federal, state, and local regulatory agencies.

David Volkert & Associates also offers a full range of architectural design services. The award-winning design team's expertise includes educational facilities, transportation terminals, office and commercial buildings, parking garages, and medical facilities.

One of the most important factors in Volkert's success is the firm's ability to manage the total planning, design, and construction process for projects of any size or scope and to deliver the projects on time, within a set budget. An example is the three-phase, 10-year project to design and construct the McDuffie Coal Terminal for the Alabama State Docks. McDuffie was inducted into the State of Alabama Engineering Hall of Fame in 1994.

Over the years such ability, coupled with superior performance, has earned Volkert many local, state, and national awards. The National Society for Professional Engineers named two Volkert projects as Outstanding Engineering Achievement in the United States—the Cochrane/Africatown USA Bridge over the Mobile River in 1992 and the Interstate 10 Twin Bridges over Mobile Bay in 1978. The Cochrane Bridge was chosen by the Federal Highway Administration in 1992 for Excellence in Highway Design, and the I-10 Bridges were inducted into the Alabama Engineering Hall of Fame in 1990.

Volkert's site development and utilities design for Naval Station Mobile was presented the Design Excellence Award from the United States Navy in 1991. The United States Department of Defense selected the Visitors Center at Arlington (Virginia) National Cemetery, a project directed by Volkert, to receive the department's 1990 Design Award.

Commenting on Volkert's corporate philosophy, CEO King says: "As one of the earlier leaders and advocates of total quality management and team building, we have renewed our focus on the customers we serve. They are the reason we exist, and we will continue to cultivate meaningful relationships between our associates and our customers."

Volkert has a strong commitment to active community involvement. In addition to sponsoring an Engineering Explorer Post and adopting Forest Hill Elementary School as a Partner in Education, Volkert participates in activities to support education, civic and professional organizations, the Chamber of Commerce, and the United Way. Employees are encouraged to volunteer for the firm's activities and other community-service projects. ❧

Volkert's design team expertise includes educational facilities, transportation terminals, office and commercial buildings, parking garages, and medical facilities such as the University of South Alabama Health Services Building in Mobile.

The National Society for Professional Engineers named the Cochrane/Africatown USA Bridge over the Mobile River as Outstanding Engineering Achievement in the United States in 1992. The bridge was also chosen by the Federal Highway Administration for Excellence in Highway Design.

A Gulf Coast Treasure

VANCE McCOWN CONSTRUCTION COMPANY, INC.

Vance McCown Construction has completed numerous projects including multi-family, office, warehouse, retail, and institutional facilities.

Incorporated in June of 1983, Vance McCown Construction Company, Inc. (VMC) is licensed for general contracting and related work in Alabama, Florida, Mississippi, North Carolina, South Carolina, Louisiana, and Tennessee.

The Mobile-based firm has completed numerous projects, including multifamily, office, warehouse, retail, and institutional. T. Vance McCown, president, states, "We are a company that can give personal attention to each project and have the expertise to build large projects as well as small projects." During a 10-year period, VMC completed contracts for such companies as AmSouth Bank, World Omni Financial Center, CIBA-GEIGY, Southeast College of Technology, and Rex TV & Appliance.

VMC is committed to providing quality construction for its clients and, as a result, has several clients for whom they have constructed multiple projects, with one client in particular, Rex TV & Appliance retail stores. Having completed 55 successful Rex projects over the past eight years,

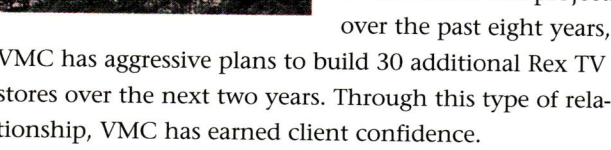

VMC is committed to providing quality construction for its clients.

VMC has aggressive plans to build 30 additional Rex TV stores over the next two years. Through this type of relationship, VMC has earned client confidence.

Always looking for a solution to a client's needs, including site acquisition, selection of architects/engineers, and recommendations for construction types and methods, VMC is also experienced in developing the site, handling permit requirements, and offering design/build services.

McCown believes that the owners of his projects realize an opportunity for innovation through open communication and trust, especially in the development of value engineering changes and constructability improvements. Often the owner, architect/engineer, and contractor can become adversarial to one another on projects where the contractor is not an active team member of the decision-making process in providing interpretation of design intent and solutions to problems. A quality project has never been built in an adversarial condition.

VMC suggests that the contractor assist the owner with the preliminary engineering and design to create conceptual plans for the purpose of better defining the land use requirements, site-development costs, and construction costs. This information allows the owner the opportunity to complete the pro forma, financing, and other necessary negotiations for his project prior to obligating himself to full-service design and even the purchase of the property.

McCown realizes how important it is to respond quickly through this process. McCown explains, "Five years ago we made a commitment to develop a computer estimating program and database that would allow us to calculate site work and material quantities with accuracy and speed. The estimating program is integrated with the job cost accounting program and allows the owner to track his project's estimated cost as compared to actual cost from design to completion. The company offers single-source responsibility, serving as the owner's agent for the design and construction of the project. The owner will realize a lower risk of cost overruns and delays because of better time and cost control over the project."

To enhance the design capacity of the company, VMC is a dealer for Butler Manufacturing—the giant manufacturer of pre-engineered structures. Butler allows VMC to capitalize on the tremendous engineering staff and product line that is available through Butler Manufacturing.

A comprehensive safety program, hazardous materials policy, and drug policy are in place to provide a safe environment for all VMC employees. These programs will increase the skills of the workers and protect the interest of VMC's customers.

Vance McCown Construction Company, Inc. is known throughout the Mobile area as a concerned corporate citizen. Besides being an active member of the Mobile Area Chamber of Commerce, the firm is a member of Associated Builders and Contractors, South Alabama Chapter, of which Vance McCown is a past president.

McCown comments, "I am proud of the VMC staff and their talents. We look forward to a future in which we will implement those talents in even better ways than ever before." ⚜

BRETT REAL ESTATE

In 1970 Brett Real Estate opened its first sales office in Chickasaw, Alabama, and in 1972 Tillis and Gene Brett formed a partnership with Tommy Robinson. Presently, the firm of Brett Real Estate /Robinson Development Company, Inc. operates three offices, one each in Gulf Shores and Orange Beach, with headquarters located in Saraland.

This versatile firm specializes in real estate sales, home building, residential subdivision development, and property management, while the company's general contracting arm constructs such projects as churches, shopping strips, branch banks, and many and varied commercial buildings. Presently, Brett/Robinson has $70 million in construction projects working in Mobile and Baldwin Counties, primarily along the Gulf Coast.

Brett/Robinson has built their business by offering the best available products at reasonable prices while providing long-range service to their clients. Nothing travels faster than the word of a satisfied customer, and since the beginning, the firm has been able to count on a large volume of repeat business. Their "Family Tree" is the foundation of Brett/Robinson's business.

Brett/Robinson's family-oriented business has built a reputation for reliable rental management and personal service. Gulf Shore's Phoenix and Orange Beach's Island Winds East, beachfront resort condominiums, are managed by Brett/Robinson and represent their commitment to family atmosphere and convenience in vacation rentals.

Brett Real Estate/Robinson Development Company, Inc. specializes in real estate sales, home building, residential subdivision development, and property management, while the company's general contracting arm constructs such projects as churches, shopping strips, branch banks, and many and varied commercial buildings.

Whether building or enlarging a business, buying or selling a new or pre-owned home, or just getting away from it all in a condo overlooking the Gulf of Mexico, look to Brett/Robinson for that personal service. ⚜

Gulf Shore's Phoenix and Orange Beach's Island Winds East, beachfront resort condominiums, are managed by Brett/Robinson and represent their commitment to family atmosphere and convenience in vacation rentals.

SOUTHERN EARTH SCIENCES, INC.

Southern Earth Sciences, Inc. (SES) was established by Dr. James E. Laier, P.E. in 1976 to provide innovative solutions to difficult and unusual foundation engineering problems.

What began as a local geotechnical engineering and materials inspection company has grown into a regional, full-service, professional engineering, testing, and environmental services organization utilizing the area's best professionally trained people, including registered engineers, environmental scientists, and geologists. SES now operates throughout the southeastern United States.

Since its inception, the company's principal objective has been to provide the construction industry with complete geotechnical consulting and materials testing services in a timely manner for reasonable fees. Their success along these lines is evidenced by their long list of satisfied clients.

SES provides comprehensive professional services in the fields of geotechnical engineering and environmental services.

The company operates under the philosophy that engineering technical services should be directed by registered professional engineers who have technical experience in that specific area. Therefore, SES's professional staff of registered engineers, environmental scientists, and geologists ably provide this expert supervision for their well-trained technicians.

The company's geotechnical engineering professionals are accustomed to solving a wide range of difficult and unusual geotechnical problems on land and over water.

(Seated) Diana K. Laier, treasurer, (left to right) Dr. James E. Laier, Ph.D., P.E., president, and William H. Brenner, geologist, vice president, have established Southern Earth Sciences as a company known for providing services in a timely manner for reasonable fees.

Southern Earth Sciences, Inc. has a reputation for tradition, integrity, and pride.

Typically, these services are in one of the following categories: engineering and geological services, field drilling/site investigation services, laboratory testing services, and instrumentation, with construction services divided into laboratory and field operations. Laboratory testing of materials is performed in a modern facility which is equipped for testing concrete, soils, asphalt, and steel. Field testing and inspection are performed by a group of experienced field technicians able to monitor the quality of new construction.

The company is also able to provide a wide range of environmental services which fall into one of four categories: underground storage tanks (UST) services, site assessments and evaluations, landfills and solid waste management, and asbestos abatement services. In 1988 the analytical testing division of Southern Earth Sciences, Inc. became a separate corporation equipped with state-of-the-art analytical equipment, allowing SES to respond quickly and accurately to a client's environmental needs. When necessary, SES can provide courier service for clients who collect their own samples on ground water, wastewater, hazardous waste, sludge, air, soils, paint, wipes, and other matrices. Their Asbestos Laboratory is proficient at identifying asbestos fibers in bulk samples taken from suspect structures and is capable of managing air sampling programs during asbestos removal operations.

Southern Earth Sciences, Inc. was founded with excellence in service in mind. That tradition, as well as their reputation for integrity, continues to grow, inspiring confidence among their growing number of clients. ⚜

The Buyer's Agent of Mobile, Inc. was founded in January 1993 by Harriet H. Person, who remains company president of the first franchise in Alabama for the Memphis-based national franchise firm.

A relatively new concept in the real estate field, the firm exclusively represents the buyer in any transaction involving real estate. Although the company is "the new kid on the block," Person is not new to the real estate business. She brings to the company 22 years of experience as a buyer's representative in a commercial area of real estate. Person felt that the time was right for Mobile-area buyers to enjoy representation equal to that of the seller in real estate transactions.

All associates of The Buyer's Agent are licensed Realtors. Furthermore, the franchise requires additional training as buyer's agents.

Person says, "We represent people, not property. We were the first, and are the only, real estate franchise in the Mobile area to represent the buyer only. This concept is very much the coming thing."

The company does not list any real property; therefore, its agents are free to work in the best interest of the buyer. This concept is decidedly different from traditional real estate companies that list and sell real property. These companies are obligated to represent their "sellers" in any transaction where there is a listing.

Just as a conventional real estate firm signs a listing agreement with the real estate seller, thereby obligating them to act in the seller's best interest, The Buyer's Agent signs an agency agreement making it legally accountable to the buyer.

Since they represent no seller, The Buyer's Agent associates have no conflict of interest. There is no dual agency, no compromise in their advocacy of the buyer, leaving them free to negotiate prices with no repercussions. Because they owe no loyalty to the property's sellers, they are free to point out a property's weaknesses as well as its strengths.

One company slogan is, "If you are serious about buying a home—we are serious about saving you money." In addition to negotiating for the lowest price for the property, The Buyer's Agent also assists in securing the most competitive financing and homeowner's insurance.

Person says, "If we save a client $10,000 on the purchase of a home, our associate would earn only approximately $150 less commission. The client's goodwill and word-of-mouth advertising will be worth much more to us than $150."

The company's agents save the buyers time by pre-qualifying them financially and showing only the properties that fit the buyer's criteria.

THE BUYER'S AGENT

With the exception of property listings, The Buyer's Agent offers their clients a full-service real estate firm. The Mobile office is a member of both the Mobile County Board of Realtors and Baldwin County Association of Realtors, and subscribes to their Multiple-Listing Services (MLS). The associates are able to show and help buy homes listed in the MLS as well as "for sale by owner." Also, they often help buyers choose building lots and builders for custom-built homes. The company also has full relocation services. Besides residential and commercial purchases, the company represents tenants in office leases.

While most conventional real estate companies recognize the accomplishments of their sales agents by their total amount of gross sales, The Buyer's Agent recognizes its agents by the "total amount of money they have been able to save their buyer clients" through negotiation.

Although The Buyer's Agent of Mobile, Inc. is a young company, it already sponsors a youth softball team and participates in several scholarship fund-raising events. As the company expands, so will its involvement in Mobile's civic arena.

Whether shopping for a home or a business in the Mobile area, The Buyer's Agent provides an edge. The Buyer's Agent saves money, time, and effort. Its loyalty is solely to its client—the buyer. ⚜

Whether shopping for a home or a business in the Mobile area, The Buyer's Agent provides an edge. The Buyer's Agent saves money, time, and effort. Its loyalty is solely to its client—the buyer.

ROBERTS BROTHERS, INC.

Roberts Brothers, Inc., one of Mobile's finest comprehensive real estate companies, was founded in 1946 by David and John Roberts. Over the years, these two brothers built a solid reputation of integrity and honesty, coupled with an expertise in real estate matters. This reputation, as well as community involvement, has made the Roberts Brothers name one of "the most trusted in real estate."

Today, the company's tradition of excellence and professionalism continues under the direction of a second Roberts generation, John A. Roberts Jr., David D. Roberts Jr., and Ben Tom Roberts, all of whom serve as senior executive vice presidents.

"People You Know, A Name You Trust," one of the company's slogans, tells volumes. The people of Mobile and Baldwin counties have grown to know Roberts Brothers and trust it with all their real estate needs. The company, now recognized as one of the state's largest, offers not only residential and commercial sales, but also property management, insurance, mortgages, real estate counseling, real estate development, and relocation services.

Offices are located in both Mobile and Baldwin counties, and the Mobile offices are members of both Mobile and Baldwin County Boards of REALTORS® and MLS Systems. With more than 200 professional agents and staff and five conveniently located sales offices, Roberts Brothers consistently captures the largest share of the Mobile area's real estate market. The company's annual sales figures now total nearly $150 million, a long way from the $20,000 total sales of 1946.

Roberts Brothers remains the first choice of buyers and sellers in Mobile, evidenced by data taken from a 1993 study. By a wide margin, Roberts Brothers REALTORS® listed and sold more Mobile-area homes than any other firm. For more than 50 years, Roberts Brothers, Inc. has helped thousands of families moving to and from the Mobile Bay area. It is their objective to provide the finest services available in order to make the move an enjoyable and memorable experience.

Every detail involved in the transfer of real estate can be handled by Roberts Brothers while offering such specialties as their "Guaranteed Sales Plan," enabling buyers to "trade-in" their present home while purchasing another; their Estate Homes Division, offering an exclusive upscale approach to marketing homes priced in the upper 10 percent of the market; the Mobile Bay area's only locally owned and operated home warranty company, Homeguard Home Warranty; and our own "in-house" mortgage company, Mortgage Mobile.

There's hardly an honor in the real estate community that has not been accorded one of the Roberts'. Among the many professional memberships and honors are REALTOR® of the Year, President of the Mobile County Board of REALTORS®, President of the Alabama Association of REALTORS®, and even President of the National Association of REALTORS®.

Roberts Brothers owners, management, and employees are actively involved in the community, both individually and as a company. A few of their many interests are the United Way Campaign, YMCA, Boy Scouts of America, Better Business Bureau, American Red Cross, America's Junior Miss, First Night Mobile, Junior Achievement, Historical Development Committee, as well as local schools, churches, and colleges.

The company's progress over nearly a half century is not the result of professional skill and hard work alone, but is primarily from the confidence of its faithful clients and the reputation attained in the Mobile community by its dedicated employees. Whether it's real estate needs or civic duties, Roberts Brothers, Inc. is a name the Mobile community can count on. ✤

David D. Roberts Jr., John A. Roberts Jr., and Ben Tom Roberts represent the leadership for Roberts Brothers, Inc.

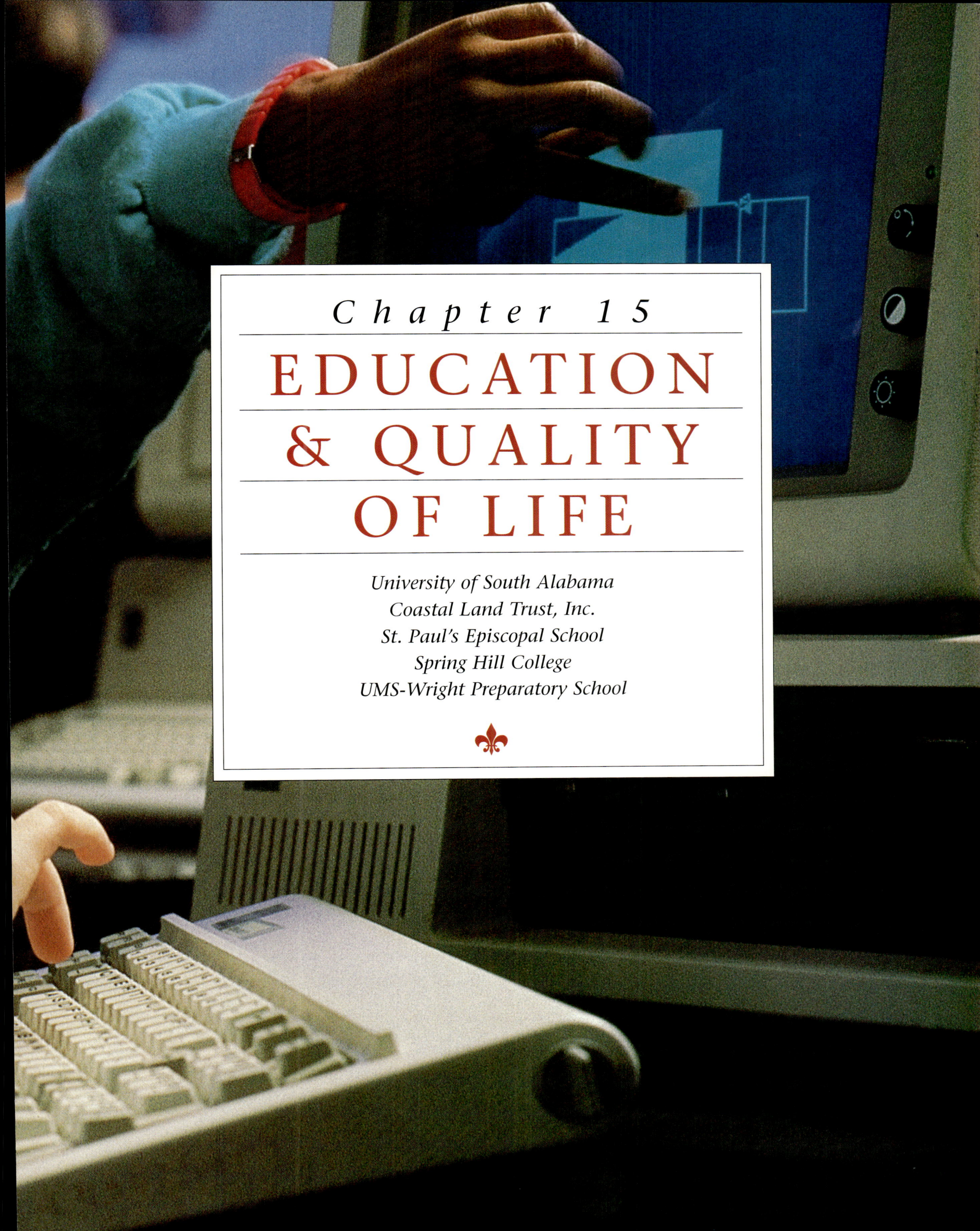

Chapter 15
EDUCATION & QUALITY OF LIFE

University of South Alabama
Coastal Land Trust, Inc.
St. Paul's Episcopal School
Spring Hill College
UMS-Wright Preparatory School

UNIVERSITY OF SOUTH ALABAMA

When it was announced in May 1963 that an act of the Alabama Legislature had chartered the University of South Alabama, there was great rejoicing in Mobile. Prior to that time, the area's only two schools of higher education were private. In order to attend a state-supported school, area students had to look elsewhere.

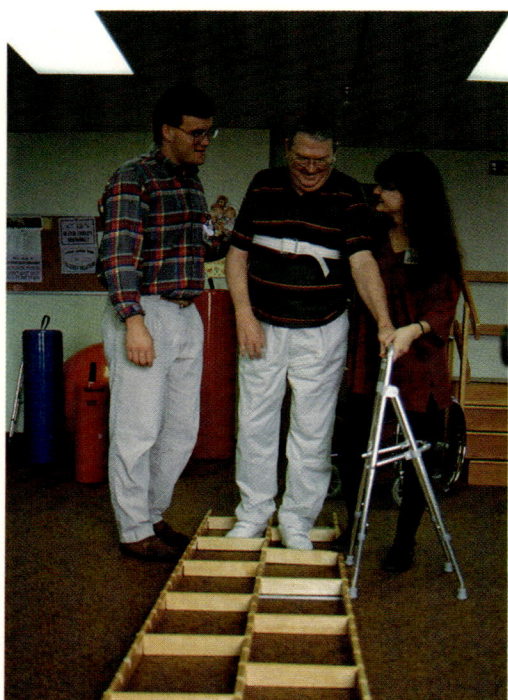

The University's occupational therapy programs train students to work with individuals having physical, emotional, mental, or developmental disabilities.

Since Mobile, Alabama's oldest city (founded 1702), was the birthplace of the state's education system, locating a university here seemed natural. In 1836 Alexander B. Meek, a pioneer Alabama educator, organized Barton Academy, a facility which serves today as the offices of the Mobile County Board of School Commissioners. In 1853-1854 the Alabama State Legislature drafted the state's first public school law, and today the Mobile County Public School System is the state's largest.

In October 1963, at the first meeting of the Board of Trustees, Dr. Frederick P. Whiddon was named president of the University of South Alabama, a post which he still holds.

Today the University hardly resembles its humble beginnings. The first classes began in June 1964 with only 276 students, and 88 baccalaureate degrees were conferred at the first commencement ceremonies in June 1967.

To say that the University has grown is an understatement. The diverse student body has become a multicultural community with students from 46 states and 79 foreign countries, reaching a total enrollment of over 12,000.

In a relatively short time, the University has progressed from a few classrooms in a downtown location to a beautifully landscaped 1,200-acre campus in west Mobile which includes the following colleges and schools: Allied Health Professions, Arts and Sciences, Business and Management Studies, Education, Engineering, Nursing, Computer and Information Sciences, Continuing Education and Special Programs, and Medicine.

The University's innovative Ph.D. program in Instructional Design and Development, the only program of its kind in Alabama, provides students with skills to plan, implement, and evaluate instructional programs in many educational settings.

The University of South Alabama's mission is to remain a comprehensive, coeducational, state-assisted institution serving as a major center of undergraduate, graduate, and professional education for Alabama, the Gulf Coast region, and the southeastern United States. Three traditional academic functions of this mission encompass teaching, research, and public service.

The University is proud of its undergraduate curricula, designed to expose students to a variety of subjects in order to develop communication and thinking skills which will thoroughly prepare them for their chosen professions and make their lives more rewarding.

Through the years the University's enrollment has diversified. Currently, nearly 20 percent of USA's students are minorities, and 34 percent of USA's students are age 26 or older.

There is no "typical" student at USA. Elderly students hardly rate a second glance from USA's younger ones, as they have become accustomed to attending classes with grandfathers "going back for that degree" or grandmothers taking a class to enhance their writing skills so they can "write that prize-winning novel."

The aim of the University is to attract "the brightest and the best." To enroll at USA, an applicant must have scored a minimum of 19 on the American College Test (ACT), but the average incoming freshman has an ACT score of 22. Scholarships are awarded to students who have a score of 26 or above, enabling the University to attract top students from all over the nation. In addition to scholarships, other opportunities for financial aid exist, such as grants, work, and loan programs.

Since not everyone's IQ ranges in the stratosphere, USA has special programs to help those students deficient in certain subjects. Numerous programs are designed to aid foreign-speaking students and those with less academic preparation.

Students enrolling at USA expect the very best when it comes to instructors, and they get what they ask for. USA's quest for excellence in teaching, as well as research, is evidenced in its 650-plus faculty members, 80 percent of whom have doctoral degrees. Many of these faculty members have received national recognition for their intellectual accomplishments. Also, instruction is by faculty members only. No graduate students are allowed to teach academic courses.

A Gulf Coast Treasure

A unique closeness between USA faculty and students reaches outside the classroom. Instructors serve as student organizational sponsors, mentors, and tutors. Perhaps one reason for this closeness is that the average class size is only 22, and the faculty-to-student ratio holds steady at 1 to 15.

In addition to 53 undergraduate degrees, the University offers 27 masters' programs, three specialist programs, four doctoral programs, and one medical doctor program.

At USA graduate programs are aimed solely at preparing students in every possible way for their professional and academic careers. They provide students with opportunities for independent investigation, creative achievement, and the advancement of knowledge.

The choices at USA are many. Ranked according to popularity, the top programs for graduates are counselor in education, MBA-general, nursing, elementary education, computer and information sciences, special education, interdepartmental education, educational leadership, basic medical sciences, secondary education, and public administration.

Newly approved for the University's doctoral program by the Alabama Commission on Higher Education are doctorates in marine sciences and instructional design and development, and the newest Ph.D., in communication sciences and disorders, accepted its first students in 1993.

Offered through the College of Allied Health Professions, the Ph.D. in communication sciences and disorders will produce academicians and researchers who will teach at the college level and generate research leading to new treatments for persons with communication disorders.

USA is the only university in Alabama fully accredited by the American Speech, Language, and Hearing Association for both academic and clinical programs.

The modern facilities at the USA Speech and Hearing Center contributed to landing this doctoral program, unique among Alabama schools.

Additionally, the University's new bachelor's degree program in Occupational Therapy enables USA students to pursue one of America's fastest-growing careers. Occupational therapists are health care professionals who work with individuals with acute and chronic physical, emotional, mental, or developmental disabilities, and in so doing, help them achieve independence in their daily lives and activities.

In 1969 the Alabama Legislature once again made an announcement which would have a monumental impact on the Mobile area. There would be a new medical school established under the auspices of the University of South Alabama.

Medical education is nothing new to Mobile. In 1859 the Medical College of Alabama was founded here and operated until 1920, with the exception of the Civil War years of 1861-1865.

The USA College of Medicine admitted its first class in 1973 and has, to date, trained more than a thousand physicians. College of Medicine students receive their medical training in the largest health care system in the region. Serving as teaching facilities are USA Hospitals, including the USA Medical Center, USA Doctors Hospital, and USA Knollwood Park Hospital.

Serving as an academic health center, the University is dedicated to educating physicians, health scientists, allied health professionals, and nurses who will provide the very highest quality health care and leadership in the practice of medicine.

USA's campus has had to expand to meet the needs of its ever-growing medical community. Additional space was provided for ambulatory services of specialized medicine, internal medicine, orthopaedics, and student health services.

Medical research projects at USA have attracted large sums of outside funding, making additional research possible. In 1993 alone, over $11 million was contributed, evidence that others recognize the caliber of those involved in research and the merit of their endeavors.

Besides their importance to the University, these outside funds have also provided

This addition to the Health Services Building provides more space for ambulatory services of specialized medicine, internal medicine, orthopaedics, and student health services.

The University has claimed the Sun Belt Conference Commissioner's Cup, which is awarded to the best all-around athletic program, five of the last six years through 1993.

a significant boost to the area's economy. The same level of participation is expected in the future.

Enrollment in USA's College of Nursing has raised it to a ranking of seventh largest in the nation. The program is expected to continue its phenomenal growth, as USA nursing alumni heartily endorse the curriculum which now includes an Advanced Nurse Education Program.

It's not easy to enter USA's nursing program. Students must have a minimum 2.5 grade point average even to apply. Since only top students are accepted, it is often the case that those with a 3.0 or above are the ones admitted.

Everything from Broadway musicals to international acrobats are featured at the University's historic Saenger Theatre in downtown Mobile.

Most impressive is the nursing faculty, of which more than 30 percent hold doctoral degrees. Many faculty members are also involved in service and scholarly activities which keep them in touch with the community.

The College of Business and Management Studies is active and community-minded. With a host of talented research professors, it has a very clear impact on the area.

The Center for Business and Economic Research often works with state and regional governing bodies to produce facts and fig-

USA's enrollment has increased by over 70 percent in the last 14 years to the current level of more than 12,000 students.

ures which chart the business development of the state.

The Small Business Development Center has a direct impact on the small business community through help with grant programs and necessary information.

And, the Alabama Banking School at USA is recognized as one of the most successful of its kind in the nation.

Meanwhile the University's School of Computer and Information Sciences boasts the only program of its kind in the Mobile area, offering students three areas of specialization: computer science, information science, and computer systems design.

Students are surrounded by a rich computing atmosphere. The full range of computing facilities includes personal computers, work stations, and a supercomputer. This environment provides superior learning tools that guarantee the best preparation possible. The USA School of Computer and Information Sciences is one of the few full-range computing facilities in the country.

With the University's growth, more and more students, both full-time and part-time, are able to take advantage of classes offered at locations other than the main campus.

A variety of off-campus classes are taught at USA's 327-acre Brookley Center, USA Springhill Campus (which houses the College of Nursing), and the USA Baldwin County Campus at Fairhope.

Located in downtown Mobile, the Saenger Theatre (ca. 1928), long considered a treasure by generations of Mobilians, was acquired by the University in 1971 for its Theatre for the Performing Arts, part of USA's School of Continuing Education and Special Programs.

Newly renovated, the theatre, featuring one of Mobile's most beautiful interiors, offers productions designed to meet the varied tastes of the Mobile community. Performances run the gamut from Chinese acrobats and rock 'n' roll to Broadway musicals. Most shows are sellouts.

Athletics are also an important part of campus life at USA. Since becoming a charter member of the Sun Belt Conference in 1976, student athletes have excelled in the 15 intercollegiate sports. In a recent two-season period, USA earned nine Sun Belt championships and received the Sun Belt Conference Commissioner's Cup, which is awarded to the best all-around athletic program, three consecutive years and five of the last six.

USA's highly touted basketball, baseball, and soccer programs are nationally recognized. The Jaguars have played in five consecutive NCAA baseball tournaments and have been within one victory of the College World Series.

In addition, the Jaguars have had winning programs in golf and track and field, and in 1993 were champions in such sports as women's cross country and men's and women's tennis.

Jaguar athletes win not only on the field of play, but in the classroom, too. In 1993, 50 student athletes were named to the Sun Belt Commissioner's All-Academic List.

For the disabled, even the smallest task can be an overwhelming obstacle. In an effort to eliminate some of these obstacles which hinder the lives of the physically challenged, seniors in USA's College of Engineering work with patients from the State Adult Vocational Rehabilitation Service. As part of a design course, these engineering students have worked on projects ranging from playground equipment for wheelchair-confined children to modifying sewing machines.

A Gulf Coast Treasure

A new program designed to draw minorities into the engineering field introduces area high school students to the principles and practices of engineering. Students obtain experience visiting local industries, where they observe civil, electrical, mechanical, and chemical engineering in action.

Through efforts of the Mobile County Public School System's Southeastern Consortium for Minorities in Engineering, local industry, and USA, minorities will be recruited into the field of engineering and, upon graduation, choose an employment opportunity in the Mobile area.

In keeping with its commitment to the disabled, USA's College of Arts and Sciences' new $2.5 million Visual Arts Building is equipped for the handicapped/disabled, making classes, lectures, and darkroom facilities easily accessible to everyone.

The Gulf Coast is the perfect location for the College of Arts and Sciences' new doctoral program in Marine Sciences with specializations in biological, chemical, and geological disciplines. Students are able to take full advantage of the Marine Environmental Sciences Consortium headquartered at Dauphin Island Sea Lab, just 35 miles south of USA's main campus.

With its 33 programs, the University's College of Arts and Sciences has a place for everyone, whether it be foreign languages, anthropology, art, music, or criminal justice.

"Visionary" is a word frequently used to describe USA's College of Education, which stays at the forefront of educational technology in the classroom.

These University faculty actually go into area classrooms, give technical assistance, provide staff development principles, and work directly with students.

Other than academics, there are many reasons a student should place the University of South Alabama at the top of his list when considering where to attend college. USA has many special programs and facilities for students, such as well-equipped computer labs, excellent libraries, state-of-the-art science and engineering laboratories, and modern, extensive clinical facilities for allied health, pre-professions, and nursing programs, all of which provide support for USA's academic programs.

Of special benefit are programs which offer advanced credit options, course exemptions for outstanding students, personalized studies, adult studies, interdisciplinary programs, cross-college minor programs, developmental studies programs, Army and Air Force ROTC, and many other options.

Studies have shown that students who are involved in extracurricular activities fare better, both socially and academically. To that end over 120 different organizations are available for out-of-class activities, ranging from student government to Greek sororities and fraternities, honor societies, special interest groups, professional and departmental clubs, and student publications.

More and more students recognize the advantages of attending the University of South Alabama as evidenced by the last 14 years. During that time USA's enrollment has increased by over 70 percent, credit hour production has grown by almost 60 percent, while the budget has leaped from about $58 million to almost $304 million.

According to the USA fact book, "Expansion of the range of the University's programs and services and of the institution's reputation for excellence in instruction, research, health care, and public service, has been as rapid as the increase in enrollment."

University of South Alabama President Dr. Frederick P. Whiddon says, "I am encouraged by the vitality and enthusiasm shown by the entire University community, the Board of Trustees, the faculty, staff, alumni, legislators, and friends as they work together to make the University of South Alabama flourish."

Making the right choice is the goal of every student selecting a college. For an outstanding educational opportunity, with the support of diverse and nationally recognized academic programs, outstanding faculty, and an abundance of student services and campus activities, "the right choice" is the University of South Alabama. ⚜

The new Student Recreation Center offers basketball, volleyball, racquetball, handball, weight lifting, exercycling, and an indoor track in a pleasant, climate-controlled environment.

USA's beautiful main campus is located in west Mobile, and provides a scenic and restful educational environment.

COASTAL LAND TRUST, INC.

Located just north of the busy seaport of Mobile is one of nature's most extensive and magnificent wetlands, the Mobile-Tensaw Delta, the nation's third largest estuary.

The Delta area, with its rich, organic soil reaching depths of 70 feet, serves as nature's aviary for 250 kinds of birds, as an aquarium for 234 species of fish, and as a hothouse or habitat for plants and wildlife, including 37 endangered species.

The five-to-seven-mile southern area is mostly shallow bays, creeks, lakes, bayous, and small marsh-grass and cane-covered islands, while the remainder of the 200,000 acres is hardwood swamp. The atmosphere is one of sublime serenity, a natural welding of plants and animals.

But all is not well with the Delta. Man, in his never-ending search for prosperity, has intruded upon Mother Nature, and the Delta is suffering.

Although nature allows some of this stress to be absorbed, there are fears that careless management, population increases, or industrial expansion may cause the collapse of the Delta's naturally balanced ecological system.

In an effort to prevent this catastrophe, Coastal Land Trust, Inc. was formed in 1984 and shortly thereafter acquired 18,000 acres of the Mobile-Tensaw Delta. This non-profit organization hopes to acquire sufficient acreage to form an Independent Wildlife Management Area and educate the public and government and industrial agencies on the Delta's crisis.

Coastal Land Trust believes that saving the Delta will not only benefit the environment, but will also benefit local industries such as forestry, seafood, restaurant, and recreation. Almost 100 percent of the fish and shellfish in Mobile Bay and the Gulf of Mexico depend on the Delta's estuaries. Many young species of seafood begin life in the Delta and are nurtured by its rich food supply. Eventually, they end up in the bay and gulf for harvesting. Destruction of the Delta would devastate the multimillion dollar seafood industry, which ships local seafood worldwide.

Alabama's chief employer, the timber industry, would also suffer if the Delta's upper region's prime hardwood forests were damaged. The forests support over 13,000 area workers and contribute over $600 million yearly to the area's economy.

Only recently has the importance of United States wetlands been recognized. The State of Alabama has set aside 4,000 acres of Delta land in addition to Coastal Land Trust's 18,000 acres. The United States Army Corps of Engineers has now purchased approximately 14,000 acres from Coastal Land Trust and an additional 6,000 acres from a private landowner under the Tennessee-Tombigbee Waterway Mitigation Program, all of which is now under management by the Alabama Department of Conservation and Natural Resources. Although more and more Delta acreage is being rescued (to date, over 35,000 total acres) through one project or another, much work is left to be done. But this difficult task cannot succeed without the help of concerned citizens who want to preserve and protect this natural treasure.

Coastal Land Trust's efforts to protect the wetlands have not gone unnoticed. In 1985 Gulf Oil Corporation's Conservation Awards Program presented an award to Coastal Land Trust's president, G. Sage Lyons, in recognition of Coastal Land Trust's efforts which "resulted in the protection of thousands of acres of wetlands near Mobile and raised the awareness of local citizens about the importance of the Bay and Tensaw Delta and the threats facing it." And in 1992 Coastal Land Trust, Inc. was named by Alabama Wildlife Federation as "Conservation Organization of the Year."

Coastal Land Trust, with the cooperation and contributions of environmentally concerned corporations and citizens, strives to ensure that the Mobile-Tensaw Delta flourishs for the enjoyment of man and nature for many succeeding generations. ⚜

COASTAL LAND TRUST BOARD OF DIRECTORS
The current board of directors for Coastal Land Trust, Inc. are shown left to right: Arthur C. Dyas—president, Southeastern Natural Resources, Inc., Mobile, Alabama; Henry Bryars—timber, farming, cattle, oil, and gas investments, Bay Minette, Alabama; G. Sage Lyons—president, Lyons, Pipes & Cook, P.C., Mobile, Alabama; Winthrop Hallett III—president, Mobile Area Chamber of Commerce, Mobile, Alabama; Arthur Tonsmeire III—president, Tonsmeire Development Corporation, Fairhope, Alabama; Fred T. Stimpson—president, Gulf Lumber Company, Inc., Mobile, Alabama; Not shown David E. Morine—author and former vice president, The Nature Conservancy, Arlington, Virginia.

A Gulf Coast Treasure

ST. PAUL'S EPISCOPAL SCHOOL

Students from St. Paul's Upper and Lower School pose by the gate at the school's main entrance.

St. Paul's Episcopal School, founded in 1947, lies nestled among 35 acres of oaks, dogwoods, and pines in Springhill, one of Mobile's loveliest and most historical areas.

In the beginning it was known as St. Paul's Day School, with a kindergarten, one teacher, and a dozen children, operating as a part of the educational mission of St. Paul's Episcopal Church in Mobile.

In 1961 a first grade was formed, and with each succeeding year an additional grade was added, and in 1968 the school was incorporated as a separate entity under its own board of trustees.

Today the campus houses grades three through twelve in the eight major campus buildings, with Pre-K through 2 remaining at St. Paul's Church. The Louise R. Moorer Library contains over 19,000 books and reference volumes, the A. S. Mitchell Science Laboratory provides modern laboratory space for chemistry and physics, and the Dr. Monte L. Moorer Theatre boasts a 500-seat capacity and adjoining classrooms.

This modern educational facility has evolved from its humble beginnings into one of the area's premier schools with a present-day enrollment of over 1,400 students and a staff and faculty of over 135. The first class graduated in 1974, and since that time over 1,500 students have become proud alumni of St. Paul's.

St. Paul's educational mission continues to focus on student growth and development. The school is committed to nurturing individual talents within the context of a caring community of people with common values and shared goals.

St. Paul's curriculum is college preparatory in character. Honors courses and advanced placement work are available for students of exceptional ability and motivation. Typically, during any given year, 100 percent of St. Paul's graduates enroll in four-year colleges or universities.

St. Paul's students have excelled from the very beginning. Their college preparatory programs and liberal arts tradition enabled the school to be named an "Exemplary School" by the United States Department of Education in 1989. Student honors range from a United States Presidential Scholar, Mobile County Young Woman of the Year, Westinghouse Science Scholar, Tandy Technology Scholar to various and prestigious writing awards, among others.

The school's "Individualized Study Program" is geared toward the special needs of children with disabilities or attention disorders and is aimed at helping them adapt to the conventional classroom.

A healthy mind needs a healthy body, and that philosophy is carried over into St. Paul's athletic programs. Recently, St. Paul's "Field of Dreams" became a reality with the opening of the E. E. Delaney Memorial Stadium and Athletic Complex, adjacent to the campus. The gridiron, surrounded by the Dr. Monte L. Moorer Track and the Bussie Greer Baseball Field nearby, is home to St. Paul's football, baseball, soccer, and track teams.

Championship teams abound at St. Paul's. Since becoming a part of interscholastic athletic competition in 1969, their girls' volleyball teams have traveled to the Alabama state championships for 21 consecutive years, which is a state record. In a like number of years, the "Saints," a member of the Alabama High School Athletic Association, have collected a total of 68 state championships in 10 sports. The school offers programs in football, volleyball, soccer, cross country, track and field, baseball, softball, basketball, tennis, and golf.

There's no finer Fine Arts program than that offered at St. Paul's. Six full-time and numerous part-time, talented and dedicated arts instructors teach students visual arts, music, and speech and theater arts. Students from the advanced speech class comprise a strong forensics team. In fact, the school's team members have won more trophies at state competition than any other school in Alabama. Students enrolled in the Fine Arts program are prize winners all, receiving many and varied honors.

St. Paul's Episcopal School continues its commitment to educational excellence by offering a high quality, college preparatory education in a Christian environment. Students in grades Pre-K through twelve are educated spiritually, academically, civically, socially, physically, and emotionally. ⚜

The school's athletic complex provides practice and playing fields for both girls' and boys' sports. Three members of the girls' championship track and field team practice at the Dr. Monte L. Moorer Track.

A Gulf Coast Treasure

SPRING HILL COLLEGE

> *Spring Hill College is a Jesuit, Catholic liberal arts college founded on the principles of faith in God, the necessity of knowledge, academic excellence, spiritual instruction, and social responsibility.*

With more than 3,559 colleges and universities in the United States, the ability to narrow the field down to one choice is worthy of a degree in itself. Students at Spring Hill College in Mobile, Alabama, explain how they narrowed their choice. "I wanted a small liberal arts college where I was a person, not a number," expresses one high school senior.

"I wound up at Spring Hill College by accident. Mobile is my hometown. That's why I chose to go off to school. I was unhappy away and came home to decide what to do. I took some courses at Spring Hill, fell in love with the school, and stayed on to graduate," reveals an editor of a national magazine.

"I chose Spring Hill College because the school's Communication Arts Department offered internships in broadcast journalism that larger schools didn't," explains a local television anchorwoman.

These students chose Spring Hill College. They may never have realized that Spring Hill College also chose them. *USA Today* labeled Spring Hill College one of the "choosiest" colleges in the nation. The national newspaper did so because Spring Hill College has high expectations for the students it "chooses" to join its student body. These students represent a diverse blend of backgrounds, religious beliefs, and academic abilities.

> *Labeled as one of the "choosiest" schools in the nation, Spring Hill College has high expectations for the students it "chooses" to join its student body. These students represent a diverse blend of backgrounds, religious beliefs, and academic abilities.*

Spring Hill College is a Jesuit, Catholic liberal arts college with a rich 164-year tradition and is non-sectarian in its recruiting of students and teachers. The college was founded on the principles of faith in God, the necessity of knowledge, academic excellence, spiritual instruction, and social responsibility.

Being the oldest Catholic college in the Southeast, the third oldest Jesuit college in the United States, and the oldest four-year college in Alabama, Spring Hill has survived more than its share of hardships including wars, fires, the Great Depression, and hurricanes. These challenges have only served to strengthen the college's mission to educate students to become responsible leaders in service to others.

At Spring Hill, education takes place within a moral context, therefore students are expected to develop a higher appreciation of service to mankind and to learn more than just facts and figures. To carry out this mission, the college attracts an extraordinary faculty. Ninety percent hold degrees that place them at the top of their fields, and 82 percent have earned doctorates. Spring Hill College's reputation for academic excellence extends throughout the nation, which explains why a majority of the school's student body is from out of state.

"Our dedication to academic excellence is not unlike other institutions," comments college president William J. Rewak, S.J. "Our difference is Spring Hill's combination of excellence, the Jesuit adherence to religious values and to principles of academic and personal discipline, concern for the individual student, and a strong liberal arts curriculum."

This curriculum offers the bachelor of arts and bachelor of science degrees, and the interdivisional studies in general studies and international studies. Graduate degrees include the master of business administration, master of science in education, master of arts in teaching, and master of theological studies.

Numerous degree-related internships offer students the opportunity to explore many career options. A long list of student clubs, organizations, and activities provides opportunities for social and community involvement.

"When I visited Spring Hill College, I didn't feel awkward even though I was from out of state. I didn't know one person when I started school there, but I graduated with many friends and a special love for Mobile and the Gulf Coast," is a common testimony of Spring Hill College graduates. ⚜

UMS-WRIGHT PREPARATORY SCHOOL

On October 2, 1893, Dr. Julius Tutwiler Wright introduced his school as an institution dedicated to building character of the highest order in its students. By providing a tailored curriculum which met the needs of each student while nurturing their mental, moral, and physical talents, the University Military School for Boys, became a beacon of learning and innovation. Its elementary school was the first in the state to be accredited by the Southern Association of Colleges and Schools.

In 1988 UMS-Preparatory School merged with J. T. Wright's School for Girls to create UMS-Wright Preparatory School. Today more than 100 years after its founding, the school continues its tradition of educational excellence as a private pre-kindergarten through twelfth grade co-educational college preparatory school that welcomes students who have a desire to learn. The school remains committed to providing a supportive environment conducive to the development of the total student.

Mr. Ervin S. Cooper, class of 1928 for whom the Ervin S. Cooper Football Stadium is named, eulogized, "It isn't where we are that counts, but where we are going." And the "going" forecasts clear and sunny for UMS-Wright. The school's 60-acre campus offers students a wide variety of educational and athletic stimuli. Ten buildings house both grade and special interest classrooms such as a math and science building as well as individual laboratories for biology, chemistry, computers, foreign language, life science, and physics. The school's two libraries feature state-of-the-art CD-Rom reference materials.

One of the most exciting facilities is the new $2.2 million, 25,000 square foot multi-purpose physical activities complex. This facility includes a 1,000-seat arena, which makes it possible for several athletic activities to play simultaneously. It provides boys' and girls' locker rooms, physical education classrooms, and athletic training rooms.

The campus also includes a large cafeteria, a 900-seat auditorium, a football stadium, coed exercise and weight/training rooms, a swimming pool, and baseball, soccer, and softball playing fields as well as several athletic practice fields.

The school's credibility and stability are enhanced by a $2 million, and constantly growing, foundation fund and an endowment fund used primarily to support an aggressive scholarship program.

Headmaster Dr. Tony Havard believes that UMS-Wright is one of the finest private institutions in the country. He adds, "Nothing surpasses the exhilaration one feels when considering the unlimited possibilities of an exciting educational future. We look ahead to a second 100 years full of challenges and opportunities."

A distinguished faculty includes recipients of Woodrow Wilson Fellowships, National Endowment for the Humanities Fellowships, National Science Foundation Fellowships, Fulbright Fellows, National Gallery of Art Fellows, Presidential Scholar Teachers, and Who's Who in American Education. In keeping with the high standards set by Dr. Wright, over 70 percent of UMS-Wright's faculty hold master degrees and above.

All students take advanced placement courses and generally, 100 percent of UMS-Wright graduates attend college. On average, 50 percent of graduates are awarded merit-based scholarships. UMS-Wright is a member of the National Association of Independent Schools and accredited by the Southern Association of Colleges and Schools.

Dr. Wright gave UMS-Wright life. He gave it purpose. He left it with a message, "A thought becomes an act; an act becomes a habit; a habit becomes a character; a character becomes a destiny."

The school's 60-acre campus offers students a wide variety of educational and athletic stimuli.

UMS-Wright Preparatory School is committed to providing a supportive environment conducive to the development of the total student.

Chapter 16
HEALTH CARE

University of South Alabama Hospitals
Bay Area Plastic Surgery
Saad Enterprises
Providence Hospital
Cardio-Thoracic and Vascular Surgical Associates
PrimeHealth
Mobile Infirmary Medical Center
Blue Cross and Blue Shield of Alabama
Springhill Memorial Hospital
Mobile Bay OB-GYN Associates
Partial Hospital Institute of America, Inc.
Cardiology Associates of Mobile, P.C.
Pulmonary Associates of Mobile, P.A.
Cogburn Health Center, Inc.
The Mobile Heart Center
Anesthesia Services, P.C.
Mobile Orthopedic Center

A Gulf Coast Treasure

UNIVERSITY OF SOUTH ALABAMA HOSPITALS

University of South Alabama Hospitals make up the largest, most comprehensive health care system in our region.

In 1970 the University of South Alabama purchased Mobile General Hospital to serve as a teaching facility for the USA College of Medicine. With a lineage dating back to colonial Mobile, this hospital's rich tradition of providing medical care to the citizens of the area served as the foundation for the USA hospital system. In 1990 the University purchased Knollwood Park Hospital and Doctors Hospital.

With a total of 880 beds, USA Hospitals bring together the skills of a vast array of highly trained and caring medical professionals, state-of-the-art equipment, and the advantages of a major research institution.

"The Medical Center has a long and proud tradition of service, but we are most proud of where the USA hospital system is today and where we are headed," says Steve Simmons, senior administrator of USA hospitals. "Our team of dedicated health care professionals provides the best care available to each and every patient. As a teaching institution, USA is training the health care providers of tomorrow, and as a research institution we are able to offer our patients the most up-to-date treatments available."

USA hospitals provide many specialized and unique services to the citizens of Alabama, northwest Florida, and southern Mississippi. The USA Medical Center is the region's only Level I Trauma Center, providing the highest level of emergency care, 24 hours a day. The hospital is also home to medical, surgical, coronary, neonatal, and neurotrauma intensive care units.

The USA Burn Center is one of the leading centers of its kind in the nation and is noted for its research in burn treatment.

The USA Genetics/Birth Defects Center collects data and researches inherited disorders. It serves as a resource for physicians throughout our region and country.

USA specializes in the delivery and care of babies. In fact, more babies are born every year at USA than at any other hospital in the state of Alabama, and many high risk infants are transferred from other area hospitals to USA's Level III neonatal intensive care unit. Labor/delivery/recovery suites are an added option for expectant parents.

SouthFlite USA, based at USA Medical Center, serves all three hospitals and has been instrumental in saving many lives. Flying at speeds of more than 120 miles per hour, SouthFlite is staffed by specially trained nurses

More babies are delivered at USA than any other hospital in Alabama . . . each with tender, loving care.

The University of South Alabama stands as a leader in health care.

A Gulf Coast Treasure

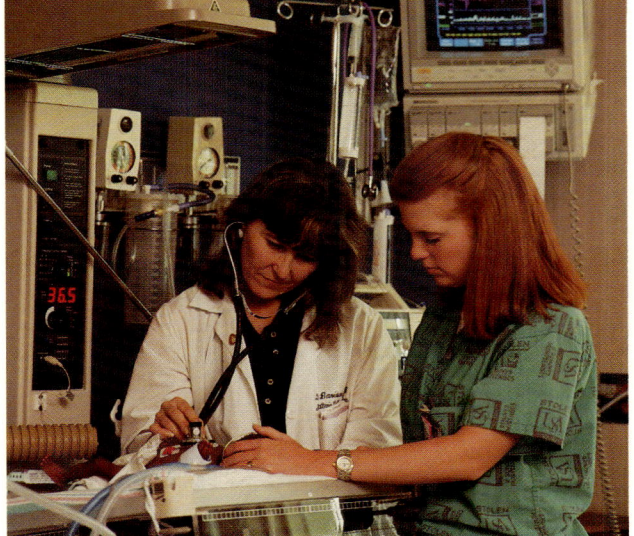

The Pediatric Intensive Care Unit at USA provides the highest level of care available for seriously ill children.

and paramedics able to administer intensive care treatment to the critically ill or injured while en route to the hospital.

USA Regional Cancer Center is waging war on this disease through its research into effective methods of detection and treatment. The Center developed the first radiation facility in the Mobile area and employs leading researchers in the treatment of cancers. These researchers include oncologists, radiation oncologists, surgeons, and pulmonologists who treat both children and adults.

The USA Cancer Center is a member of the Southwest Oncology Group and the Pediatric Oncology Group. As a research institution and member of these two organizations, USA is able to provide patients clinical protocols not available elsewhere in the region.

Mobile's first open-heart surgery program was at the Medical Center, and today USA's Cardiovascular Diseases Center offers the most up-to-date diagnosis and treatment available. It includes state-of-the-art cardiac catherization and electrophysiology laboratories, and a Heart Station for outpatient EKG's, echocardiography, and exercise testing.

The Comprehensive Sickle Cell Center is one of only 10 such centers in the United States to be chosen for funding from the National Institutes of Health. The Center is involved in researching all aspects of sickle cell disease and providing treatment and counseling to victims of the disease.

USA Doctors Hospital is a 159-bed, acute care hospital located near downtown Mobile. Plans are underway to move all of USA's children's and women's services to this facility, making it one of five freestanding hospitals in the country dedicated solely to the special needs of children and women. The necessary construction for this move will be complete in 1995.

"Our goal is to provide quality and cost-effective care to our patients," says Tom Gibson, administrator of Doctors Hospital. "We recognize the needs of the individual and combine the latest technology with a personal touch to address those needs. We believe this sets us apart from other hospitals. As we move toward our future as the USA Children's and Women's Hospital, we will have even greater opportunity to accomplish these goals."

Deeply rooted at USA Doctors Hospital is "The Treehouse," a special place where hospitalized kids can just be kids. The Treehouse is supervised by a certified child-life specialist, who addresses the psycho-social needs of our young patients. Certified teachers help young patients of all grade levels keep up with their school work during extended stays in the hospital.

USA's Pediatric Intensive Care Unit and the Children's Evaluation Center provide the highest level of care available for seriously ill children. These specialized areas are medically directed by physicians with board certification in pediatric intensive care and pediatric emergency care.

USA Knollwood Park Hospital and USA Knollwood Park Long-Term Care Hospital, with a total of 315 beds, are located on the same campus in west Mobile.

"Our goal is to provide personal, hands-on treatment in a modern facility for the citizens of our community,"

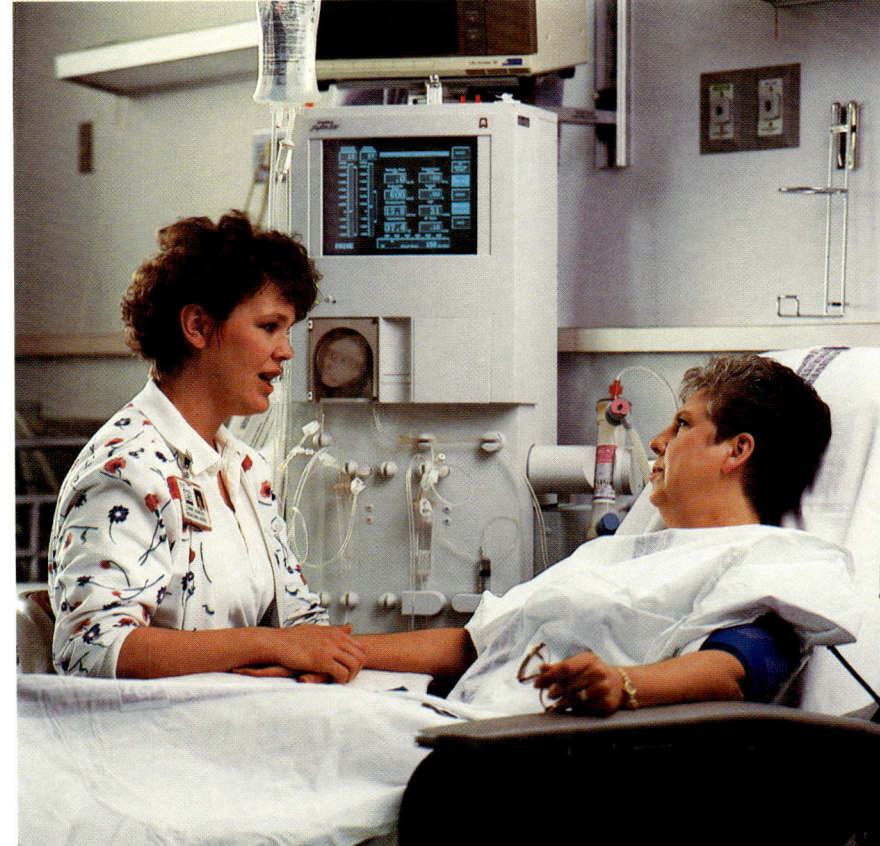

Compassion and technology come together in a vast array of specialties at USA Hospitals.

says Stan Hammack, administrator of USA Knollwood Park. "We offer a community-hospital setting, with all the advantages of a major research institution. In addition to quality medical care, we are also committed to community education and accessibility of our specialized programs."

USA Knollwood Park Hospital is a full-service hospital offering acute medical care and many specialized services.

One such service is the One Day Surgery Center, providing quality, economic, and convenient outpatient surgical procedures.

The GI Lab provides patients with the latest technology in endoscopic procedures.

Other services include a physician-staffed emergency room, Breast Care Center, Sleep Disorders Center, Child and Adolescent Psychiatry, and a physicians' office complex with specialists in family care, internal medicine, pediatrics, dermatology, general surgery, plastic surgery, rheumatology, vascular surgery, orthopaedics, neurology, gastroenterology, and cardiology.

USA Knollwood Park Long-Term Care Hospital is charting new ground in restorative care. It is the first hospital of its kind in the region and one of only two in the state. The hospital combines the services of an inpatient facility and a rehabilitation hospital. Its goal is to provide hospital-level care to patients who require rehabilitative care and/or intensive management of medically complex conditions and to help these patients be self-sufficient upon their discharge from the hospital.

Standing as a leader in health care, USA hospitals look to the past with pride and to the future with commitment—commitment to serving the citizens of our community . . . commitment to the education of health care professionals . . . and commitment to medical research. ⚜

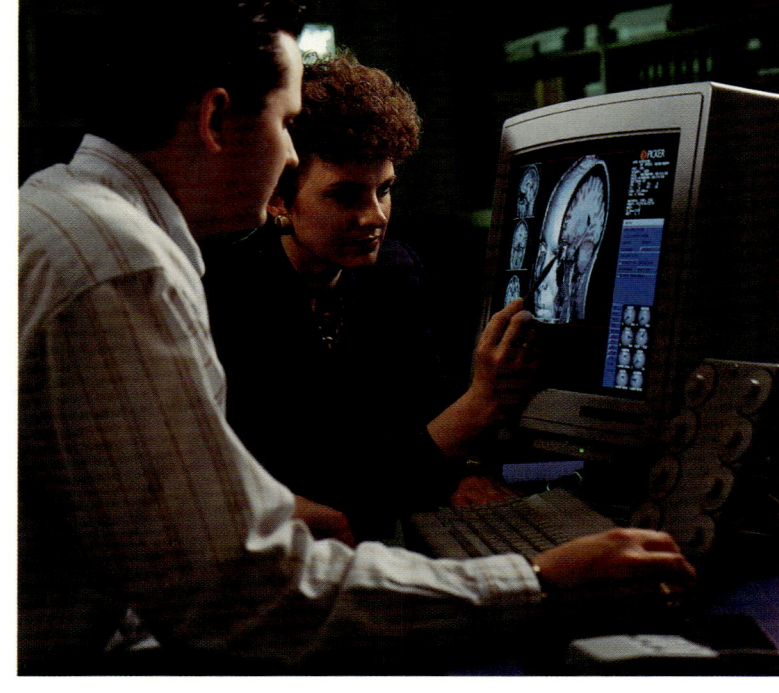

As a teaching institution, USA Hospitals bring together the skills of many highly trained health care professionals.

USA Hospitals make up the largest, most comprehensive health care system in the region.

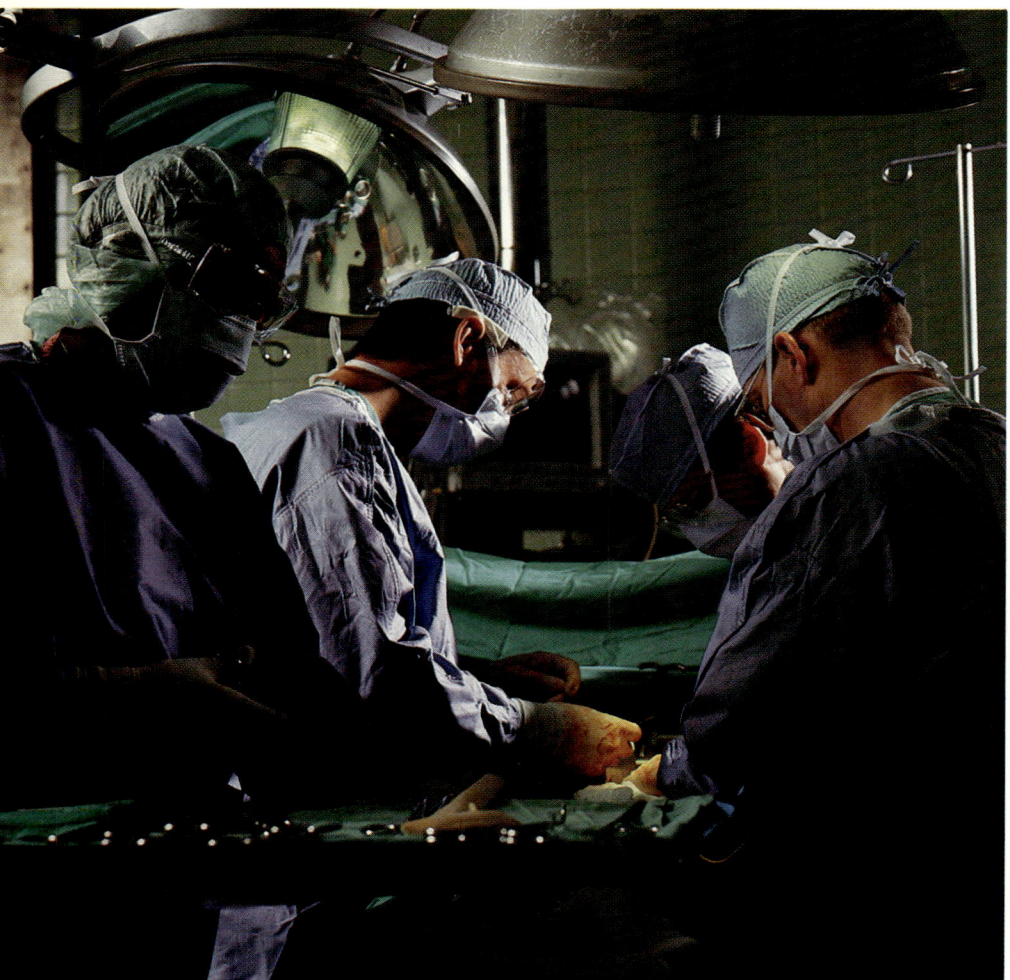

Interstate 65 was slick from the hard rains the night before as Cheryl Guy, owner of Camelia Construction Company of Mobile, drove home from a trip to Birmingham. Suddenly, her car hit a bump, hydroplaned over a concrete embankment and came to a rest, wedged between two pine trees.

A call for help from a passing motorist brought paramedics, fire department personnel, and two jaws-of-life vehicles to the scene. It was clear that Cheryl's only hope for survival was air transport to a hospital able to treat her multiple injuries.

SouthFlite USA was called and touched down at the scene just as Cheryl was cut from her mangled vehicle. She was loaded onboard the helicopter and treatment was begun enroute to USA Medical Center, the region's only Level I Trauma Center.

When SouthFlite arrived at USA, Cheryl was "hot unloaded" and rushed to a waiting surgery suite.

The trauma team was faced with a serious challenge. Cheryl was suffering from a ruptured spleen, numerous broken ribs, a damaged liver, a crushed pelvis, a left arm broken in two places, and a punctured heart that required immediate open heart surgery.

Her prognosis that morning was dim, but today Cheryl Guy—businesswoman and mother of three—bears few scars from her close brush with death. She credits SouthFlite and USAMC with saving her life.

"What makes USAMC different from all other hospitals is that they have to diagnose and treat at the very same time," says Cheryl. "They knew me only as Jane Doe. Refusal to attempt to save my life was not an option. I would be dead without SouthFlite and USA Medical Center."

Combining the services of an inpatient facility and a rehabilitation hospital, USA Knollwood Park Long-Term Care Hospital is the first of its kind in the region.

Cheryl Guy–businesswoman and mother of three–credits Southflite and USAMC with saving her life. Photo by Ric Moore.

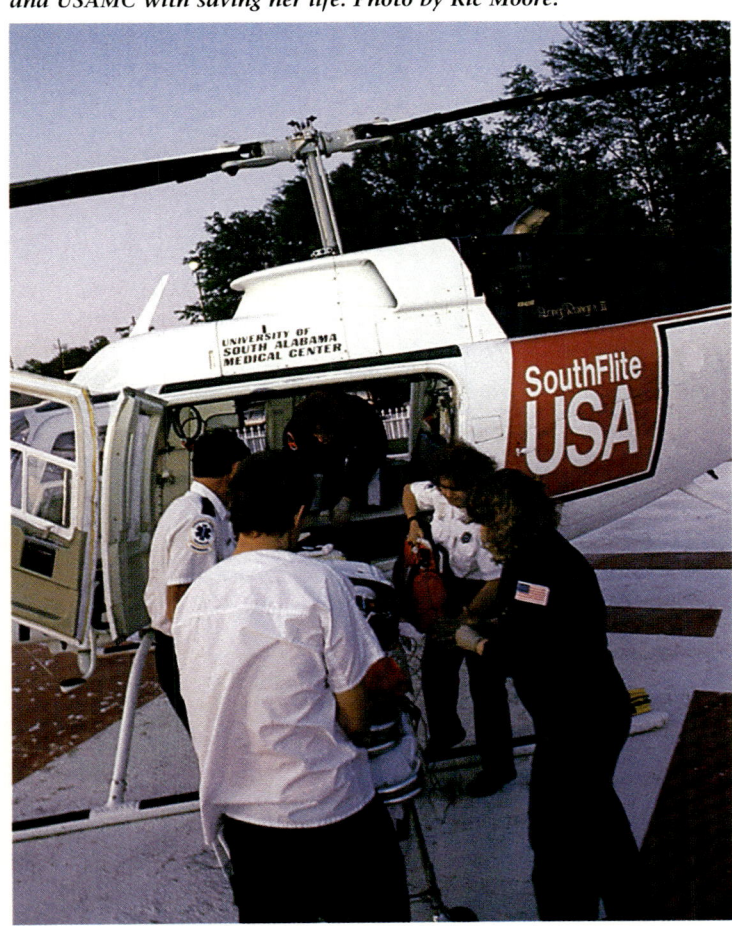

BAY AREA PLASTIC SURGERY

Bay Area Plastic Surgery opened in 1980 with (left to right) Dr. Charles L. Dyas Jr. as the sole physician. Dr. Daniel A. Dennis joined the practice in 1987 and Dr. Randy D. Proffitt in 1994.

The office staff of Bay Area Plastic Surgery help patients receive quality, professional care.

"Most consider plastic surgery to be beautiful surgery. In reality, plastic surgery deals with a lot of ugliness," begins Dr. Charles Dyas, founder of Bay Area Plastic Surgery.

The public has a narrow view of what they perceive plastic surgery and plastic surgeons to be. Dr. Dyas describes plastic surgeons by what they do: "We operate on the skin and all its contents." He continues by adding: "We do everything from removing moles and suturing minor lacerations to extensive reconstruction following cancerous disfigurement or traumatic mutilation. We deal with complex wound care and are frequently called upon to assist other surgeons in a variety of operations such as open heart surgery, where the sternum has become infected, and we correct it by either transferring body tissue to the sternum or simply rewiring it. We are also frequently involved in surgeries that are the result of serious injuries."

Plastic surgery is a surgical subspecialty designed either to improve the patient's physical appearance or to make the abnormal more acceptable. It involves the treatment of a number of different entities beyond general surgery. These include aesthetic surgery—for which the field is most recognized—reconstructive surgery in a number of areas such as burns, congenital defects, multiple cancerous conditions, body contouring, breast reconstruction, arthritic surgery, hand surgery, and microvascular surgery.

Dr. Dyas introduced microvascular surgery to the state of Alabama. This specialized surgery usually involves the reattachment of traumatically amputated or surgically removed parts from one part of the body to another, as in breast or jaw reconstruction or the rebuilding of a nose. Both Dr. Daniel Dennis and Dr. Randy Proffitt, Dr. Dyas's partners in Bay Area Plastic Surgery, have completed additional training in microvascular surgery. Dr. Proffitt was fortunate enough to have studied under Dr. Robert Acland, considered by most to be the father of microsurgery.

Becoming a doctor of plastic surgery is difficult. Becoming certified by the American Board of Plastic Surgeons goes beyond difficult, requiring some of the most extensive undergraduate and postgraduate training of all the medical subspecialties. The thin slip of paper hanging on Dr. Dyas's wall, for instance, represents 14 years of medical training which includes medical school, certification in general surgery, residency in plastic surgery, and in Dr. Dyas's case, an additional fellowship in hand surgery.

Bay Area Plastic Surgery opened in 1980 with Dr. Dyas as the sole physician. Dr. Daniel Dennis joined the practice in 1987 and Dr. Randy Proffitt in 1994. The group wishes to remain small enough to be able to communicate with and care for patients in a personal manner. The goal of Bay Area Plastic Surgery is to provide the best plastic surgical care possible in the country in the most efficient and cost-effective manner.

All three doctors at Bay Area Plastic Surgery realize the importance of body image, one of the most important aspects of plastic surgery. There is no doubt that the aesthetic side of the profession is equally as important as the medically traumatic. Reducing a full neck, sculpting a heavy jowl, minimizing a redundant eye lid are all important procedures and have an immensely positive effect upon patient self-esteem.

Dr. Dyas comments, "If it can be done simply and safely and it is important to the patient, then it is important that it be done." He adds, "It is never neces-

The goal of Bay Area Plastic Surgery is to provide the best plastic surgical care possible in the country in the most efficient and cost-effective manner.

sary to be heroic if a simpler procedure will work just as well."

Dr. Dyas admits that most of his work does not involve life-or-death situations. Instead, "Our work is elective and is meant to improve the quality of life of our patients." He adds, "We promise uniform care that assures our patients that when they need help, we will be there to provide it."

Dr. Dennis adds, "Our work may not be life-threatening, but it is lifestyle altering. We are always honest and straightforward with our patients, for, after all, our job is to make our patients feel better about themselves."

Bay Area Plastic Surgery splits its talents between the public and private sectors. For many years Dr. Dyas managed the plastic surgery care at the University of South Alabama and directed the university's burn unit. Continuing in its interest in promoting education, the group sponsors several high school and college scholarship programs, as well as offering community service seminars to both professional and public groups on a variety of topics related to their profession.

All three doctors donate their time and talents to the crippled children of Alabama. The group conducts monthly clinics in its work with a state program that deals with childhood birth defects and trauma-related situations.

Bay Area Plastic Surgery is constructing a new office at Dauphin Street and Interstate 65 that will be completed in 1995. This office will offer added privacy and convenience, as well as significantly reduced operating room costs, for its patients. The office will be equipped with an operating room, recovery room, and overnight recovery accomodations, including private sleeping areas, a kitchenette, and limited nursing care.

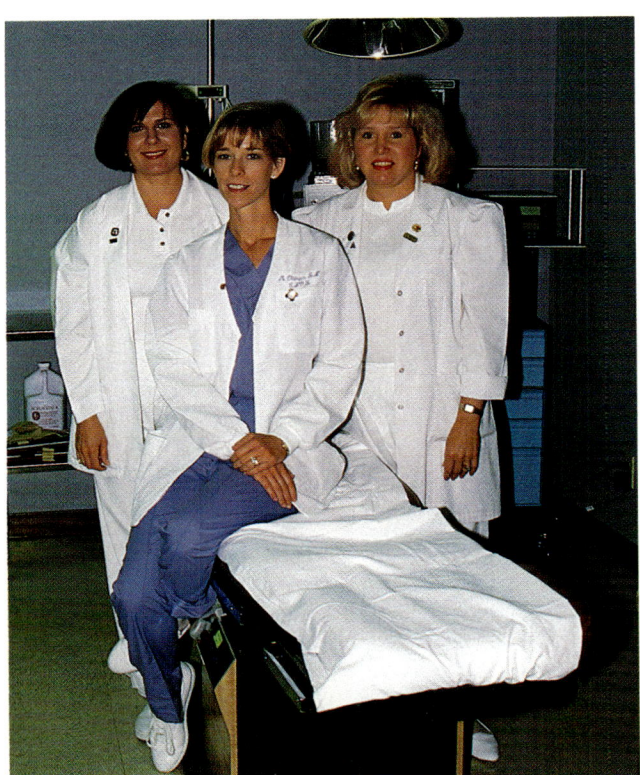

The group is small enough to communicate with and care for patients in a personal manner and the operating room staff of Bay Area Plastic Surgery assists in this goal.

SAAD ENTERPRISES

From a humble beginning, John and Dorothy Saad began providing health care for Mobilians in 1967. Today John serves as CEO and Dorothy serves as President of one of the largest providers of home health care on the Gulf Coast.

"As a boy growing up, I thought my father only knew four letters of the alphabet, W O R K," declares Alexander Saad, Senior Vice President for Saad Enterprises, Inc. "But as I got older and wiser, I realized he knew eight letters, W O R K and L O V E."

From a humble beginning, John and Dorothy Saad began providing health care for Mobilians in 1967 with the opening of Heritage Nursing and Convalescent Center. Mrs. Saad's expertise in geriatric nursing and Mr. Saad's administrative and management skills helped Heritage Nursing Home become the premiere long-term care facility in the area. It also became the training ground for the Saad's children, providing the foundation of the work ethic and the love of their work that still continues.

Today, Saad Enterprises is one of the largest employers and the largest provider of home health care services on the Gulf Coast. Collectively with its subsidiaries, Saad provides health care services through its various office locations in southern Alabama and Mississippi. Each branch location is staffed with trained professionals dedicated to providing quality care, comfort, and service to its patients and customers. Saad Enterprises, Inc. has been accredited by the Joint Commission on Accreditation of Healthcare Organization (JCAHO) facilities, the most recognized accreditation body in the country. Administration for the Alabama and Mississippi operations are centralized in Mobile, managed by Barbara Saad Fulgham, and Biloxi, managed by Dorothy Saad Dunning, respectively.

Saad's subsidiaries include home health care services, medical equipment, the state's largest assisted-living facility, senior apartments, many specialized medical services, including case management and private duty nursing, and a new skilled nursing facility under development.

Saad's Healthcare Services, the largest division, is a leader in physician-prescribed home health services, employing more than 400 licensed RNs and LPNs for both in-home service as well as relief staff for facilities and physicians' offices. Other certified professionals providing quality care and comfort include nurses' aides, companions, and homemaker and personal care attendants. Saad's offers rehabilitation specialists, medical social workers, and hospice care with trained professionals who provide comfort to the terminally ill.

"We use a seamless approach to make our patient's transition from hospital to home as smooth as possible," says Saad's Healthcare Services Senior Vice President, Henry Fulgham. "Working in conjunction with the attending physician, our professional staff work with the patient and patient's family from admission to discharge."

Certified nursing assistants also play a vital role in patient comfort and care. Nursing assistants provide a variety of services, including bathing, housekeeping, meal preparation, and many times make it possible for patients to remain in the comfort of their own homes instead of the hospital or other medical institutions.

Saad's Healthcare Services is an alternative source of health care provided in the patient's home. The Saad name is recognized for quality and cost-effective care, with a tradition of excellence that physicians, hospitals, patients, and families have come to depend upon and trust.

Located on a beautiful 12-acre campus, Gordon Oaks Retirement Community represents the senior housing and assisted living division of Saad Enterprises. Unlike a lifecare community, Gordon Oaks offers a wonderful

Administration for the Alabama operation is centralized in Mobile, managed by Barbara Saad Fulgham, Administrator of Saad's Healthcare Services.

alternative where residents can lease a unique lifestyle on a daily, monthly, or yearly basis. Divided into three levels of service, Gordon Oaks provides independent living, assisted living, and skilled nursing care.

Independent living is provided in the senior apartment complexes with a total of 88 units. The apartments are designed to provide residents with peace of mind and comfort and feature emergency call systems, security guard service, maintenance for living, and additional amenities available, such as transportation, a full-time recreation director, and much more.

At 164 beds, the assisted-living facility is the largest in the state. It is designed for residents who want to have some independence but need help or assistance on a daily basis. This may include help in the areas of bathing, meals, dressing, housekeeping, medicating, and/or other personal service. Gordon Oaks is also able to provide many additional services, such as housekeeping services, exercise facilities, recreation facilities, transportation, a private dining room, in-house pharmacy, beauty and barber shop, a registered dietician, and medical social workers to meet the needs of our residents.

A 100-bed, high tech sub-acute nursing home facility devotes 71 beds to skilled nursing, with the remainder devoted to a specialized assisted-living facility. The facility provides skilled short-term stay for those rehabilitating or long-term stay as needed.

Saad Enterprises is dedicated to providing only the best trained, most qualified health care professionals possible and sponsors on-going professional training programs which are CEU certified in the state of Alabama. Saad employees are required to participate in programs from comprehensive orientation to a variety of specialized training in order to perform their duties and meet the needs of the future in their continuing education studies. Saad's Education Department offers physicians and other representatives in the medical field a wide variety of educational topics. These seminars are not only an on-going training for Saad employees, but are also offered free of charge to the public. Subjects range from nutrition to acute wound care, as well as pediatric and geriatric care.

The managed care and case management system developed by Saad Enterprises is devoted to helping workers who have been injured on the job to return to work quickly and, in most cases, in better physical and mental health than before. This service assigns trained personnel to assist clients in efficiently coordinating necessary therapy. This deals not only with the management of the recovery but also cost management related to the recovery. Case management counselors deal with permanent injury cases and usually manage their clients' medical care on a lifetime basis.

As modern technology continues to allow increased physician-directed services to be provided in the home environment, Saad Enterprises will remain committed to providing quality home health care services to assist in the healing process of each person. With the current demand for health care services now and new needs in the future, Saad Enterprises is dedicated to providing the highest quality of services, professional health care workers, and caring management to meet the changing needs of their patients and clients.

The people who are Saad Enterprises will continue the W O R K and L O V E characteristics taught them in the past. They work hard for their patients and love the comfort the work brings to so many. ⚜

Saad's Healthcare Services, the largest division, is a leader in physician-prescribed home health services, employing more than 400 licensed RNs and LPNs for both in-home service as well as relief staff for facilities and physicians' offices.

Divided into three levels of service, Gordon Oaks provides independent living, assisted living, and skilled nursing care.

Providence Hospital's unique floor plan design ensures that each patients's room is only nine feet away from a nurse's station. The new facilities completed in 1987 are adjacent to the Providence Medical Office Plaza, home to many of the hospital's medical staff.

PROVIDENCE HOSPITAL

Where Age-Old Values Meet Modern Care

When the Daughters of Charity founded Mobile's Providence Hospital in 1854, could they have imagined that it would grow from a 60-bed central city infirmary to a 349-bed full-service tertiary care hospital? Yes, they probably could, because the kind of faith it took for them to dedicate their lives to quality health care has been the guiding principle for Providence ever since—faith in the future of health care, faith in the future of each patient as an individual.

This faith is probably best expressed in the "five core values" which our staff, administrators, and physicians have upheld from the beginning:

- ◆ *Respect*—A high regard for the worth of each person
- ◆ *Quality Service*—Excellence in duty or work performed for others
- ◆ *Simplicity*—Honesty, integrity, and straightforwardness
- ◆ *Advocacy for the Poor*—Supporting the cause of those who lack resources for a reasonable quality of life
- ◆ *Inventiveness to Infinity*—Boundless creativity

These aren't just words to put on a plaque; they are our living philosophy, and we strive to fulfill them every day.

By the 1980s the westward growth of the city of Mobile had made it clear that in order to best serve the needs of our community, we would have to grow with it. A tremendous advantage of this move was the opportunity to update our facilities to accommodate the most modern technology and care.

Our present facility, completed in 1987, is located in west Mobile on Airport Boulevard. It is adjacent to the 157-acre Providence Park, which is being developed for commercial and residential uses. The unique design ensures that each patient's room is only nine feet away from a nurse's station.

Adjacent to the hospital, via a skyway bridge, is the Providence Medical Office Plaza, which is home to physicians representing cardiology, family practice, internal medicine, obstetrics and gynecology, oncology, orthopedics, surgery, other specialties, and sub-specialties. What attracts physicians to Providence Hospital? Access to all the latest equipment, technology, and methods for one thing. Another, equally important, is the cooperation and expertise they receive from the Providence staff. It is a combination of these—physicians, the technology, the staff—that allows Providence to excel in its various "centers" of special needs: the Heart Care Center, the Diabetes Center, the Family Birth Center, and a 24-hour Emergency Room.

Providence's staff of more than 1,900 employees strives to provide patients with the best possible care. It is not an accident or a case of luck that the people at Providence are such special individuals. It is a conscious effort of Providence Hospital to encourage and foster that kind of care for the whole person. For this hospital, since its founding, it is not just an idea, but a way of life.

Yes, it's a long way from 60 beds, but the same faith on which we began sustains us today as we enter a new era of health care reform. ⚜

The combination of the physicians, the technology, and the staff allows Providence to excel in its various 'centers' such as the Family Birth Center.

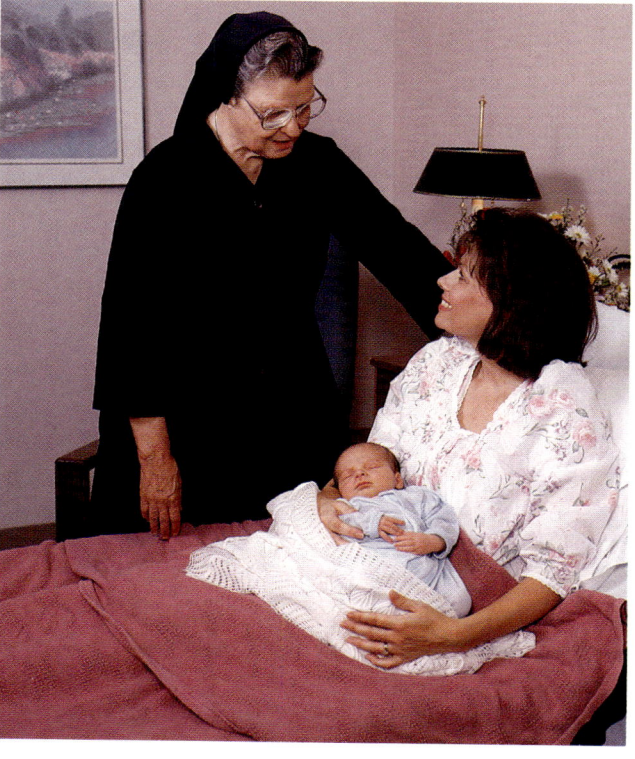

CARDIO-THORACIC AND VASCULAR SURGICAL ASSOCIATES

Cardio-Thoracic and Vascular Surgical Associates (CTVSA), a group of surgeons, nurses, and physicians' assistants specializing in cardiac, thoracic, and vascular surgery, has offices at Mobile Infirmary Medical Center and Providence Hospital, with privileges at all Mobile hospitals.

Dr. Louie Wilson founded CTVSA in 1971 upon entering private practice in Mobile. Since that time, CTVSA has been responsible for initiating open-heart surgery programs at the Mobile Infirmary and Providence Hospital and has served as the cardiothoracic surgical staff at the University of South Alabama, where their physicians remain on the clinical faculty.

Group physicians, Drs. Louie C. Wilson, John E. Stone Jr., William E. Johnson III, and Mark A. Goncalves, head the CTVSA group which presently performs about 1,000 major operations each year, with 700 of these being open-heart procedures. They are especially proud of their overall surgical results and overall outcomes, which are comparable to any major center around the country.

All CTVSA physicians are certified by the American Board of Surgery and American Board of Thoracic Surgery, and all are members of the Mobile County Medical Society, Medical Association of the State of Alabama, American Medical Association, and Society of Thoracic Surgeons.

In addition, Dr. Wilson has a special certificate in vascular surgery from the American Board of Surgery and, along with Drs. Stone and Johnson, is a Fellow of the American College of Surgeons, the American College of Cardiology, and the American College of Chest Physicians, with Dr. Goncalves being an Associate Fellow of these same groups. Dr. Wilson is a member of the Alton Ochsner Surgical Society, and along with Dr. Stone, is a member of the Southern Thoracic Surgical Association and the Nathan Womack Surgical Society. Additionally, Dr. Stone is a member and past president of the John W. Kirklin Surgical Society, with Dr. Johnson being a member of the Denton A. Cooley Cardiovascular Surgical Society.

Besides being licensed to practice in Alabama, one or more of the group's physicians are licensed to practice in Texas, North Carolina, Louisiana, Tennessee, Georgia, and Florida.

One of the most important aspects of CTVSA's successful practice is the extensive contributions rendered by their nurses and physicians' assistant. Lisa Anderson, RN, clinical coordinator for the Mobile Infirmary service, and Sarah Roberts, RN, MSN, coordinator of the Providence Hospital service provide invaluable help, not only to the CTVSA surgeons, but, more importantly, to the patients, cardiologists, and primary care physicians. They also provide preliminary evaluation of problems and organize the complicated scheduling that is a part of the daily practice. Marie Jeffrey, RN, BSN, provides the same skills in the office and outpatient setting. Melissa Bearden, SA, PAC, is the primary first assistant in surgery and provides additional help in both in-patient and office settings. All work many long, hard hours each week along with the surgeons.

Physicians (left to right) Drs. Stone, Johnson, Goncalves, and Wilson head the CTVSA group, which presently performs about one thousand major operations each year.

CTVSA is fortunate to have a very capable and experienced clerical staff headed by office manager Lee Adams. Julia Middleton and Carolyn Thompson handle patient accounts, JoAnn Bell is transcriptionist and secretary to the physicians, and Paula Reed is receptionist and appointments secretary. These ladies all do an outstanding job keeping the office running smoothly.

The entire staff of CTVSA, physicians and employees, is dedicated to providing the very best service to their patients and their families. From careful preoperative evaluation to meticulous surgical technique and attentive postoperative management, Cardio-Thoracic and Vascular Surgical Associates is committed to excellence and to inspiring confidence and trust in the patients and their referring physicians.

CTVSA physicians perform over 700 open-heart procedures annually and are responsible for initiating open-heart surgery programs at the Mobile Infirmary and Providence Hospital.

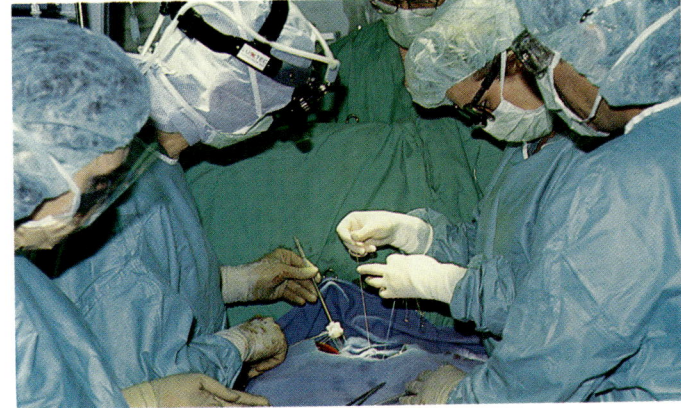

A Gulf Coast Treasure

PrimeHealth, a Mobile community managed-care organization, is attentive to the needs of the members it serves.

PRIMEHEALTH

From its inception in 1984, PrimeHealth's mission has been to offer the highest quality medical care available, as well as provide comprehensive coverage at a reasonable cost. The growth and success of this relatively young company can be attributed to its commitment to this goal.

What began 10 years ago as a small staff model health maintenance organization has grown into the PrimeHealth Companies. This thriving managed care organization offers employers a variety of benefit plan designs and funding options. The PrimeHealth Companies include both a federally and state qualified HMO, as well as a company providing third party administrative services to self-funded employer health plans.

Sensitive to the ever-changing healthcare environment, PrimeHealth has been a leader in the development of innovative products and services such as an open-ended HMO, or point-of-service plan. The PrimeChoice plan allows members to go outside the HMO network for medical services. PrimeChoice is available for employers who want to have the cost savings of an HMO, while retaining the freedom to choose non HMO providers. PriMed 2/25 meets the healthcare needs of employers with 2 to 25 employees, offering comprehensive healthcare benefits at an affordable cost. The latest product, PrimeComp, is bringing PrimeHealth's managed care expertise to Workers Compensation medical claims. As the only staff model HMO in Alabama, PrimeHealth has taken the staff model concept a step further by offering its own psychiatric and substance abuse facility, TriCare. Tricare is a center for family counseling and treatment within the managed-care company, with a full staff of physicians, counselors, and nurses.

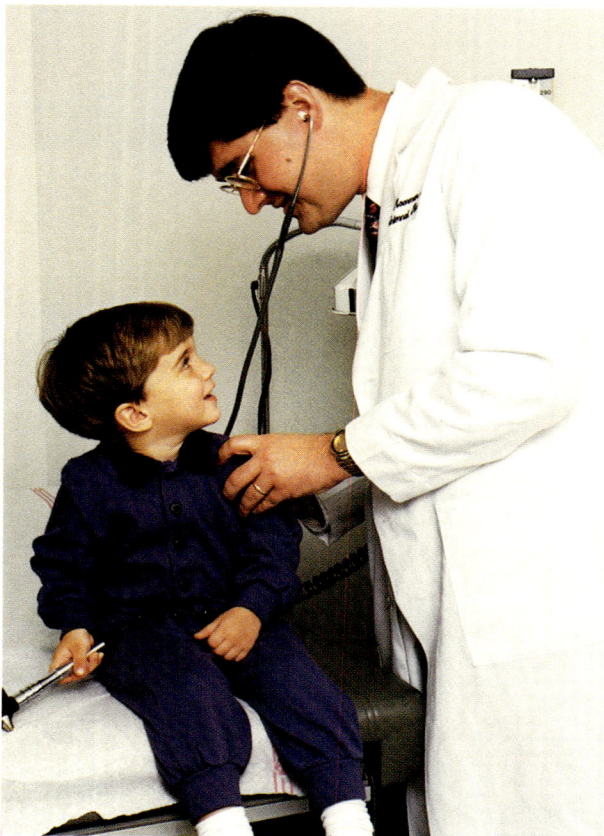

With over 160 employees, PrimeHealth provides high quality, cost-effective healthcare to their members.

The success of the PrimeHealth Companies can be attributed to the fact that the plan was established with two fundamental purposes: first, to introduce the community to the many resources of the University of South Alabama Medical System and second, to bring the alternative concept of managed care to Mobile's business and industry and to assist employers in containing the spiraling cost of healthcare.

As PrimeHealth completes its first decade of service to the people of southern Alabama, it is only appropriate to look back upon the decisions and events that provided the opportunities for the growth and development of the plan.

On July 19, 1984, Mobile Health Plan was officially formed as a not-for-profit corporation. On October 1, 1984, Mobile Health Plan, doing business as PrimeHealth, commenced operations as an HMO and began servicing its enrolled membership. On November 27, 1985, PrimeHealth became Alabama's first federally qualified health maintenance organization serving Mobile County, Baldwin County, and portions of south Washington County. The plan's service area has now been expanded to include Clarke and Escambia Counties as well.

The relationship between PrimeHealth and the community has continued to flourish, with the plan growing to a membership of over 35,000 comprised of individuals from over 250 employer groups. PrimeHealth operates five modern primary care facilities where members receive the majority of their healthcare. The Adult, Pediatric, and OB/GYN Care Centers are located at the PrimeHealth complex in West Mobile, along with Pediatric and Adult facilities in Daphne and Fairhope.

To further enhance our services, PrimeHealth has networked extensively with over 300 physicians in the community, utilizing 8 area hospitals, 51 pharmacies, and other healthcare providers.

Today PrimeHealth stands ready to meet the challenges the next decade will surely bring. As in the past, each step forward will be motivated by the ongoing mission that began 10 years ago with the inception of the plan: to provide premier, community-oriented healthcare services to a family of members. ⚜

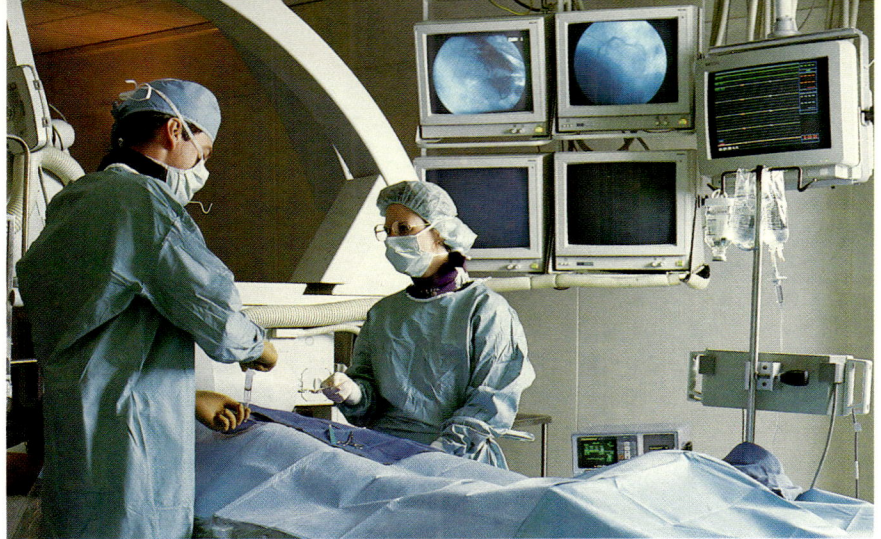

MOBILE INFIRMARY MEDICAL CENTER

Sigmund Freud once admitted, "I have not yet been able to answer . . . the great question that has never been answered: What does a woman want?"

Well, in 1896 a group of determined women knew exactly what they wanted—to establish an infirmary and a school of nursing for Mobile. And they did. They held numerous bazaars and "entertainments" to raise the money to make Mobile Infirmary a reality in 1910.

The Mobile Infirmary of today is best described by a 41-year employee, Geraldine James, who has since retired, "You've come a long way, baby!"

Mobile Infirmary Medical Center is now a 704-bed, acute care facility offering services and specialty areas not found in the average community hospital. It is the largest private, not-for-profit community hospital in Alabama and is staffed by more than 500 physicians and 3,000 employees.

Mobile Infirmary is a leading surgical center and performs more surgical procedures than any hospital in the state. It initiated the city's first outpatient surgery center and is the only area hospital offering 24-hour, seven-day-a-week anesthesia coverage.

The Infirmary's Center for Women and Children offers a nurturing environment for patients, their families, and staff. Family-centered care highlights the labor and delivery area, which provides individualized nursing care. The Level II nursery houses state-of-the-art equipment in a nurse-friendly environment. The postpartum unit continues the family-centered philosophy and provides an aesthetically pleasing environment, coupled with a nursing staff that is dedicated to providing the finest medical, physical, and emotional care for each individual patient.

The Infertility Center at Mobile Infirmary Medical Center provides the latest in reproductive technology by combining a reproductive endocrinologist and special laboratory facilities with the University of South Alabama College of Medicine's Infertility Clinic.

Mobile Infirmary's PRO Health Fitness and Rehabilitation Center is the only medically-oriented wellness facility providing the region's only comprehensive outpatient rehab services offering treatment for stroke, spinal cord injury, traumatic brain injury, neuromuscular disorders, orthopedic injury, amputation, and arthritis, as well as a full range of conditioning programs for the healthy individual.

Mobile Infirmary is a leading surgical center and performs more surgical procedures than any hospital in the state.

The Rotary Rehabilitation Hospital, a division of Mobile Infirmary Medical Center, offers the region's only comprehensive physical medicine and rehabilitation program. Inpatient and outpatient programs enable individuals to return to a productive lifestyle.

The Infirmary's sophisticated Cardiology Services Division gets its reputation through the coordination of many departments, including the heart cath lab, open-heart surgery, nuclear cardiology, electrodiagnostic services, telemetry, coronary care, and surgical intensive care units and the state's largest cardiac rehab program, Operation Bounce-Back.

The Pulmonary Rehabilitation Education Program (PREP) is one of the conditioning programs offered through Mobile Infirmary to improve overall health and fitness for those suffering from lung disease and related illnesses. It is the largest program of its kind in Alabama and the second largest in the United States.

Mobile Infirmary Medical Center's Industrial Medicine program utilizes wellness, prevention, and education to help control industry health care costs in our region while efficiently assisting the injured worker to return to the workforce.

The Infirmary 65 Diagnostic Center, located just off Interstate 65 at Dauphin Street, offers the community the opportunity to receive the latest technological testing in a comfortable and convenient setting.

Mobile Infirmary Medical Center has a proven formula for success. Dedicated staff plus advanced technology multiplied by a sincere commitment to the community equals a hospital that cares with a commitment to excellence and a passion to heal. ⚜

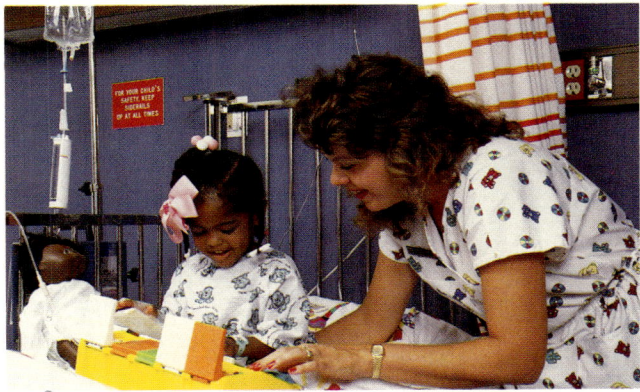

A family-centered philosophy of providing a nurturing environment for patients is Mobile Infirmary Medical Center's commitment to the community.

BLUE CROSS AND BLUE SHIELD OF ALABAMA

Blue Cross and Blue Shield of Alabama's Mobile District Office is the southern base for one of Alabama's leading corporations. The Mobile Blue Cross office opened in the mid-60s with one phone, one clerical worker, one CRT computer terminal, and two sales representatives.

Today the Mobile office serves the 15 counties making up southwestern Alabama. Its staff of 30 includes marketing and customer service representatives, administrative personnel, and a PBX operator. Also working from the Mobile District Office are four managed-care nurses and three reimbursement auditors.

Blue Cross and Blue Shield of Mobile moved into its attractive new "home" at 4750 Airport Boulevard in 1985, becoming the first free-standing Blue Cross district office in the state. The office is constructed on a piece of land separating residential and corporate neighborhoods. In order to blend aesthetically into the community, Blue Cross asked its residential neighbors to collaborate with the architects to develop a design that would be both pleasing and functional. The Mobile Blue Cross office reflects the time, thought, and effort put into this project. This building has received numerous accolades from neighbors and organizations, including landscape and architectural awards from the Azalea Trail Festival, the Mobile Area Jaycees, Keep Mobile Beautiful, and the Tree Commission.

Mike Phillips, district sales manager for Blue Cross and Blue Shield of Mobile, explains the company's purpose: "We are in business to do what our customers want us to do. Commitment to our customers is the foundation of Blue Cross' success."

Blue Cross and Blue Shield of Mobile responds to more than 2,300 customer service calls per week. These calls come from employees of huge corporations to businesses with a payroll of three or less.

Blue Cross and Blue Shield of Alabama is headquartered in Birmingham, Alabama. The company now has four district marketing and customer service offices and six satellite marketing offices scattered throughout the state.

Blue Cross and Blue Shield of Alabama provides health and dental care coverage to over 2 million people and covers over half the state's population. The Alabama Plan is a member of the national Blue Cross Blue Shield Association, which helps Blue Cross and Blue Shield Plans across the nation by providing research and cost containment information, national lobbying support, and protection of the use of the Cross and Shield name and logo.

Blue Cross and Blue Shield of Alabama offers several specialized programs that are designed to control rising health care costs. The Preferred Provider Organization controls costs by asking physicians to accept reduced fees for specific procedures. Blue Cross and Blue Shield was Alabama's first company to put together a statewide network of physicians. Today this network of Preferred Medical Doctors (PMD) is the largest network in the state. The program includes over 5,000 doctors and 130 participating hospitals.

Blue Cross and Blue Shield also introduced Managed Care Programs, which enhance the quality of care while saving health care dollars. Managed Care Programs involve Blue Cross registered nurses working with the doctor, patient, family, and employer in making the best decisions for the subscriber.

Blue Cross and Blue Shield is finding better ways to manage health care costs and services through the specially developed ACE (Analyze, Compare, and Explore) software system. ACE is a computer program that tracks health-related information according to factors such as demographics and geography and helps Blue Cross to pinpoint and research unusual or problem areas.

Blue Cross and Blue Shield of Mobile cares about the community and is particularly active in the United Way and many health-related charities. The company's major commitment, however, has been the establishment and support of the Alabama Child Caring Foundation. The foundation provides health coverage which allows thousands of Alabama children to receive needed health care. It meets the needs of the children whose parents are not eligible for Medicaid, yet do not make enough to buy insurance. Blue Cross Blue Shield matches dollar-for-dollar all contributions, in addition to absorbing all administrative costs. Since its March 1988 inception, the Alabama Child Caring Foundation has served over 20,520 children in Alabama.

Blue Cross and Blue Shield of Alabama's corporate purpose is: "To be the market leader in design, development, marketing, purchase, and delivery of employee benefits and other services in a caring, ethical, and financially viable manner." Blue Cross and Blue Shield of Mobile will continue to be known as "The Caring Company" by responding to the needs of every customer with a sense of urgency and compassion and by working hard to make the Port City of Mobile and surrounding areas a terrific place to live. ⚜

Located on a piece of land separating residential and corporate neighborhoods, the Mobile Blue Cross office reflects the time, thought, and effort put into making the building blend aesthetically into the community. This building has received numerous accolades from neighbors and organizations.

A Gulf Coast Treasure

At Springhill Memorial Hospital quality health care in a family oriented atmosphere is instilled in every employee.

SPRINGHILL MEMORIAL HOSPITAL

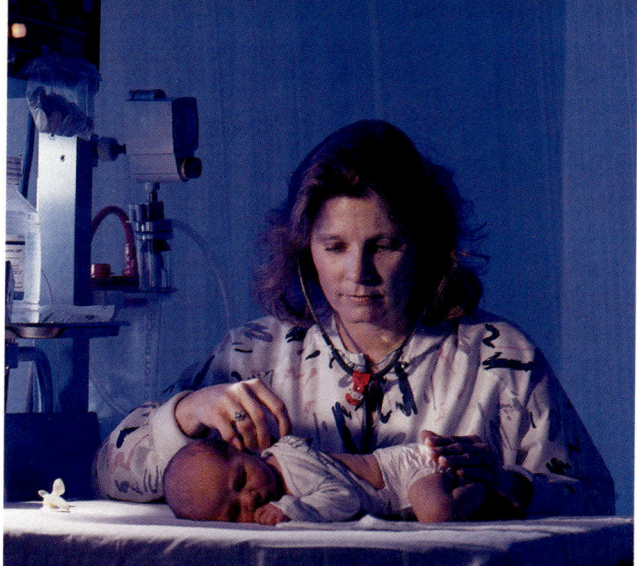

Springhill Memorial Hospital was founded by Gerald L. Wallace, M.D. in 1975 as a private, tax-paying, acute-care medical and surgical facility. The hospital began with 35 beds, grew to 252, and the prognosis for continued growth is promising. Springhill Memorial has incorporated the services and technology of a big health care facility into the de-institutionalized, family-friendly environment of a small hospital.

Bill Mason, President of the hospital adds, "Springhill Memorial Hospital is the area's finest medical facility. Springhill Memorial has earned an enviable reputation for its quality of care, convenience of location, and courtesy to patients. The hospital successfully blends a family-oriented atmosphere with state-of-the-art technology."

Springhill Memorial has always been a leader and is proof positive that, "there's a first time for everything." Springhill Memorial was first on the Gulf Coast to equip its Urology Center with a non-invasive lithotripter to treat kidney stones and the first regional medical center within a 500-mile radius to offer cryosurgery for prostate cancer victims.

Springhill Memorial Hospital was the first to offer the Mobile community the services of a Hyperbaric Oxygen Chamber. The pressurized oxygen treatments provided by this chamber speed the healing of problem wounds, resolve stubborn infections, and increase healing in certain toxic poisoning or critical care cases.

The first private Mobile area emergency room was located at Springhill Memorial. Today it is the only private hospital emergency room in the city with 24-hour staffing by emergency room board-certified physicians and provides radio medical control for Mobile County.

The hospital's WorkMed program led the way in Mobile's effort to help control workers' compensation costs. Springhill Memorial also blazed the trail in home health care by offering the area's only hospital-based Home Health Agency providing intermittent medical service to home-bound patients.

In 1984 Springhill Memorial Hospital opened the first family oriented OB Center in Mobile and now delivers more babies than any other private hospital in the city. In 1994 the hospital became the first regional hospital to open a Family Center as an educational and resource center area. The center offers to the community a variety of complimentary educational seminars. Topics range from childcare and parenting skills to personal safety and financial management.

The Health Information Library at the Family Center is Mobile's most extensive collection of health care information written and produced in a language that can be understood by the entire family. The library offers general health literature, videos, physician information, and national directories which list various health associations and government clearinghouses and their toll-free information hot lines.

Springhill Memorial is environmentally conscious and was the first area hospital to invest in environmental protection by installing a progressive medical waste disposal system.

Other services include Springhill Memorial's comprehensive laser surgery, which is equipped with state-of-the-art equipment and staffed by experienced medical personnel trained to perform many laser surgical procedures, primarily gallbladder removal and endometriosis treatment. Rounding out the menu of services is Springhill's MRI and CT diagnostic equipment and its Sleep/Wake Disorders Center.

A stroll down any of Springhill Memorial's corridors treats visitors, patients, and hospital staff to a delightful display of children's art—the product of the Color by Kids Program sponsored by the hospital. Springhill Memorial provides area schools with the necessary art supplies for the contest. The children's works are judged, and the winners are framed and hung on walls throughout the hospital. Winning schools receive additional financial support from the hospital.

Springhill Memorial Hospital is equipped with 252 beds, 3 medical office buildings, and complete medical-surgical services.

Springhill Memorial is a supporter of public education in the Mobile area and has adopted Mary B. Austin Elementary School as its partner in education. The hospital enthusiastically participates in Junior Achievement, Coalition for a Drug-Free Mobile, and the United Way.

Springhill Memorial Hospital keeps growing in its reputation as the hospital that presents the latest in medical services and technology while providing quality health care with a family feel. ⚜

MOBILE BAY OB-GYN ASSOCIATES

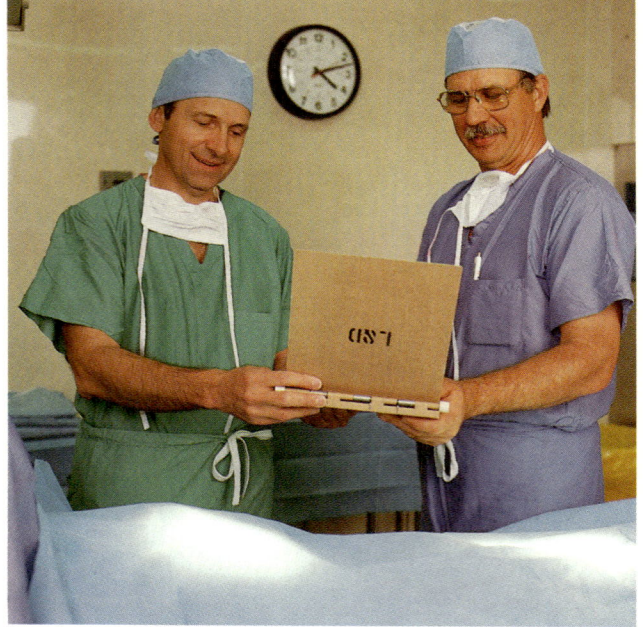

Dr. Frank H. Long and Dr. John B. Howell discuss the operative care of a Mobile Bay OB-GYN patient.

In 1975 Dr. William H. Curtright originated an obstetrical and gynecological practice in Mobile and was subsequently joined by Dr. Frank H. Long and later by Dr. J. Randy Bentley. Dr. John B. Howell soon joined them merging his practice, and eventually following was Dr. Erin C. Neal. Since that time, the group, now known as Mobile Bay OB-GYN Associates, has evolved into one of the most recognized and respected medical groups in Southwest Alabama.

With their patients' health foremost in mind, the five physicians and supporting staff of Mobile Bay OB-GYN Associates strive to provide the finest medical care available.

All of the physicians within the group are certified by the American Board of Obstetrics and Gynecology and have many society affiliations, including the American College of Obstetricians and Gynecologists, American Fertility Society, American Association of Gynecologic Laparoscopists, Gynecologic Laser Society, American Medical Association, and state and local OB-GYN societies.

The obstetrical practice of Mobile Bay OB-GYN Associates includes the total management of pregnancy, not only routine prenatal care, labor, and delivery, but also the management of any medical or surgical problem associated with pregnancy.

The group's gynecology practice deals with the health of the genital tract of the nonpregnant female, including the evaluation and correction of factors associated with infertility, menstrual disorders, birth control, pelvic pain, premenstrual syndrome, and sexuality.

While the group is on staff at all Mobile hospitals and services Springhill Memorial's out-patient facility, their primary hospital is the Mobile Infirmary, where they have the significant advantage of being on the same floor as the Infirmary's labor and delivery facilities. During office hours, this affords the doctors the benefits of being just down a corridor, only steps away from their hospitalized patients.

The group's office has a fetal monitor connected to the labor and delivery unit which enables the physicians to follow their patients' labor with the capability to continuously monitor baby and mother. Mobile Bay OB-GYN offers not only the expected, or "usual" care for the pregnant and nonpregnant female, but they also offer such extras as glucose screening and mammography and are able to handle most of their lab work in office.

The physicians at Mobile Bay OB-GYN are trained in the most recent advances within their field, which includes minimally invasive surgery (Laser surgery and Laparoscopic Assisted Vaginal Hysterectomy or LAVH) and gynecologic cancer screening, providing their patients with the finest in diagnostic and therapeutic procedures available. Also, the group performs Loop Electrosurgical Excision Procedures (LEEP), an effective treatment for the removal of the abnormal cell growth called dysplasia from the cervix or mouth of the uterus.

Affording quality health care for women is the goal at Mobile Bay OB-GYN. From adolescence through the reproductive years, the menopause through the postmenopausal period, women have and can continue to depend on Mobile Bay OB-GYN for their comprehensive health care. The physicians and staff of Mobile Bay OB-GYN Associates are dedicated to providing their patients the very latest in medical care, along with the individual attention they've come to expect. ⚜

Mobile Bay OB-GYN founder, Dr. William H. Curtright, along with his staff, is dedicated to providing the latest in medical care technology and individual attention for the organization's patients.

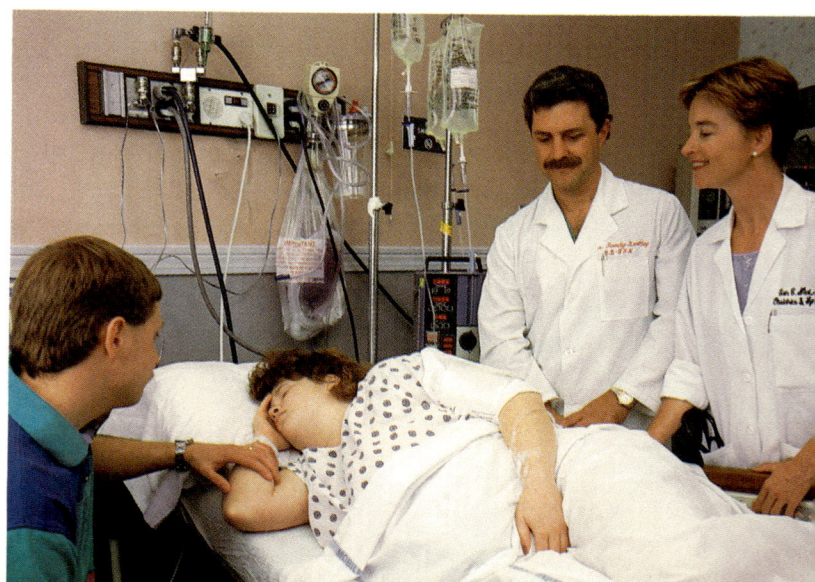

Dr. J. Randy Bentley and Dr. Erin C. Neal monitor the progress of an obstetrical patient's labor.

PARTIAL HOSPITAL INSTITUTE OF AMERICA, INC.

Since the early 1960s, it has been evident that large numbers of patients with severe psychopathology could be treated with a high quality of care and at decreased costs in a partial hospital, as opposed to an inpatient psychiatric unit.

With this idea in mind, James S. Harrold Jr., M.D., founded Mobile's Partial Hospital Institute of America, Inc., of which he serves as president, CEO, and medical director. The Mobile facility is the third such institute founded by Dr. Harrold.

PHIA offers five areas of day hospital and day treatment: psychiatry, chemical dependency, dual diagnoses (psychopathology and chemical dependency), chronic pain management, and medical review officer services.

According to Dr. Harrold, approximately 85 percent of patients now treated in a traditional inpatient psychiatric hospital setting can be treated more effectively in the Partial Hospital Institute of America at half the price. A properly constructed partial hospital can also prevent from 70-80 percent of patients who would otherwise require hospitalization from ever entering an inpatient unit.

PHIA offers day hospital care for those patients who have more acute pathology than those in day treatment. These patients require more intensive care in the areas of nursing care, psychiatric follow-up, supervision in medication, recreation therapy, dietary, and others.

In contrast, day treatment patients are more stable, but still sub-acute and too ill for traditional outpatient care. Day treatment is more focused on readiness to return to work or to begin the process of disability.

PHIA's intensive and comprehensive partial hospital program seeks to achieve and/or reverse certain qualities in its patients. They have developed a unique programmatic construct they call SAFE, by which they achieve:

S—STRENGTH. They strive for patients to become strong. Often psychological wounds take much longer to heal than physical wounds.

A—AUTONOMY. They also strive to bring their patients to autonomous functioning. An important facet of the program is that the patient can go home at the end of each day and be home on weekends.

F—FREEDOM. They find that many of their patients have been psychologically ill or under intense stress for so long that they have forgotten what it is to feel good.

E—EQUALITY. There are those who feel stigmatized if they seek treatment for their illness. PHIA works actively to dispel these myths leading to a feeling of equality.

PHIA's full multi-disciplinary staff includes the following: psychiatry, psychology, social work, dietary therapy, senior chemical dependency rehabilitation counselors, nursing, recreation therapy and leisure activities, biofeedback, mental health specialists, and a full compliment of administrative support staff.

In all areas of treatment, PHIA stresses the importance of family involvement, which they consider to be a vital component of the treatment process. Families, and significant others, are much easier to engage, for they can see the changes in their loved ones on a daily basis because they (patients) come home each night. They are also able to contact the psychiatrist directly and talk with him at any hour.

For their chemical dependency patients, PHIA offers a once-a-week aftercare group, which includes spouses, and twice-a-week AA (Alcoholics Anonymous) and NA (Narcotic Anonymous) meetings, accompanied by a chemical dependency counselor. Families who participate in these groups are better able to understand the illness and recognize any early warning signs of a relapse.

The long list of professional organizations to which Dr. Harrold and his staff belong, as well as their many credentials, number almost as many as the advantages offered by Partial Hospital Institute of America, Inc. (PHIA).

When it comes to treatment for the mentally ill or chemically dependent, Partial Hospital Institute of America, Inc., because of their original concept and innovative approach, could be an option to traditional hospitalization.

PHIA is Medicare approved and has achieved accreditation from the Joint Commission on Accreditation of Health Care Organizations. PHIA is also certified by the Alabama Department of Mental Health and Mental Retardation and is a member of the Alabama Partial Hospital Association; the American Association for Partial Hospitalization, Inc.; the Alabama Association for Healthcare Quality; and the Alabama Hospital Association. All major insurances are accepted.

Their mission is to provide a superior quality treatment at a fraction of the usual cost. ✣

Dr. James S. Harrold, Jr. founded Mobile's Partial Hospital Institute of America to treat patients with a high quality of care in a partial hospital, as opposed to an inpatient psychiatric unit.

Through PHIA's intensive and comprehensive partial hospital program called SAFE, patients can regain a sense of peace that comes from a psychological well-being.

CARDIOLOGY ASSOCIATES OF MOBILE, P.C.

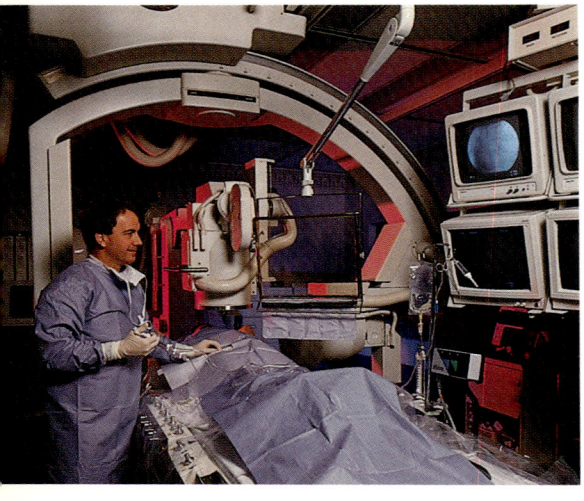

Dr. Phillips is shown at work in the Cardiac Cath Lab.

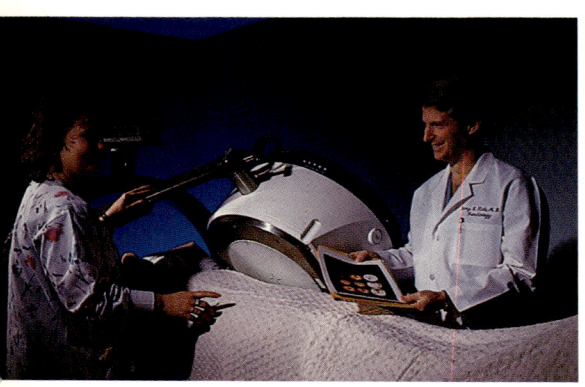

Dr. Hale evaluates a nuclear stress patient.

Cardiology Associates was founded by Gerry M. Phillips, M.D. in 1985, shortly after finishing his training in invasive cardiology. Since then the group has grown dramatically both in size and in scope. The group currently consists of six cardiologists. The other physicians are Kenneth E. Francez Jr., M.D., Terence E. Hale, M.D., J. Andrew Morrow Jr., M.D., Charles W. Parrott, M.D., and William D. Denney, M.D.

Cardiology Associates provides comprehensive invasive and non-invasive cardiology services to patients in Mobile County, Baldwin County, and other surrounding areas. New patients are referred to the group through their primary physician or are seen directly at the patient's request.

Cardiology Associates provides invasive cardiology services, including cardiac catheterization, percutaneous transluminal coronary angioplasty (PTCA), directional coronary atherectomy, laser angioplasty, and intracoronary stent placement.

Non-invasive cardiology services provided include inpatient and outpatient consultation, EKGs, echocardiograms, holter monitor scans, nuclear cardiology studies, exercise stress testing, pacemaker management, transtelephonic monitoring, cardiac rehabilitation, preventive and educational programs, and nutritional counseling.

The group has five office locations. The main office is located in the Providence Medical Office Building adjacent to the Providence Hospital. The other two office locations in Mobile are in the professional office buildings at the Springhill Memorial Hospital and at the Mobile Infirmary Medical Center. The two office locations in Baldwin County are in Fairhope near Thomas Hospital and in Foley near South Baldwin Hospital.

Cardiology Associates has taken an aggressive stance with regard to outreach and to providing cardiology services to areas outside of Mobile. The practice is involved in outreach in the Baldwin County area with offices in Fairhope and Foley. This outreach activity provides Baldwin County residents with cardiology services that would not otherwise be available.

A number of the physicians of the Cardiology Associates group have additional special interests in the area of cardiology. Dr. Phillips has special interests in atherectomy and laser angioplasty. Dr. Francez's special interests are in mitral valve prolapse, balloon angioplasty, and stress echocardiography. Dr. Hale's special interests are in nuclear cardiology and invasive cardiology. Dr. Morrow also has special interests and is trained in nuclear and invasive cardiology. Dr. Parrot has received special training in angioplasty and is also nuclear trained. Dr. Denney is trained in nuclear cardiology and has an interest in echocardiography.

The practice is supported by an administrative staff and employees numbering approximately 30, including cardiac nurses, echocardiography technicians, nuclear cardiology technicians, and clerical and business office personnel. The staff and the physicians strive to remain abreast of the latest advances in cardiology by participating in continuing education programs and seminars in order to provide the most up-to-date and effective care available.

Whenever possible, the physicians speak to other physicians and to the general public about the prevention and treatment of heart disease. The group also co-directs the Providence Hospital's Fit For Life Cardiac Rehabilitation Program. At Fit For Life patients who have suffered a heart attack or other serious heart-related problems are encouraged to undergo lifestyle changes and begin exercise programs that will lead to their recovery. Cardiology Associates has plans to continue to expand its services in the area of education and prevention. "Patient education is all important to us, and prevention is the number one thing we can do in cardiology to reduce the incidence of heart disease and prevent death. The answer is prevention up front instead of treatment after the fact," says Dr. Phillips.

Cardiology Associates' physicians continually strive to maintain the highest standards of care in the area of cardiology and provide the most up-to-date services to their patients in Mobile and surrounding areas. They are committed to improving their patients' overall cardiovascular health through proper education, effective diagnostic procedures, and the application of cardiology's most current technologies.

Although there are major changes on the horizon with regard to health care, Cardiology Associates sees these changes as opportunities and plans to continue to expand and change as necessary to provide the most comprehensive cardiology-related services in the area. The group is positioned for the future to meet the needs of referring physicians and patients in all aspects of cardiology.

PULMONARY ASSOCIATES OF MOBILE, P.A.

Pulmonary Associates of Mobile, P.A. is a pulmonary and critical care medicine practice specializing in the treatment of diseases of the lungs and critically ill patients. Founded by Dr. John N. McAtee in 1980 as the first board-certified pulmonary practice in Mobile, Pulmonary Associates operates under the philosophy of providing immediate care for the critically ill patient. Pulmonary Associates is known for its availability, both to its patients and referring physicians.

The group attends patients in all Mobile area hospitals and has initiated outreach offices and consultative services in Atmore and Foley, Alabama. In addition, the group has three fully staffed offices located throughout Mobile.

Pulmonary Associates is considered a premier pulmonary and critical care medical group. The doctors associated with Pulmonary Associates are known to work long hours caring for critically ill patients, and many of the group members have developed special interests in unique procedures and techniques relative to pulmonary medicine.

After attending an educational program at the Stanford University Sleep Disorder Center, Dr. McAtee helped develop the Sleep Disorder Center at the Mobile Infirmary Medical Center. With the generous help of the Florence Foundation, Dr. McAtee was instrumental in forming the second largest pulmonary rehabilitation program in the nation located at the Mobile Infirmary Medical Center, known as the Pulmonary Rehabilitation and Education Program, or PREP.

Dr. Gottlieb has developed distinctive skills in laser bronchoscopy and nuclear implants after attending educational seminars for such procedures. He is a medical director of the USA Knollwood respiratory therapy department.

After attending a transtracheal oxygen course in Denver, Colorado, Dr. Saucier introduced the technique of transtracheal oxygen delivery to the Mobile area. In addition, he has been instrumental in providing the mechanism for assessing the details of nutritional support in the hospitalized patient. He also serves as a medical director of the USA Knollwood respiratory therapy department.

Dr. Sindel has a unique interest in cystic fibrosis and has been director of the regional Cystic Fibrosis Center since 1989. He has a strong interest in allergies and their effects on children and adults. He also coordinates and conducts a number of medical research projects.

Dr. Schulte has a special concern in medical ethics and issues relating to death and dying. Dr. Patterson and Dr. Dotson are the two latest members of the group, and they complete the profile for providing pulmonary care to the Mobile area.

In 1991 Pulmonary Associates established its own home oxygen service and is one of the very few pulmonary groups in the country to have undertaken the development of such a program. The main goal of the service is to provide quality home respiratory care and oxygen services that are second to none in the Mobile area.

The future for Pulmonary Associates of Mobile, P.A. is continued growth in the areas of services and expertise. Emphasis is placed on providing the most effective and innovative method of treatment in striving to create, to research, and to evaluate new ideas, enabling patients to lead healthy, productive lifestyles. Dr. McAtee states that "in order to have the existence and persistence of quality pulmonary care, there must be a continued mixing of competent physicians with similarly competent allied health professionals to direct the health care of the pulmonary patient." The physicians at Pulmonary Associates have been committed to this simple philosophy in the past and continue to hold this as their principal for providing quality health care in the future.

Pulmonary Associates is considered a premier pulmonary and critical care medical group. The doctors associated with Pulmonary Associates are (first row) William J. Schulte, M.D.; Scott H. Patterson, M.D.; (second row) Lawrence J. Sindel, M.D.; Randy G. Dotson, M.D.; Marc S. Gottlieb, M.D.; K. Scott Saucier, M.D.; and (third row) John N. McAtee, M.D.

Dr. McAtee instructs a patient at PREP, the second largest pulmonary rehabilitation program in the nation, located at the Mobile Infirmary Medical Center.

COGBURN HEALTH CENTER, INC.

In 1939, when the United States was on the brink of World War II, Mrs. Maude Roberts Cogburn opened a home on Church Street to care for patients who required long-term nursing care.

Ten years earlier Mrs. Cogburn had graduated from Providence School of Nursing as a registered nurse. From graduation in 1929 to the opening of the Church Street home, she worked as a private duty nurse, developing a preference and skill for nursing the elderly.

In five short years the Church Street facility was outgrown, and Mrs. Cogburn moved to Garnett Avenue near Five Points. Just two years later she bought the old Davis Estate on Tuscaloosa Street and incorporated the business as Cogburn Nursing Home, Inc. Over the years, Mrs. Cogburn developed a reputation as a provider of long-term care who placed the patient's needs first and foremost.

In 1959, as a result of 20 years of hard work, often working continuous shifts of 48 hours without any rest, Mrs. Cogburn suffered a heart attack. At this point, her son and daughter-in-law, Mr. and Mrs. W. L. Roberts Sr., became involved in the business. The quality of patient care was sustained and improved upon under their supervision. Soon, Mrs. Cogburn returned to work.

The Cogburn Health Center, Inc. was now a family business. In 1963 the demand for quality nursing care had outgrown the existing facilities, which included several smaller cottages constructed since the 1946 move to Tuscaloosa Street.

Cogburn's commitment is giving those who need it the best care they can get.

That year a 98-bed modern long-term nursing care facility was constructed around the old Davis Home. Once the new structure was completed, the patients were moved from the old building to the new, and a more up-to-date era in skilled nursing care was begun in Mobile.

By 1971 the smaller cottages were replaced by a 52-bed addition, creating a 150-bed facility. William L. Roberts Jr., Suzanne Roberts Hughes, and L. Steven Roberts, Mrs. Cogburn's grandchildren, were now the third generation involved, making it Mobile's oldest continuous private operation of its kind.

Mrs. Cogburn died in 1984, after living several years in what is now known as Cogburn Nursing Center. Several months before her death, she could be seen visiting other patients and residents, directing nurses and aides, and demanding her own particular brand of excellence in caring for patients. She was 92 at the time of her death.

Mrs. and Mrs. W. L. Roberts Sr. are retired, and the three grandchildren are now responsible for the mission of Cogburn Nursing Center, giving people the best long-term care they can receive.

Suzanne Roberts Hughes is the administrator, having received her state license in 1987 after serving as assistant administrator for many years.

From 1970 to 1986, Steve Roberts served as administrator. Today, he is administrator of Roberts' Nursing Center, a new 100-bed long-term care facility.

Bill Roberts, administrator from 1965 to 1970, is now Director of Development of Cogburn's and Roberts' new and expanded services. Cogburn Health Services is the oldest provider of long-term care in Mobile.

After more than half a century, Cogburn Health Services, Inc. is renewing its commitment to excellence in health care and related services. Being at Cogburn's should be the second best thing to being in one's own home. Being the oldest doesn't mean being the best, but being the oldest and being committed means Cogburn has a tradition to build on and a commitment to keep. The tradition is almost 55 years of nursing service to the community. The commitment is doing what Cogburn says it will do—give those who need it the best care they can get. ✤

Dr. Gary M. Rich established The Mobile Heart Center in 1978 to provide the Mobile area with experienced, readily available services devoted to the subspecialty of cardiology.

As planned, The Mobile Heart Center's wide range of services provides all aspects of clinical, diagnostic, invasive, and interventional cardiology. Included are consultative cardiology, cardiac catheterization; all aspects of interventional cardiology, including PTCA, atherectomy, stent placement, and laser angioplasty; echocardiography, including transesophageal echocardiography; arrhythmia detection and management, including electrophysiologic studies, catheter ablation, automatic defibrillator placement and management, pacemaker placement and management; nuclear cardiology, including in-office nuclear capabilities; treadmill stress testing; and dietary counseling.

All Mobile Heart Center physicians are first and foremost clinical cardiologists, but each has special areas of expertise.

Dr. Bedwell specializes in arrhythmias and performs electrophysiologic testing. He installs pacemakers, which prevent abnormal slowing or stopping of the heart, and automatic defibrillators, which treat potentially lethal fast heart rhythms. He also treats some arrhythmias by using a catheter and radio waves to ablate (destroy) abnormal electrical pathways.

Drs. Davis, Rich, Eyrich, and Jordan perform angioplasty, whereby a balloon is used to unclog an artery. This procedure saves many patients from having to undergo coronary artery bypass graft surgery, or from taking large doses of medications chronically.

Dr. Massing does transesophageal echocardiography, which uses an ultrasound probe inserted through the mouth and passed into the esophagus to image the heart. He, along with Drs. Davis and Jordan, performs and interprets nuclear procedures, a technique which involves using radioisotopes injected through a vein in the arm to obtain images of the heart non-invasively.

The list of physicians' credentials at The Mobile Heart Center is an extensive, but one of the most important requirements is that each physician be a caring, personable individual.

The group's physicians pride themselves in taking a personal interest in their patients from diagnosis to discharge. They participate in most phases of care for critically ill patients, beginning with the initial treatment in the emergency room or in consultation, until their problem is resolved as completely as possible.

Whatever the procedure, The Mobile Heart Center's physicians are on hand to counsel and comfort. They are immediately available to their patients and consulting physicians, providing experienced, expert advice and treatment in all aspects of cardiology.

Mobile Heart Center's physicians including (left to right) Jerry D. Jordan, M.D. and Gary M. Rich, M.D., pride themselves in taking a personal interest in their patients from diagnosis to discharge.

THE MOBILE HEART CENTER

True to their commitment to offer complete cardiac care, including patient education, the practice employs a dietitian who privately counsels their outpatients regarding special cardiovascular risk-reducing diets. In the hospital, prior to discharge, one of the group's critical-care trained nurses discusses at length home activity, medications, and special instructions with the patient and family.

Fifteen years ago, three physicians, including Dr. Rich, formed the Operation Bounce Back Cardiac Rehabilitation Program. Today Dr. Rich continues as medical director for this exercise and educational program for patients who are recovering from a cardiac problem.

Just as they feel a responsibility to their patients and colleagues, The Mobile Heart Center group, individually and collectively, feels a responsibility to the citizens of the Mobile area. They support a wide range of charitable organizations, including hospital foundations, The American Heart Association, Camp Rap-A-Hope, Keep Mobile Beautiful, the Exploreum, and many others.

The physicians and staff of The Mobile Heart Center remain prepared for the many changes that are forthcoming in medicine with plans to expand the educational and preventive aspects of the practice, as well as expanding to areas surrounding Mobile. No matter what changes occur, they will always be committed to providing quality cardiology care and advice to their patients and consulting physicians. ⚜

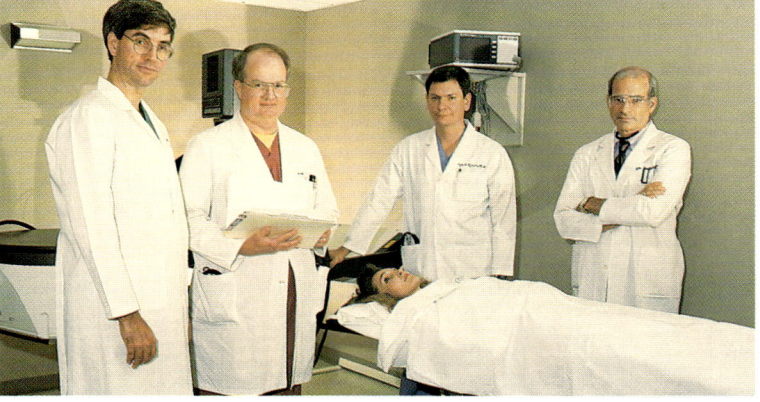

It is the goal of Mobile Heart Center to offer more than just diagnostic and invasive techniques, but to encompass all phases of cardiology care. (Left to right) Noel W. Bedwell, M.D., Archie G. Davis, M.D., George A. Eyrich, M.D., and George K. Massing, M.D. work hard to carry out this goal.

ANESTHESIA SERVICES, P.C.

Anesthesia Services, P.C. is the largest group of its kind in the state and the second largest in the Southeast.

Anesthesia Services, P.C. is a network of caring, dependable clinicians and office staff working together as a team. Anesthesia Services, P.C. was founded on this philosophy in 1957. The group has flourished and today has 28 board-certified or board-eligible physicians and 50 certified registered nurse anesthetists (CRNA) stationed in major hospitals and surgical centers in the Mobile area providing the community with continuous around-the-clock service. Because Anesthesia Services, P.C. personnel are always available, they are frequently called upon to perform hospital services such as inserting difficult IVs when hospital staff are unable to do so. The physicians, CRNAs, and RNs of Anesthesia Services, P.C. are always willing to extend a helping hand. This is the company's philosophy in action.

Anesthesia Services, P.C. is the largest group of its kind in the state and the second largest in the Southeast. In addition to a medical staff consisting of 80 professionals who administer both general and regional anesthesia, the company employs an office staff operating both the primary office in Mobile and its branch office in Fairhope.

The company's primary purpose is to provide quality anesthesia and pain management services to its patients. Perhaps this is best stated through the mission statement adopted by Anesthesia Services, P.C.: "To deliver comprehensive anesthesia in an efficient manner to serve the needs of the community."

The introduction of patient-controlled analgesia (PCA) for post-operative pain management to area hospitals further demonstrates the commitment to quality patient care by Anesthesia Services, P.C. PCA allows the patient to control the frequency of administering pain medication by pressing a handheld button connected to a pump. Safeguards insure that no patient is overmedicated. And interestingly enough, patients on the pump require less pain medication, partly due to the control they have and the rapid response time. Patients without the pump tend to anticipate their pain in order to allow for the time it takes a nurse to obtain and administer their prescribed medication. PCA pumps may be connected through intravenous (IV) or epidural catheters, depending on the surgical site and the patient's needs.

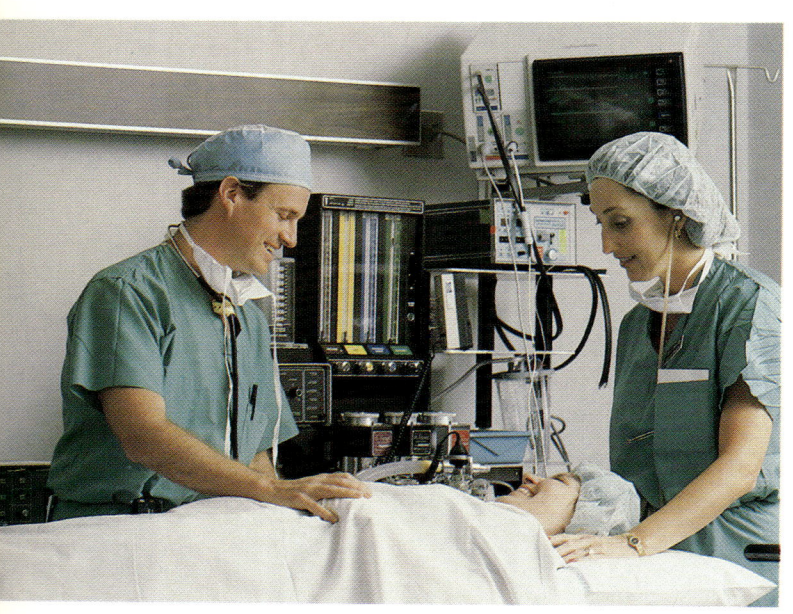

Anesthesia Services, P.C.'s primary purpose is to provide quality anesthesia and pain management services to its patients.

The anesthesia "care team" is the predominant method of practice at Anesthesia Services, P.C. Under this program, pre-operative assessment, intra-operative management, and post-operative care are provided by anesthesiologists, CRNAs, and RNs in a collaborative effort. As a result, patients are afforded a safe, convenient, and cost-effective anesthetic experience.

Utilization review and continuing medical education are two techniques promoted by Anesthesia Services, P.C. Utilization review is conducted by the various hospitals to review each patient's experience to see what aspects, if any, could have been handled more efficiently. Continuing medical education is an in-house program conducted by Anesthesia Services, P.C. for the benefit of its employees. Reviews are led by individual employees who have expertise and knowledge in specific areas as well as by those assigned to research and present topics for discussion. Many lectures are also offered by various professionals from across the country. These programs provide continuing medical education credits which enable the physicians and nurse anesthetists to maintain their certification, as well as to stay abreast of new developments in anesthesia and patient care.

Community involvement is important to Anesthesia Services, P.C. The practice supports numerous medical-related charities as well as civic organizations such as Keep Mobile Beautiful, the Mobile Area Chamber of Commerce, Newspaper in Education, Mobile Opera, September Celebration, and youth athletic teams. The group also enthusiastically provides the clinical rotation training for students from the Manley Cummins School of Nurse Anesthesia in Dothan as well as from the School of Nurse Anesthesia at the University of Alabama at Birmingham.

Anesthesia Services, P.C. personnel are carefully selected on the basis of their knowledge and dependability. The practice has been built over the years through the acquisition of employees with strong character and whose ultimate goal is meeting the special needs of each individual patient. ⚜

A Gulf Coast Treasure

MOBILE ORTHOPEDIC CENTER

Mobile Orthopedic Center, under the direction of Joseph B. Ray, M.D., was established in 1965 as a single physician practice dedicated to the evaluation and treatment of general orthopedic problems. Having completed medical school and orthopedic training at the University of Alabama and Crippled Children's Hospital in Birmingham, Dr. Ray was prepared to handle most musculoskeletal injuries, diseases, and illnesses of adults and children. He is certified by the American Board of Orthopaedic Surgeons and has served as an orthopedic surgeon in the United States Air Force before coming to Mobile.

Dr. Ray's practice has been influenced by attendance at medical educational meetings and by visits to physicians with recognized expertise. Early in his career, he received instruction from Dr. Robert Salter of Toronto in innominate osteotomy, a surgical treatment of Legg-Perthes disease, and congenital hip dislocation. He has followed these young patients to adulthood to monitor the excellent long-term effects of the surgery.

Traveling to England, Dr. Ray observed early total hip replacement surgery by surgeons John Charnley and Peter Ring. These techniques offered dramatic and long-term functional improvement for patients, as there was no good solution for advanced arthritis of joints prior to joint replacement surgery.

While attending a U.A.B. arthritis seminar in 1969, Dr. Ray learned of the development of arthroscopy. A small telescope or endoscope allows the surgeon to look directly into joints to diagnose and treat diseases. The arthroscope enhances visualization of the entire joint and eliminates the need for large surgical incisions which are painful and take longer to heal. The evolutionary development of video-arthroscopy enables Dr. Ray to evaluate and treat injuries and diseases of almost all joints through small puncture incisions. In recent years he has added the routine use of laser energy to his arthroscopic procedures to treat a greater variety of orthopedic problems with better clinical results.

A long-standing interest in less-invasive surgical methods and in problems of the lumbar spine has led Dr. Ray to study "percutaneous discectomy," which allows removal of disc material without a large incision. Its use is extremely beneficial in the treatment of uncomplicated lumbar disc problems with open surgery reserved for more severe cases.

As chairman of the foot committee of the Alabama Orthopaedic Society, Dr. Ray has been involved in a state-wide educational effort in the care of orthopedic problems of the foot. Dr. Ray, with the help of Dr. Kenneth Hannon, was active in the formation of the Southeastern Orthopedic Foot Club, which he presently serves as program chairman. In addition to routine care of foot and ankle problems, he has been actively involved in the extension of less-invasive endoscopic and laser methods of treatment in soft tissue areas of knees, elbows, wrists, hands, and feet.

A native Alabamian, Dr. Ray received undergraduate education at Duke University and graduated from the University of Alabama and the Medical College of Alabama. He holds an appointment as Associate Clinical Professor of Orthopedics at the University of South Alabama. He has worked with USA orthopedic residents in a hand clinic, an arthritis clinic, the Crippled Children's Clinic, and the Southeastern Orthopedic Foot Club. A founding member of the International Arthroscopy Association and a charter member of the North American Spine Society, Dr. Ray is also an active member of the Orthopaedic Laser Society of North America and the American Orthopaedic Foot and Ankle Society.

The natural and architectural beauty of the Mobile region and the encouragement of friends caused Dr. Ray to open his medical practice here. Dr. Ray and his experienced and long-term staff are committed to continuing to provide concerned comprehensive orthopedic care to the people of the Mobile area. ⚜

Mobile Orthopedic Center provides patients with evaluation and treatment of general orthopedic complaints. A caring, experienced, and long-term staff, acting as the patient's advocate, provides assistance in the scheduling of diagnostic tests and treatments, as well as in the filing of insurance claims.

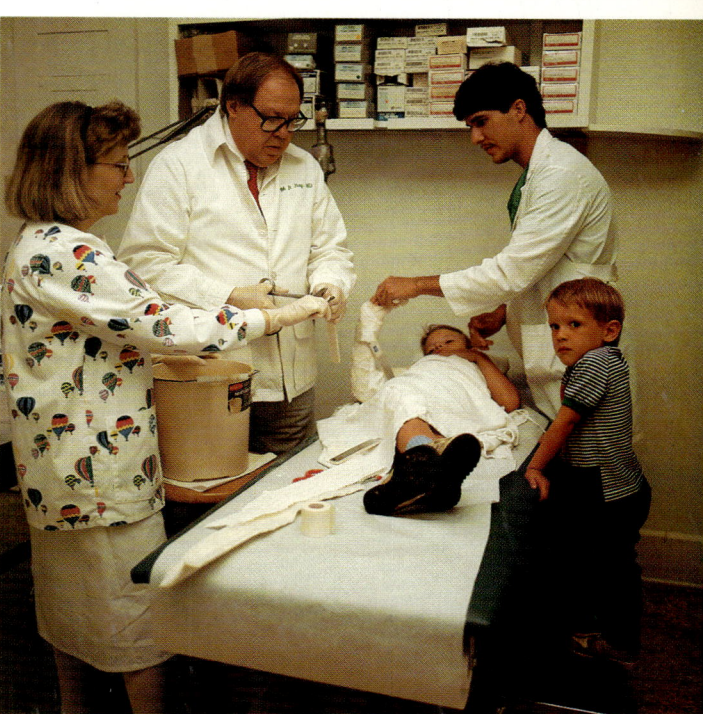

Dr. Ray and his staff are prepared to handle most musculoskeletal injuries, diseases, and illnesses of adults and children.

Chapter 17
THE MARKET PLACE

Barber Dairies
Holiday Inn Downtown
Delchamps

BARBER DAIRIES

Quality, excellence, and Barber's have been partners for over 70 years. George H. Barber founded Barber Brothers Dairy in Birmingham, Alabama, with his brother, Warren Barber, in 1923.

George Barber was a pioneer in the dairy industry. He supported bulk pasteurization and the distribution of milk from centrally located, sanitary milk processing plants and was influential in developing the United States Public Health Service Grade A Pasteurized Milk Ordinance, which originated in Alabama in late 1920. This ordinance set the stage for change in the dairy business, both in Alabama and across the nation.

When George H. Barber passed away in 1938, his son, George W. Barber, assumed control of the company. He helped establish the Alabama Milk Control Board for the purpose of setting high standards of milk quality throughout the state.

All Barber ice cream products are produced in the ultra-modern Birmingham ice cream plant. This cutting-edge-of-technology facility produces over 75,000 dozen ice cream novelties per day, as well as several million gallons of ice cream per year. Barber's is also a major licensed manufacturer/distributor of a large variety of national brand ice cream products; in fact, Barber's is the worlds' largest manufacturer of Eskimo Pie products, Weight Watcher frozen desserts, and Nestle's ice cream confections.

Quality is the top priority in Barber's Mobile, as it is for all of Barber's. There is never a discussion of ingredient pricing when formulas are being developed—Barber milk is packaged in opaque plastic jugs rather than less expensive translucent jugs because light destroys vitamins and taste in milk—and all Barber delivery vehicles are carefully maintained to insure cold delivery of our delicate dairy products.

George Pilgrim, vice president and general manager of Barber's Mobile, explains: "Barber people take great pride in helping to produce and deliver Barber's award-winning milks and ice creams; they really try to perform as though each of our customers is family."

Barber Dairies Mobile is the amalgamation of several small and large dairy processors which began with the purchase of Ruffin Graham Dairy in 1956. From this base on Moffat Road, Barber's has steadily added to its Mobile production base—Coleman Dairy in 1959, Fairhope Creamery in 1961, Shoreline Foods in 1976, Woodhaven Dairy in 1978, plus several additional Alabama and Mississippi processors who have become part of the Barber family.

Today, Barber's Mobile processes a full line of white and chocolate milks, buttermilk, fruit juice and drinks, egg nog, and specialty seasonal items. It distributes its milk and ice cream products throughout southern Alabama and Mississippi, as well as the panhandle of Florida, to a huge variety of customers, including all major supermarkets, convenience stores, fast-food operations, schools, and nursing homes.

Barber's is indeed thankful for its good fortune and works diligently to give back to its communities. As an example, The Barber Dairies' Scholarship Program awards several very generous scholarships in the Mobile area. These scholarships are given to college seniors in business-related curricula and are based on need, scholastic achievement, campus involvement, and entrepreneurial spirit. The point, of course, is to reward those special achievers and possibly induce them to remain a part of our community. Barber's is continually involved in worthwhile community projects where it feels it can make a difference.

Barber's Mobile will continue to offer its customers delicious, highest quality milk and ice cream products because it will continue its history of investment in the latest technology and encouraging of its employees to participate, to accomplish, to be recognized, and to grow.

Barber's ultra-modern milk processing facility produces the highest quality milk products.

HOLIDAY INN DOWNTOWN

The historic marker planted at 301 Government Street in front of the Holiday Inn in Mobile's Downtown Historic District was one of the first treasures uncovered in the renovation of the abandoned downtown landmark that had once been occupied by the Sheraton Hotel. The magnificent transformation of this once vacated building resulted in an attractive rotunda, the style of which is reminiscent of old Mobile French design and representative of a proper downtown Mobile address.

Original photos of old Mobile highlight the walls of the hotel's main dining room. Elaborate French grill work accentuates the stairwells and hallways of the first and second floors. The unique lobby-level gazebo and ever-flowing fountain serve as the hotel's center piece and is within viewing and penny-tossing range from second floor balconies.

The historic marker tells the story of Lafayette's visit to Mobile in 1825. Mobile's mayor, Samuel H. Garrow, entertained the French officer, statesman, and hero of the American Revolution in his home on that very spot. The marker also describes the enthusiastic welcome the city extended to this distinguished general.

Today the Holiday Inn Downtown Historic District considers all its guests "distinguished" and welcomes them accordingly. All of the hotel's 210 tastefully decorated rooms are more spacious than the standard hotel room as they treat guests to a spectacular panoramic view of Mobile Bay and Mobile's Historic District. Other hotel amenities include an outdoor pool, gameroom, gift shop, hair salon, business center, and guest privileges at a nearby health club, along with numerous Holiday Inn promotions.

The Executive Club Floor spoils VIP guests by providing personalized service through our concierge department. A complimentary continental breakfast is served each morning and hors d'oeuvres and cocktails each evening in the club lounge, located on the top floor of the hotel, offering a magnificent panorama of Mobile.

The Holiday Inn Downtown is "meeting friendly," offering a generous 10,000 square feet of function space, 13 meeting rooms, and a foyer ideal for registration and exhibits. Complete audiovisual and meeting-planning services are readily available. The 6,120-square-foot Bienville Ballroom easily accommodates groups as large as 900, and the elegant rooftop lounge doubles as a popular reception area.

Mobile is known for its many fine restaurants, and in keeping with Mobile's culinary reputation, the hotel proudly offers Lafayette's, a full-service dining room, and 24-hour dining through room service and its deli, Garrow's. The Bayview Lounge, with its breathtaking view, on the 17th floor provides toe-tapping entertainment and a fabulous seafood and prime rib buffet on weekends.

The Holiday Inn Downtown Historic District is ideally located in the heart of Mobile's central business district, offering the business and leisure traveler the ideal stay. It is within comfortable walking distance of the Mobile Civic Center, the Mobile Convention Center, numerous historic attractions, and a variety of bars, restaurants, and shops. It is a mecca for Mardi Gras visitors and places guests in the midst of all the thrills of Mardi Gras madness.

The Holiday Inn was the first major business to undertake the renovation process downtown. The refurbishment of what most considered an outdated eyesore and the establishment of the Holiday Inn Downtown Historic District served as a catalyst in the rejuvenation of downtown Mobile. Nearly everyone involved in the project, from the owners and designers to the suppliers and laborers, were Mobilians.

David Lindsey of MRS Architect viewed the project as a "gem." John Whiddon, President of Downtown Mobile Hotels Inc., agreed and commented, "David's fire got us involved. He lit our excitement in the potential of the project."

David Lindsey explains: "Fortunately the building was structurally sound. What we first considered deficits quickly reverted into assets. The whole renovation process developed into the finding of a series of nice spaces that somebody years before had planned for us to find and redesign. The space was there . . . we just had to uncover it." ⚜

The unique lobby-level gazebo and ever-flowing fountain serve as the hotel's center piece.

The Holiday Inn Downtown Historic District is ideally located in the heart of Mobile's central business district, offering the business and leisure traveler the ideal stay.

A Gulf Coast Treasure

DELCHAMPS

Seldom has a company experienced such success and growth as Delchamps, Inc., the Mobile-based grocery chain. In 1921 brothers Alfred and Oliver Delchamps, along with their widowed mother and the aid of their three sisters, founded the first "cash and carry" Delchamps store with a mere $1,000 investment.

Previously, the better grocery stores were higher-priced and offered credit and delivery. The new cash-and-carry concept was successful, and Delchamps opened a new store every year for the first five years of business, each managed by a family member.

From the beginning, the Delchamps philosophy has been directed toward five fundamental priorities: prime locations, newer stores, bigger stores, better merchandising, and quick assimilation of new technology.

Today, Delchamps operates 120 supermarkets in Alabama, Louisiana, Mississippi, and the Florida Panhandle, employing over 8,000 system wide, with 3,000 of those associates in Alabama.

In April 1994 Delchamps opened its state-of-the-art flagship supermarket in Mobile and dedicated it to the company's founders: Alfred F. Delchamps Sr., Oliver H. Delchamps Sr., and Annie Delchamps Moore.

Located in the McGregor Square Shopping Center, the store has over 58,000 square feet of shopping space and features a full-service dry cleaner and laundry; full-service pharmacy; one-hour film developing; sit-down or take-out pizza parlor; sit-down or take-out Delchamps Diner serving hot or cold meals, including breakfast prepared by the expansive deli-bakery; walk-in beer and ale cooler featuring domestic and imported beers; and a special warehouse-type area where items can be purchased in bulk.

The Delchamps philosophy has been directed toward five fundamental priorities: prime locations, newer stores, bigger stores, better merchandising, and quick assimilation of new technology.

The Delchamps family's interests reach far beyond the grocery-business arena into the surrounding community, where they involve their stores in various fund-raisers for local charities and civic organizations.

One of the most successful is the "Cash Back for Schools" program, which allows participating public, private, and parochial schools to collect Delchamps cash register receipts and redeem them for one percent cash back to use for anything the school needs, such as air conditioners, computers, copy machines, teacher supplies, or books. This widely-popular program has proven to be a very successful way for schools to acquire important educational tools and equipment that would be otherwise unobtainable.

Another successful fund-raiser is the Delchamps Senior Bowl Charity Run—a 10-K road race and one-mile fun run—held annually in downtown Mobile which has earned $592,000 for 67 area charities during a six-year period.

In an agreement reached in 1993, the official name of the 44-year-old all-star, post-season football classic, previously known as the Senior Bowl, was changed to the "Delchamps Senior Bowl," making Delchamps Supermarkets the title sponsor. This sponsorship agreement covers the 1994-1997 bowl games.

Says Randy Delchamps, "Delchamps believes in the importance of working for our communities as well as our company. In that way we return something to our communities and say thank you to our customers. This was a priority of our founders and has been instilled in all of us through the generations. I believe it is one of the reasons for Delchamps' success." ❧

Delchamps operates 120 supermarkets in Alabama, Louisiana, Mississippi, and the Florida Panhandle, employing over 8,000 system wide, with 3,000 of those associates in Alabama.

Mobile's Enterprises Index

Adams and Reese 166-167
Alabama Power Company 133
AmSouth Bank 158
Anesthesia Services, P.C. 226
Barber Dairies 230
Bay Area Plastic Surgery 210-211
Blue Cross and Blue Shield of Alabama 218
Brett Real Estate 189
The Buyer's Agent 191
Cardio-Thoracic and Vascular Surgical Associates 215
Cardiology Associates of Mobile, P.C. 222
Coastal Land Trust, Inc. 200
Cogburn Health Center, Inc. 224
Colonial Bank 162
Contel Cellular 130
Cooper/T. Smith Corporation 143
Courtaulds Fibers 142
Cummings and White-Spunner, Inc. 180
David Volkert & Associates, Inc. 187
Degussa Corporation 147
Delchamps 232
Equity Technologies Corporation 148
First Alabama Bank 156
Gottlieb, Barnett, & Bridges Engineering Consultants 174
Hiller Investments Incorporated 157
Hoechst Celanese 144
Holiday Inn Downtown 231
Hosea O. Weaver & Sons, Inc. 185
Inchcape Shipping Services 136-137
J. S. Walton & Co., Inc. 184
Jeffreys Steel Company 138-139
Johnstone, Adams, Bailey, Gordon and Harris 170-171
Lane, Lyons, Burton & Bullock, Inc. Real Estate 182
Lewis Communications, Inc. 172
Lyons, Pipes & Cook, P.C. 173
McAleer-Rogers-Willard, Inc. 186
Miller, Hamilton, Snider & Odom L.L.C. 168-169

Mobile Aerospace Engineering, Inc. 150
The Mobile Airport Authority 124-125
Mobile Area Chamber of Commerce 154-155
Mobile Bay OB-GYN Associates 220
Mobile Gas 122-123
The Mobile Heart Center 225
Mobile Infirmary Medical Center 217
Mobile Orthopedic Center 227
Mobile Paperboard/Recycled Fibers of Alabama 145
Partial Hospital Institute of America, Inc. 221
Pete Peters and Associates 161
PrimeHealth 216
Providence Hospital 214
Pulmonary Associates of Mobile, P.A. 223
QF, Inc. 149
QMS 140-141
Richardson, Daniell, Spear & Upton, P.C. 176
Roberts Brothers, Inc. 192
Saad Enterprises 212-213
St. Paul's Episcopal School 201
Sirote & Permutt, P.C. 175
South Central Bell 126-127
Southern Earth Sciences, Inc. 190
SouthTrust Bank 160
Spring Hill College 202
Springhill Memorial Hospital 219
ST&T, Inc. 132
Thompson Engineering 183
UMS-Wright Preparatory School 203
University of South Alabama 196-199
University of South Alabama Hospitals 206-209
Vance McCown Construction Company, Inc. 188
Warranty Corporation 159
Warrior & Gulf Navigation Company 146
WBLX AM and FM Radio Stations 131
White-Spunner Construction, Inc. 181
WKRG-TV 128-129

Cytec Industries, Inc.—Patron

Bibliography

Aaron, Hank and Lonnie Wheeler. *I Had a Hammer.* New York: HarperCollins, 1991.

Amos, Harriet E. "Social Life in an Antebellum Cotton Port: Mobile, Alabama, 1820-1860." Ph.D. diss., Emory University, 1976.

Dean, B. Wayne Sr. *Mardi Gras: Mobile's Illogical Whoop-De-Doo.* Chicago: Adams Press, 1970.

Greene, Carolyn Brandon. *Brandon, Sibert and the Alabama State Docks 1923-1928.* Printed by the author.

Hamilton, Peter J. *Colonial Mobile.* Edited by Charles G. Summersell. Reprint, Tuscaloosa: University of Alabama Press, 1976.

Hearin, Emily Staples. "Let the Good Times Roll!" Printed by the author: 1991.

Higginbotham, Jay. *Old Mobile, Fort Louis de la Louisiane, 1702-1711.* Mobile: 1977.

Inabinett, Mark. "Big Time Baseball, Alabamians in the Major Leagues." *Alabama Heritage,* (summer 1993): 26-39.

Ludlow, M. Noah. "Dramatic Life as I Found It." New York: Noble Offset Printers.

Martin, Thomas W. *Doctor William Crawford Gorgas of Alabama and the Panama Canal.* New York: The Newcomen Society of England, American Branch, 1947.

McWilliams, R. G., translator and editor. *Iberville's Gulf Travels.* Tuscaloosa: University of Alabama Press, University of Alabama, 1981.

Melton, McLaurin and Michael Thomason. *Mobile, The Life and Times of a Great Southern City.* Woodland Hills: Windsor Publications, Inc., 1981.

The Mobile Chamber of Commerce and Business League. "Mobile, Alabama, A Rapidly Growing Port." Mobile: Wood Printing Co., Circa 1912.

The Mobile Chamber of Commerce and Business League. "Mobile." Circa 1912.

Semmes, Raphael. *Memoirs of Service Afloat.* Baltimore: Baltimore Publishing Co., 1887.

Toulmin, Mary Morgan. *Antebellum Theatre in Mobile for Elderhostel*, Faulkner State, January 5-10, 1992.

National Oceanic and Atmospheric Administration Estuary-of-the-Month Seminar Series No. 15. "Mobile Bay: Issues, Resources, Status, and Management." Proceedings of a seminar held November 17, 1988, at the Herbert C. Hoover Building of the U.S. Department of Commerce. Washington, D.C.: Government Printing Office.

In addition to the above publications, current and past issues of the *Mobile Press*, the *Mobile Register*, the combined Sunday issues of those papers, as well as *Alabama, Business Alabama Monthly, Mobile Bay Monthly*, and *Port of Mobile* magazines were helpful.

Hank Aaron, Judy Culbreth, Winston Groom, Carolyn Haines, Ed Scott, Colman McCarthy, and others kindly submitted to interviews and provided the author with updated biographical information for the Chapter 3.

Index

A Walk Across America 102
Aaron, Hank 42-44
Aaron, Tommie 43
Adams and Reese 166-167
Adams Mark Hotel 31
Admiral Semmes Hotel 31
Africaine 21
Agee, Tommie 43
Alabama 22, 29
Alabama Aviation and Technical College 117
Alabama Department of Natural Resources 89
Alabama Dry Dock and Shipbuilding Company (ADDSCO) 24, 26, 96-97
Alabama Game and Fish Division 82, 89
Alabama Institute for Deaf and Blind Mobile Regional Center 110
Alabama magazine 48
Alabama Power Company 133
Alabama red-bellied turtle 82-83
Alabama Review, The 24
Alabama River 82-83
Alabama School of Mathematics and Science 112, 117
Alabama State Docks 92-94, 96-98
Albright, E. Roy 97
Allen, Winston A. 75
alligators 82-83
Altus Bank 38
America's Junior Miss 62
American Bowling Congress 35
AmSouth Bank 31, 158
Amtrak 102, 107
Anesthesia Services, P.C. 226
Arts Coalition of Mobile 114
Ash Wednesday 70, 75
Ashland Place 54
Athelstan Club 35
Atlanta 42, 44
Atlantic Marine 97, 102
Auburn University 48, 51, 86
Azalea City Golf Club 48, 67
Azalea Festival 54
Azalea Trail Maids 114
Azalea Trail Run 66

Baldwin County 21, 26, 51, 66-67, 84, 86, 107
Bankhead Tunnel 82
Barber Dairies 230
Barkett, Rosemary 50, 116
Barton Academy 21, 24, 112
Battle House 21-22, 36
Battle, James 22
Battle, John 22
Battle, Samuel 22
Battle of Horseshoe Bend 21
Battle of Mobile Bay 22-23, 57
Battles, Mary (Vaultz) 50
Battleship Memorial Parkway 83, 86
Bay Area Plastic Surgery 210-211
Bay Oaks Golf Club 67
Bayley, Bill 50
Bayou La Batre 54, 72, 86, 98, 106
Bayway 107
Bebo's Car Wash 103
Becker, Julius 23
Bedsole, Ann 50
Beebee, William S. 24
Bel Air Mall 75
Bellingrath Gardens 54, 59-60
Bellingrath, Walter D. 50
Belmont, Alva E. Smith Vanderbilt 50
Belrose Wharf 24
Bender Shipbuilding & Repair Co., Inc. 94, 102
Besteda, Samuel 75
Bienville Square 18, 30, 32, 35-36, 38
Bienville Water Works 36
Biloxi 19
Biloxi Bay 19
Birmingham 25, 66, 94, 96, 110-111
Birmingham News 50
Bishop State Community College 116-117
Black Warrior River 83
Blakeley 23
Blakeley Island 98
Blakely Terminal 98
Blessing of the Fleet 54
Blue Cross and Blue Shield of Alabama 218
Blue College 21
Bottle Creek Indians 84-86
boutique marketing 98
Boykin, Frank 50
Bragg-Mitchell Mansion 57
Brandon, Sibert and the Alabama State Docks, 1923-1928 97
Brandon, William Woodward 96-97
Brett Real Estate 189
Brookley Complex 106-107, 117, 124
Brookley Field 25-26
Brooklyn 23

Brown Bag in Bienville 38
Brown, Milton 50
Buchanan, Franklin 22
Buffett, Jimmy 42, 46, 48, 50
Burlington Northern 92, 94
Busby, Jim 45, 140-141
Buyer's Agent, The 191

Cain, Joseph S. 70, 72
Camellia Ball 75
Campbell, John 21
Campbell, William Edward 51
Cancer Crusader 62
Cardio-Thoracic and Vascular Surgical Associates 215
Cardiology Associates of Mobile, P.C. 222
Carlen House 57
Carver Park 43
Cathedral of the Immaculate Conception 36
Cathedral Square 39
Cathedral Square Arts District 32, 36
Catholic Cemetery 49
Causeway 107
Cedar Point 50, 93
Center for International Trade and Commerce (CITC) 92
Central High School 50
Chamberlain, "Black Bart" 50
Charlie G 61
Chattahoochee River 94
Chickasabogue 96
Chickasabogue Creek 116
Chickasaw 26, 82
Chickasaw Indians 72
Chief Slacabamorinico 70, 72
Church Street East 31, 54
Church Street Graveyard 21, 70, 72
Citronelle Municipal Golf Club 67
Civil War 21, 49, 70, 72-73, 82, 94
Claiborne 93
Clay, Henry 21, 51
Clinton, Bill 50
Clotilde 21
Coastal Land Trust, Inc. 89, 200
Cochrane/Africa Town U.S.A. Bridge 105, 107
Cogburn Health Center, Inc. 224
Colonial Bank 162
Colored Carnival Association of Mobile 75
Comic Cowboys 75
Conde Cavaliers 75
Conde-Charlotte House 57

Contel Cellular 130
Cooper/T. Smith Corporation 94, 143
Coosa River 83
Corey, Winthrop 54
Cortés, Hernando 18
cotton 21-24
Country Club of Mobile 67
County of Mobile 106
Courtaulds Fibers 142
Cowbellion de Rakin Society 70
Cowbellions 72-73
Creek Indians 21
Crewe of Columbus 75
CSX Transportation 92, 94
Culbreth, Judsen "Judy" 42, 44-45
Cummings and White-Spunner, Inc. 180

Daphne 24, 48, 51
Daphne Wharf 24
Daughters of Charity 111, 214
Dauphin Island 19, 31, 67, 83, 93
Dauphin Island Audubon Bird Sanctuary 66-67
Dauphin Island Race 67
David Volkert & Associates, Inc. 187
de Soto, Hernando 19, 85-86
Dean, Wayne 70
Deep Sea Fishing Rodeo 67
Deerhound 49
Degussa Corporation 147
Delchamps 106, 232
Delchamps' Senior Bowl 61-62, 232
Denny, David E., Jr. 21
Denton, Jeremiah 50
DeTonti Square 27, 31, 54-55
Do Dah Day Parade 39
Dothan 66
Dow, Mike 31, 79, 155
Downs, Bunny 44
Downtown Redevelopment Commission 31-32
Drought of '88 97
Dryer Wharf 24
duck population 82, 84, 89

Eastern Shore 23-24, 82, 87
Eddie Stanky Field 64
Edgar F. Luckenbach 96
Edison, Thomas 45
Eichold-Heustis Medical Museum of the South 57
Elexis 75
Emerson Institute 21

Equity Technologies Corporation 148
estuaries 86-87
Excelsior Band 70, 72, 75
Exploreum Museum of Discovery 31, 56
Exxon 103

Facade Program 36
Faggard, Don 66
Fairhope 75, 107
FAMOS Downtown 32, 38, 56
Farragut, David G. 22-23
Fave, Bernard 26
Fellini, Federico 48
Fenollosa, Ernest F. 51
Fine Arts Museum of the South 32, 43, 56, 67
Finlay, Carlos Juan 46
Fire of 1919 21
First Alabama Bank 156
First Baptist Church 49
First National Bank Building 31
First Night Mobile 38-39
fishing tournaments 65, 67
Fitzpatrick, Robert J. 50
Flowerwood Nursery, Inc. 106
Folly chasing Death 71, 75
Fonvielle Elementary School 114, 116
Fort Biloxi 85
Fort Condé 19, 21
Fort Gaines 22, 67
Fort Maurepas 19
Fort Mims 21
Fort Morgan 22-23, 93
Foster, Red 70
Fowler, John 24
Franklin, James Alexander, Sr. 112
Franklin Memorial Primary Health Center 112
Freeman, Lauretta 51
Friend, Jack 23

Gadsden 66
Gaines 22-23
Gálvez, Bernardo de 21
Gayfers 106
Gayle, John 48
Gibson, General 23
golf 62, 64, 66-67
Gorgas, William C. 42, 46
Gottlieb, Barnett, & Bridges Engineering Consultants 174
Grand Hotel 24

Granger, Gordon 23
Great Depression 24-25, 97
Greater Gulf States Fairgrounds 79
Greene, Carolyn Brandon 97
Greyhound Bus Station 30, 32
Groom, Winston 42, 51
Gulf Coast Classic 64
Gulf Coast Military Academy 50
Gulf Coast Survey 85
Gulf Intracoastal Waterway 94
Gulf Pines Golf Course 67
Gulf Shipbuilding Corporation 26, 50, 97
Gulf Shores 26

Hafner, John 51
Haines, Carolyn 42, 51
Hamilton, Peter Joseph 18
Hartford 22-23
Hartwell, Harry T. 96
Head Start 79
Henderson, Beryl 51
Heritage Tree Ordinance 35
Herman, Alex 75
Herman, Alexis 50
Hersey, Jean 60
Higginbotham, Jay 51
Hiller Investments Incorporated 157
Historic Mobile Preservation Society 30
Hodgson, Sam 46
Hoechst Celanese 144
Holiday Inn Downtown 31, 231
Holmes, Nicholas H. 46
Hosea O. Weaver & Sons, Inc. 185
Howard's Wharf 24
Huger, Daniel E. 75
Huls America, Inc. 102
Hunley 57
Hurricane Frederic 31, 87, 94
Hutchison, Miller Reese 45

I Had a Hammer 42-43
Illinois Central 92, 94
Inchcape Shipping Services 95, 136-137
Infant Mystics 75
International Paper Company 106, 113
International Trade Center 97
Isle Dauphine Golf Course 67

J. S. Walton & Co., Inc. 184
Jackson, Andrew 21
Jeffreys Steel Company 138-139

Jenkins, Aliene 75
Jenkins, Peter 102
JJ Blue Dancer 61-62
Joe Cain Processional 70, 72
Joe Cain Society 75
Johnstone, Adams, Bailey, Gordon and Harris 170-171
Jones, Cleon 43
Jordan Pile Driving 102
jubilees 87
Judge Roy Bean's 46, 48

K's Clown 61
Kearsarge 49
Kelley, William "Pig Iron" 24
Ketchum, George A. 36
Kettering, Charles F. 46
Kids Creating Opera 113
King Elexis I 75
Knights of Columbus 75
Knights of May Zulu Club 75
Knights of Revelry 75
Krafft, Michael 70, 73
Krewe of Columbus 75
Krewe of Marry Mates 75
Krewe of Out-of-Towners 79

Lackawanna 23
LaClede Hotel 31
Ladd Memorial Stadium 61-62, 64
Lane, Lyons, Burton & Bullock, Inc. Real Estate 182
Langan Park 55-56
Le Krewe de Bienville 79
Le Moyne, de Bienville, Jean Baptiste 18-19
Le Moyne de Iberville, Pierre 19, 85-86
Le Vert, Octavia Walton 21, 51
LeFlore High School of Advanced Studies/Communication & Arts 112, 115
Leinkauf 54
Levi, Dave 75
Lewis Communications, Inc. 172
Linksman Golf Club of Mobile, The 67
Little Eva 75
Lower Dauphin Street Commercial 54
Ludlow, Noah 21
Luna, Tristan de 19
Lyons, Pipes & Cook, P.C. 173

Madison, James 21

Magnolia Cemetery 18, 73
Magnolia Grove Golf Complex 67
Maids of Mirth 75
Main Street Mobile 36, 39
Mammoth 73, 75
Mardi Gras 50, 57, 70-79
Marine Environmental Sciences Consortium 83
Marine Spill Response Corp. 102
Matching Grant Fund 36
Maury, D. H. 23
May, A. S. 75
McAleer-Rogers-Willard, Inc. 32, 186
McCarthy, Colman 48, 116
McCovey, Willie 43
McDonald's 114, 116
McDuffie Coal Terminal 95, 98-99
McDuffie Terminal Bulk Coal Plant 97
McGill Institute 46, 48
McLaurin, Melton 24, 96
McLean, Malcom 93, 95
McNeil, Mary 51
McWilliams, R. G. 85
Medical Society of Mobile County 117
Memoirs of Service Afloat 48-49
Merrimac 22
Midnight Revellers, The 70
Miller, Hamilton, Snider & Odom, L.L.C. 168-169
Mississippi River 18, 21, 70, 83, 85, 93, 97, 111
Mobile Aerospace Engineering, Inc. 102, 150
Mobile Airport Authority, The 124-125
Mobile Area Chamber of Commerce 31, 38, 106, 154-155
Mobile Area Mardi Gras Association 75
Mobile Arts Council 30, 39
Mobile Ballet 32, 54
Mobile Bay 18-19, 21, 60, 83, 86, 89, 93-94
Mobile BaySharks, 64
Mobile Bay OB-GYN Associates 220
Mobile Black Bears 43
Mobile Carnival Association 75
Mobile City Council 35
Mobile Civic Center 31, 78-79
Mobile Commerce Park 103, 106
Mobile Convention and Visitors' Bureau 32, 35
Mobile Convention Center 31-32, 35, 98

Mobile County 19, 24, 31, 50, 67, 72, 86, 98, 103, 105-107
Mobile County Health Department 112
Mobile County Parking Garage 32
Mobile County Public School System 106, 110, 112, 114
Mobile County Training School 21
Mobile Daily Register 73
Mobile Downtown Redevelopment Commission 31
Mobile Gas 122-123
Mobile Government Plaza 30-32, 106
Mobile Greyhound Park 54, 60, 62
Mobile Harbor 94
Mobile Heart Center, The 225
Mobile Historic Development Commission 30, 36
Mobile Homeport Reuse Committee 98
Mobile in Motion 106, 154
Mobile Infirmary Association 50
Mobile Infirmary Medical Center 217
Mobile International Carnival Ball 79
Mobile, Miami, and Gulf Steamship Company 95
Mobile Mystics 75
Mobile Oceanic Line 95
Mobile Opera 32, 51, 56, 113
Mobile Opera Chorus 51
Mobile Opera Workshop 51
Mobile Orthopedic Center 227
Mobile Paperboard/Recycled Fibers of Alabama 145
Mobile Press Register 26, 46, 51, 66, 97, 102
Mobile Public Library 38
Mobile Regional Airport 107, 125
Mobile Register 46, 79
Mobile Revolving Fund for Historic Properties 36
Mobile River 18-19, 89, 93, 97-98
Mobile River Industrial Park 106
Mobile River Valley 87, 89
Mobile Ship Channel 92, 94, 98
Mobile SPCA 39
Mobile Symphonic Pops Band 54-55
Mobile Symphony Orchestra 48
Mobile-Tensaw Delta 19, 82-89
Mobile, The Life and Times of a Great Southern City 24, 96
Mobile Theatre 21
Mobile Tree Commission 35

Monitor 22
Montgomery 23, 50, 66
Montrose 45
Moon Pie 68, 70, 78-79
Moore, Dot 50
Morgan 22-23
Morgan, Ruby 75
Morphy, Paul 51, 116
Morrissette, H. Taylor 50
Mosely, Brett Culbreth 44
Mosely, Charles Boykin 44
Mound Island 84
Murphy High School 24, 44, 50
Museum of the City of Mobile 57
Mystic Stripers Society 75
Mystics of Children 75
Mystics of Time 75

National Merit Scholarship 114
Naval Station Mobile 98
New Mobilians, The 79
New Orleans 18-19, 70, 72, 75, 78-79, 93
New Orleans Daily Picayune 46
Nicholas, Florina 75
Norfolk Southern 92, 94
North American Waterfowl Management Plan 89
Nott, Josiah C. 46

Oakleigh 57
Oakleigh Garden District 54
Office of Special Events 38-39
Old Dauphin Way 54
Old Shell Road School for Creative & Performing Arts 113
Omnimax Theatre 31
Order of Athena 75
Order of Doves (ODD) 75
Order of Inca 75
Order of LaShe's 75
Order of Myths 71-73, 75
Order of Polka Dots 75
Original Utopia Club 75
osprey 82
Otis, Amos 43
Outlaw, Authur 31
Ozark 117

Paige, Satchel 43
Pan Atlantic Steamship Co. 95, 97
Panama Canal 35, 46, 60, 96
Partial Hospital Institute of America, Inc. 221
Partners in Education 113-114, 116

Pensacola 18, 21, 46, 49, 85
Perdido River 49
Pete Peters and Associates 161
Petticoat Rebellion 19
Pharaohs 75
Phoenix Fire Museum 57
Pine Hills Golf Club 67
Pineda, Alonso Álvarez de 18
Plateau 43
Point Clear 24, 49, 51
Pope, John A. 75
Pope, John C. 75
Port City 27, 70, 96
Port City Brewery 32
Port City Puppy Classic 62
Port City Symphony 32, 39, 54-55
Port of Bayou La Batre 98
Port of Mobile 92-94, 97-98
Port of Mobile 94
powder magazine explosion 23-24
Prichard 75, 105, 107
PrimeHealth 216
Providence Hospital 106, 111, 214
Pulmonary Associates of Mobile, P.A. 223

QF, Inc. 149
QMS 45, 113, 140-141
Queens of Mobile Mardi Gras 1893-1986 78

Rayford, Julian Lee "Judy" 51, 70, 72
Reed, Walter 46
Resurrection Cowbellion de Rakin Society 73
Richards DAR House 57
Richardson, Daniell, Spear & Upton, P.C. 176
River Rhapsody Gala 32
Robert Trent Jones Trail 67
Roberts Brothers, Inc. 192
Roberts, E. A. 95
Roberts, Ed 50
Robinson Iron 36
Ruth, Babe 42, 44
Ryan-Walsh 94-95

Saad Enterprises 106, 212-213
Saenger Theatre 36, 56, 198
Saint Joseph's Chapel 116
St. Paul's Episcopal School 201
Schele, Linda 50
Schwartz, Maryln 51
Scott, Ed 43

Scott Paper Company 45, 89, 106
seafood industry 86, 89
Sea-Land Service, Inc. 95
Sears TeleCenter 102, 106
Selma 22-23
Semmes, Raphael 22, 48-49
September Celebration 38
Shakespeare Club 117
shipping industry 92-98
Shonts Wharf 24
Show Business Mobile 106
Sibert, William 96
Singapore Aerospace 102, 150
Sirote & Permutt, P.C. 175
sister cities 93
Ski's Gallo 61
Skyline Country Club 67
Smith, A. J. 23
Smith, Carter C. 22
Smith, Ozzie 43
Soost, Chief of Police 79
South Central Bell 114, 126-127
Southeastern Consortium for Minorities in Engineering (SECME) 114
Southern Earth Sciences, Inc. 190
Southern Steamship Agency 95, 136-137
SouthFlite USA 111-112, 206, 209
SouthTrust Bank 160
Spanish Fort 21, 23
Spitz Planetarium 31
Spring Hill College 45, 48, 50-51, 114-116, 202
Springdale Plaza 75
Springhill Memorial Hospital 106, 111, 219
ST&T, Inc. 132
Stanky, Eddie 51
StarBright Concerts 55
Steele, Frederick 23
Stocking, John 70
Strikers Independent Society 72
String of Pearls 31
sturgeon 82
Sumter 49
Sunday Concerts 38
Sundays in the Square 38-39
Symphony Concerts of Mobile 36

Tallapoosa River 83
Taylor, Laurie 78
Teague, Joe 48
Tecumseh 23
Tell the World 106

Tennessee 22-23
Tennessee River 94
Tennessee-Tombigbee Waterway 92, 94, 97
Tensaw River 83
Theodore Industrial District 106
Theodore Industrial Park 97
Theodore Middle School 114
Theodore Ship Channel 94
Thomas A. Edison Laboratories 45, 116
Thomason, Michael 24, 96
Thompson Engineering 183
Thurber Company 95
Thurber, Win 95, 136-137
Tillman's Corner 75
Tombigbee River 83
Toulminville 42, 45, 48
Townsend, Barney & Patrick Advertising, Inc. 106
Tuesdays at Twelve 38
Tuscaloosa 66, 110
Twenty-Seven Mile Bluff 19, 70
Two Naval Journals at the Battle of Mobile Bay 22

UMS-Wright Preparatory School 203
Underwood, Oscar 94
United States Coast Guard 98-99, 106
U.S. Corps of Engineers 94, 106
United States Fish and Wildlife Service 89
United States Navy 49, 98
University Military School 50-51
University of Alabama 48, 85, 111
University of Mobile 116
University of South Alabama (USA) 36, 44, 51, 56, 92, 97, 106, 110, 115, 196-199
University of South Alabama Hospitals (USA) 106, 110-112, 206-209

USS Alabama 54, 57, 60
USS Drum 60
USS Oneida 57

Vance McCown Construction Company, Inc. 188

Walter, Eugene 48
Warranty Corporation 159
Warrior & Gulf Navigation Company 146
Warrior-Tombigbee River 94
Washington, George 21
Washington Post 48, 116
Waste Management of Alabama 114
Waterman, John Barnett 50, 93-94
Waterman Steamship Corporation 50, 95, 97
WBLX AM and FM Radio Stations 131
Weeks Bay 86
Westlawn Elementary 114
Whistler 43, 75
White-Spunner Construction, Inc. 181
Wiggins, Sarah Woolfolk 24
Williams, Billy 42-43
Williamson High School 51
Wilson, Augusta Evans 51
Winchester Steamship Agency 95
Wisconsin Ice Age 87
WKRG-TV 128-129
Working Mother 42, 44
World Omni Financial Corp. 102
World War I 24, 96
World War II 25-27, 33, 50, 57, 60, 97
Wragg Swamp 75
WZEW 38

yellow fever 21, 45-46, 117

This book was set in Stone Serif Book and Stone Serif Semibold Italic at Community Communications, Montgomery, Alabama, and printed on 80lb. Warren Flo Text.